Scribes and the City

London Guildhall Clerks and the Dissemination
of Middle English Literature, 1375–1425

YORK MEDIEVAL PRESS

York Medieval Press is published by the University of York's Centre for Medieval Studies in association with Boydell & Brewer Limited. Our objective is the promotion of innovative scholarship and fresh criticism on medieval culture. We have a special commitment to interdisciplinary study, in line with the Centre's belief that the future of Medieval Studies lies in those areas in which its major constituent disciplines at once inform and challenge each other.

EDITORIAL BOARD (2012)

Professor Peter Biller (Dept of History): General Editor
Dr T. Ayers (Dept of History of Art)
Dr J. W. Binns (Dept of English and Related Literature)
Professor Helen Fulton (Dept of English and Related Literature)
Dr K. F. Giles (Dept of Archaeology)
Professor Christopher Norton (Dept of History of Art)
Professor W. M. Ormrod (Dept of History)
Professor J. G. Wogan-Browne (English Faculty, Fordham University)

CONSULTANT ON MANUSCRIPT PUBLICATIONS

Professor Linne Mooney (Dept of English and Related Literature)

All enquiries of an editorial kind, including suggestions for monographs and essay collections, should be addressed to: The Academic Editor, York Medieval Press, University of York, Centre for Medieval Studies, The King's Manor, York, YO1 7EP (e-mail: gmg501@york.ac.uk).

Publications of York Medieval Press are listed at the back of this volume.

Scribes and the City

London Guildhall Clerks and the Dissemination
of Middle English Literature, 1375–1425

LINNE R. MOONEY

&

ESTELLE STUBBS

THE UNIVERSITY *of York*

YORK MEDIEVAL PRESS

© Linne R. Mooney and Estelle Stubbs 2013

All rights reserved. Except as permitted under current legislation
no part of this work may be photocopied, stored in a retrieval system,
published, performed in public, adapted, broadcast, transmitted,
recorded or reproduced in any form or by any means,
without the prior permission of the copyright owner

First published 2013
Reprinted 2014, 2015

A York Medieval Press publication
in association with The Boydell Press
an imprint of Boydell & Brewer Ltd
PO Box 9, Woodbridge, Suffolk IP12 3DF, UK
and of Boydell & Brewer Inc.
668 Mt Hope Avenue, Rochester, NY 14620-2731, USA
website: www.boydellandbrewer.com
and with the
Centre for Medieval Studies, University of York

ISBN 978-1-903153-40-6

A CIP catalogue record for this book is available from the British Library

The publisher has no responsibility for the continued existence or
accuracy of URLs for external or third-party internet websites referred
to in this book, and does not guarantee that any content on such
websites is, or will remain, accurate or appropriate.

Papers used by Boydell & Brewer Ltd are natural, recyclable
products made from wood grown in sustainable forests

Designed and typeset in Adobe Minion Pro by
David Roberts, Pershore, Worcestershire

Printed and bound in Great Britain by
CPI Group (UK) Ltd, Croydon, CR0 4YY

CONTENTS

List of Illustrations   vi

Acknowledgements   viii

Introduction   1

1 The Clerks of the London Guildhall   7

2 Richard Osbarn, Chamber Clerk, 1400–37   17

3 John Marchaunt, Chamber Clerk, 1380–99, Common Clerk, 1399–1417   38

4 Adam Pinkhurst, Scrivener and Clerk of the Guildhall, c. 1378–1410   66

5 John Carpenter, Common Clerk, 1417–38   86

6 Other Scribes Associated with the Guildhall or its Clerks   107

7 Conclusions   132

Epilogue   141

Bibliography   142

Index of Manuscripts Cited   150

General Index   152

ILLUSTRATIONS

2.1 San Marino, CA, Huntington Library, MS HM 114, fol. 192r. Reproduced with permission of the Henry E. Huntington Library. 20

2.2 San Marino, CA, Huntington Library, MS HM 114, fol. 49r. Reproduced with permission of the Henry E. Huntington Library. 20

2.3 London, British Library, MS Harley 3943, fol. 15r. Reproduced with permission of the British Library. 22

2.4 London, Lambeth Palace Library, MS 491, fol. 184r. Reproduced with permission of the Lambeth Palace Library. 22

2.5 London Metropolitan Archives, COL/AD/01/009, Letter Book I, fol. 223r. Reproduced with permission of the London Metropolitan Archives. 22

2.6 London Metropolitan Archives, COL/CS/01/012, *Liber Albus*, fol. 320r. Reproduced with permission of the London Metropolitan Archives. 24

2.7 London, Goldsmiths' Company Archives, MS 1642, Register of Deeds, fol. 1r. Reproduced with permission of the Goldsmiths' Company of London; © The Goldsmiths' Company. Photograph: Richard Valencia. 25

2.8 London Metropolitan Archives, COL/AD/01/008, Letter Book H, fol. 256r. Reproduced with permission of the London Metropolitan Archives. 26

2.9 Plan of the Guildhall precinct, *c.* 1400. From D. Bowsher, T. Dyson, N. Holder and I. Howell, *The London Guildhall: An Archaeological History of a Neighbourhood from Early Medieval to Modern Times*, 2 vols (London, 2007), vol. 1, pp. 170–1, fig. 165. Reproduced with permission of The London Guildhall. 29

3.1 London, British Library, Additional MS 27944, fol. 196rb. Reproduced with permission of the British Library. 40

3.2 London, Senate House Library, MS SLV/88 (the Ilchester manuscript), fol. 93r. Reproduced with permission of the University of London. 40

3.3 Princeton, NJ, Princeton University Library, Department of Rare Books and Manuscripts, MS Taylor 5, fol. 170r. Reproduced with permission of the Department of Rare Books and Special Collections, Princeton University. 41

3.4 Manchester, John Rylands University Library, MS Eng. 103, fol. 86r. Reproduced by courtesy of the University Librarian and Director, John Rylands University Library, University of Manchester 41

3.5 Graphs of **g** found in manuscripts written by Scribe D (= John Marchaunt) 42

3.6 Graphs of **a, d, g,** and **h** in the handwriting of Scribe D (= John Marchaunt) 43

3.7 Graphs of **r, s, w** and **y** in the handwriting of Scribe D (= John Marchaunt) 44

3.8 Distinctive graphs of yogh, **I** and **N**, and tags after letters in the handwriting of Scribe D (= John Marchaunt) 45

3.9 Distinctive treatments of upper case letters in the handwriting of Scribe D (= John Marchaunt) 46

3.10 Oxford, Corpus Christi College, MS 198, fol. 263v. Reproduced by permission of the President and Fellows of Corpus Christi College, Oxford. 47

3.11 London Metropolitan Archives, COL/CS/01/012, *Liber Albus*, fol. 231v. Reproduced with permission of the London Metropolitan Archives. 47

3.12 London Metropolitan Archives, COL/CS/01/012, *Liber Albus*, fol. 197v. Reproduced with permission of the London Metropolitan Archives. 48

3.13 London Metropolitan Archives, COL/CS/01/012, *Liber Albus*, fol. 233v. Reproduced with permission of the London Metropolitan Archives. 49

3.14 London Metropolitan Archives, COL/AD/01/009, Letter Book I, fol. 5r. Reproduced with permission of the London Metropolitan Archives. 49

3.15 London Metropolitan Archives, COL/AD/01/008, Letter Book H, fol. 52r. Reproduced with permission of the London Metropolitan Archives. 50

3.16 London Metropolitan Archives, COL/AD/01/008, Letter Book H, fol. 42v. Reproduced with permission of the London Metropolitan Archives. 52

3.17 Kew, National Archives, E 40/2360, dorse. Reproduced with permission of The National Archives. 53

3.18 London Metropolitan Archives, COL/AD/01/007, Letter Book G, fol. 232v. Reproduced with permission of the London Metropolitan Archives. 54

List of Illustrations

3.19 London Metropolitan Archives, CLA 023/DW/01/117, mem. 10v, item 96. Reproduced with permission of the London Metropolitan Archives. 55

3.20 London, British Library, MS Harley 7334, fol. 180r. Reproduced with permission of the British Library. 56

4.1 Scriveners' Company Common Paper, London, Guildhall Library, MS 5370, p. 56. Reproduced with permission of the Guildhall Library and the Scriveners' Company of London. 66

4.2 Cambridge, Trinity College, MS R.3.20, p. 367. Reproduced with permission of the Master and Fellows of Trinity College, Cambridge. 70

4.3 Kew, National Archives, C 81/1394/87. Reproduced with permission of The National Archives. 72

4.4 Cambridge, Trinity College, MS R.3.2, fol. 11v. Reproduced with permission of The Master and Fellows of Trinity College, Cambridge. 75

4.5 London Metropolitan Archives, COL/AD/01/009, Letter Book I, fol. 87r. Reproduced with permission of the Corporation of London Record Office, London Metropolitan Archives. 76

4.6 London Metropolitan Archives, COL/AD/01/009, Letter Book I, fol. 36r. Reproduced with permission of the Corporation of London Record Office, London Metropolitan Archives. 77

4.7 Kew, National Archives, Ancient Petitions, SC 8/21/1001B. Reproduced with permission of the National Archives. 78

4.8 Cambridge, University Library, MS Kk.1.3, Part XX, fol. 1r. Reproduced with permission of the Syndics of Cambridge University Library. 80

4.9 London, British Library, Additional Charter 40542. Reproduced with permission of The British Library. 81

5.1 Kew, National Archives, E 40/12349, dorse. Reproduced with permission of The National Archives. 87

5.2 London Metropolitan Archives, COL/AD/01/009, Letter Book I, fol. 212v. Reproduced with permission of the London Metropolitan Archives. 88

5.3 London Metropolitan Archives, COL/AD/01/009, Letter Book I, fol. 212r. Reproduced with permission of the London Metropolitan Archives. 90

5.4 London Metropolitan Archives, COL/AD/01/009, Letter Book I, fol. 222v. Reproduced with permission of the London Metropolitan Archives. 91

5.5 London Metropolitan Archives, COL/CS/01/012, *Liber Albus*, fol. 1v. Reproduced with permission of the London Metropolitan Archives. 92

5.6 New York, Pierpont Morgan Library & Museum, MS M.817, fol. 43v. Reproduced with permission of The Pierpont Morgan Library & Museum. 94

5.7 London Metropolitan Archives, COL/CS/01/012, *Liber Albus*, fol. 17v. Reproduced with permission of the London Metropolitan Archives. 95

5.8 Philadelphia, Rosenbach Museum and Library, MS 1083/29, fol. 1r. Reproduced with permission of the Rosenbach Museum and Library. 96

5.9 Cambridge, University Library, MS Dd.8.19, fol. 7v. Reproduced by permission of the Syndics of Cambridge University Library. 97

6.1 London Metropolitan Archives, Charter 50. Reproduced with permission of the London Metropolitan Archives. 109

6.2 London Metropolitan Archives, COL/CS/01/012, *Liber Albus*, fol. 60r. Reproduced with permission of the London Metropolitan Archives. 110

6.3 San Marino, CA, Huntington Library, MS HM 19920, p. 173. Reproduced with permission of the Henry E. Huntington Library, San Marino, California. 113

6.4 Kew, National Archives, DL 42/1, fol. 1r. Reproduced with permission of The National Archives. 114

6.5 Oxford, Bodleian Library, Bodley misc. 2963 (Rolls 9), top of m. 1. Reproduced with permission of the Bodleian Library. 117

6.6 Aberystwyth, National Library of Wales, MS Peniarth 392D, fol. 150r. Reproduced with permission of The National Library of Wales. 125

ACKNOWLEDGEMENTS

We would like to thank the Arts and Humanities Research Council which funded the research for this book from 2007 to 2011, and the Neil Ker fund of the British Academy for assistance with preparation of images and permissions for their use in 2012. We would also like to thank Joel Fredell, Ralph Hanna, Simon Horobin, Michael Bennett, Matthew Davies and Daniel Mosser for reading and commenting on individual chapters or passages, and Ian Doyle and Felicity Riddy for reading the whole manuscript and offering useful suggestions for its improvement. In addition we thank Caroline Barron for suggesting that we examine the wills of John Marchaunt and John Carpenter as an indicator of the close connections among these clerks and their mutual interest in books. We would also especially like to thank Derek Pearsall and other readers and editors for the York Medieval Press for their helpful comments, corrections and encouragement. The views expressed here, and any errors remaining, are our own.

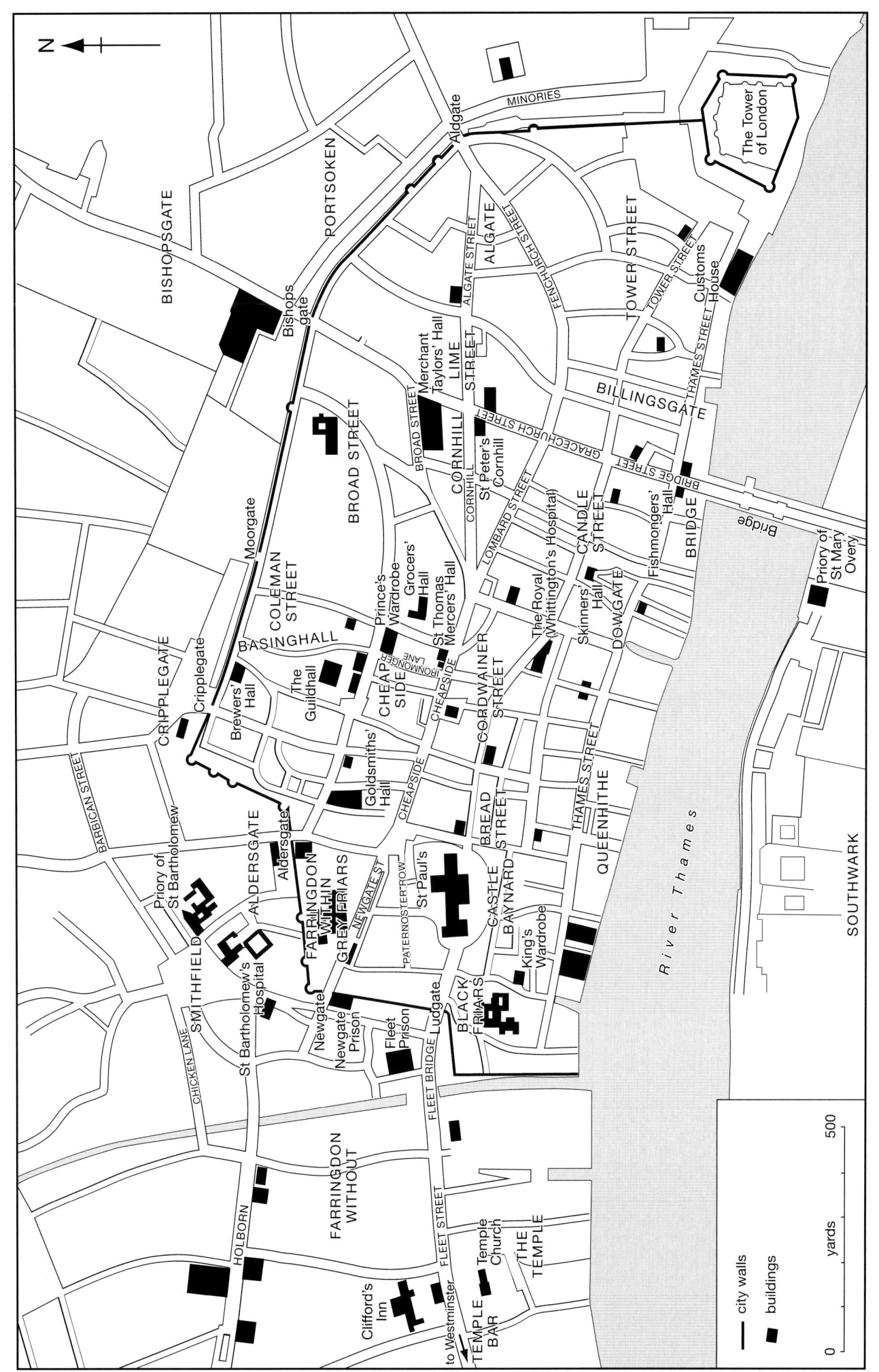

London in the late fourteenth century

*Dedicated to
Norman Blake
and
Ian Doyle*

Introduction

OVER THE LAST FEW DECADES scholarly endeavours to discover the identity or place of work of late medieval English literary scribes have helped develop a new image of what it meant to be a professional text-writer in late medieval England. Linne Mooney's discovery in 2004 of the identity of the scribe of the so-called Hengwrt and Ellesmere manuscripts of Chaucer's *Canterbury Tales* as Adam Pinkhurst, member of the Scriveners' Company of London, shifted the focus of these endeavours from viewing scribes of literary manuscripts as pure text-writers, copying Middle English literary manuscripts as their principal line of business, to investigating whether they were instead clerks for royal or civic government, livery companies or their wealthy masters, copying literary texts as a side-line.[1] Mooney has since published two further articles outlining her vision of the principal occupations and places of work for these scribes of English vernacular literature,[2] and Andrew Prescott has recently highlighted the absurdity of analysing English literary manuscripts in a vacuum in seeking to identify their scribes:

> there have been few studies ... of the production and characteristics of administrative records. The result is that the overwhelming majority of manuscripts produced in medieval England – perhaps more than 90% of the surviving handwritten products of medieval England – remain effectively unexamined from the point of view of the scribal characteristics of their production. While a small proportion of well known manuscripts of such celebrated texts as the *Canterbury Tales* or *Piers Plowman* are endlessly revisited, thousands of documents from the same period, many written by the same scribes who produced manuscripts of Chaucer and Langland, are effectively forgotten and remain uninvestigated.[3]

Drawing on exactly this kind of attention to the hands of government documents produced in London at this period, we here offer a new vision for the copying and dissemination of Middle English literature in the age of Chaucer and continuing into the first few decades of the fifteenth century. Through matching idiosyncratic elements of the handwriting of certain scribes in London documents and in literary manuscripts, we have discovered that many of the earliest and most authoritative manuscripts of works by Geoffrey Chaucer and his contemporaries John Gower, John Trevisa, and William Langland were copied by clerks employed at the London Guildhall. Whereas scholars had previously speculated that these manuscripts were produced by teams of scribes in the lay scriptoria that arose in the fourteenth century to supplement monastic book production, or by individual

---

[1] See L. R. Mooney, 'Chaucer's Scribe', *Speculum* 81 (2006), 97–138; and earlier, L. R. Mooney, 'Professional Scribes? Identifying English Scribes who had a Hand in More than One Manuscript', in *New Directions in Later Medieval Manuscript Studies*, ed. D. Pearsall (York, 2000), pp. 131–41.

[2] L. R. Mooney, 'Locating Scribal Activity in Late-Medieval London', in *Design and Distribution of Later Medieval Manuscripts in England*, ed. M. Connolly and L. R. Mooney (York, 2008), pp. 183–204; and L. R. Mooney, 'Vernacular Literary Manuscripts and their Scribes', in *The Production of Books in England, 1350–1500*, ed. A. Gillespie and D. L. Wakelin (Cambridge, 2011), pp. 192–211.

[3] A. Prescott, 'Administrative Records and the Scribal Achievement of Medieval England', *English Manuscripts before 1400*, ed. A. S. G. Edwards and Orietta da Rold, English Manuscript Studies 17 (London, 2012), pp. 173–99 (p. 190).

scribes working as freelance textwriters sometimes subcontracted by stationers, we have now identified that the scribes of many of these early and important copies of works by the London poets were clerk attorneys of the Guildhall, working for the mayor, aldermen, and sheriffs of the City of London and acting as attorneys in their courts, and later in their careers holding the most important clerical positions in the city.[4] Just as Geoffrey Chaucer wrote poetry around his day jobs as king's esquire, controller of customs, justice of the peace, keeper of the king's works, and royal forester, and Thomas Hoccleve wrote poetry around his day job as one of the four chief clerks of the royal office of the Privy Seal, these clerk-attorneys must have copied manuscripts of Middle English literature after hours or between jobs.[5] This book will identify who they were and set forth our evidence for these identifications; it will identify which manuscripts are written by their hands, and what we know of the ownership of those manuscripts; it will explain what it meant to hold the positions that they did in city government, and how the clerks positioned themselves in the politics of late fourteenth- and early fifteenth-century London.

In the first half of the twentieth century scholars such as Aage Brusendorff and Germaine Dempster argued for the existence of lay scriptoria, or workshops, where teams of scribes produced manuscripts of Middle English writings.[6] G. C. Macaulay argued that John Gower himself oversaw the production of copies of his *Confessio Amantis* and 'that there was some organized system of reproduction, which was wanting in the case of Chaucer'.[7] John Fisher took this idea further to argue that there was a scriptorium at St Mary Overie in Southwark where Gower oversaw the copying of manuscripts of his writings.[8]

An article by A. I. Doyle and M. B. Parkes in the 1978 memorial volume of essays for N. R. Ker exploded these theories of lay scriptoria, replacing them with an alternative theory that English literary scribes worked in small workshops of one or two, or operated freelance and only collaborated to the extent that a third party like a stationer might distribute portions of a text to two or more scribes for simultaneous copying.[9] Only a few studies of manuscripts produced from the middle of the fifteenth century onwards have offered evidence of commercial scriptoria for literary texts, and Linne Mooney has suggested an alternative view that scriptoria and commercial copying existed in London not for literary texts but for the copying of books in high demand such as prayer books, lectionaries, and school

---

[4] See Mooney, 'Locating Scribal Activity'; and Mooney, 'Vernacular Literary Manuscripts and their Scribes'. Previous studies included that by J. M. Bowers, 'The House of Chaucer & Son: The Business of Lancastrian Canon-Formation', *Medieval Perspectives* 6 (1991), 135–43.

[5] *Chaucer Life-Records*, ed. M. M. Crow and C. C. Olson (Oxford, 1966), pp. 94–122, 148–270, 348–63, 402–76, 494–9; D. Pearsall, *The Life of Geoffrey Chaucer: A Critical Biography* (Oxford, 1992), pp. 98–9, etc.; L. R. Mooney, 'Some New Light on Thomas Hoccleve', *Studies in the Age of Chaucer* 29 (2007), 293–340.

[6] A. Brusendorff, *The Chaucer Tradition* (Oxford, 1925; repr. 1967), 54–5; G. Dempster, 'Manly's Conception of the Early History of the *Canterbury Tales*', *PMLA* 61 (1946), 379–415 (p. 404).

[7] *The English Works of John Gower*, ed. G. C. Macaulay, 2 vols., EETS ES 81 and 82 (1900–1), I, xlvii.

[8] J. H. Fisher, *John Gower: Moral Philosopher and Friend of Chaucer* (New York, 1964), pp. 66, 116–17, 124–7, 303–6.

[9] A. I. Doyle and M. B. Parkes, 'The Production of Copies of the *Canterbury Tales* and the *Confessio Amantis* in the Early Fifteenth Century', in *Medieval Scribes, Manuscripts, and Libraries: Essays Presented to N. R. Ker*, ed. M. B. Parkes and A. G. Watson (London, 1978), pp. 163–210; repr. in M. B. Parkes, *Scribes, Scripts and Readers: Studies in the Communication, Presentation and Dissemination of Medieval Texts* (London, 1991), pp. 201–48.

books.[10] Some studies based on script, owners' names or decoration have suggested a Westminster clientele and site for vernacular manuscript copying, especially in relation to manuscripts of *Piers Plowman*.[11] Others have examined London and Westminster documentary culture more broadly to find connections to the production of medieval English manuscripts.[12]

One of the most celebrated scribes of late medieval England was Doyle and Parkes's 'Scribe B', the second scribe of Cambridge, Trinity College, MS R.3.2, whom J. S. P. Tatlock had identified as the scribe common to the earliest surviving manuscript of Geoffrey Chaucer's *Canterbury Tales*, the Hengwrt manuscript, now National Library of Wales, MS Peniarth 392D, and the most authoritative manuscript of the *Tales*, the Ellesmere manuscript, now Huntington Library, MS EL 26 C9.[13] The importance of these two manuscripts was further emphasized when Kathleen Scott argued that the decoration of the Ellesmere manuscript could not be dated later than the first decade of the fifteenth century, and would more likely fit a pattern of decoration popular at the end of the fourteenth century.[14] With this redating of Ellesmere it seemed probable that the Hengwrt manuscript, which almost all scholars accepted as predating the Ellesmere, might have been produced around the time of Chaucer's death in 1400.[15] In 2004 Linne Mooney, identified this scribe as Adam Pinkhurst, showing that the handwriting of his manuscripts matched that of certain documents in the archives of the Mercers' Company of London, in the royal petitions now stored in the National Archives at Kew, and in the Common Paper of the Scriveners' Company of London, where he had signed his name beside an oath of loyalty as a scrivener in or around 1392.[16] The discovery that this important scribe of Middle English literature was employed as a scrivener in the City of London shifted the search for London literary scribes east from Westminster and still further from the shops of textwriters. We sought their hands instead in the documents associated with the livery companies of London and in the Guildhall itself. There Estelle

---

[10] E.g., L. M. Matheson and L. R. Mooney, 'The Beryn Scribe and his Texts: Evidence for Multiple-Copy Production of Manuscripts in Fifteenth-Century England', *The Library*, 7th series 4 (2003), 347–70; Mooney, 'Locating Scribal Activity'; Mooney, 'Vernacular Literary Manuscripts and their Scribes'.

[11] J. H. Fisher, '*Piers Plowman* and the Chancery Tradition', in *Medieval English Studies Presented to George Kane*, ed. E. D. Kennedy *et al.* (Cambridge, 1988), pp. 267–78; C. Grindley, 'The Life of a Book: British Library Add. 35157 in Historical Context' (unpublished PhD dissertation, University of Glasgow, 1997); K. Kerby-Fulton, 'Professional Readers of Langland at Home and Abroad: New Directions in the Political and Bureaucratic Codicology of *Piers Plowman*', in *New Directions in Later Medieval Manuscript Studies: Essays from the 1998 Harvard Conference*, ed. D. Pearsall (York, 2000), pp. 103–29 (pp. 107–17); etc.

[12] R. Hanna, *London Literature, 1300–1380* (Cambridge, 2005), pp. 44–103; E. Steiner, *Documentary Culture and the Making of Medieval English Literature* (Cambridge, 2003).

[13] Doyle and Parkes, 'Production of Copies', pp. 170–4, 185–92 (repr. pp. 201–47); J. S. P. Tatlock, 'The Canterbury Tales in 1400', *PMLA* 50 (1935), 100–39 (p. 128); and others including *The Text of 'The Canterbury Tales': Studied on the Basis of All Known Manuscripts*, ed. J. M. Manly and E. Rickert, 8 vols. (Chicago, 1940), I, 23, 268.

[14] K. L. Scott, 'An Hours and Psalter by Two Ellesmere Illuminators', in *The Ellesmere Chaucer: Essays in Interpretation*, ed. M. Stevens and D. Woodward (San Marino CA, 1995; repr. 1997), pp. 87–119 (pp. 104–6).

[15] Estelle Stubbs argues that the Ellesmere manuscript was being written and compiled at the same time as the Hengwrt manuscript. See *The Hengwrt Chaucer Digital Facsimile*, ed. E. Stubbs, Scholarly Digital Editions (Leicester, 2000), and see further pp. 63–5 below.

[16] Mooney, 'Chaucer's Scribe', pp. 97–138.

Stubbs found the hand of Doyle and Parkes's 'Scribe D' who had copied eight manuscripts of John Gower's *Confessio Amantis* and the other two earliest copies of Chaucer's *Canterbury Tales*, and there we identified the scribe of the Huntington Library manuscript HM 114, whose hand Ian Doyle had found in documents of the London Guildhall and had identified as either a freelance scribe or an employee of the city. We knew that these two scribes must have been employed directly by the Guildhall because of their access to the city's archives, which was limited to the common clerk and the chamberlain of the city.

Our next step was to learn more about the duties and responsibilities of the clerks of the city, and fortunately these were set forth in detail in one of the books containing their handwriting, the *Liber Albus* of the City of London, which collects in one volume the rules and precedents for governing the city as they were understood in 1419. Our first chapter summarizes pertinent facts about the compilation of the *Liber Albus* and its descriptions of the offices of city government that allowed us to identify these men.

The longest serving of these men was Richard Osbarn, clerk of the chamber, or 'controller' of the city from around 1400 until his retirement in 1437. (He died the following year, 1438.) We have been able to identify him as the scribe of San Marino, CA, Henry E. Huntington Library MS HM 114 (including, among many other Middle English texts, copies of Langland's *Piers Plowman* and Chaucer's *Troilus and Criseyde*) of Lambeth Palace Library MS 491 (including, again among other Middle English texts, the prose *Brut* and the *Siege of Jerusalem*) and a portion of British Library, MS Harley 3943 (including another copy of Chaucer's *Troilus and Criseyde*). Chapter 2 sets forth our evidence for this identification, based on the appearance of his hand in the London Letter Book H in entries specifically associated with the office of chamberlain.

Another clerk who apparently served the city throughout his career was John Marchaunt, clerk of the chamber from 1380 and common clerk from at least 1399 until his retirement in 1417. (He died in 1422.) By the same method of matching his hand in scattered entries in Letter Books G, H and I with the roles of the chamber clerk and common clerk, Estelle Stubbs was able to identify him as Doyle and Parkes' Scribe D, an important scribe of Middle English literary manuscripts whom Doyle and Parkes had characterized as a 'full-time [literary] scribe'.[17] Kathryn Kerby-Fulton and Steven Justice described him as a key player in the 'marketing' of Middle English literature.[18] Chapter 3 sets forth the evidence we have found to identify John Marchaunt as Scribe D and explains his importance as a copyist of Middle English literature.

Adam Pinkhurst also appears to have been employed at the Guildhall for at least part of his career, perhaps as a mayor's court clerk or as the recorder's clerk, since his hand appears in Letter Book I. In Chapter 4 we add his name to this group of clerks centred around the Guildhall, revealing new material about his life and writings discovered since the publication in 2006 of Mooney's article 'Chaucer's Scribe'.

The man who succeeded John Marchaunt as common clerk of the City of London was John Carpenter, known to medieval historians as the compiler of the *Liber Albus* and as executor of the will of Richard Whittington, four times mayor of the City of London. Carpenter was a book collector who had a keen interest in education and public access to

---

[17] Doyle and Parkes, 'Production of Copies', p. 185 (repr. p. 223).

[18] K. Kerby-Fulton and S. Justice, 'Scribe D and the Marketing of Ricardian Literature', in *The Medieval Professional Reader at Work: Evidence from Manuscripts of Chaucer, Langland, Kempe and Gower*, English Literary Studies 85 (Victoria BC, 2001), pp. 217–37.

books.[19] We discovered that, like his fellow clerks of the Guildhall, Carpenter too copied manuscripts of Middle English literature. Ian Doyle had suggested that the hand of a letter copied into London Letter Book I, on fol. 209r–v, signed by John Carpenter, was similar to that of New York, Pierpont Morgan Library, MS M.817, the so-called Campsall manuscript of Chaucer's *Troilus and Criseyde* with the arms of the future Henry V in its border.[20] By matching his hand in signed documents and in Book I of the *Liber Albus* with that manuscript and others, we have identified him as the scribe not only of Pierpont Morgan M.817 but of two important copies of John Gower's *Confessio Amantis*. Chapter 5 describes this identification and explains Carpenter's importance as both a copyist and a book collector.

Another clerk who shared literary exemplars with these men appears to have worked primarily for the Duchy of Lancaster. Malcolm Parkes has written about Richard Frampton, characterizing him as a 'freelance literary scribe' before he was employed by the Duchy of Lancaster in the reign of Henry IV. We have found the hand of Richard Frampton in further documents that were not known to Parkes, and argue that he had access to exemplars also used by Guildhall clerks in the earlier part of his career. Chapter 6 begins with an outline of his career as clerk and literary copyist.

Chapter 6 also discusses other clerks who copied manuscripts of Middle English literature having worked for London livery companies, either as clerks of the companies or on an *ad hoc* basis. Osbarn appears to have done this for the Goldsmiths, and Marchaunt and Pinkhurst for the Mercers. The poet Thomas Usk was a clerk of the Goldsmiths in the 1370s and early 1380s before his rise to higher office in the city and his demise at the hands of the Appellants in 1388.[21] Another clerk who recorded the annual accounts in the first portion of the medieval record-book of the Skinners' Company also wrote a number of literary manuscripts, including two of Chaucer's *Canterbury Tales*. A clerk recently identified by Simon Horobin worked for the Brewers' Company. The elusive scribe 'Delta' was identified by Doyle and Parkes as a major copyist of Middle English literature.

Chapter 6 ends by considering the relationship of the poet Thomas Hoccleve to these clerks at the Guildhall. Hoccleve had been identified by Doyle and Parkes as the fifth scribe in the Cambridge, Trinity College, MS R.3.2 copy of Gower's *Confessio Amantis*.[22] We consider his involvement in that multi-scribe production and as probable corrector of the Hengwrt manuscript of *The Canterbury Tales* written by Pinkhurst, and ask how he might have been known to scribes of the Guildhall in order for his hand to be found in these two important manuscripts.

Our final chapter will place these clerks of the Guildhall in their historical context: they began their careers in the turbulent last decades of the fourteenth century when factions tore apart both city and royal government, and it would be unusual if they had managed to remain neutral. Thomas Usk rose and fell in importance as he supported first one side of these factions and then the other; John Marchaunt is named as having been present at

---

[19] M. Davies, 'Carpenter, John (d. 1442)' in *Oxford Dictionary of National Biography* (Oxford, 2004); and W. Scase, 'Reginald Pecock, John Carpenter, and John Colop's "Common-Profit" Books: Aspects of Book Ownership and Circulation in Fifteenth-Century London', *Medium Aevum* 61 (1992), 261–74.

[20] A. I. Doyle, letter to Michael Benskin, 1997, related to us by Doyle, private communication, 2002. For more on Letter Books, see Chapter 1 below.

[21] C. M. Barron, 'New Light on Thomas Usk', *Chaucer Newsletter* 26:2 (2004).

[22] Doyle and Parkes, 'Production of Copies', pp. 182–5 (repr. pp. 220–3).

the secret meetings of one faction, and Pinkhurst wrote petitions and acted as attorney for the same group. Osbarn and Carpenter came onto the scene later, being younger than Usk, Pinkhurst or Marchaunt, so they had just reached maturity in their careers in 1400 as the Lancastrians introduced a period of greater stability; nevertheless they clearly embraced the principles of the use of English and of making the written word and its teachings available to more members of English society than had had access to books before. We shall here discuss the place these scribes held in the political and social upheavals, and speculate about how this fits with their copying of literary manuscripts.

1

The Clerks of the London Guildhall

THIS BOOK offers a new vision for our understanding of the copying and dissemination of Middle English literature in the age of Chaucer and the first few decades of the fifteenth century. Through matching idiosyncratic elements of the handwriting of London documents with those of literary manuscripts, we have discovered that many of the earliest and most authoritative manuscripts of works by Geoffrey Chaucer and his contemporaries John Gower, John Trevisa, and William Langland were copied by clerks employed at the London Guildhall.[1] To understand who these men were, it will be necessary first to outline the structure of London government in the Middle Ages and describe the offices of the civil servants who ran its day-to-day business.

The London Guildhall employed a number of clerks to record and enact the business of the mayor and aldermen and their courts. Caroline Barron estimates that there were eight clerks in the Guildhall at the beginning of the fourteenth century, with this number rising to twenty-four by the end of the fifteenth century, not including the 'various serjeants and valets in the households of the mayor and sheriffs who were paid by the officials themselves'.[2] Highest in rank was the recorder of the City of London, who was primarily concerned with maintaining and recording the decisions of the Husting court, but who by the fourteenth century also sat in the mayor's court and advised the annually elected mayors, represented the city in any disputes, and was the returning officer for mayoral elections.[3] The recorder was the highest paid of the civic officers, and from around 1320 it was customary that he should become an alderman of the city on his election to this office. He was specifically required not to accept fees from any other persons or institutions while in office, a stipulation that was meant to ensure his impartiality in carrying out his legal duties and his full attention to the needs of the city's courts. The oaths of the other civic officers included no such prohibition on accepting fees, which suggests that they could take in work on the side. In keeping with this distinction, we have not been able to identify recorders as copyists of English literary manuscripts; but we have found evidence that Adam Pinkhurst may have served as one of the clerks who worked for the recorder.[4]

---

[1] Our research, supported by a major research grant from the Arts and Humanities Research Council of the UK, focused on the manuscripts of vernacular writings by five Middle English authors, the four named here and Thomas Hoccleve. Linne Mooney's previous research (and assembly of information on scribes from the work of many scholars) shows that these scribes also copied other authors' works, and writings in other languages. Because of the limited focus for this grant, we have not investigated widely for other samples of their hands in medieval manuscripts, literary or not. There is much more scope for finding their hands in further manuscripts: for instance, we have not systematically researched the early manuscripts of John Lydgate's writings, copies of the prose *Brut*, the *Speculum Vitae*, Nicholas Love's *Mirrour of the Blessed Life of Jesus Christ*, manuscripts of Wycliffite tracts or sermons or English bibles.

[2] C. M. Barron, *London in the Later Middle Ages* (Oxford, 2004), p. 196.

[3] Ibid., pp. 173–6, describes the office and its duties, providing the information for this paragraph.

[4] See Chapter 5 below.

The second office in the civic hierarchy was that of chamberlain, the city's chief financial officer. In the period with which we are concerned, the chamberlain was an amateur chosen by the commonalty, who might elect two candidates from whom the mayor and aldermen selected one. This office-holder was re-elected every year, though men might, and did, hold it for several consecutive years. Most of those who held this office were members of the great mercantile companies, the Mercers, Grocers, Fishmongers and Goldsmiths. Because they were already established guildsmen, according to Barron, 'The chamberlain was not provided with a house, nor was he given a livery or any perquisites'.[5] The duties of the chamberlain increased significantly in the fourteenth and fifteenth centuries as Londoners left properties to the city which needed to be maintained and whose rents needed to be collected and recorded.[6] He was assisted in this work by three serjeants who were elected by the common council. The chamberlain was ultimately responsible for the accuracy of the city's ledgers, but their keeping would have been deputized to the clerk of the chamber, or 'controller', a professional civil servant who could hold his office for life.[7] The best-known chamberlain is Andrew Horn, who was re-elected many times, serving in this office from 1320 until his death in 1328. Horn compiled or oversaw the compilation for the city of both a *Liber Legum* (*c.* 1321) and a *Liber Custumarum* (1324).[8]

Next in the civic hierarchy was the common clerk, after the recorder the highest of the permanent, professional, paid officers at the Guildhall. The common clerk archived the records of the courts of assize and the Husting, and kept some of the city's legal records. The common clerk received an annual salary of £10, but, as Barron notes, citing the *Liber Albus*, 'the common clerk also received 10*d.* for every deed or will recorded in the Husting, 2*s.* for every deed enrolled in the mayor's court rolls, and 6*d.* for every writ drawn up for assizes of nuisance and freshforce'.[9] These fees, like the modern collection of stamp taxes, would have provided a very comfortable income to common clerks. Besides this income, the common clerk could receive rewards from individuals and livery companies for 'helping companies to draw up petitions for presentation to the mayor, writing letters, or offering good advice and counsel'.[10] In other words, he could accept gratuities for such work from individuals or institutions, whereas the recorder was forbidden to do so. The role of common clerk seems to have been enlarged in the early fifteenth century, when the office was held first by John Marchaunt (1399–1417) and then by John Carpenter (1417–38). During this period the custody of city records seems to have been shifting towards the common clerk, who took over some responsibility for archives from the chamberlain. As we explain in Chapter 2, this transfer of duties may have had something to do with the building works in the Guildhall close in the early decades of the fifteenth century, when records formerly held in the Guildhall itself may have needed safekeeping while it was partly torn down and reconstructed. It may also have had something to do with the conscientious holders of the office of common clerk, John Marchaunt and John Carpenter, along with Richard Osbarn, who held the office of

---

[5] Barron, *London in the Later Middle Ages*, p. 176, citing B. R. Masters, *The Chamberlain of the City of London, 1273–1987* (London, 1988), p. 87.

[6] Barron, *London in the Later Middle Ages*, pp. 178–9.

[7] For description of the duties of the chamber clerk, or controller, see p. 9 below.

[8] N. R. Ker, '*Liber Custumarum*, and Other Manuscripts Formerly at the Guildhall', in *Books, Collectors and Libraries: Studies in the Medieval Heritage*, ed. A. G. Watson (London, 1985), pp. 135–42 (pp. 135–7). See also Hanna, *London Literature*, pp. 67–79.

[9] Barron, *London in the Later Middle Ages*, p. 185.

[10] Ibid., p. 186.

controller, or chamber clerk, during virtually the whole period of both men's tenure, 1400–37. These three men were particularly highly esteemed in the city, Carpenter the most of all. Carpenter served as common clerk for the most famous mayor of London, Richard Whittington, Mercer, in Whittington's last term as mayor, 1419–20. It was in this year, as Carpenter pointedly mentions in his introduction, that he completed the compilation of a book of the city customs and indices to other records of city charters and privileges held at the Guildhall called the *Liber Albus*, or White Book of the Customs and Charters of the City of London.[11]

Next in seniority within the Guildhall was the clerk of the chamber, or chamberlain's clerk, also called the 'controller'. Since the chamberlain was not a professional clerk but a member of one of London's livery companies elected for a year at a time to keep the city's finances, the chamber clerk, or controller, had the ongoing responsibility for managing the city's financial affairs and keeping its financial records. Chamber clerks were paid 100s., or £5, per annum, but Barron notes that they were also 'entitled to half the fee paid for the enrolment of entries to the freedom [of the city], and also to whatever sum for his work the auditors of the chamberlain's annual account considered appropriate.'[12] A chamber clerk might bring in significant income from this activity, as we have discovered Richard Osbarn doing when he made a copy of their charters for the Goldsmiths' Company.[13]

Other professional long-term office-holders at the Guildhall were the common serjeant-at-law, the common serjeant-at-arms (or common crier), the mayors' esquires or swordbearers, the waterbailiff, the common hunt, the serjeant of the channel, and the coroner and deputy coroner. Of these, the only one that relates to our study of clerks writing literary manuscripts is the common serjeant-at-law, also called the common pleader. He acted as spokesman and prosecutor for the freemen of London and their orphans in the city courts, and he kept a close eye on the chamberlain's activities on behalf of city orphans.[14] Chaucer's friend or acquaintance, Ralph Strode, held this office from 1373 to 1382, more or less coinciding with the period of Chaucer's service as controller of the wool custom on behalf of Richard II, 1374–86. Both men were granted houses by the city, Chaucer's perhaps as a gesture to please Richard II or as an acknowledgement that, though formerly a member of the king's household and still in royal employment, Chaucer was yet one of themselves, the son of a Vintner. Strode was granted the apartments built over Aldersgate for the term of his office, and then in 1375 he was granted them for life; but he was deprived of these apartments in 1382/3 and in another turnabout was awarded 4 marks per annum in compensation for loss of the residence.[15] Over a similar span of years, 1374–85, Geoffrey Chaucer resided in the apartments built over Aldgate while he served as controller of customs. Chaucer named Strode, together with the poet John Gower, as men who should read and amend his great love poem, *Troilus and Criseyde*, which he completed around 1385, towards the end of his employment as controller of customs; it may be that the city formed the link between

---

[11] London Metropolitan Archives, CLRO, COL/CS/01/012 (Cust. 12). *Liber Albus* was so called by the mid-fifteenth century, and the name continued in use even after the volume was bound in black leather in the sixteenth century; since then it has been rebound at least once, in tanned leather.

[12] Barron, *London in the Later Middle Ages*, p. 183.

[13] See pp. 24–5 below.

[14] Barron, *London in the Later Middle Ages*, p. 189.

[15] Ibid., citing Letter Book H, in the *Calendar of Letter-Books of the City of London, A–L*, ed. R. R. Sharpe, 11 vols. (London, 1899–1912), VIII, 15, 83, 208, 245.

these men.[16] Gower is thought to have had a legal career but no one has discovered in what capacity he served.[17] John Marchaunt, chamber clerk from 1380 and common clerk from c. 1399 until 1417, occupied a similar elevated city apartment over the middle gate to the Guildhall yard, and as copyist of eight manuscripts of Gower's *Confessio Amantis*, including those considered closest to Gower's original, it is likely that he knew the poet personally.[18]

Barron notes that 'There were clearly close links between the chamberlain's clerk and the common clerk', and cites the example that John Carpenter acted as feoffee for Richard Osbarn.[19] Osbarn and Carpenter served together as executors for Marchaunt's will.[20] In his own will Carpenter bequeathed a large number of books, some to members of the civic secretariat with whom he had worked all his life, with the remainder to be given to the newly built Guildhall Library. In this will he stated that at least one of the books had been given to him by his predecessor in the office of common clerk, John Marchaunt. Their common interest in books is also attested by the number of literary manuscripts we have identified written in the hands of these three men.

The handwriting of all three of these men appears in the *Liber Albus*, compiled by John Carpenter and completed in 1419 during the fourth mayoralty of Richard Whittington. Barron states that Carpenter's work on the *Liber Albus* was 'in his capacity as the city's common clerk' and 'with the encouragement of the then mayor, Richard Whittington', and further that 'This was not a private project on Carpenter's part (unlike Horn's compilations a century earlier), but a public task undertaken for public use.'[21] As she says, there had been several attempts in the fourteenth century to compile a book of customs, rights, and privileges of the City of London,[22] but this one had the longest influence on London governance. William Kellaway noted that 'for centuries [it was] regarded as a major source for the law and custom of the City of London [and] it was still considered to be of sufficient importance to merit an elaborate transcript [in the sixteenth century]'.[23] The *Liber Albus* is a compilation, a *repertorium* as Carpenter himself calls it, drawn from the archival documents held at the Guildhall and compiled in several booklets each focused on a different aspect of city governance. Its structure is consequently very complex. William Kellaway's article offers the best description of the constituent parts of this complicated volume, so we shall use his divisions of its contents as our base in describing where the hands of literary scribes occur in the manuscript.[24]

---

[16] See Chaucer, *Troilus and Criseyde*, V.1856–9, in *The Riverside Chaucer*, gen. ed. L. Benson (Oxford, 1987). All further quotations or citations from Chaucer's works are taken from this edition unless otherwise indicated.

[17] Fisher, *John Gower*, pp. 55–8.

[18] See Chapter 3 below.

[19] Barron, *London in the Later Middle Ages*, p. 184.

[20] We thank Prof. Barron for calling our attention to this will. For more on the close working relationships among these men, see pp. 11–16, 28–30, 86–7, 96–9, 134–5, 138–40 below.

[21] C. M. Barron, 'The Political Culture of Medieval London', in *Political Culture in Late Medieval Britain*, ed. L. Clark and C. Carpenter, The Fifteenth Century 4: (Cambridge, 2004), pp. 110–33 (p. 126).

[22] These are described briefly by Barron: ibid., pp. 122–6.

[23] W. Kellaway, 'John Carpenter's *Liber Albus*', *Guildhall Studies in London History* 3:2 (1978), 67–84 (p. 67).

[24] Ibid., pp. 74–84.

The *Liber Albus* consists of four separate books, some in multiple portions and some created well before 1419. There is significant evidence that the volume was conceived as early as the 1390s and built up over several decades. Kellaway set out the organization of these booklets as follows.

Book I, written last of all the booklets, begins with Carpenter's introduction, explaining why he was preparing this *repertorium*, or finding aid, for the officials of the City of London. Kellaway translates and summarizes this introduction:

> Since human memory is fallible and life is short, we are unable to learn everything worth remembering even though it has been committed to writing, especially if such writing is without order or arrangement. Furthermore, since the aged and most experienced rulers of the City have frequently perished by pestilence at the same moment, their successors have, at various times, been at a loss for written information and disputes have arisen as to what decisions should be taken. The superior authorities of the City, as well as their inferiors, have long deemed necessary the compilation of a Repertorium containing the regulations of the City compiled from the more noteworthy memoranda that lie scattered without order or classification throughout the books, rolls and charters of the City. Such a project, not previously undertaken perhaps because of the extreme laboriousness of the task, is now at length compiled in the mayoralty of Richard Whittington, i.e. November 1419. It contains not only those praiseworthy observances which, though not written, have been usually followed and approved in the City, but also the written memoranda already referred to, so that the superior authorities and their inferiors may know henceforth more precisely what should be done in rare and unusual emergencies.[25]

This introduction (fol. 2r) is followed by the table of contents for Book I (fols 2v–4v), also written by Carpenter.[26]

Next comes Part 1 of Book I (fols 5r–19v), written in Carpenter's hand, containing a description of how the city is governed, of the officers of the Guildhall and their duties,

---

[25] Ibid., p. 69. The original text, fol. 2r of the *Liber Albus*, reads [with lacunae where the left side of the leaf has been damaged], 'Quia labilitas humane memorie brevitas *que* vite de singulis rebus memorandis licet scriptis presertim irregulari*ter* & confuse multo magis de non Scriptis certam h*abere* noticiam non *per*mittunt Civiique *per* frequentes pestilencias subtractis velut insimul cunctis gubernatoribus longevis magis ex*per*tis & discrecioribus Civitatis regal*is* londo*ni* Juniores eis in Civitatis regimine succe[....]s[..]ii variis casibus *per* defectu scripture [nume]ru*m* sepius anbigebit*ur* [....su]*per* iudiciis reddend*is* controversia & *per*plexitas int*er* eos pluries causa [....] Necessariu*m* videbat*ur* adiutam sup*er*ioribus quia subditis d*icte* Civi[] quoddam volumen quod Reportoriu*m* a contento in eo Civitatis [....]re di[..]reti[..] ex notabilib*us* memorandis tam in libris Rotulis [...] cartis d*icte* Civitatis inordinate diffuse q*ue* positis compilari. Et [....] c*ter* proposit*is* qua de causa nescitur nisi *propter* laborem num*erum* hactenus [...] erat execu*te* tempore Majoratus nobilis viri Ricardi Whityng[ton] [Ma]ioris d*icte* Civitatis Anno vide*licet* Incarnacionis d*omi*ni Mill*essi*mo qua[drages]simo decimo nono Regni vero Regis Henrici quinti post con[questu]m septimo Mense Novembris huiusmodi volumen annuente [....] compilatur continens in se tam laudabiles observancias no*n* [......]as in d*icte* Civitate fieri solitas & approbatas ne post*er*ius deleat[...] [......]imo q*uam* notabilia memoranda modo quo *per*dicitur sparsim & mor[...] [......]e scripta ut securius *per* ea cognita \sciant/ tam superiores q*uam* subditi d*icte* [Civit]atis quid in casib*us* raris & insolitis dec*ete*ro sit agendu*m* & c*etera*.

[26] All our references to folios in the *Liber Albus* will disagree with those used by Kellaway, 'John Carpenter's *Liber Albus*', since we use the newer foliation, marked in pencil at the centre of the lower margin of rectos.

described in his introduction as 'those praiseworthy observances which, though not written, have been usually followed and approved in the City'.[27] It includes references to the items of Books II to IV, so it was clearly written last, probably in 1419.[28] Book I, Part 2 (fols 20r–43v), consists of two quires extracted from the *Liber Custumarum* (London, Metropolitan Archives, CLRO COL/CS/01/006), compiled and written in the 1320s by the Fishmonger Andrew Horn.[29] The portion here extracted from *Liber Custumarum* concerns visitations of justices in eyre.

Book II (fols 44r–174v) is largely made up of the *Inspeximus* of Henry IV renewing the royal charters granted to the city by previous monarchs (fols 60r–105v), and a table summarizing their contents. Kellaway comments that since the *Liber Albus* was completed in 1419 we might instead expect to find the *Inspeximus* of Henry V from 12 July 1414, and that therefore this portion of the book must have been written before then.[30] We have identified the writer of the *Inspeximus* as Richard Frampton, Lancastrian clerk (see Chapter 6), who also wrote the original *Inspeximus*. This suggests that this second copy was also written at the beginning of Henry IV's reign. The *Inspeximus* itself is preceded by a table (fols 44r–57v), *Tabula super cartis de libertatibus civitatis*, giving extracts or summaries of the contents of the *Inspeximus*.[31] The original portion of the table (fols 44v–55v) is written in the hand of Richard Osbarn, who also added marginal finding aids on the leaves of the *Inspeximus*, keyed to his table. This table was probably prepared before 1414, since it summarizes only the charters of Henry IV's *Inspeximus*. Copies of charters granted to the city by later monarchs, Henry V to James I, are added by later hands to the folios immediately following the *Inspeximus*, fols 105v–137v, and abstracts or summaries of these are added to Osbarn's table on fols 55v–57v.[32] Because neither the abstracts nor the copies of charters for Henry V are written in Osbarn's hand, it appears that he completed his work on Book II before 1414.

Book III (fols 175r–267v) consists of a list of contents in a hand we have not identified (fols 175r–184r), followed by four parts containing transcripts of documents illustrating

---

[27] Kellaway, 'John Carpenter's *Liber Albus*', p. 69. Barron, 'Political Culture of Medieval London', p. 126, comments that in fact Carpenter was 'writing an account of how he believes the city should be governed'. See further Chapter 4 below. Fols 18v–19v are left blank.

[28] Kellaway, 'John Carpenter's *Liber Albus*', p. 75, notes that it must have been written after 1416, referencing Cap. XIII.

[29] These are fols 16–39v of the older foliation used by Kellaway; N. R. Ker, *Medieval Manuscripts in British Libraries*, 4 vols. (Oxford, 1969–92), I, 27–34; the text of these leaves is edited in *Munimenta Gildhallae Londoniensis: Liber Albus, Liber Custumarum et Liber Horn*, ed. H. T. Riley, 3 vols. in 4, Rolls Series 12 (London, 1859–60), pp. 45–113, and described in the introduction, pp. xxi–xxii. For Andrew Horn see J. Catto, 'Andrew Horn: Law and History in Fourteenth-Century England', in *The Writing of History in the Middle Ages: Essays Presented to Richard William Southern*, ed. R. H. C. Davies and J. M. Wallace-Hadrill (Oxford, 1981), pp. 367–91; Hanna, *London Literature*, pp. 67–79. For the break-up of the volume, see N. R. Ker, '*Liber Custumarum* and other Manuscripts Formerly at the Guildhall', *Guildhall Miscellany* 1:3 (London, 1954), 37–45 (p. 39, n. 11); and P. R. Robinson, *Catalogue of Dated and Datable Manuscripts, c. 888–1600, in London Libraries*, 2 vols. (London, 2003), I, no. 20; II, plate 44.

[30] Kellaway, 'John Carpenter's *Liber Albus*', p. 70.

[31] Fols 58r–59v are blank.

[32] Osbarn had left blank spaces for these additions, and they do not fill the blanks he left: fols 55v–57v at end of the table and fols 138r–174v after additions of later charters are still blank.

London customs.[33] Kellaway describes this portion of the volume as having 'no clear principles of selection' and adds, 'nor is it always evident why one text was chosen in preference to another' and 'Furthermore, [that] much of the material is arranged in a somewhat haphazard fashion.'[34] Kellaway further remarks that,

> Book III, apart from later interpolations, contains no document later than 1394. The hand in which it is written appears nowhere else in the volume and is, perhaps, the earliest in *Liber Albus* (book I part ii excepted). Unlike Books I, II and IV it does not commence with an illuminated initial and border.[35]

Because it may have been prepared as a draft for internal use, or a first draft from which a clean copy was intended to be made, the handwriting in Book III is very informal, making identification of the scribes more difficult. (Unlike Kellaway, we find more than one hand at work in Book III.) Estelle Stubbs identified one of the hands that appears in scattered occurrences throughout Book III as the literary scribe identified by Doyle and Parkes and known after their appellation as 'Scribe D':[36] he is John Marchaunt, who served as common clerk of the city from at least 1399 until 1417, when he was succeeded by John Carpenter (see Chapter 3). Although not involved in either the original compilation of texts or the table of contents of Book III, Richard Osbarn added more marginal headings throughout Book III and heavily annotated the table to link its entries to his additional headings. Furthermore, he added to the end of Book III, Part 4 material describing the laws governing kidells,[37] immediately after the end of the original texts (fols 254r–259v), and he added entries at the end of the table of contents on fol. 183r to include references to this new material.

Book IV (fols 268r–356r) begins with another preface by Carpenter where he states that he had intended to transcribe more important documents (i.e. continuing the work of Book III) but that he feared he would be thought presumptuous to devote so much of his time to such a task rather than attending to the city's business, so instead he proposed a calendar (or list) of the important documents with references to where they could be found in the city's archives. This calendar, or finding list, occupies the rest of Book IV. It is not written in Carpenter's hand but rather that of Richard Osbarn, who wrote the table of contents for Book II and the marginal references throughout the volume that are tied to the tables.

❦

---

[33] Kellaway, 'John Carpenter's *Liber Albus*', p. 77, notes that this table could have been compiled at any time before 1419. Blank leaves were again left for additions, some filled at the end of Book III, Part 4 (fols 261r–263r) with additional matter by Osbarn and other fifteenth-century scribes, and some still blank (fols 184v–186r at the end of the table, fol. 260r–v before the later additions, and fols 263v–267v after the additions at the end of Book III).

[34] Ibid., p. 70.

[35] Ibid.; although Kellaway refers to a single hand here, Book III is actually written by several hands.

[36] Doyle and Parkes, 'Production of Copies', pp. 174–82 (repr. pp. 212–20).

[37] Kiddells are fish-weirs, and the mayor and aldermen regularly ordered their inspection to ensure that the Thames was not being over-fished. John Carpenter served on commissions of enquiry into kiddells, including one in 1440, very late in his life. See Kellaway, 'John Carpenter's *Liber Albus*', p. 68, and pp. 82–3, where he describes Osbarn's hand (Book III, Part 4, fols 254r–259v [250r–55v in the older foliation he used]) without knowing the writer's identity: 'A collection of material in another hand (15th cent.) arranged with unusual care' (p. 83).

Kellaway had commented that portions of the *Liber Albus* had been written by John Carpenter well before the 1419 date of its completion. He recognized that the inserted portions, from Horn's *Liber Custumarum* and Henry IV's *Inspeximus*, were written earlier, and speculated that Book III had been written in the 1390s. Our identifications of the scribes complements his theory that the volume was conceived as early as the 1390s and the work on it carried out from time to time during the decades leading up to 1419. Richard Osbarn's table to Book II must have been prepared for the city before Henry V's *Inspeximus* in 1414, so a version of Book II, including Osbarn's table and marginal finding aids, had been completed in the previous reign. The documents compiled in the original portion of Book III can be dated up to 1394 and not later, so it is clear that this portion of the *Liber Albus* had been begun before the rest, and long before Carpenter or even before his predecessor John Marchaunt held the office of common clerk.[38] Carpenter's comments at the beginning of Book I show that the superior officers of the city had long seen the need for compiling a book of its laws and customs, and it seems clear that the work of compiling this had been begun in the 1390s, probably under the direction of the previous common clerk, Henry Perot, who died in 1394. It appears that Marchaunt, probably working under Perot, had taken part in this transcription of documents and memoranda, and that its simple red and blue decoration and lack of organization point to its having been the first attempt at a book of customs, perhaps intended for reorganization or even recopying to compile a more orderly and neat, decorated, version. Then, just as Carpenter suggested in his preface to Book IV, these officials found it difficult to complete the task of gathering all the material, having 'enter[ed] upon such an inextricable wilderness and a chaos so vast'.[39] At Perot's death the office of common clerk remained empty, or at least not officially filled, until the accession of Henry IV in 1399, when records show that it was held by John Marchaunt. It is likely that in those intervening years Marchaunt was fulfilling the duties of common clerk, though perhaps not officially named, and therefore might not have found the time to continue the work he had begun under Perot. Finally, Carpenter, on taking up the task of completing the *Liber Albus*, equally found it too laborious to select and organize documents from the rough drafts of Book III but deemed that the transcripts gathered in the 1390s would be better than nothing. Thus the portions were compiled by successive civil servants over a considerable period:

- *c.* 1321–8 Andrew Horn, Chamberlain, compiled his *Liber Custumarum*, from which Book I, fols 20r–43v, are taken (two quires extracted from Horn's volume), relating to visitations of justices in eyre.

- *c.* 1388–94 Henry Perot (?), John Marchaunt and others transcribed documents relating to London's customs from various sources, perhaps intending to organize and rewrite them but never finding time to do so, now Book III (fols 174r–267v). This work may have been begun after the burning of the Jubilee Book in 1387.

- *c.* 1399–1400 Richard Frampton prepared a second copy of the *Inspeximus* of Henry IV in codex form, perhaps commissioned specifically to be incorporated as Book II of the *Liber Albus* (fols 60r–105v), containing copies of royal charters

---

[38] Ibid., p. 70; Kellaway further remarks, pp. 70–1, 'Although inconclusive, the evidence suggests that Book III was written at the very end of the fourteenth or early in the fifteenth century. It follows, then, that Book I part ii, Book II (fols 56a–101b) and the text of Book III were already in existence when Carpenter became common clerk.'

[39] Ibid., p. 70.

granted to the City of London from William the Conqueror up to the accession of Henry IV.

c. 1400–14   Richard Osbarn compiled the abstracts or summaries to Book II, fols 44r–55v; he may also have written the marginal finding aids in Books II and III, the table to Book II and annotations to the table of Book III at this time. His work on Book III could have been done at any time up to 1419.

c. 1417–19   John Carpenter wrote the preface to Book IV (fol. 268r), and Richard Osbarn, at John Carpenter's instruction, prepared the rest of Book IV; and Osbarn could have added the additional headings and annotations to the table of Book III if he had not done so already.

1419   John Carpenter wrote the preface to the whole volume and the first part of Book I, Part 1 describing the officers of the Guildhall and their duties, including a table of contents to Book I at the beginning of the volume. Richard Osbarn added marginal headings as finding aids, fols 7r–8v.

15th century and later   Clerks of the Guildhall added material to Book II, at the end of the table and after the inserted *Inspeximus*, and to the end of Book III, Part 4.

The collection of London customs was thus conceived in the 1390s and prepared over three decades by the common clerks and chamber clerks, some of the most senior officers of the civic secretariat whose successors were meant to benefit from its compilation. Additions continuing to the early seventeenth century suggest that the book continued to be used by the clerks as a reference work for centuries.

Besides the *Liber Albus*, other documents written in the Guildhall (and now held there, as part of the London Metropolitan Archives) have helped us to identify these literary scribes who were employed in the city. To test whether hands in the *Liber Albus* were clerks employed at the Guildhall itself we searched the London Letter Books, since the common clerk had chief responsibility for these, and other clerks of the Guildhall might also be expected to make entries in them. The Letter Books are so called because the volumes are designated by letters of the alphabet, indicating chronological order, and were so referenced even in medieval documents. They begin with Letter Book A early in the reign of Edward I (1275).[40] They continue through the alphabet, A–Z, plus some odd extra volumes, and again through double letters, AA–ZZ, to near the end of the reign of James I; but Letter Books A–H, for the period 1275–1399, are the most important, because they are virtually the only record that survives of the decisions of the court of common council and court of aldermen relating to the government of the City of London. Beginning in the fifteenth century the decisions of these courts were recorded separately in volumes called Journals and Repertories, but the more important decisions were also still recorded in Letter Books I, K and L, covering the reigns of Henry IV and Henry V (Book I), Henry VI (Book K), and Edward IV to Henry VII (Book L).[41] Examining Letter Books G (1352–74), H (1375–99), I (1400–23) and K (1423–61), we recognized the hands of Richard Osbarn (formerly called 'The HM 114 Scribe'), John

---

[40] *Calendar of Letter-Books*. See also *Memorials of London and London Life in the Thirteenth, Fourteenth and Fifteenth Centuries*, ed. and trans. H. T. Riley (London, 1868).

[41] *Calendar of Letter-Books*, I, i and n. 1. In the fifteenth century there was considerable duplication, since the journals began in 1416 but the letter books for a time continued to record much of the same material. In 1495 the decisions of the court of aldermen began to be recorded separately in

Marchaunt (formerly called 'Scribe D'), John Carpenter, and Adam Pinkhurst (formerly called 'Scribe B' or 'the Hengwrt-Ellesmere scribe').

The content of the entries written by their hands were the key for us to match the names of these clerks with the duties and responsibilities of the offices, as described by John Carpenter in Book I of the *Liber Albus*. John Carpenter served as a control, since we knew his name and office, and the part he played in compiling the *Liber Albus*. His hand in Books I and IV of the *Liber Albus* also matched a signed record on the dorse of the will of John Marchaunt.[42] Mooney had already identified the hand of manuscripts of Chaucer's *Canterbury Tales* as Adam Pinkhurst, scrivener of London, but new identifications of his hand in Letter Books H and I have enabled us to connect him to the Guildhall.[43] H. T. Riley had concluded that a single hand had written the table of contents for Book II and the calendar summarizing the content of records at the Guildhall that forms the bulk of Book IV, but had mistakenly assumed this to be Carpenter's own hand.[44] Doyle corrected this by contrast with a signed piece of Carpenter's work, showing instead that it was the hand of Huntington Library MS HM 114 and other literary manuscripts. Doyle added that this hand could also be found in Letter Book I, fols 223r, 224v, 226v–27r, 228r, 229r–31v.[45] We discovered his greater involvement in compiling the *Liber Albus* by adding the marginal finding aids to Books II and III, and found his hand adding entries dated after 1400 to Letter Book H (1375–99) through which we identified him as the chamber clerk after 1400, and thus as Richard Osbarn.[46] The hand of John Marchaunt had been identified with the sobriquet of 'Scribe D' in twelve literary manuscripts. After recognizing his hand in Book III of the *Liber Albus* Stubbs examined Letter Books G (1352–74) and H (1375–99) and found his hand adding occasional entries relating to decisions of the chamberlain in the 1380s and 1390s, which identified him as the then clerk of the chamber, John Marchaunt, who later served as common clerk of the city before John Carpenter.[47]

Thus in the Guildhall records we have traced several of the scribes of late fourteenth- and early fifteenth-century manuscripts of the works of Geoffrey Chaucer, John Gower, William Langland, John Trevisa and other anonymous vernacular literary authors of the late fourteenth and early fifteenth centuries. Remarkable as it seems, these busy clerks found time to prepare copies of vernacular literary writings. They sometimes had access to early authorial copies of these writings, and often to more than one exemplar. The following chapters will focus on each clerk-scribe in turn to describe the documents where we have found his handwriting among the records of the City of London, and the manuscripts of literary writings to which we can therefore link him.

---

the repertories, whereas for most of the fifteenth century the journals recorded decisions of both courts.

[42] For Carpenter as copyist of literary manuscripts see Chapter 4 below. Marchaunt's will is Kew, National Archives, E 40/12349; Carpenter writes and signs a note on the dorse, as executor, to say that the will has been enrolled at the Husting Court.

[43] Mooney, 'Chaucer's Scribe'. For a discussion of his hand in the Letter Book see Chapter 5 below.

[44] *Munimenta Gildhallae Londoniensis: Liber Albus*, p. xxii, n. 2.

[45] Personal communication to Ralph Hanna, cited in *The Siege of Jerusalem*, ed. R. Hanna and D. Lawton, EETS OS 320 (2003), p. xxii.

[46] See Chapter 2 below.

[47] See Chapter 3 below.

2

Richard Osbarn, Chamber Clerk, 1400–37

THE SCRIBE who wrote the manuscript anthology of Middle English literary works now in the Huntington Library, MS HM 114, and other literary manuscripts, was previously known as the 'the scribe of Huntington HM 114' or 'the HM 114 Scribe'. We present here the evidence we have discovered for identifying him as Richard Osbarn, the man who held the position of controller, or clerk of the chamber, at the London Guildhall from 1400 to 1437.

The HM 114 Scribe is acknowledged to have played an important role in recording and thus preserving copies of Middle English literature in the first half of the fifteenth century. The three literary manuscripts attributed to his hand are London, Lambeth Palace Library, MS 491; San Marino, CA, Huntington Library, MS HM 114; and the first half of London, British Library, MS Harley 3943.[1] The latter manuscript records a portion of *Troilus and Criseyde* prepared on parchment, while the other two manuscripts are anthologies of Middle English verse and prose containing originally separate booklets of mixed paper and parchment construction. These include the following texts, drawn from Ralph Hanna's 1989 article, 'The Scribe of Huntington Library HM 114', and listed in the chronological order he suggested, that is, with both Lambeth 491 and Harley preceding HM 114, but with no indication of whether Lambeth or Harley came first:[2]

⁋ London, Lambeth Palace Library, MS 491

   Booklet 1: 16 quires of 16, some with leaves missing: Middle English prose *Brut*, acephalous and ending in reign of Edward III (fols 1r–205v); Alliterative *Siege of Jerusalem*, lines 1–632 (fols 206r–216v)

   Booklet 2: 4 quires of 16, some with leaves missing: *Siege of Jerusalem* concluded (fols 217r–227v); unique Middle English prose translation of *The Three Kings of Cologne* (fols 228r–274v)

   Booklet 3: 1 quire of 16, presumably once longer to complete the text: *The Awntyrs of Arthure* (fols 275r–286v); Middle English verse *Book of Hunting*, incomplete, ending at line 349 (fols 287r–290v)

⁋ San Marino, CA, Henry E. Huntington Library, MS HM 114

   Booklet 1: 8 quires of 16, some with leaves missing: Langland, *Piers Plowman* (fols 1r–130v)

   Booklet 2: 4 quires of 16, some with leaves missing: *Mandeville's Travels* (fols 131r–184v); Alliterative *Susanna* (fols 184v–190v); excerpt from *The Three Kings of Cologne* (fols 190v–192v)

---

[1] A. I. Doyle, 'The Manuscripts', in *Middle English Alliterative Poetry and its Literary Background*, ed. D. A. Lawton (Cambridge, 1982), pp. 88–100, 142–7 (pp. 94, 144, nn. 22–3).

[2] R. Hanna, 'The Scribe of Huntington HM 114', *Studies in Bibliography* 42 (1989), 120–33; see also R. Hanna, 'The Manuscripts and Transmission of Chaucer's *Troilus*', in *The Idea of Medieval Literature: New Essays on Chaucer and Medieval Culture in Honor of Donald R. Howard*, ed. J. M. Dean and C. K. Zacher (Newark, 1992), pp. 173-88. The order of the manuscripts is discussed in greater detail at pp. 32–7 below.

Booklet 3: 8 quires of 16, some with leaves missing: Chaucer, *Troilus and Criseyde* (fols 193r–318v); unique Middle English translation of Peter Ceffons, *Epistola Luciferi ad Cleros* (fols 319r–325v)

¶ London, British Library, MS Harley 3943, fols 2r–7v, 9r–56v, 63r–67v

Chaucer, *Troilus and Criseyde*, completed by later hands to 116 folios.

Besides these literary manuscripts, the scribe's hand has been identified in London Letter Book I writing in 1418–19 and in the *Liber Albus* compiled by John Carpenter in 1419.[3]

It seems remarkable that this important preserver and disseminator of Middle English texts could be identical with such an important and busy officer of the Guildhall as Richard Osbarn, an attorney in the Husting courts in the 1390s and clerk of the chamber for the City of London from 1400 until 1437, but there is very strong evidence for this identification.[4]

In his article on this scribe, Hanna pointed out that the HM 114 Scribe's language was 'fairly consistent', indicating an origin (or at least training) in a small area of the Thames estuary in south-eastern Essex, but he argued that all three of his manuscripts were written after the scribe had migrated to London.[5] Identification of the scribe as Richard Osbarn suggests that he was a Londoner, or migrated to London at an early age, since he had served as an attorney in the city's courts from 1390 to 1403, and probably as a clerk at the London Guildhall before and concurrently. In 1400 he was raised to the important position of controller, or clerk of the chamber, which he held for almost forty years.[6]

Hanna sought to estimate the period of the HM 114 Scribe's productivity in London, though he acknowledged that the hand 'cannot be dated very precisely' on palaeographical grounds.[7] Lambeth 491 and HM 114 could be dated by their paper stocks, and Hanna's appendix set forth his descriptions of the watermarks, and their similarities to those in Briquet.[8] Consuelo Dutschke's catalogue of the manuscripts in the Huntington Library identifies some of these watermarks differently and therefore assigns different dates to them.[9] Combining their evidence, it appears that Lambeth 491 contains papers similar to those produced from 1405 to the 1410s (the *Brut*), to another produced 1414–20 (Booklet 1: end of the *Brut* and fragment of *Siege of Jerusalem*), and to one produced from 1397 with variants to 1413 (Booklets 2 and 3: *Siege of Jerusalem*, excerpt of *Three Kings of Cologne*, *The Awntyrs of Arthure*, *Book of Hunting*). HM 114 contains two papers similar to ones produced in the early 1420s, one similar to a paper produced in 1410, and another similar to one produced from

---

[3] These appearances were identified by A. I. Doyle, whose discovery is recorded in the description of Lambeth Palace Library, MS 491, in *Siege of Jerusalem*, ed. Hanna and Lawton, p. xxii. We argue below for his greater involvement in the compilation of the *Liber Albus*.

[4] For dates of Osbarn's service as chamber clerk see Barron, *London in the Later Middle Ages*, p. 363; for serving as a city attorney, P. Tucker, *Law Courts and Lawyers in the City of London, 1330–1550* (Cambridge, 2007), p. 386.

[5] Hanna, 'Scribe of HM 114', p. 122. Hanna took his localization in southeastern Essex from *A Linguistic Atlas of Late Medieval English*, ed. A. McIntosh, M. L. Samuels and M. Benskin, 4 vols. (Aberdeen, 1986), LP 6030, grid 578 190. See also Hanna, *London Literature*, pp. 29, 244.

[6] Tucker, *Law Courts and Lawyers*, p. 386 for serving as attorney, pp. 298–9 for the attorneys being clerks of the Guildhall.

[7] Hanna, 'Scribe of HM 114', p. 121.

[8] Ibid., pp. 122, 129–31; C.-M. Briquet, *Les Filigranes* (Leipzig, 1923).

[9] C. W. Dutschke, *Guide to the Medieval and Renaissance Manuscripts in the Huntington Library*, 2 vols. (San Marino CA, 1989), I, 150–2; watermarks identified p. 151.

1378 with variants to 1412.[10] Hanna noted that one had to take into account the time it took papers to reach England and the shelf time before a paper stock was used up, and argued for a period in the late 1420s or early 1430s for this scribe's activities.[11] Hanna was writing before Ian Doyle had discovered the hand writing in London documents of 1418 and 1419. Even dating to the late 1420s to 30s, Hanna was arguing for an earlier date for the manuscripts of the HM 114 Scribe than had earlier scholars, such as R. K. Root, who estimated the scribe's activities to have taken place in the third quarter of the fifteenth century, based on dating the Harley manuscript by its later additions.[12] With the additional evidence of his hand in the *Liber Albus* and Letter Book I, we would move his literary activity back still earlier in the century: the paper need not have taken a decade to reach England nor sat on the shelves for decades before use in these booklets. Based on the dates of watermarks alone, Lambeth 491 could have been written at any time after 1414, and HM 114 at any time after 1421, even if they were all written at one sitting, as it were, rather than in booklets produced at different times.[13]

These earlier dates for the activity of the HM 114 Scribe fit well with our identification of the scribe as Richard Osbarn. Since the hand of the HM 114 Scribe had been discovered by Doyle in the London *Liber Albus* and Letter Book I, he was already known to have worked in London and to have written these brief portions of books associated with the Guildhall. We discovered that his involvement in compiling the *Liber Albus* was greater than Doyle had surmised, and we found his hand not only in Letter Book I, but also making additions to Letter Book H; the context in which he was working pointed to his identity as Richard Osbarn, the clerk of the chamber in the first few decades of the fifteenth century.

These identifications depend upon recognition of his hand in the London documents as being the same as the hand of the literary manuscripts. The writing of the three literary manuscripts attributed to him has been described by Hanna as 'a rather splayed anglicana' script.[14] This 'splayed' aspect of his hand is quite distinctive, and allows one to recognize his hand in spite of the wide variance of aspect and letter-forms in pieces of his writing. One finds a similar variance in the writing of Thomas Hoccleve, for instance, depending upon the formality of the occasion of writing.[15] Figs 2.1 and 2.2 illustrate the range of his hand within HM 114. Characteristics common to these samples are the distance between

---

[10] Hanna, 'Scribe of HM 114', pp. 129–31; see further discussion pp. 31–4 and nn. 42–4 below.

[11] Hanna, 'Scribe of HM 114', p. 122, and n. 6, citing J. Irigoin, 'La Datation des filigranes du papier', *Codicologica* 5 (1980), 9–36 (pp. 21–22) for the shelf-life of paper stocks.

[12] R. K. Root, *The Manuscripts of Chaucer's 'Troilus'*, Chaucer Society 1st series 98 (London, 1914 for 1911), p. 17, and R. K. Root, *The Textual Tradition of Chaucer's 'Troilus'*, Chaucer Society 1st series 99 (1916), p. lv, said his hand 'seem[ed] to be earlier than' the date of the hands that completed Harley 3943, third quarter of the fifteenth century; but Hanna argued that the scribe's portion of Harley 3943 was left fragmentary for some decades before two other scribes completed the text of *Troilus* by adding an outer bifolium to quire 1 (fols 1r–8v), quire 8 (fols 57r–62v) and the remainder of the manuscript (fols 71r–116v) in the middle or third quarter of the fifteenth century. M. C. Seymour, *A Catalogue of Chaucer Manuscripts*, vol. 1: *Works before 'The Canterbury Tales'* (Aldershot, 1995), p. 56, following Hanna, dated HM 114 to 1425–50.

[13] The dating of booklets is discussed later in this chapter: see pp. 31–7, esp. 33–4, below.

[14] *Siege of Jerusalem*, ed. Hanna and Lawton, p. xxi.

[15] See J. A. Burrow and A. I. Doyle, intro., *Thomas Hoccleve: A Facsimile of the Autograph Verse Manuscripts*, EETS SS 19 (Oxford, 2002), p. xxxiv: 'He was a very accomplished scribe in several modes appropriate to the different contexts of his tasks, in some tightly disciplined, in others fluent and relaxed.' See also Mooney, 'Some New Light on Thomas Hoccleve', and L. R. Mooney,

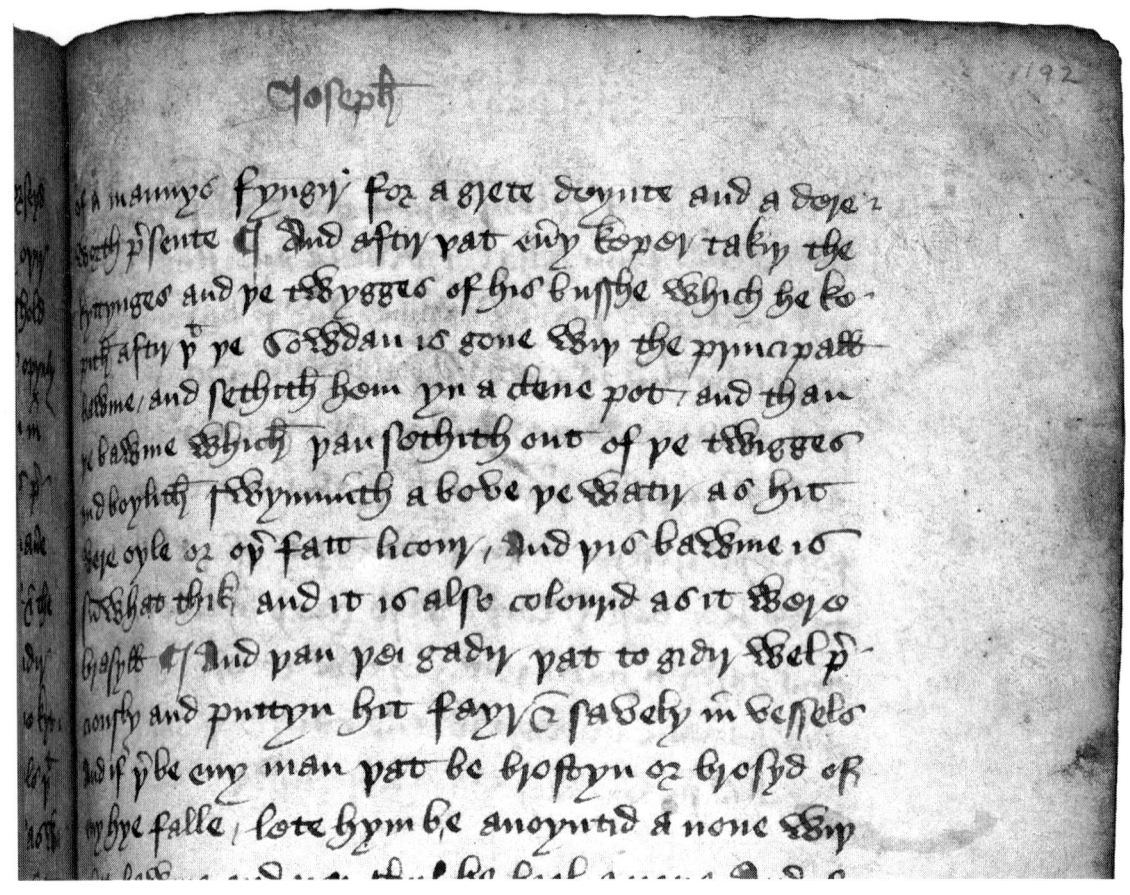

Fig. 2.1 San Marino, CA, Huntington Library, MS HM 114, fol. 192r (top half): illustrating the hand of Richard Osbarn

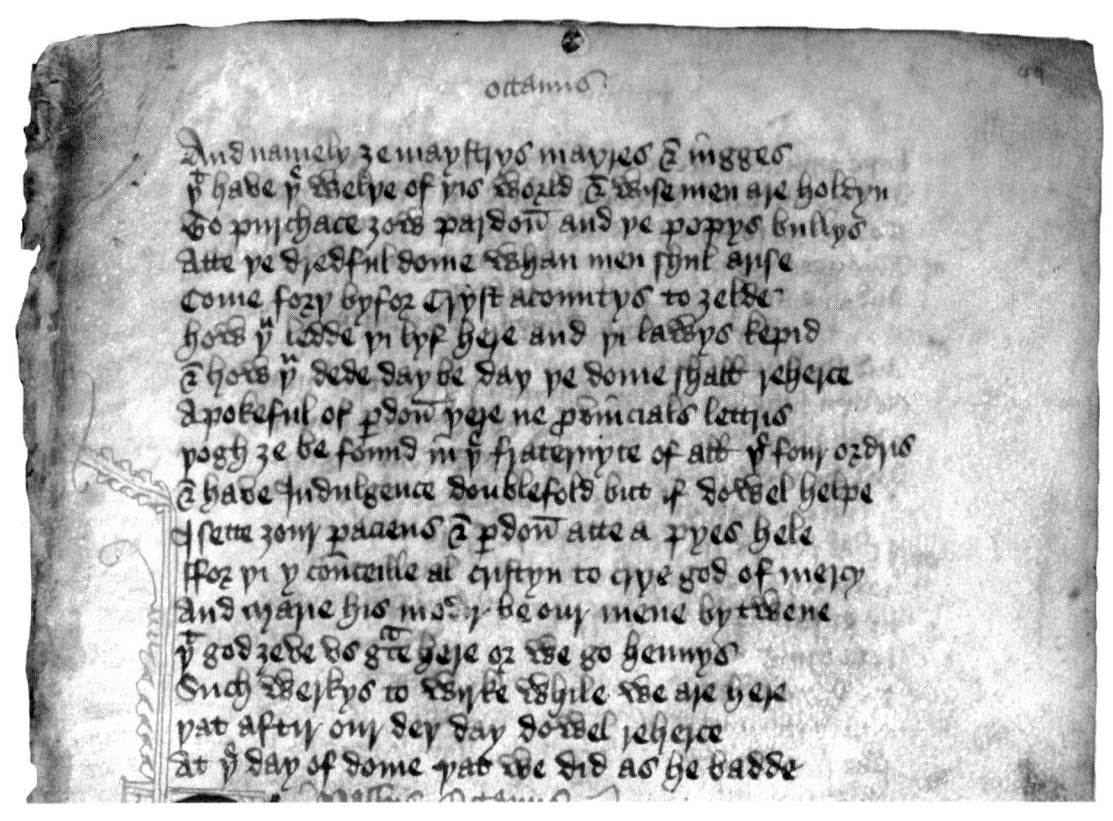

Fig. 2.2 San Marino, CA, Huntington Library, MS HM 114, fol. 49 (top half): illustrating the hand of Richard Osbarn

lines and the relationship of the minim height to the height and depth of the ascenders and descenders; roundedness of forms of the graphs; and (in most of his literary copying) what we would describe as an awkwardness, an unpolished appearance at variance with what we would expect from a professional scribe like Scribe D or Adam Pinkhurst. The horizontal splay changes significantly from sample to sample, according to the care with which he writes the text: at times he seems to be writing in haste, such as one would do in writing to preserve a fair copy for personal reading or for use as an exemplar rather than to produce a copy for sale. When he writes prose, as in the *Brut* in Lambeth 491, his letters are more closely packed into a line; when he writes verse, especially alliterative verse, they are written with greater horizontal spread.[16]

Not only the aspect but the letter-forms vary from one piece of writing to another. Fol. 192v of HM 114 shows a marked preference for rounded anglicana **e** (see fig. 2.1, line 1, 'deynte', or line 2, 'keper'), a letter-form that does not appear at all in other texts in the manuscript (compare fig. 2.2, line 1, 'namely'). The two-compartment form of letter **g** (see fig. 2.1, line 3, 'twygges', or fig. 2.2, line 1, 'iugges') is often a small letter with both lobes about the same size, both ovoid, so it looks like a numeral '8', but in the sample of Harley 3943, fol. 15r (see fig. 2.3, line 7, 'gladyd', or line 8, 'right'), the lower lobe is quite angular, pointed toward the left. Letter **h** can have a looped descender (fig. 2.2, line 7, 'reherce'), or just curl toward the left (fig. 2.1, line 3, 'which', or line 13, 'hym'), be completely straight (fig. 2.2, line 16, 'reherce', or fig. 2.3, line 8, 'the'), or curl more sharply to the right with a little hook at the bottom (see fig. 2.3, line 8, 'have'). Letter **w** can have two looped approach strokes (fig. 2.2, line 6, 'How'), one looped approach and one arched stroke (fig. 2.1, line 3, 'twygges' and 'which'), touching at the widest point of their loops or fully intersecting at this point; and it can have a distinct foot at the base of the left stalk (fig. 2.1, line 3, 'twygges'), or be fully rounded on this first stalk (fig. 2.3, line 6, 'wyser'). At times these forms appear in the same piece of writing.

The point we are making is that the HM 114 Scribe's writing is not as consistent as some professional scribes' writing, so we need to look harder for what can be taken as evidence of his hand. Certain letter-forms appear regularly in his writing. His lower-case **d** has an angular lobe and loop (fig. 2.3, line 9, 'good'); when it is a terminal letter in a word or especially ending a line of verse, it often has an otiose finishing stroke (fig. 2.4, heading, 'Edward'), sometimes looking like a backward **s** or sometimes more angular, turning sharply and dropping straight down. The anglicana **g** with equal-sized ovoid lobes is typical, though, as noted above, not a constant form. Lower-case **h** often has a distinct foot at the base of its stalk (fig. 2.3, line 3, 'hope'; fig. 2.4, line 9, the first 'h' of 'which'); in other samples of his handwriting the shoulder of **h** is detached from the stalk (fig. 2.2, line 2, 'holdyn' or line 15 'here'). Z-shaped **r** has a large hook (fig. 2.1, line 1, 'for'; fig. 2.2, line 9, the first 'r' of 'ordris'; fig. 2.4, line 4, 'victorie'), sometimes not quite from the lower left corner but springing from the base of the z-shape just to right of the corner (fig. 2.3, line 1, the second 'r' of 'therfor'). Sigma-shaped **s** in terminal position is more than usually open and often leans over to the right (fig. 2.2, heading, 'Octauus"). Finally, the upper-case **I** often has a waving or even closed

---

'A Holograph of Hoccleve's *Regiment of Princes*', *Studies in the Age of Chaucer* 33 (2011), 263–96 (pp. 265–75).

[16] For discussion of this same difference of scribes' spacing when they are writing alliterative verse, giving examples from the handwriting of Scribe D and Adam Pinkhurst, see S. Horobin and L. R. Mooney, 'A *Piers Plowman* Manuscript by the Hengwrt/Ellesmere Scribe and its Implications for London Standard English', *Studies in the Age of Chaucer* 26 (2004), 65–112 (pp. 70–1).

Fig. 2.3 London, British Library, MS Harley 3943, fol. 15r (extract): illustrating the hand of Richard Osbarn

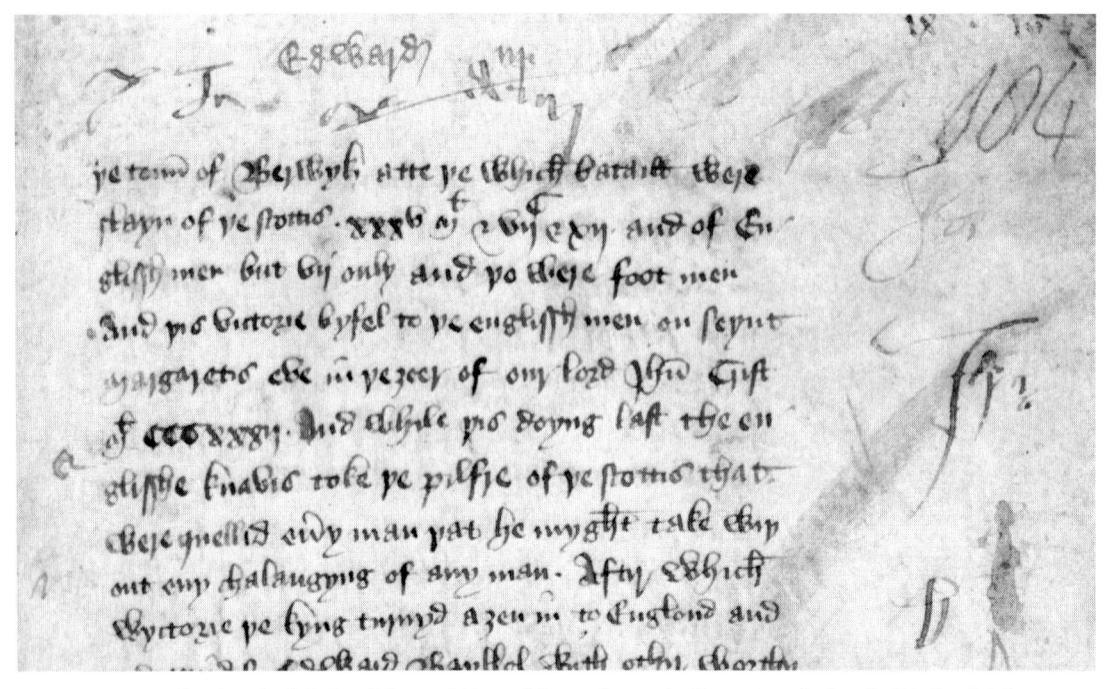

Fig. 2.4 London, Lambeth Palace Library, MS 491, fol. 184r (extract): illustrating the hand of Richard Osbarn

Fig. 2.5 London Metropolitan Archives, COL/AD/01/009, Letter Book I, fol. 223r (lower page, extract, reduced): illustrating the hand of Richard Osbarn

loop approach stroke toward the upper left side of the letter (fig. 2.1, heading, 'Ioseph'; fig. 2.2, line 11, 'I').

Ian Doyle, as cited by Hanna, had identified this hand in documents of the London Guildhall. It appears in Letter Book I (from the reigns of Henry IV and Henry V), fols 223r (lines 9–37), 224v, 226v (last six lines), 227r (lines 2 – bottom), 228r, and probably 229r–231v (line 25) (see fig. 2.5, fol. 223r), and in *Liber Albus*, Book II, fols 40r–51v, headings on fols 7r–8v, addition on fols 179r, 213r–214r?, 250r–255v [1 Hen V], 267r–322v.[17] In addition to these instances we have identified the hand of the HM 114 Scribe in the running titles and rubric glosses written as finding aids virtually throughout the volume, and tied to his table in Book II, his annotations to the table in Book III and the calendar of Book IV. In this capacity of writing indices and the whole calendar of Book IV, with marginal finding aids throughout, he seems to have been the compiler of the *Liber Albus*, under Carpenter's direction, rather than Carpenter being the compiler himself. At the very least, this book shows the two men working very closely together, and at the Guildhall.

Fig. 2.5 shows an extract from Letter Book I, fol. 223r, identified by Doyle as written by the HM 114 Scribe. This extract illustrates his characteristic ductus, and the forms of letters **h**, **g**, rounded **e**, **w**, **d** and sigma **s** described above. The extract records the decree of the mayor and aldermen prohibiting people from walking in the streets in disguise even if they are mummers during the Christmas season, but urging people to be merry within their own houses. It further requires those who live in the high streets to put out a lantern with a candle to light the streets each night during the festive season. The scribe of HM 114 often writes into the *Liber Albus* such proclamations relating to keeping the peace and law and order within the city; even more often his entries relate to money. For example, fig. 2.6 shows him writing in the *Liber Albus*, where we see him writing a list of commodities whose sale was regulated by the city, together with references to earlier Letter Books in which city regulations for these commodities had been recorded.

These identifications by Doyle certainly demonstrated that the scribe of HM 114 was an employee of the Guildhall, but their significance became clear only with an understanding of the duties of the Guildhall officers. The contents of the *Liber Albus* demonstrate an intimate knowledge of the older custumals and records of the city, access to which was limited to a few officers of the civic secretariat. Although in the time of Andrew Horn in the 1320s the chamberlain alone was responsible for the city's records, by the time of John Carpenter this responsibility was shared between the chamberlain and common clerk. Barron notes that anyone 'who wished to consult the records had to ask permission of either the chamberlain or the common clerk; if the request seemed reasonable then the chamber clerk would show him the records and provide a copy as required, for a fee'.[18] The chamberlain was chosen from the members of the city's more important guilds, and by the end of the fourteenth century would not have been expected to do clerical work; for such tasks the clerk of the chamber, also called the controller, would be called upon. To have had such access to the city's archives as to be able to index and contribute to the *Liber Albus*, the HM 114 Scribe must, then, have been either the chamber clerk or the common clerk of the city. The holders of these two clerical offices in 1419 were Richard Osbarn and John Carpenter, respectively.

---

[17] *Siege of Jerusalem*, ed. Hanna and Lawton, p. xxii, citing for the instances in *Liber Albus* the identification that these leaves were by a single hand, made by Riley, *Munimenta Gildhallae Londoniensis: Liber Albus*, p. xxii, n. 2.

[18] Barron, *London in the Later Middle Ages*, p. 181.

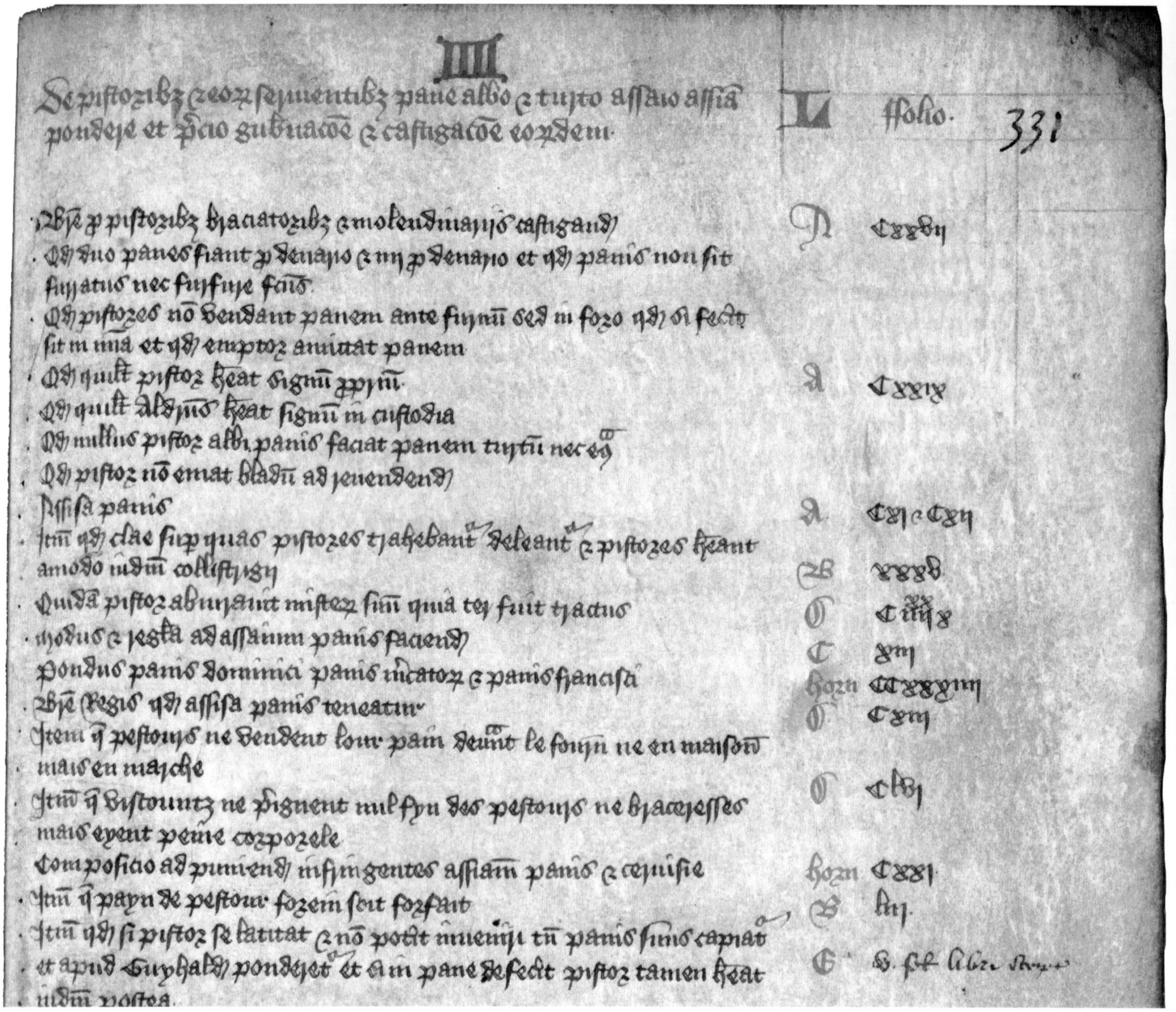

Fig. 2.6 London Metropolitan Archives, COL/CS/01/012, *Liber Albus*, fol. 320r (extract, reduced), from Book III, Part 4

The hand of the HM 114 Scribe could not be identified with Carpenter himself because he wrote the preface to the *Liber Albus* in which he set out his reasons for its compilation, and the handwriting in that portion of the *Liber Albus* does not match the HM 114 Scribe's hand. Thus, if not the common clerk, the HM 114 Scribe must be the chamber clerk, Richard Osbarn.

Further evidence that the HM 114 Scribe must be an important officer of the Guildhall came in our identification of his hand in the Register of Deeds and Charters written for the Goldsmiths' Company, prepared c. 1418.[19] As he had done in the *Liber Albus*, the scribe carefully organized the contents of the Register and provided a detailed table of contents as a finding aid.[20] The clerk who prepared them had to have had a knowledge of, and ready access to, the city's records. We know of Carpenter's lament at the beginning of the *Liber Albus*

---

[19] London, Goldsmiths' Company Archives, MS 1642, Register of Deeds and Charters.

[20] Osbarn also provided an English translation of the Prologue to the Register of Deeds and Charters 1642 and noted in a rubric at the top of the first folio that the English translation could be found

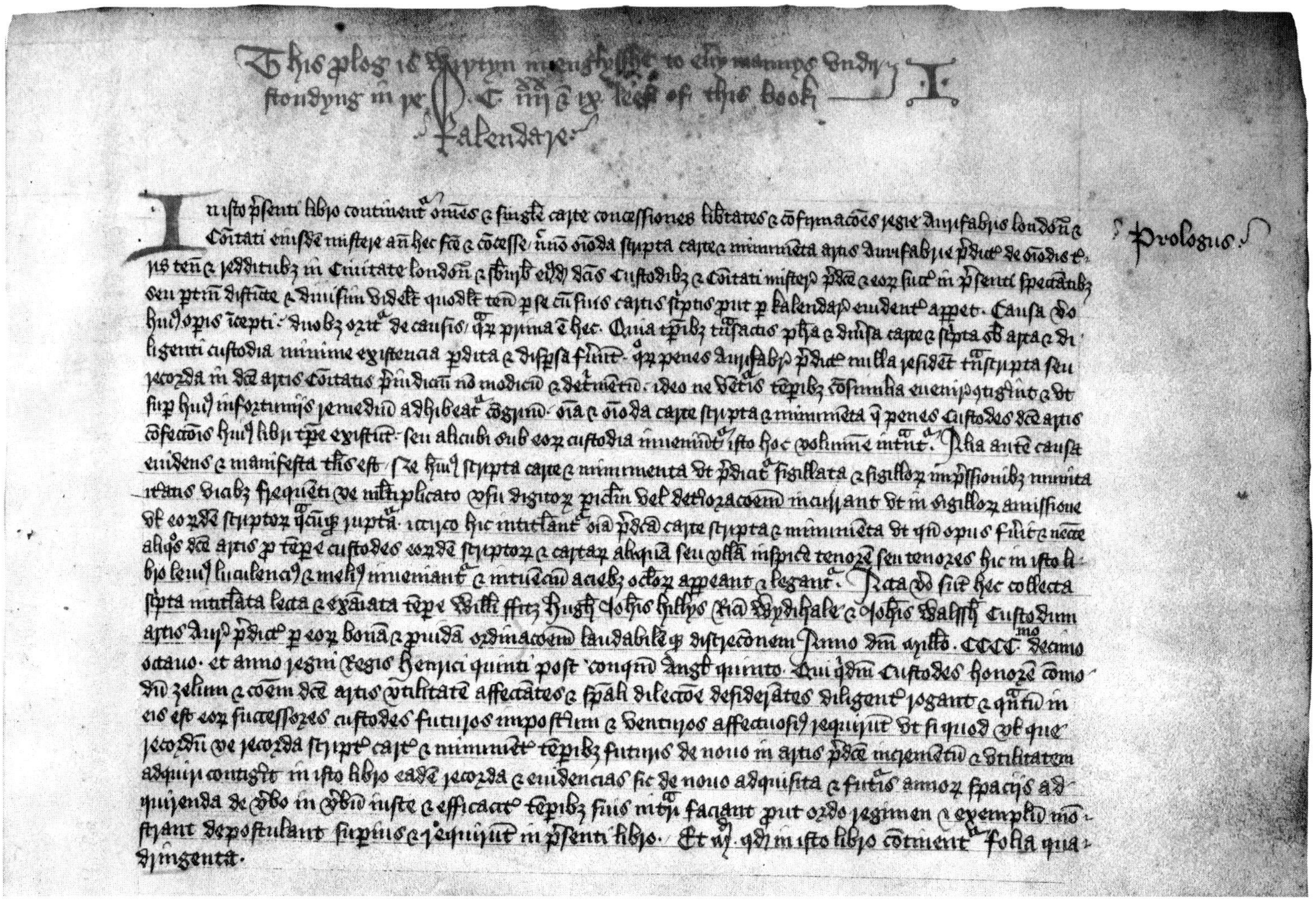

Fig. 2.7 London, Goldsmiths' Company Archives, MS 1642, Register of Deeds, fol. 1r (top half, reduced): illustrating the hand of Richard Osbarn

that the material collected for its compilation was retrieved from memoranda contained in the many uncatalogued books, rolls and charters at the Guildhall; the same applies to the material entered into the Goldsmiths' Register. The Goldsmiths had commissioned this volume recording their landed possessions because, as they record in the memorandum at the beginning of the Register, valuable items such as charters had been 'embesylez et detraez' (embezzled and removed) from the Company (see fig. 2.7).[21] The same memorandum goes on to record that for the missing material they had had to resort to the Guildhall, where copies of their original documents were held. As we have just noted, permission to copy would have been given by the chamberlain or common clerk and the copying itself would have been the task of the common clerk or the clerk of the chamber. In 1418, when the Register was prepared, the clerk of the chamber was Richard Osbarn.

We have also found samples of the HM 114 Scribe's hand in Letter Book H, which records the decisions and decrees of mayor and aldermen from 1375 to 1399. At first it seemed improbable that his hand would be found in a Letter Book of such an early date, given the much later dating of his literary manuscripts. However, on examination of the specific

at the end: 'This prolog is wrytyn in englysshe to every mannys vndyrstondyng in þe C iiij (xx) ix [189] leef of this book'.

[21] *Wardens' Accounts and Court Minute Books of the Goldsmiths' Mistery of London, 1334–1446*, ed. L. Jefferson (Woodbridge, 2003), p. xvi.

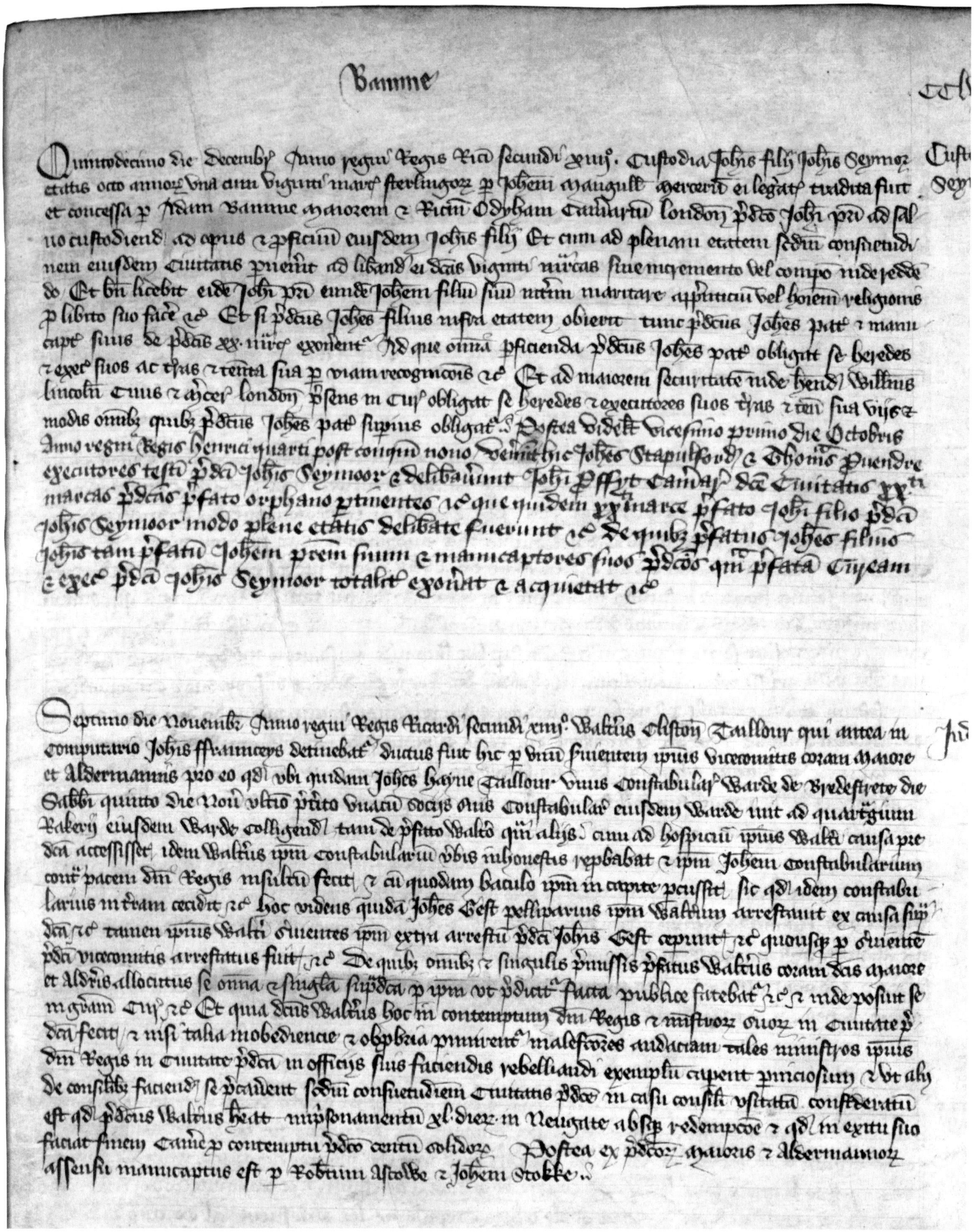

Fig. 2.8 London, Metropolitan Archives, COL/AD/01/008, Letter Book H, fol. 256r (excerpt). The hand of the HM 114 Scribe (= Richard Osbarn) begins with the ninth word of line 12 with 'Postea videlicet vicesimo primo die Octobris …' and continues to the break after line 17.

entries in his hand, we found that they had been added to Letter Book H at several dates *after* 1400. Furthermore, we recognized that in the main they pertained to proceedings of the office of the chamberlain. As noted in Chapter 1, the chamberlain's principal responsibility was care of the finances of the City of London; but another related responsibility, shared at the beginning of the fifteenth century by the chamberlain and common serjeant, was care of the orphans of deceased freemen.[22] The chamberlain would arrange for their care by a warden or executor who would retain (safeguard) any goods or money bequeathed to those children until they achieved their majority. The arrangements would then be recorded in the Letter Books. When the orphan came of age, which could be many years later, he would present himself at the Guildhall for the return of his rightful possessions. The arrangements for their return would also be recorded in the Letter Books, not in the sequence appropriate to the date when the return took place but attached to the initial entry, recorded some years earlier; the second (and subsequent) record was frequently squeezed into a gap left for the purpose by the original clerk years before. Fig. 2.8, lines 11–17, shows the hand of the HM 114 Scribe recording that the executors handed over an estate to the orphan John Seymour, son of John Seymour. The original arrangements (lines 1–11) had been made and recorded on the death of the father in December 1390, when the boy was eight years old. The transfer was recorded almost seventeen years later, on 21 October 1407. The hand that wrote these additional sentences in 1407 can be identified as that of the HM 114 Scribe by the aspect, the 'splayed anglicana' described by Hanna. This is the most telling characteristic of the hand, but some of its characteristic letter-forms are also evident in this short passage: lower-case **d** with an angular lobe and pointed loop (fig. 2.8, line 11, 'die'); an anglicana **g** whose two lobes are of equal size and slightly ovoid (fig. 2.8, line 12, 'Regis'); a variety of treatments of the descenders of letter **h** (fig. 2.8, line 12, 'Henrici' with a sharp curl to right at the bottom; line 12, 'hic' with a curve to the left; line 15, 'Joh*annes*', with the curve extending under the letter and almost completing a loop); letter **h** invariably having a distinct foot at the base of its stalk (fig. 2.8, each of the letters in the preceding example); sigma **s** in terminal position which is open and leans slightly to the right (fig. 2.8, line 12, 'Joh*annes*'); and initial **I** with a waving or even closed loop as approach stroke (fig. 2.8, line 17, 'Joh*annes*'). Many other decisions of the chamberlain regarding orphans recorded in Letter Book H after 1400 are also the hand of the HM 114 Scribe; they would have been entered into the Letter Book not by the chamberlain (since his was not a clerical office) but by the chamber clerk himself. Thus we were able to identify the hand as that of Richard Osbarn, who was chamber clerk in the years 1400–37 when these additional entries were made to Letter Book H.

Taken together, these occurrences of the hand of the HM 114 Scribe in positions where the controller, or clerk of the chamber, would have been the most likely writer, provide quite conclusive evidence of his identity as Richard Osbarn. As chamber clerk, he would have had the intimate knowledge of custumals and records required to organize and copy the materials in the *Liber Albus*; as chamber clerk he would have had a close working relationship with John Carpenter, under whom the *Liber Albus* was compiled in the years leading up to 1419; as chamber clerk he would have been one of the few people with knowledge of and access to the city's guarded records who was available to be commissioned by the Goldsmiths in 1418 to collect and recopy their charters, the sole remaining copies of which were held at the

---

[22] Barron, *London in the Later Middle Ages*, p. 181, states that the chamberlain and common serjeant shared this responsibility for orphans, and describes the process we outline in the next few sentences.

Guildhall; and as chamber clerk he would have been the man who added the decisions of the chamberlain relating to orphans into Letter Book H after 1400.

Richard Osbarn is first mentioned in the city's records in the 1390s as an attorney in the Husting court, alongside John Marchaunt.[23] In 1400 he rose to the high position of clerk of the chamber, or controller of the City of London, while Carpenter combined work for the city's courts with the position of assistant to Marchaunt (who was first officially recorded as common clerk in 1399 although he may have been fulfilling the duties of common clerk since the death in 1394 of the previous officer, Henry Perot).[24] As attorneys for the city, both Carpenter and Osbarn would have been members of one of the elite groups of clerk-attorneys who serviced the mayor, the common serjeant-at-law, the chamberlain, and the common clerk. Osbarn's name is also connected with Carpenter's in several land transactions from the early part of the fifteenth century; this association continues to 1437 when Osbarn retired.[25] (He died the following year.) Holding various offices as clerk-attorney for the city courts before 1400, Osbarn may have served as one of the chamber serjeants or clerk-attorneys who worked for the chamberlain.[26] With promotion to clerk of the chamber he would be paid twice the annual salary of the serjeants and would have been in a position to add to his income by charging fees for whatever copying work he undertook as part of his office.[27] The chamber clerk might be promoted to higher city offices, as Marchaunt had been, progressing from that position in the early 1380s to become the common clerk by 1399; but Osbarn remained in the position of clerk of the chamber, or controller, possibly because Carpenter was preferred for the position of common clerk at the retirement of Marchaunt in 1417. Both Carpenter and Osbarn were executors of the will of Marchaunt (d. 1422), who, having held the office of clerk of the chamber as early as 1380–1, may have been a generation

---

[23] Tucker, *Law Courts and Lawyers*, p. 386.

[24] Perot served as common clerk from 1375 until his death in 1394, and Marchaunt is recorded as holding this office by c. 1399: see Barron, *London in the Later Middle Ages*, p. 364; Perot left money to both Osbarn and Marchaunt in his will, Kew, National Archives, PCC, PROB11/1/9, fols 68v–69r.

[25] Carpenter was one of the executors for Osbarn's will; Carpenter resigned his position as common clerk of the city the following year, 1438. Barron, *London in the Later Middle Ages*, p. 184, notes that 'There were clearly close links between the chamberlain's clerk and the common clerk', adding by way of example that 'John Carpenter acted as feoffee for Richard Osbarn (chamber clerk 1400–37)' and citing *Calendar of Wills Proved and Enrolled in the Court of Husting, London, 1258–1688*, ed. R. R. Sharpe, 2 vols. (London, 1889–90), II, 484–5. Together with other men, Osbarn and Marchaunt held properties in London, including St Pancras Soper Lane 145/30 (see *Historical Gazetteer of London before the Great Fire: Cheapside; Parishes of All Hallows Honey Lane, St Martin Pomery, St Mary le Bow, St Mary Colechurch, and St Pancras Soper Lane*, ed. D. J. Keene and V. Harding (London, 1987), pp. 766–7; the manor of Oldeford called 'Marlawe Maner' or 'Badby Maner' in Middlesex and a messuage in Henley on Thames, Oxfordshire (*A Calendar to the Feet of Fines for London and Middlesex, vol. 1: Richard I – Richard III*, ed. W. J. Hardy and W. Page (London, 1892), pp. 235–6); and property in Thames Street which was owned in part by Osbarn and Carpenter together with Marchaunt and others (Kew, National Archives, E 40/1292, in *A Descriptive Catalogue of Ancient Deeds in the Public Record Office*, ed. H. C. Maxwell Lyte, 6 vols. (London, 1890–1915), I, 515). These are only four of the many properties in which Osbarn and Carpenter together held part interests, but they may have been doing this in an official capacity for the city, for some properties appear to have been held on behalf of widows or orphans. Nevertheless their linked names show them to have been working closely together.

[26] Office-holders of these positions are not listed by Barron, *London in the Later Middle Ages*, app. 2, so work remains to be done here.

[27] Ibid., pp. 182–3.

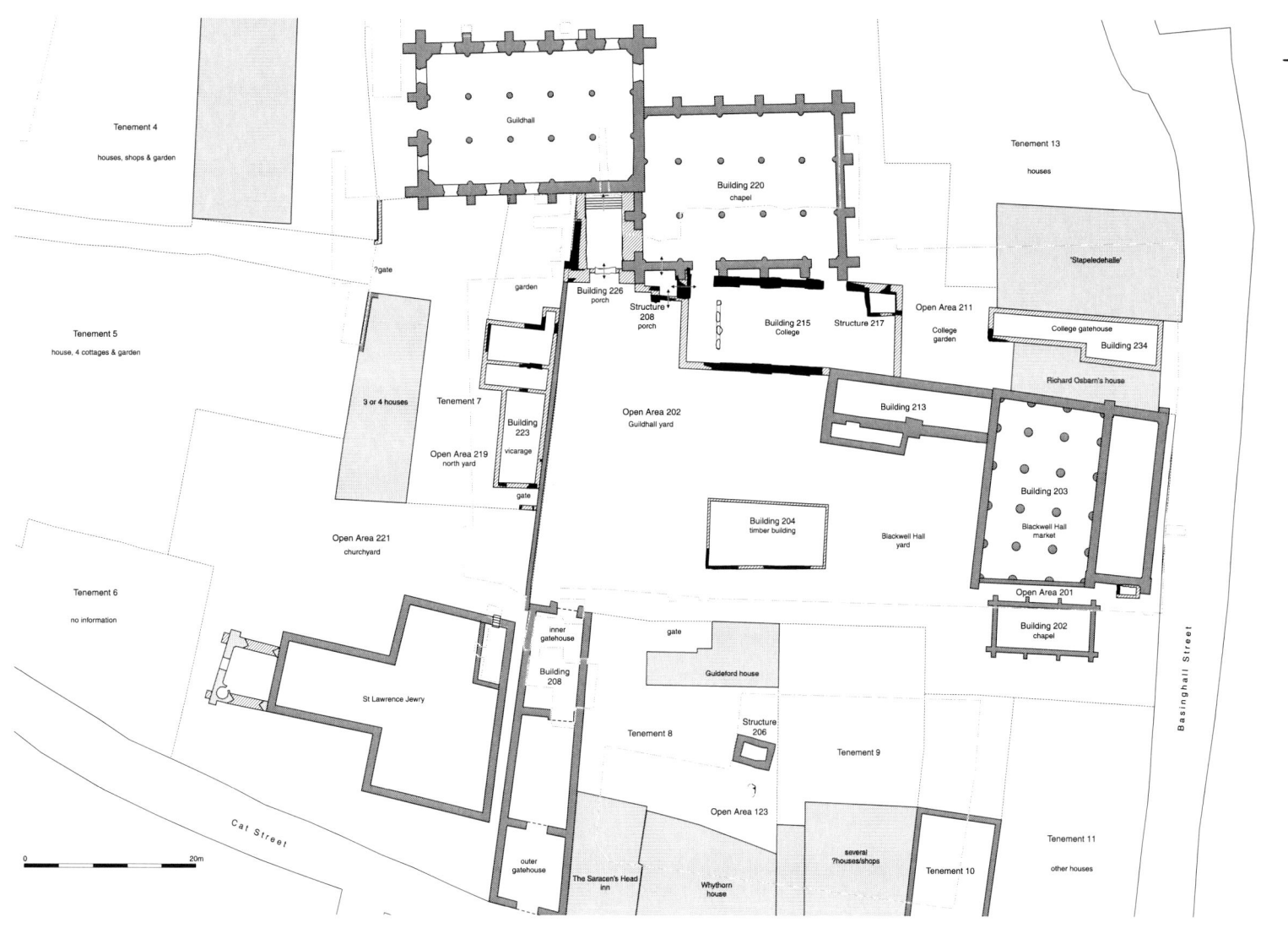

Fig. 2.9 Plan of the Guildhall precinct, *c.* 1400. Richard Osbarn's house is the lower of the two shaded areas in the upper right quadrant.

older than they were.[28] Osbarn held the office of clerk of the chamber for virtually the whole period during which Marchaunt and Carpenter held the office of common clerk (1399–1417 and 1417–38 respectively). Barron observes that 'These men must have been extremely experienced, and they held the job for life. When Richard Osbarn retired from office in 1437 after serving since the beginning of the century he was provided with a house, an annual robe and a pension of £6 13s 4d.'[29]

Osbarn's house, to which Barron refers, must have been the one built for his use within the close of the Guildhall. Work began in 1400 at the city's expense except for 20 marks provided by Osbarn himself. He was granted a fifty-year lease on the property, at an annual rent of 40 *s*.[30] The property contained a house, two shops, and a vacant plot adjoining. It was on such a scale that, later in the century, after Osbarn's occupancy had ended and the city had changed its mind about building new housing for its college north of the Guildhall, the site of Osbarn's 'house' provided accommodation for the whole college of priests who served the Guildhall chapel. (See fig. 2.9.)

[28] The will is Kew, National Archives, E 40/12349, written in 1421 and proved in July 1422.

[29] Barron, *London in the Later Middle Ages*, p. 183.

[30] Ibid., p. 183 and n. 76, citing *Calendar of Letter-Books*, IX, 6–7, 10–11. The text of this concession is on fol. 2 (ii) of Letter Book I. See also C. M. Barron, *The Medieval Guildhall of London* (London, 1974), p. 57, fig. 1 and item 5 of the notes to fig. 1.

The building of this house on land adjoining two shops was part of a major redevelopment project inside the Guildhall precinct in the first four decades of the fifteenth century, which was to see the old chapel of the Guildhall torn down and replaced by a huge extension to create the eastern half of Guildhall, new city courts built on the north side of the Guildhall, and the building that housed the college demolished to make way for a new chapel and a library on the southeast side.[31] Osbarn's property, east of the old chapel lying just beyond the south-east corner of the Guildhall, was apparently built first, before the other demolition and rebuilding projects began.[32] A secondary purpose of this new building, more than large enough to accommodate Osbarn and his family, may have been to provide secure storage for some of the city's records during the period when the Guildhall precinct was to become a construction site, with open walls where the Guildhall itself was to be extended, the college and chapel torn down, and the north side of the Guildhall also exposed to create doorways into the new courts. After this construction, towards the end of Osbarn's tenure of office, the archive might be stored in the accounts room between the Guildhall and the new aldermen's court, or in the new library, a separate building. It may not be a coincidence that this period of construction was also exactly the time when Osbarn was organizing materials for the *Liber Albus*.

Osbarn's own manuscripts, especially the booklets gathered together in HM 114 and Lambeth 491, offer evidence for the existence of exemplars circulating among Guildhall clerks. He and his fellow clerks seem to have had access to a wide range of English vernacular literary texts. Osbarn made two copies of Chaucer's *Troilus and Criseyde*, and one each of Langland's *Piers Plowman*, the anonymous *Siege of Jerusalem*, *The Awnters of Arthure*, *Susanna*, the *Brut*, and *Mandeville's Travels*. He also copied a unique prose translation of *The Three Kings of Cologne*, a verse *Book of Hunting*, and a unique translation of Peter Ceffons's *Epistola Luciferi ad Cleros*. His manuscripts share distinct textual traditions with Richard Frampton's *Siege of Jerusalem* and Scribe D's (John Marchaunt's) *Piers Plowman* and prose *Brut*, both of whose hands are also to be found in the *Liber Albus*.[33] His copies of *Troilus and Criseyde* and of *Siege of Jerusalem* are witnesses to distinct versions of the poems circulating in London; his *Piers Plowman* is itself a distinct copy in which a scribe attempts to combine all three versions of the text; his copies of *The Awntyrs of Arthure* and *Susanna* are the only surviving ones written in London. His manuscripts also include three unique Middle English texts, perhaps circulating only in the very small circle of clerks with literary interests in and around the Guildhall.

Hanna has commented upon the compiling tendency of this scribe and on his access to a large library of vernacular literary texts: '[The] contents [of his literary manuscripts] suggest that either the scribe or his director was intensely aware of textual contents and capable of assembling a number of archetypes with ease.'[34] He also characterized Osbarn's manuscripts as exemplars, noting that the material used for the manuscripts copied by this scribe (two of them comprising booklets of mixed paper and parchment)

> look cheap and as if produced in the expectation that they might remain unbound for

---

[31] Barron, *Medieval Guildhall of London*, pp. 25–33; D. Bowsher, T. Dyson, N. Holder and I. Howell, *The London Guildhall: An Archaeological History of a Neighbourhood from Early Medieval to Modern Times*, 2 vols. (London, 2007), I, 181–225.

[32] Barron, *Medieval Guildhall of London*, p. 57, fig. 1 and item 5 of the notes to fig. 1.

[33] For further discussion of the relationships mentioned here see pp. 31, 58, 60, 116–17 below.

[34] Hanna, 'Scribe of HM 114', p. 123.

a protracted period … These small packets of quires, minimally decorated (the scribe did nearly all his own rubrication, including running titles), look as if they might form a small in-house bookseller's stock – cheap copies of popular items in heavy demand.[35]

In the introduction to *Siege of Jerusalem* Hanna and Lawton moved away from the exemplar argument, offering instead evidence of ownership of Lambeth 491 in Barking in the sixteenth century.[36] Indeed, if his manuscripts HM 114 and Lambeth 491 were intended to preserve texts for him (or others) to prepare further bespoke copies from, they do not seem to have been used in this way: no other surviving manuscripts of these texts preserve copies made from Osbarn's exemplars, with the possible exception of Frampton's *Siege of Jerusalem*, which Hanna and Lawton argue was more likely to have been prepared using the same exemplar as Osbarn than to have been copied from it.[37] This might show only that he intended that these copies should preserve the texts for further copies, but then never found the time to carry his project further; or he may have been preparing volumes specifically for his own, his family's or colleagues' use. Whereas his fellow clerks are seen solely preparing bespoke copies for gifts or commissions, Osbarn here appears to have been a compiler of texts, and copyist of only one fine manuscript, the Harley *Troilus*, which he abandoned.

At this point we should examine how his identification as Richard Osbarn, clerk of the chamber, or controller, at the London Guildhall from 1400 to 1437, contributes to our understanding of the context in which these literary manuscripts were produced. First of all, identification assists us with dating his manuscripts, since we now know that they must all have been completed before 1438. We can now re-examine the booklets of his two anthologies in this light, and with the knowledge that Osbarn held his office in one place for a long period. Hanna's arguments relating to the order in which the scribe prepared the manuscripts (which we discussed briefly above) depends upon evidence from texts repeated in them, while his dating of the manuscripts depends upon the watermarks of paper in two of them. He argues that Lambeth 491 must have preceded HM 114 because the brief excerpt from *The Three Kings of Cologne* that was copied into HM 114 ('probably inserted to supplement a copy of *Mandeville's Travels* in that typically defective English form which lacks much of the description of Egypt') shows that he knew of the defect in copies of *Mandeville's Travels* and that he was well enough acquainted with the text of *The Three Kings of Cologne* (perhaps through having copied a unique prose translation into Lambeth 491) to know that it contained material on Egypt that could fill the gap. Hanna concludes that the scribe must have copied the *Three Kings* in Lambeth 491 before he wrote HM 114.[38] He argues that the Harley manuscript would precede HM 114 because the scribe had realized he had a defective exemplar of *Troilus and Criseyde* when he copied HM 114 and made corrections on the page and by adding loose sheets to make up the gaps. Hanna reasons that, 'Knowing the defects

---

[35] Ibid.

[36] *Siege of Jerusalem*, ed. Hanna and Lawton, pp. xxi–xx; for the Barking connection, see J. Boffey and C. Meale, 'Selecting the Text: Rawlinson C.86 and Some Other Books for London Readers', in *Regionalism in Late Medieval Manuscripts and Texts*, ed. F. Riddy (Cambridge, 1991), pp. 143–69 (pp. 161–2 and n. 63). Their long note explains connections between the sixteenth-century names in the Lambeth manuscript, John and Thomas Patsall of Barking, and members of the Mercers' Company of London. This does not seem to preclude Osbarn's owning the manuscript up to his death in 1438.

[37] *Siege of Jerusalem*, ed. Hanna and Lawton, p. xxii, arguing they were written 'from the same archetype'.

[38] Hanna, 'Scribe of HM 114', p. 122.

of the archetype, it is difficult to imagine the scribe copying the text a second time without adding corrections: on this basis, Harley probably preceded Huntington.'[39]

Taking the second of these datings first, it seems clear to us that the scribe made up for the defects of his HM 114 copy of *Troilus* after his initial copying, since he employed a combination of corrections for minor defects, and addition of singleton sheets to the quires to make up for larger sections of the missing text. He might have done this at any time after its initial copying. But as these corrections run throughout the copy, he must have completed the initial copying first. As Hanna suggests, he would hardly have begun copying a second manuscript from the same exemplar if by that time he had recognized its shortcomings. Since he had only copied part of Harley 3943, the parchment copy, before he began to make corrections, it is clear that he had recognized that his exemplar was defective before he completed this manuscript.

He then apparently attempted to correct it with the assistance of one of the other scribes in the manuscript (C), whose work he checked and corrected, but stopped work on it altogether in the middle of the following quire. This shows that the surviving fragment in his hand was never a complete copy. Instead he either abandoned it or gave it away, to be corrected and completed by other scribes some decades after his death.[40] We see his corrections to HM 114 as occurring after Harley, when he had recognized the defects of his exemplar: he could make a mess of his cheap paper-and-parchment copy (HM 114) by adding corrections and singleton sheets, but he could not do this with the more expensive parchment copy (Harley 3943), which was probably being prepared as a bespoke copy for a wealthy client. In fact the correction to HM 114 offers additional evidence that the mixed paper-and-parchment manuscripts *were* intended to serve as exemplars, since the *Troilus* booklet remained in Osbarn's possession long enough for him to make the corrections when another, more complete, copy of the poem crossed his desk.[41] But given that he apparently recognized that his exemplar was defective while he was copying Harley 3943, it would seem that he had made the initial copy of HM 114 first rather than the other way around as Hanna suggests.

Hanna's second issue related to dating, dependent upon watermarks, assumes a single brief period of production for both Lambeth 491 and HM 114; whereas knowledge that the scribe, Richard Osbarn, had a long career in one place might allow us to stretch the period of

---

[39] Ibid.; Hanna's article describes in detail the construction of these manuscripts and changes of hand and sequence of production of Harley 3943.

[40] There is further work to be done to try to identify the other hands in the manuscript; in particular the scribe whom Osbarn supervised might be a subordinate clerk at the Guildhall. The scribes who took it up again and completed it in the 1440s or 1450s might bear further study as well, since the unfinished manuscript may have remained at the Guildhall to be completed decades later. One of these, who completed the bulk of the later additions, fols 71r–116v, is also the main hand of Oxford, Exeter College, MS 129, a manuscript of John Lydgate's *Troy Book* which shares an exemplar with the copy in British Library, MS Royal 18 D.vi, copied by one of the so-called 'hooked-g scribes'. See A. S. G. Edwards, 'A Missing Leaf from the Plimpton *Fall of Princes*', *Manuscripta* 15 (1971), 29–30; A. S. G. Edwards and D. Pearsall, 'The Manuscripts of the Major English Poetic Texts', in *Book Production and Publishing in Britain, 1375–1475*, ed. J. Griffiths and D. Pearsall (Cambridge, 1989), pp. 257–78 (p. 265); review of further references to this scribe by L. R. Mooney and D. W. Mosser, 'Hooked-g Scribes and Takamiya Manuscripts', in *The Medieval Book and a Modern Collector: Essays in Honour of Toshiyuki Takamiya*, ed. T. Matsuda, R. A. Linenthal and J. Scahill (Cambridge, 2004), pp. 179–207 (p. 179, n. 2).

[41] Additional evidence that the manuscript remained in his possession may be the name 'Richard' on the back flyleaves; Dutschke dates this as sixteenth century but it may be a hasty signature from the previous century.

Table 2.1 Four hands in London, British Library, MS Harley 3943

Hand	Folios	Concordances
A	1r–v, 8r–v, 68r–70v	Root's Hand 3*
B	2r–7v, 9r–56v, 63r–67v	Root's Hand 1 = HM 114 Scribe, Osbarn
C	57r–62v: one quire missing its centre bifolium	Root's Hand 2, corrected by B, the HM 114 Scribe, Osbarn
D	71r–116	Root's Hand 4 = scribe of Oxford, Exeter College, MS 129

* Root, *The Manuscripts of Chaucer's 'Troilus'*, p. 17, listed the scribes in the order of their work on the manuscript. He described hands 3 and 4 (our A and B) as being 'so similar that the unquestionable differences have not hitherto been noticed' and suggested that they 'had learned writing in the same school'.

production for these manuscripts over several decades, during which the manuscript booklets would remain accessible to the scribe for additions and corrections. With this greater span of time in mind, when we examine the watermarks again, it is clear that Lambeth 491 precedes HM 114 (as Hanna also argued based on the sequence of texts), because the watermarks used for its writing can be dated from 1405 to the 1410s for the first part of the *Brut*, to 1414–20 for the conclusion of the *Brut* and beginning of *Siege of Jerusalem* (two parts of Booklet 1), and to 1397–1413 for the conclusion of *Siege of Jerusalem*, the *Three Kings of Cologne*, *The Awntyrs of Arthure*, and the unique *Book of Hunting* (Booklets 2 and 3).[42] Osbarn may have begun writing the *Brut* before 1414 and completed it in the second part of Booklet 1 after that date. Hanna argues that there is a distinct break between Booklets 1 and 2, spanned by the text of the *Siege*, so he may have written Booklets 2 and 3 at around the same time, using paper produced between 1397 and 1413.

As Hanna notes, the quires and watermarks of HM 114 present a more complicated pattern that shows the scribe to have worked in a place where paper was regularly ordered and used up, with remaindered paper lying available for use as single sheets or to make up a booklet from several different stocks. The manuscript is principally made up of three paper stocks: one with a *monts* watermark (*a*) which Hanna identifies with a paper produced in Pisa in 1420–1, one with a *cloche* watermark (*d*) which he identifies with a paper produced in Udine in 1420–3, and the third, used for three quires, with a *hache* watermark (*c*) which he identifies with a paper produced in Thirlemont in 1378 with variants to 1412. Two other papers whose dates precede 1420 are used only rarely, and in only one quire each.[43] Booklet 1, quires 1–8 with a text of *Piers Plowman*, is written on papers *a* and *d* produced mainly in 1420–1 and 1420–3, with one quire made up of mixed papers from earlier dates. Booklet 2, quires 9–12 with texts of *Mandeville's Travels*, *Susanna*, and an excerpt from *Three Kings of Cologne*, is comprised of the same two principal papers as Booklet 1, *a* and *d*, dated 1420–1 and 1420–3. Booklet 3, quires 13–20 containing *Troilus and Criseyde* and the Ceffons translation, is made up of quires from the same two principal papers, *a* and *d*, dated 1420–1 and 1420–3, sometimes mixed to make up quires, and two quires made up from paper stock *c* of an earlier date (1378–1412). From these paper stocks it seems likely that the manuscript HM 114 was begun in or soon after 1420, which fits well with our identification

---

[42] Hanna discusses the break between copying of *The Siege* in 'Booklets in Medieval Manuscripts: Further Considerations', *Studies in Bibliography* 39 (1986), 100–11 (pp. 105–6). He describes the watermarks and their dating in Hanna, 'Scribe of HM 114', pp. 129–31, citing Briquet, *Les Filigranes*, which we have rendered in the form of a table (Table 2.2).

[43] Hanna's alternative paper for the *Monts* watermark, produced in Trévise in 1437, can now be ruled out as too late for use by Osbarn, who died in that year; Dutschke's alternative, produced in Florence in 1434, would mean production of this manuscript quite late in the scribe's life.

Table 2.2 Watermarks in Lambeth Palace Library MS 491 and Huntington Library, MS HM 114

Quires	Text	Watermark	Comments
¶ Lambeth Palace Library MS 491 (quoted from Hanna, pp. 130–1)			
2–13	*Brut*	*Monts*, like Briquet 11685 (Trévise 1405, with variants to 1414)	One might also compare 11687 (Padua 1408–15) and 11689 (Florence 1411–21). With the exception of the unwatermarked sheet mentioned above, this stock is the exclusive form in quires 2–13.
14–16	*Brut*	*Lettre N*, not in Briquet, most like 8431 (1414–20) but on the chain-line and lacking the cross.	With the exception of the unwatermarked sheet mentioned above, this stock is the exclusive form in quires 14–16.
17–21	Booklets 2 and 3, *Siege of Jerusalem*, excerpt of *Three Kings*, *Awntyrs of Arthure*, *Book of Hunting*	*Ciseaux*, like Briquet 3656 (Perpignan 1397, with north Italian variants to 1413)	One might also compare 3656 (Aix-en-Provence 1426). This stock is the exclusive form in quires 17–21.
¶ Huntington Library, MS HM 114 (quoted from Hanna, pp. 129–30)			
1–5, 9, 13; parts of 6, 7, 15, 16, 17, 20		*Monts*, like Briquet 11872 (Pisa, 1420–1), somewhat less like 11876 (Trévise, 1437)	This stock is the exclusive form used in quires 1–5 (although quire 3 includes an unwatermarked sheet, fols 38+39+42+43), 9, and 13 (with an unwatermarked sheet, fols 196+197+204+205); with single sheets from other sources, it also appears in quires 6, 7, and 20. There are single examples in quires 15 and 16 (the mark on fols 229+236, 247+250), and two examples (one perhaps a half-sheet) in quire 17.
singleton in 6		*Joug*, not in Briquet but most resembles 7873 (Sion 1410).	A single sheet of this stock appears in quire 6 (the mark on fols 82+95).
7, 15, 20		*Hache*, like Briquet 7505 (Tirlemont 1378, with variants to 1412)	Single sheets of this stock appear in quires 7 (the mark on fols 99+112) and 20 (the mark on fols 312+ 320). There are two sheets in quire 15 (the mark on fols 226+239, 231+234).
8, 10–12, 14, 18; *passim* in 16, 17, 19		*Cloche*, like Briquet 3982 (Udine, 1420–3).	This stock is the exclusive form used in quires 8, 10–12, 14, and 18 (including one of the insert leaves). There are two sheets in quires 16 and 17 (one example in this quire perhaps a half-sheet), and a single example in quire 19 (the mark on fols 297+302).
some sheets of 19		either *Basilic* or *Griffon*, not clearly identifiable with any Briquet stock	This stock appears only in quire 19, probably two full sheets and a half-sheet.

Note For Huntington HM 114, Dutschke's *Guide*, 1.151, differs slightly in citing only the Briquet 11895 (Florence, 1434) for the *Monts*, in citing Briquet 7514 (Genoa, 1383) for the *Hache*, and in citing Briquet 3981 (Holland 1419) for the *Cloche*.

of the scribe as Richard Osbarn, since he would have been busy compiling the *Liber Albus* in the years leading up to 1419. We believe that the evidence of his having had access to single sheets of several stocks of earlier paper to make up his booklets shows that he worked in an office where paper was bought in quantity, so that except for small amounts of back stock it would have been used up quite quickly: thus we would date the composition of his mixed paper and parchment booklets in Lambeth 491 and HM 114 to closely after the dates of the principal paper stocks used in their construction. He might have written the parchment Harley manuscript of *Troilus*, presumably a bespoke copy for a wealthy Londoner, at any time before the date of his correcting his copy of *Troilus* in HM 114.[44] Identification of the scribe of Lambeth 491 and HM 114 as Richard Osbarn, and the dating of these manuscripts to the early 1420s, suggest that, having collected and compiled books of documents for the Guildhall and the Goldsmiths, Osbarn was turning to collecting and compiling manuscripts of Middle English texts, for his own use or for use by the community of scribes in and

---

[44] The watermarks do not help us to date these corrections, since Osbarn used paper of earlier date than the original booklets for his inserted sheets. As Hanna suggests, these individual sheets must have been left as the remains of earlier papers used in the office.

around the Guildhall. We think there may be significance in the fact that this new book-producing activity coincides with plans for the new Guildhall library, which was conceived in the early 1420s and built between March 1423 and September 1425.[45]

The identification of the scribe of HM 114 as Richard Osbarn raises more questions than it answers with respect to the quality of the texts he copied. While some scholars have characterized his copying as 'wilfully refus[ing] to transmit the text of his exemplar', especially in relation to his copy of *Piers Plowman* in HM 114, Hanna argued for an appreciation of the scribe's attempts to preserve as complete a copy as he could, based on all the exemplars he could lay his hands on.[46] Understanding his efforts as an attempt to compile booklets of many Middle English texts fits well with our identification of Osbarn, with his compiling work for the Guildhall and Goldsmiths.

On the other hand, and perhaps because he *was* merely compiling texts for a library of exemplars (or for his own use) rather than fulfilling commissions for clients, he seems not to have made any efforts to acquire the best copies of either *Siege of Jerusalem* or of Chaucer's *Troilus and Criseyde* before making copies for his collection. Since he meant to keep the manuscripts in his possession, he could go back and correct them if a better text came to hand, as happened in the case of *Troilus and Criseyde* but not in the case of *Siege of Jerusalem*. Both he and Richard Frampton made copies of the *Siege* that Hanna describes as textually very close, both based on 'a quite debilitated scribal version ... which had been current since the turn of the fifteenth century.'[47] Given their associations with the Guildhall, it seems likely that the Guildhall close provided the locale where both Osbarn and Frampton gained access to a common exemplar.

Scholarly opinion regarding Osbarn's copies of *Troilus and Criseyde* has changed radically since Barry Windeatt's studies were published, from previous claims that he had had access to an early authorial version to acceptance that he merely copied an exemplar from which an earlier scribe had excised certain passages to abbreviate the text. In collating the manuscripts of Chaucer's *Troilus and Criseyde*, Root had found that the two manuscripts written by the HM 114 Scribe (Richard Osbarn) were remarkably close textually, at least in the portions surviving from the Harley 3943 manuscript that were written by him.[48] Root argued that the omission of three substantial philosophical passages from this branch of the stemma marked it out as an *alpha* version of the poem, before Chaucer had added Troilus's song, or hymn to love (III:1744–71), Troilus's soliloquy in the temple in which he questions whether man has free will, given God's omniscience (IV:953–1085) and Troilus's ascent to

---

[45] Bowsher *et al.*, *London Guildhall*, p. 208.

[46] Hanna, 'Scribe of HM 114', p. 121; he cites (n. 2) *The Vision of William Concerning Piers the Plowman in Three Parallel Texts, Together with Richard the Redeless*, ed. W. W. Skeat, 2 vols. (Oxford, 1886), II, lxx; and R. W. Chambers, 'The Manuscripts of *Piers Plowman* in the Huntington Library and their Value for Fixing the Text of the Poem', *Huntington Library Bulletin* 8 (1935), 1–27 (pp. 2, 15). Hanna also notes (p. 121) that G. Kane and E. T. Donaldson 'refused to collate the manuscript for their edition, *Piers Plowman: The B Version* (London, 1975), because of the frequency of textual deviation, not limited to conflation'.

[47] Hanna, 'Scribe of HM 114', p. 124. See also *Siege of Jerusalem*, ed. Hanna and Lawton, for stemma of the manuscripts (p. lxvii) and discussion of the delta family of manuscripts to which these two belong (pp. lxviii–lxix). For Frampton see pp. 107–18 below.

[48] Root, *The Manuscripts of Chaucer's 'Troilus'*, and *The Textual Tradition of Chaucer's 'Troilus'*; these arguments are summarized and debated by R. Hanna, *Pursuing History: Middle English Manuscripts and their Texts* (Stanford, 1996), pp. 97–114, and more broadly discussing the *Troilus* manuscripts, pp. 115–29.

the eighth sphere whence he recognizes the transitoriness of earthly love (V:1807–27). As Windeatt examined the manuscripts of *Troilus* in preparation for a new edition, he came to challenge Root's ordering of the three categories or groups of manuscripts, and thus called into question Root's postulated early authorial version of the poem preserved in the subgroup of manuscripts including the two copies made by Osbarn.[49] Windeatt's views have been repeated and refined by other scholars, notably Hanna.[50] From the evidence of all the manuscripts, Windeatt and others following him have concluded that the exemplar copied by Osbarn into HM 114 and Harley 3943 was not an authorial early draft but an abridged copy in a tradition begun by a scribe's deciding to excise these three passages from the poem as being extraneous to the courtly love theme. Windeatt concludes that

> It is unlikely ... that Chaucer intended his poem to have any completed, 'published' existence without the Boethian soliloquy. Indeed, without this soliloquy, which so affects the overall philosophical tone of the whole poem, there would have been rather less aptness in Chaucer's dedicating the poem to 'philosophical' Strode, a dedication present in all extant manuscripts.[51]

There remains the unexplained anomaly that the manuscripts in this subgroup preserve variant readings of lines or individual words that are closer to the Italian of Chaucer's source than the standard text preserved in other groups, which Root and others after him took as evidence corroborating the theory that they preserved an earlier authorial draft. Windeatt considered this problem in his discussions of the poem, especially in his *Oxford Guide*, where he referred to the group by the symbol **Ph+**, and HM 114 by the symbol **Ph**, since at the time of Root's study the manuscript was still in the Phillipps collection.[52] He gave several examples of lines from this subgroup that are closer to Boccaccio's *Il Filostrato*, and commented,

> At such points the Ph+ manuscripts – by whatever means of transmission – suggest their links with the poet's process of composition. A scattering of such instances – of very varying quality – marks Book I and part of Books III and IV, precisely where Chaucer is often working most closely from the Italian.[53]

Windeatt noted that the versions closer to the Italian may have been original Chaucerian readings altered by scribes outside the Ph+ manuscript group who found the more Latinate words too difficult and took the liberty to change them for their readers' better understanding.[54] He found in the Italianate readings of this subgroup, especially toward the beginning of the poem, some 'surviving traces of Chaucer's drafting of the expression

---

[49] B. Windeatt, 'The Text of the *Troilus*', in *Essays on 'Troilus and Criseyde'*, ed. M. Salu (Cambridge, 1979), pp. 1–22; B. Windeatt, 'The Text of the "Troilus"', in G. Chaucer, *Troilus and Criseyde: A New Edition of 'The Book of Troilus'*, ed. B. A. Windeatt (London, 1984), pp. 36–54; and B. Windeatt, *Oxford Guides to Chaucer: 'Troilus and Criseyde'* (Oxford, 1992), pp. 12–36 (pp. 19–36).

[50] Hanna, 'Scribe of HM 114', pp. 127–8; Hanna, 'Manuscripts and Transmission of Chaucer's *Troilus*', pp. 173–88; and Hanna, *Pursuing History*, pp. 98–114. See also Seymour, *Catalogue of Chaucer Manuscripts*, I, 55–9.

[51] Windeatt, *Oxford Guides to Chaucer: 'Troilus and Criseyde'*, p. 28.

[52] Ibid., pp. 28–33. The remainder of this paragraph summarizes Windeatt's arguments, based on these pages.

[53] Ibid., p. 30.

[54] Ibid., pp. 30–1.

and movement of his sense',[55] and concluded that this subgroup might preserve earlier Chaucerian readings for individual words, lines or short passages. However, this would not mark them out as copies of earlier drafts which Chaucer released for 'publication' nor would it show the absence of the philosophical passages to represent anything more than later scribal excision:

> … there will always be a fine line to be drawn in discriminating between what may be simply textual deterioration due to inaccurate scribal copying, and what may be the chance survival of authorial drafting, imperfectly preserved in a manuscript grouping or tradition that more generally shows a poor level of accuracy in transcription and a neglect of metre.[56]

How do we fit this portrait of abbreviated, inaccurate or scribally conflated copies of texts with Richard Osbarn, who worked alongside scribes at the Guildhall who had access to the best authorial exemplars? Do we postulate that, even at the Guildhall, he could not always gain access to the best exemplars, so he had to work with those he had to hand? In his going back to revise his copy of *Troilus* in HM 114, and in his providing text to fill the gap in his copy of the *Brut,* we see that he *did* care about the accuracy and completeness of his copy. The Italianate vocabulary suggests that his first exemplar descended from an earlier draft of Chaucer's poem, whether one from which a previous scribe had excised passages or not. Given our identification of the scribe as Richard Osbarn, attorney and clerk of the Guildhall, it is difficult to imagine such a man himself excising the philosophical passages from *Troilus* in a manuscript he was preparing for his own use or for use by others in his Guildhall circle. The parchment copy of *Troilus and Criseyde,* now most of the first half of Harley 3943, shows him to have also been preparing manuscripts for clients; but we argue that even here, once he recognized its deficiencies, he attempted to rectify the text and then abandoned it. He was not deliberately preparing an abbreviated copy focusing on the love story. Thus the excisions seem unlikely to have been made by him, and neither of his copies appears to have been made with these passages deliberately excised. Can such a man have been ignorant of the philosophical passages in a work dedicated to a former fellow employee of the Guildhall? Given the identification of the scribe, we wonder whether *Troilus* scholars, including Windeatt, need to revisit this issue.

Richard Osbarn, whether self-directed or at the behest or direction of some other person, appears to have copied a number of literary texts to keep as exemplars, for his own use, or for use by the community of clerks at the Guildhall; this, besides his day job, represented the bulk of his writing activity: only a portion of one manuscript survives that he may have been writing for a client, and even that he appears to have abandoned unfinished. Nevertheless, because his manuscripts bring together so many texts by both London and provincial authors, and because they are not written in high-quality manuscripts such as might be prepared for the bespoke trade, his writing offers the clearest evidence we have for a personal interest in Middle English literary texts among the highest officers of the Guildhall. The following chapters will present evidence of other members of this Guildhall circle of clerks being involved in the production of manuscripts of vernacular literature.

---

[55] Ibid., p. 32.
[56] Ibid., pp. 32–3.

3

John Marchaunt, Chamber Clerk, 1380–99, Common Clerk, 1399–1417

THE SCRIBE who wrote a portion of the copy of Gower's *Confessio Amantis* in Cambridge, Trinity College, MS R.3.2, as well as all or parts of seven other copies of the *Confessio* and two of the earliest surviving copies of Chaucer's *Canterbury Tales* was previously known as 'Scribe D' from his position in the order of copying of the surviving portion of Trinity College MS R.3.2.[1] We present here our evidence for identifying him as John Marchaunt, who was appointed chamber clerk at the London Guildhall in 1380 and who held the position of common clerk from 1399 to 1417, preceding the better-known John Carpenter.[2]

In their article on the scribes of Trinity College MS R.3.2, Doyle and Parkes listed the manuscripts which they attributed to Scribe D:

¶ Gower, *Confessio Amantis*
Cambridge, Trinity College, MS R.3.2, fols 66–73v, 113 (line 61) – 154
London, British Library, MS Egerton 1991
New York, Columbia University Library, MS Plimpton 265
Oxford, Bodleian Library, MS Bodley 294
Oxford, Bodleian Library, MS Bodley 902, fols 2–16v
Oxford, Christ Church, MS 148
Oxford, Corpus Christi College, MS 67

¶ Chaucer, *Canterbury Tales*
London, British Library, MS Harley 7334
Oxford, Corpus Christi College, MS 198

¶ Trevisa, *De proprietatibus rerum*
London, British Library, Additional MS 27944, fols 2–7v, 196rb (line 9)–335v

¶ Langland, *Piers Plowman*
London, University Library, MS SL V.88 (Ilchester manuscript)

Since the publication of that article, a further two manuscripts have been identified: all but one quire of another *Confessio* as well as a prose *Brut*:

¶ Gower, *Confessio Amantis*
Princeton, NJ, Princeton University Library, MS Taylor 5, fols 7–190[3]

¶ Anonymous, prose *Brut*
Manchester, John Rylands Library, MS Eng. 103, fols 1–126v[4]

---

[1] Doyle and Parkes, 'Production of Copies', pp. 164, 174–82 (repr. pp. 202, 212–20).

[2] See Barron, *London in the Later Middle Ages*, p. 363.

[3] Identified by J. Griffiths, '*Confessio Amantis*: The Poem and its Pictures', in *Gower's 'Confessio Amantis': Responses and Reassessments*, ed. A. J. Minnis (Cambridge, 1983), pp. 163–78 (p. 170, n. 19).

[4] Identified by S. Horobin, 'Adam Pinkhurst, Geoffrey Chaucer, and the Hengwrt Manuscript of the Canterbury Tales', *The Chaucer Review* 44 (2010), 351–67 (p. 365, n. 25).

John Marchaunt, Chamber Clerk, 1380–99, Common Clerk, 1399–1417

Although Scribe D's hand had been established in such a large number of literary manuscripts, there had been no identification of it in other contexts. To Middle English scholars, the sheer quantity and quality of his manuscript work suggested someone whose principal occupation was copying manuscripts of Middle English literature. Many theories have been advanced about his identity. G. C. Macaulay argued that he prepared manuscripts under Gower's supervision; John Fisher thought that this supervision may have taken place at Southwark.[5] Doyle and Parkes characterized him as a 'full-time scribe', presumably of vernacular literary texts, and an 'independent craftsman'.[6] Kathryn Kerby-Fulton and Steven Justice felt that on available evidence, he was 'more or less a full-time purveyor of English writing', creating a '*look* for vernacular English poetry', and they linked him with a Westminster clientele.[7] John Bowers believed him to be 'probably a professional scribe and part-time purveyor of vernacular texts'.[8]

As with Richard Osbarn, the identification of Scribe D as John Marchaunt depends on establishing that the hand copying his recognized literary manuscripts is the same as that we have found in the documentary record. Unfortunately, the hand of Scribe D in his manuscripts is notable for the lack of distinctive characteristics – one of the reasons why he has escaped detection for so long. Unlike Adam Pinkhurst's hand, whose twirly knots adorning ascenders and elaborate decoration are immediately recognizable, Scribe D gives us no such assistance. Doyle and Parkes record that there are a number of scribes at the end of the fourteenth and the beginning of the fifteenth centuries who all use a very similar version of *anglicana formata* and that they are difficult to distinguish one from another. The characteristics of these hands 'lie in the refinement, the careful proportions and disciplined qualities of the handwriting'.[9] These are all features which define the aspect of Scribe D's hand (a major feature in any identification), which is neat, controlled and consistently spaced. Examples from Scribe D's literary manuscripts demonstrate the point (see figs 3.1–3.4, 3.10).

The Manchester Rylands *Brut* manuscript (fig. 3.4) shows the scribal hand at its most casual. The London University *Piers* (fig. 3.2) and the Corpus 198 *Canterbury Tales* (fig. 3.10) demonstrate a neat, rounded hand, whereas the script for the Princeton Taylor 5 *Confessio* (fig. 3.3) is slightly more formal. Additional MS 27944 (fig. 3.1) displays the most angular of all the scripts, a feature more in evidence in the scribe's documentary hand. Despite minor variations, the scribal hand in all the examples shown is recognizably the same. The line spacing is regular, as is the space between words, the space between lines in relation to minim height, height of ascenders and depth of descenders, and the size and roundedness of individual graphs.

For the purposes of a more secure identification for this scribe, we compiled graphic profiles of almost all Scribe D's known literary manuscripts and catalogued the possible range of variation within a single graph. Scribe D's **g** graph will serve as an example. (See fig. 3.5.) Although at first sight it may appear to be exactly the same as those of many other scribes of the period, **g** consistently demonstrates sufficient difference to

---

[5] See pp. 1–2 (esp. nn. 2, 4, 7, 8) above.

[6] Doyle and Parkes, 'Production of Copies', pp. 177, 197 (repr. pp. 215, 235).

[7] Kerby-Fulton and Justice, 'Marketing Ricardian Literature', p. 223.

[8] J. M. Bowers, 'Two Professional Readers of Chaucer and Langland: Scribe D and the HM114 Scribe', *Studies in the Age of Chaucer* 26 (2004), 113–46 (p. 114).

[9] Doyle and Parkes, 'Production of Copies', p. 178 (repr. p. 216).

Fig. 3.1 London, British Library, Additional MS 27944, fol. 196rb (extract from second column):
illustrating the hand of John Marchaunt copying John Trevisa's translation of *De proprietatibus rerum*, beginning line 3, 'And it haþ kynde …'

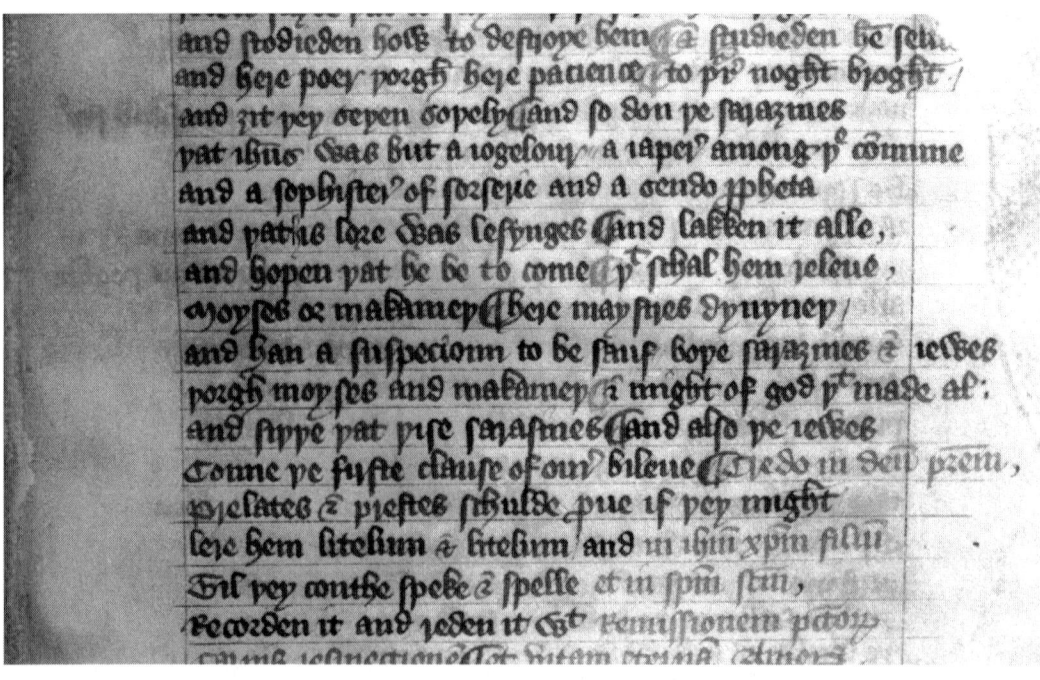

Fig. 3.2 London, Senate House Library, MS SL V.88 (the Ilchester manuscript), fol. 93r (extract):
illustrating the hand of John Marchaunt copying William Langland, *Piers Plowman*.

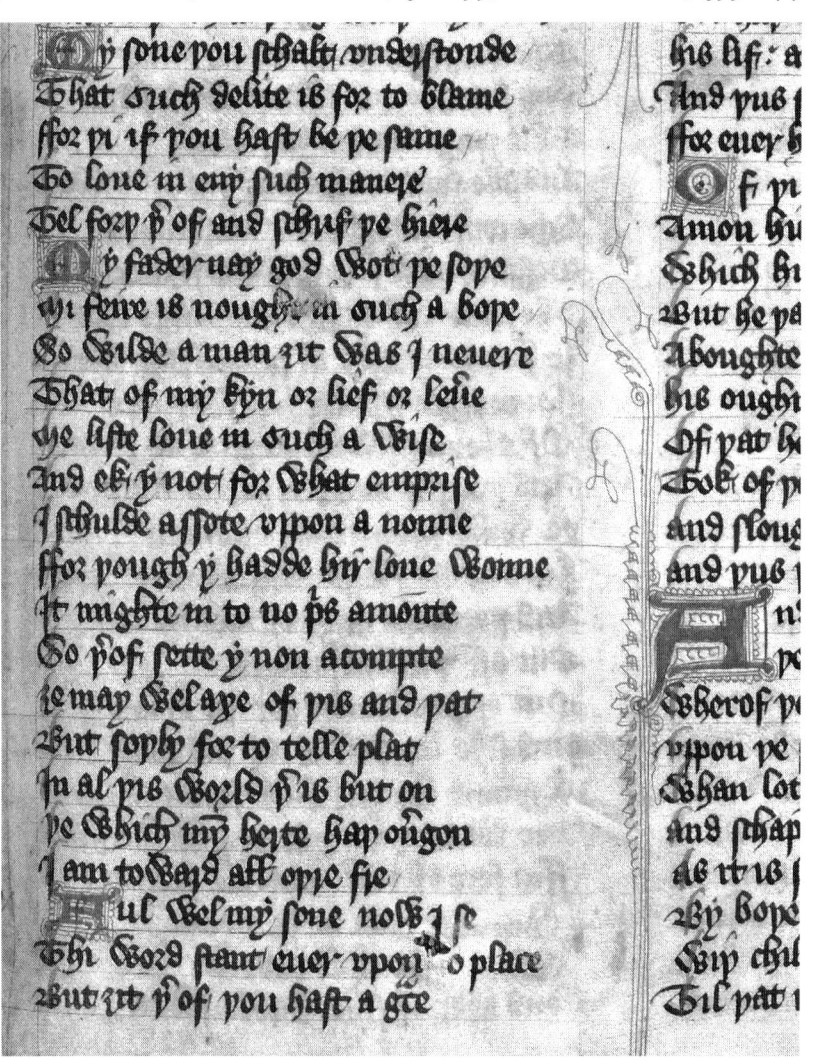

John Marchaunt, Chamber Clerk, 1380–99, Common Clerk, 1399–1417

Fig. 3.3 Princeton, NJ, Princeton University Library, MS Taylor 5, fol. 170ra (extract from first column); illustrating the hand of John Marchaunt copying John Gower, *Confessio Amantis*

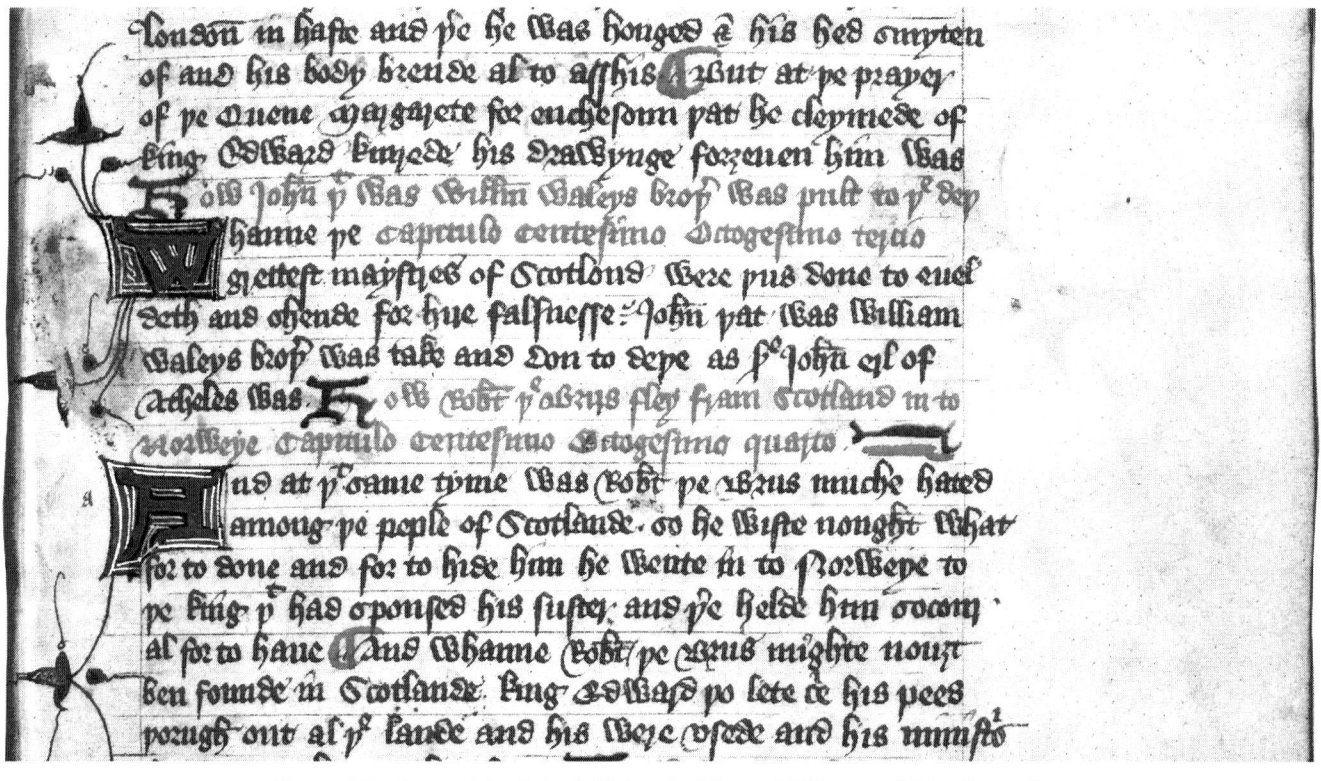

Fig. 3.4 Manchester, John Rylands University Library, MS Eng. 103, fol. 86r (extract): illustrating the hand of John Marchaunt copying the anonymous prose *Brut* (identified by Simon Horobin)

Scribes and the City

London, British Library, Additional MS 27944

London, British Library, MS Egerton 1991

Oxford, Bodleian Library, MS Bodley 294

London, British Library, MS Harley 7334

Oxford, Bodleian Library, MS Bodley 92

Cambridge, Trinity College, MS R.3.2

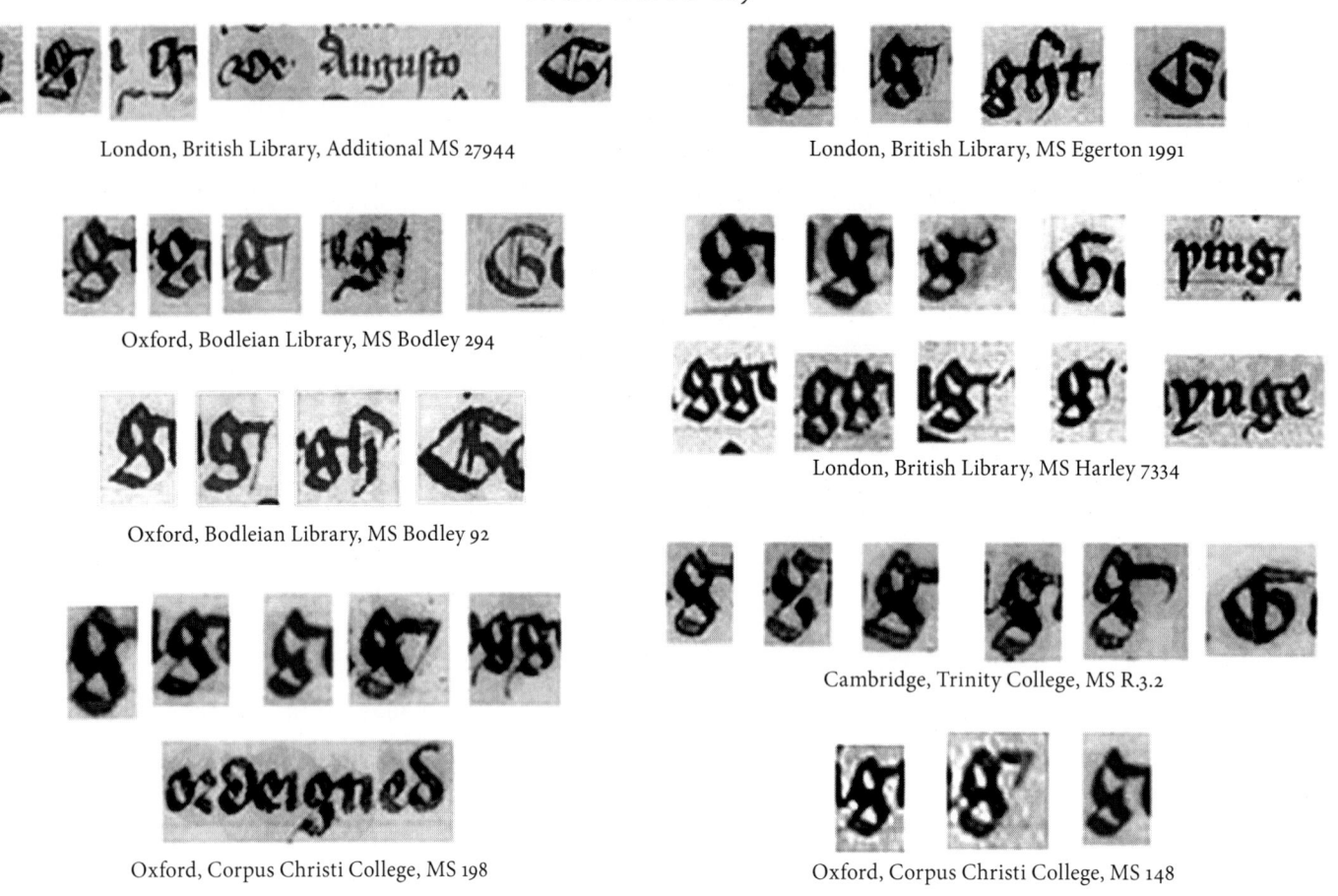

Oxford, Corpus Christi College, MS 198

Oxford, Corpus Christi College, MS 148

Fig. 3.5 Graphs of **g** found in manuscripts written by Scribe D (= John Marchaunt)

be used as a secure identifier, much as Malcolm Parkes used **g** as one of the identifiers of Richard Frampton.[10]

The lower compartment of Scribe D's **g** is generally more angular than those of his colleagues; it is often triangular, and has a horizontal aspect, sometimes appearing to be squashed up towards the more rounded upper compartment. The horizontal extension towards the next graph usually extends from the middle of the upper lobe rather than the top as in many hands. In final position, **g** often has an otiose stroke or tag attached to the end of the extension, descending vertically or at a slight angle. Sometimes the lower lobe is pointed at the left side with the addition of a variety of curled otiose strokes to finish, as may be seen in the examples selected from Corpus 198 and Bodley 294 (fig. 3.5). In the hundreds of folios from Scribe D's literary texts we have examined, we have noticed only two examples of secretary **g**; these both occur in Additional MS 27944.

Key letter-forms for the identification of late medieval scribes are **a, d, g, h, r, s, w** and **y**.[11] For Scribe D we assembled groups of variant graphs from several manuscripts to provide a basic catalogue for identification (see figs 3.6–3.9). Where the scribe's hand was remarkably consistent, as with Scribe D, we have deliberately tried to find examples on the same folio which might represent an occasional difference in the formation of a particular graph. If these 'different' graphs then occur alongside his normal graphs in other manuscripts or documents thought to be in his hand, we may have a more secure identifier than we would by merely noting the consistencies. The examples for letters **a, d,** and **h** (fig. 3.6) illustrate

[10] M. B. Parkes, 'Richard Frampton: A Commercial Scribe, *c.* 1390–*c.* 1420', in *The Medieval Book and a Modern Collector: Essays in Honour of Toshiyuki Takamiya*, ed. T. Matsuda, R. A. Linenthal and J. Scahill (Cambridge, 2004), pp. 113–24 (pp. 115–16).

[11] www.medievalscribes.com

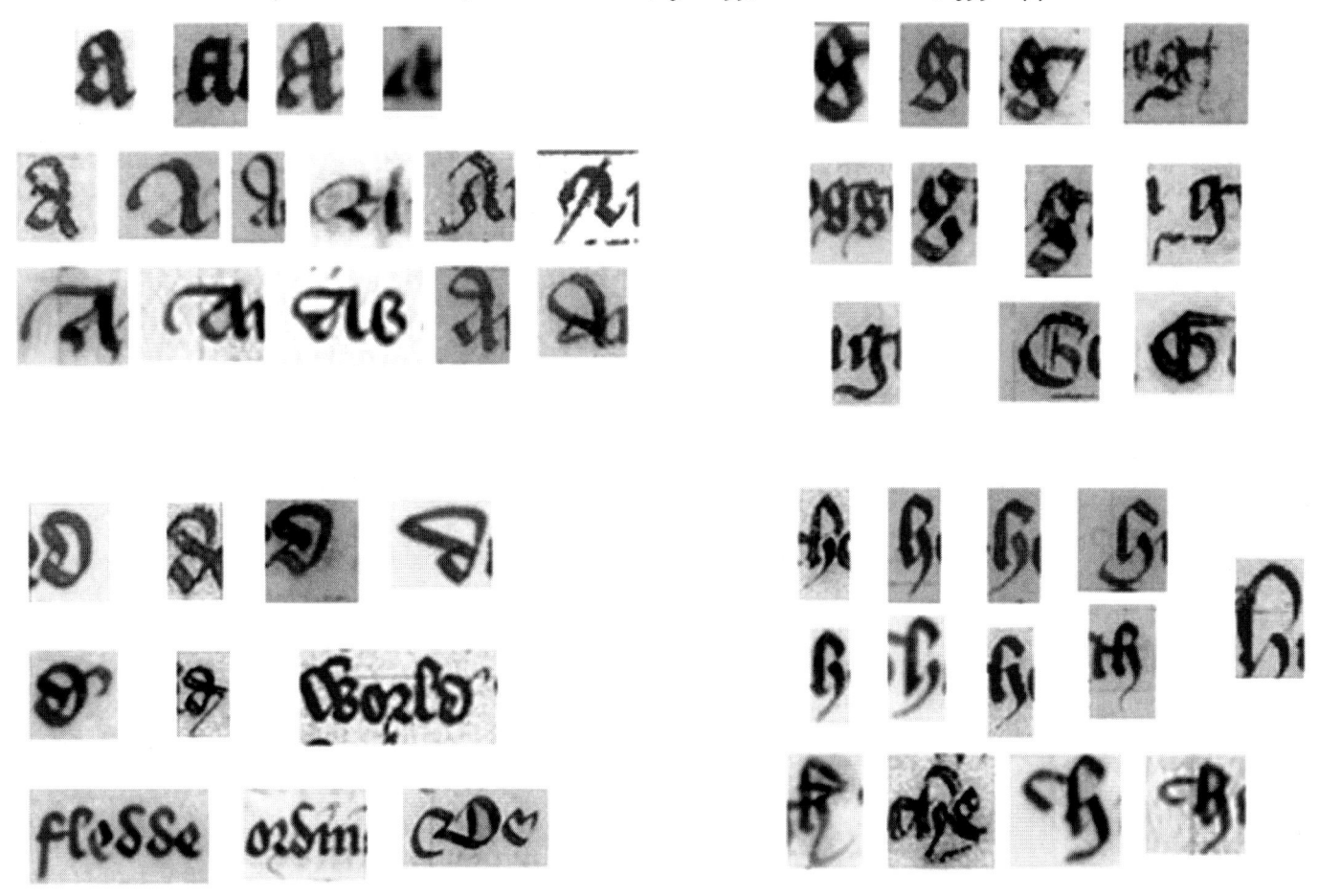

John Marchaunt, Chamber Clerk, 1380–99, Common Clerk, 1399–1417

Fig. 3.6 Graphs of **a**, **d**, **g**, and **h** in the hand of Scribe D (= John Marchaunt)

the features of these letter-forms we used for identification. For example, Doyle and Parkes remark on the number of variant forms of upper-case **A** which Scribe D uses; eleven examples may be seen here. Some examples of Scribe D's variety of **A**s may be seen in the manuscripts featured (fig. 3.10, lines 6, 10; fig. 3.1, lines 3, 25; and fig. 3.3, col. b, lines 2, 5, 8, 12 and 13). In Guildhall documents Marchaunt and other Guildhall clerks often use a special variant of **A** when writing the words 'Alderman' and 'Anglia'. So far, we have not encountered this **A** in any of Scribe D's literary manuscripts.[12] Thus, there appear to have been alphabets of specific letter-forms selected for specific purposes. Scribe D's lower-case anglicana **a** may vary slightly in its formation from manuscript to manuscript, but the upper compartment is consistently slightly smaller than the lower compartment.[13] All the manuscripts (figs 3.2–3.4, 3.10) demonstrate this quite clearly. The single example of secretary **a**, found in a Latin gloss in the Trinity College MS R.3.2, suggests that Scribe D was following the established convention for copying his manuscripts where only the anglicana form of **a** was acceptable.

The variety of **d**s (fig. 3.6) show the hand both in its rounded and in its more angular aspect. Lower-case **d** is almost always looped and generally the loop is neatly executed, in balance with the lower lobe. However, as may be seen in the last example on the top line of **d**s, occasionally the loop has a more triangular aspect, extending back over a previous graph. The first **d** illustrated, with incomplete upper loop and open centre, is very much a feature of Scribe D's hand, though it cannot be trusted as a secure identifier since he may

---

[12] We have also noticed that Marchaunt, as well as other scribes copying *Confessio* manuscripts, often use a distinctive **A** graph for the marginal gloss 'Amans', a type of **A** which may or may not be represented elsewhere in the scribal hand.

[13] Doyle and Parkes's Scribe Delta, on the other hand, consistently uses an anglicana **a** whose upper compartment is larger than the lower one.

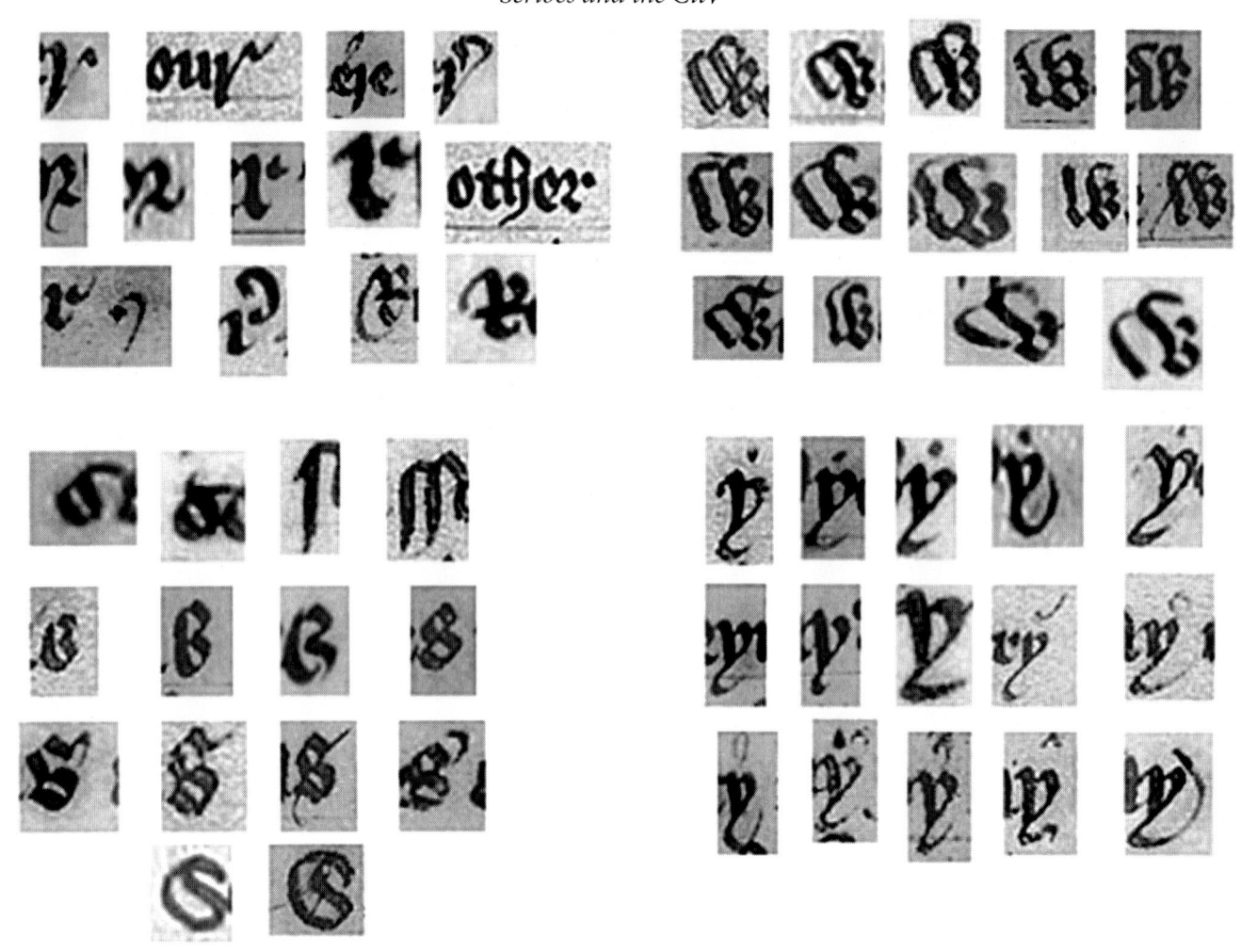

Fig. 3.7 Graphs of **r**, **s**, **w** and **y** in the hand of Scribe D (= John Marchaunt)

copy folio after folio without ever using it. It is more commonly found in English hands which predate 1400. (For other examples of this **d**, see fig. 3.4, line 2, 'and', 'brende'; line 4, 'drawynge'; line 9, 'don'; fig. 3.10, line 1, 'Iuged', line 7, 'god'.) The first group of the **h** graph demonstrates Doyle and Parkes's observation that the tail-stroke is neatly, or sometimes 'awkwardly', tucked away beneath the graph.[14] This typical feature of Scribe D's hand may be seen on almost every line of the sample manuscripts (figs 3.1–3.4, 3.10). In other examples the tail-stroke may also be flicked anticlockwise.

Fig. 3.7 collects together samples of Scribe D's letter-forms for **r**, **s**, **w** and **y**. The first example of long **r** with a downward curve of the shoulder matches Doyle and Parkes's description, but these are only occasional examples and it is much more usual to see final **r** (whether long **r** or modern **r**) with an upward flick. In the *Piers* manuscript (fig. 3.2, line 4), two examples of long **r** may be seen, one with a downward curve of the shoulder ('iogelour'), the other with a curled flourish to represent a final missing **e** ('iaper'). Z-shaped **r** often has a hook curling down from the lower left, and modern **r** sometimes has an angled foot as in the example, 'other' in fig. 3.7.

The scribe uses both sigma **s** and long **s** in initial position, and sigma, kidney and 8-shaped **s** in final position, with a preference for the kidney-shaped version. In the manuscript samples (figs 3.1–3.4, 3.10), 8-shaped **s** is the version used in final position in Corpus 198 (fig. 3.10), while kidney-shaped **s** is the preferred graph for Additional MS 27944 (fig. 3.1), London University Library, MS SL V.88 (fig. 3.2), Princeton Taylor 5 (fig. 3.3), and the Manchester Rylands manuscript (fig. 3.4). Scribe D sometimes uses an approach stroke

---

[14] Doyle and Parkes, 'Production of Copies', p. 178 (repr. p. 216).

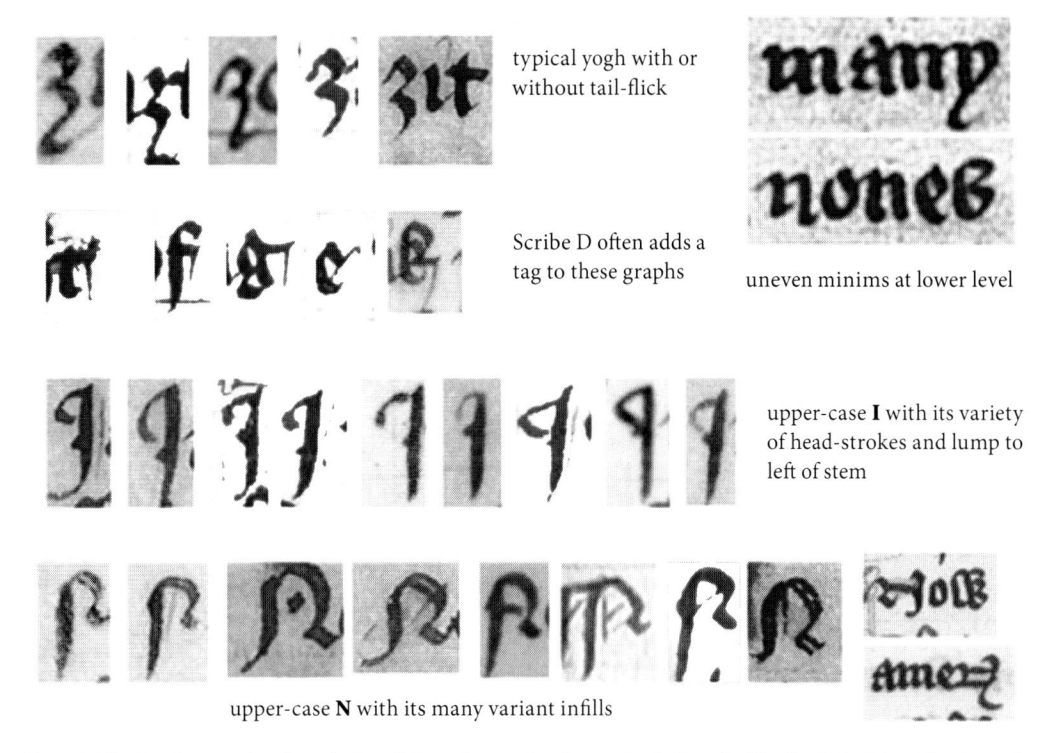

John Marchaunt, Chamber Clerk, 1380–99, Common Clerk, 1399–1417

Fig. 3.8 Distinctive graphs of yogh, **I** and **N**, and tags after letters in the hand of Scribe D (= John Marchaunt)

on long **s**, and both 8-shaped and kidney-shaped **s** sometimes exhibit angled or curled otiose strokes to finish (fig. 3.4, line 7, 'maystres', for otiose stroke on kidney-shaped **s**).

The letter-form for **w** is one graph used by Doyle and Parkes to differentiate Scribe D from Delta, but there are variations: we have found Delta, for example, using the form of **w** that they attributed only to Scribe D.[15] The top of the middle stalk of Scribe D's **w** is usually slightly higher than the left, and both turn to the right at the head. The tops of the stalks may appear as closed loops, or alternatively open strokes turning to the right, or they may have one of each type. The B-shaped element on the right side of the graph is neatly formed. The left stalk is usually smooth, with no perceptible foot. Examples of the characteristic **w** may be seen on each of the five manuscripts illustrated. Letter **y** is often dotted, but not always. The tail-stroke may be shorter or longer, or it may continue back above the body of the graph and end in a comma-like tick.[16] These, then, are the standard graphs. Many scribes used very similar graphs, but these in combination may indicate the work of Scribe D; since these are nevertheless common graphs in the late fourteenth and fifteenth centuries, it may be necessary to search further for a few of the more individual features of the hand.

A group of typical identifiers (fig. 3.8) include Scribe D's yogh, the addition of otiose tags to a number of graphs, the uneven base-line noted by Doyle and Parkes, and distinctive upper-case graphs for **I** and **N**. Yogh may occur with a sharp turn to the right at the base of its tail (Additional MS 27944, Princeton Taylor 5) or without (Egerton 1991). Several letters in final position have a hairline otiose stroke as an added tag. It has been noted on **d** and **s** (figs 3.6, 3.7), and here it is used on **t**, **f**, **g**, **e** and **k**. Two excellent examples of the unequal length of the minim strokes may be seen in the words 'many' and 'nones' (fig. 3.8). The

---

[15] Ibid. For Delta using the same **w** as Scribe D, see British Library, Additional MS 24194, fol. 148r, line 4, 'vnwytynge'.

[16] Note that this form differs from the version of the same stroke typical of Thomas Hoccleve's writing. Hoccleve's connecting stroke between tail-stroke and tick intersects the graph while Scribe D's runs up the right side of the graph. See Mooney, 'Some New Light on Thomas Hoccleve', p. 319.

upper-case letters with parallel line infill

upper-case letters with three-quarter line with turn

upper-case letters with single vertical line

upper-case **P** with oblique curved infill

upper-case **B** preceded by 2-shaped element

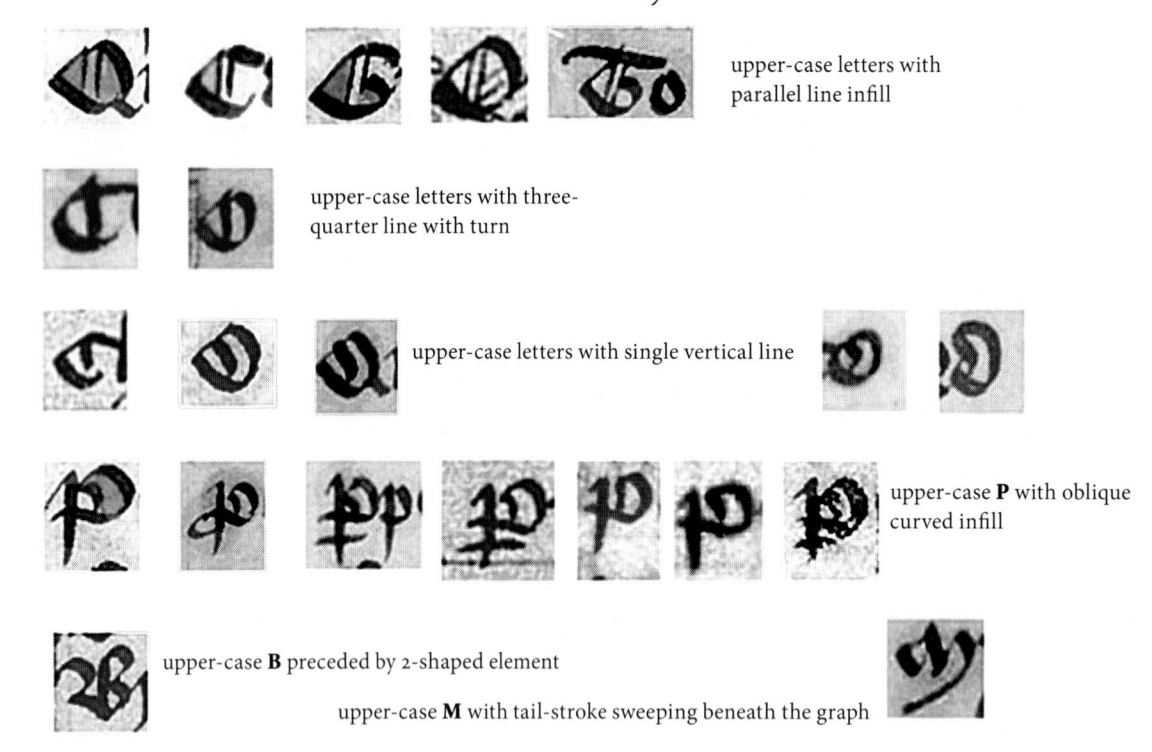

upper-case **M** with tail-stroke sweeping beneath the graph

Fig. 3.9 Distinctive treatments of upper-case letters in the hand of Scribe D (= John Marchaunt)

base line of the scribe's work appears uneven and the overall effect may be seen in all the manuscripts illustrated (figs 3.1–3.4, 3.10). However, because the upper level of minim strokes and other letters of similar height is usually well maintained, the effect is actually one of uniformity. Upper-case **I** is a distinctive feature of this hand. The approach stroke varies in length and curvature but usually joins the stem at the top. The small single protuberance on the left side of the stem is also typical (fig. 3.10, line 4 'Iugge'; fig. 3.1, line 7, 'SIluer'; fig. 3.3, col. a, lines 8, 12, 14, 'I' and 'It'). However, Scribe D also has a less formal upper-case **I** with a fine, short, curved approach stroke to the stem and no added protuberance; he uses this frequently in his documentary work (fig. 3.4, lines 8, 9, 'Iohn'). Upper-case **N** is unusual in the sheer variety and angle of the filler strokes (for instance, fig. 3.4, line 14, 'Norweye'). Dots or diamonds also inhabit the interior of this graph.

A final collection of notable features appears in fig. 3.9. Scribe D often uses parallel lines as decorative features in his upper-case graphs, as shown in fig. 3.9. However, many other scribes also use these decorative additions, so this habit must be identified in conjunction with other features of his hand. Scribe D also uses single vertical lines, but his most distinctive habit, an identifier for this hand, is a three-quarter stroke, usually set at an oblique angle, through round-bodied upper-case graphs such as **C**, **O**, **P**, and **D** (fig. 3.2, line 12 'Credo'). The stroke often turns before it reaches the lower side of the graph and resolves on the lower left side of the letter. This treatment of upper-case graphs is replicated in the formation of the scribe's lower-case round anglicana **e** and his rounded **d**. A lower-case **e** with a straight stroke on the lower left side, often descending below the base line, is also common (fig. 3.10, line 8, 'ne'). Upper-case **P** with a curved stroke within the lobe is very distinctive, as are **B** preceded by the 2-shaped element, and **M** with sweeping extension of the final minim well below the graph.

In each of these samples the scribe uses a slightly different collection of graphs, but all the samples have typical **g**s, with a particularly triangular appearance of the lower lobe in Additional MS 27944. The **d** graph may have rounded or angular lobes; two manuscripts show the rounded form of **d** so typical of the hand (fig. 3.4, line 2, 'and', 'brende'; fig. 3.10, line 7, 'god'). The **w** graph in all examples shows the head of the middle stalk standing proud

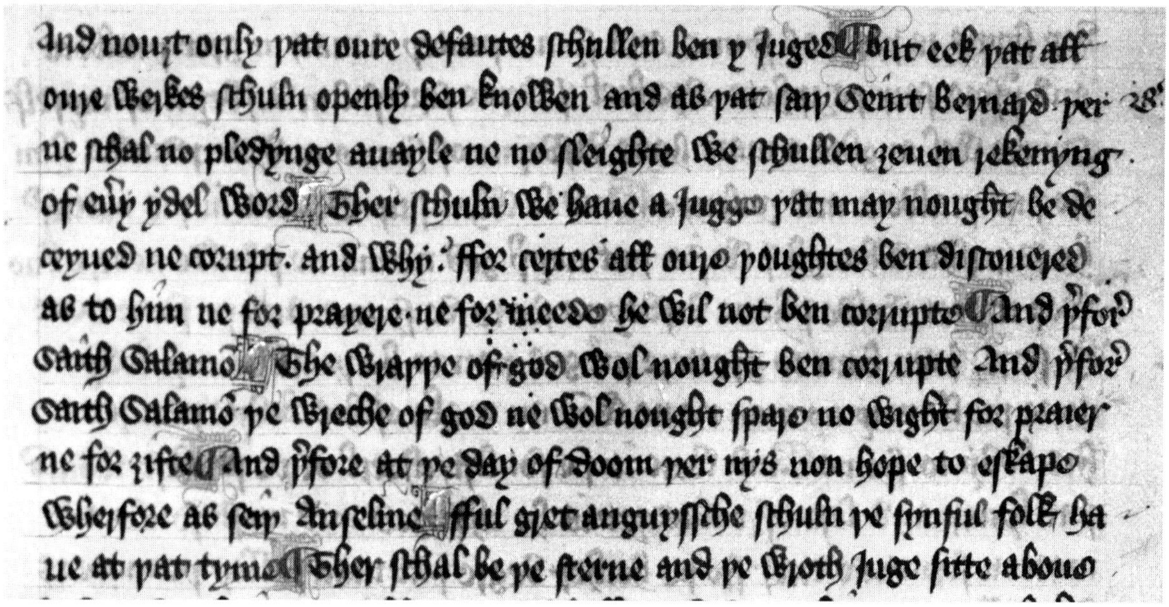

Fig. 3.10 Oxford, Corpus Christi College, MS 198, fol. 263v (extract):
illustrating the hand of John Marchaunt copying Geoffrey Chaucer, *The Canterbury Tales*

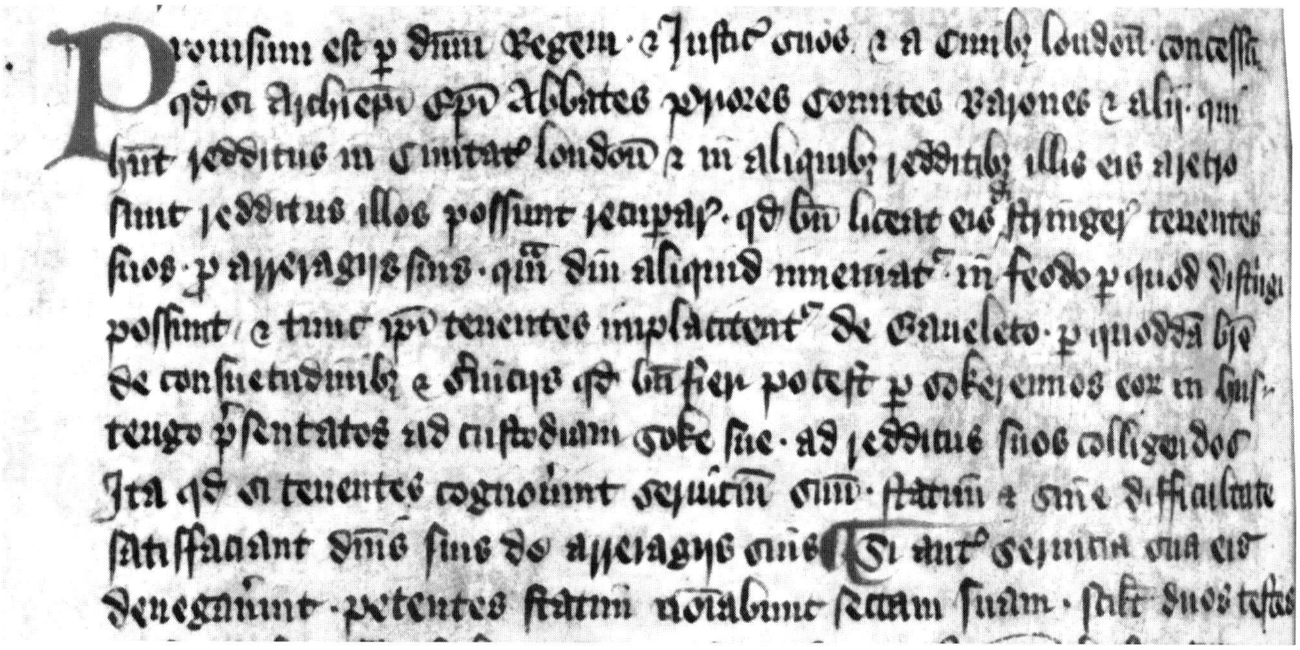

Fig. 3.11 London Metropolitan Archives, COL/CS/01/012, *Liber Albus*, fol. 231v (extract):
illustrating the hand of John Marchaunt

of the left and right elements, with a smooth left stalk and head-strokes turning to the right, with the loops either closed or left open (fig. 3.3, col. b, line 16, 'Wherof'). Graphs of **h** often show the tendency to tuck away the tail-stroke, generally within the limit of the body of the graph (fig. 3.3, col. a, line 1 'schalt', line 13, 'hir'). The uneven baseline is also visible in each manuscript example. All show some evidence of tags on **t**, **k**, **e**, **s**, **f**, **g** and **d**. Kidney-shaped final **s** is present in every sample although 8-shaped final **s** may be found occasionally in Princeton Taylor 5. Upper-case **A** is present in more than one form on each folio.

With an established 'style-sheet' for the hand, we recognized that Scribe D had contributed to several sections of Book III of the *Liber Albus*, which Kellaway described as containing 'no document later than 1394'.[17] There is a strong similarity of aspect and letter-forms, as on fol. 231v in Book III of the *Liber Albus* (fig. 3.11) and a sample of the prose from Oxford,

[17] Kellaway, 'John Carpenter's *Liber Albus*', p.70.

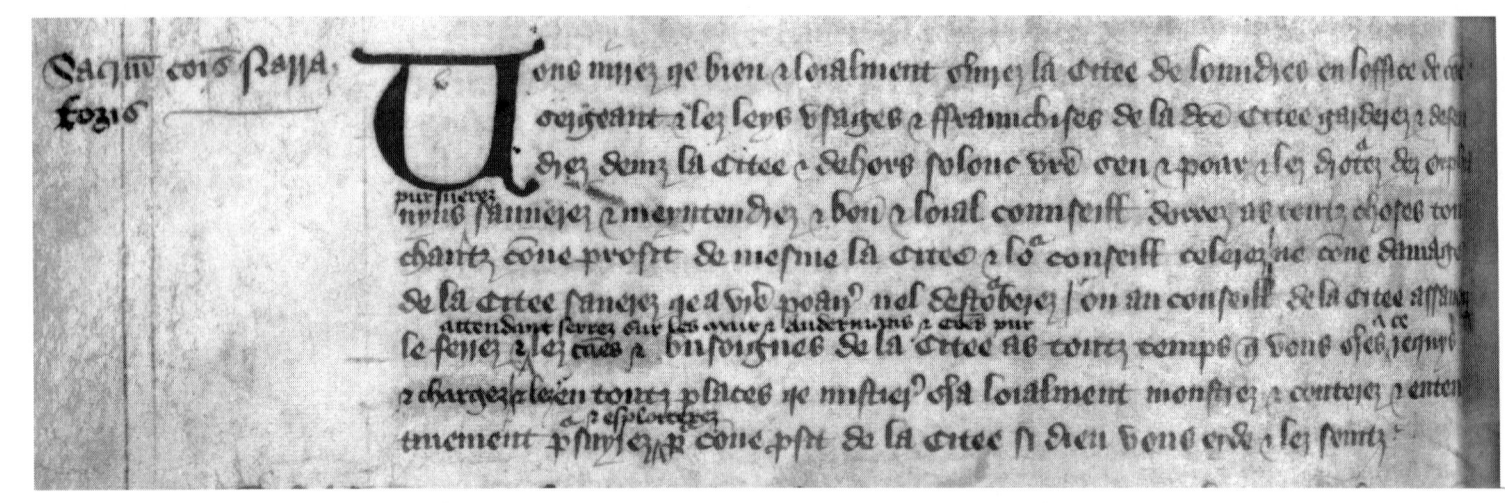

Fig. 3.12 London Metropolitan Archives, COL/CS/01/012, *Liber Albus*, fol. 197v (extract, reduced): illustrating the hand of John Marchaunt copying the oath of the common serjeant-at-law

Corpus Christi College, MS 198 (fig. 3.10). Parkes describes aspect as 'first impressions'; certainly the spacing between individual graphs and also between lines is remarkably similar in both examples, as are the forms of the letters themselves.[18] For instance in both illustrations the **g**s have a triangular lower compartment, typical use of both 8-shaped and kidney **s**, characteristic upper-case **I**, curved strokes within **P**, **G** and **C**, two versions of **A**, and **e** with sharply angled left side.

On fol. 197v of the *Liber Albus* (fig. 3.12) Scribe D records the oaths of the city's officials, here, the oath of the common serjeant. This would have been the oath sworn by Ralph Strode when he became common serjeant in 1373. A hand that may also be Scribe D's, or a later corrector, has added interlinear revisions to this oath, and it may be, as we suggested in Chapter 1, that these quires were intended to provide rough copy for a new collection. Many of Scribe D's characteristic letter-forms may be seen here, as well as some which he uses mainly in his documentary work: sigma **s** in initial position (line 2, 'sergeant'), kidney-shaped final **s** (line 3, 'dehors'), anglicana **a** with slightly smaller upper compartment (line 2, 'sergeant'), **d** with open centre (line 9, 'dieu'), the upward curl of the flourish on final **r** (line 6, 'poaire'), crossed double **l** (line 4, 'counseill'), the uneven base line, and a secretary **g** (line 2, 'vsages'), which is an exact replica of the two we have found in Additional MS 27944 (see fig. 3.5).

On fol. 235v of the *Liber Albus* (fig. 3.13) the scribe itemizes new regulations for the disposal of waste in the city. Typical examples of his letter-forms include the double parallel lines in **T** (line 1, 'Thamyse') and dotted **y** in the same word, smooth-sided **w** with taller middle stalk (line 9, 'rewes'), visible approach stroke to the left of the stem of long **s** (line 6, 'subhurbes'), the three-quarter curved stroke within upper-case **P** and **C** (line 4, 'Palys', and lines 3 and 15, 'Citee'), and an example of the idiosyncratic **A** for the word 'Aldermannes' (line 6). The typical upper-case **I** with single protuberance to the left of the stem may be seen in lines 11 and 15.

A date in the 1390s for Scribe D's work in the *Liber Albus* seems to agree with the dating of his *Piers* manuscript. The presence of his hand in a Guildhall custumal copying material in Book III, which is referred to by Carpenter in Book I on the laws and customs of the city, suggests that the scribe may, like Carpenter, have been a member of the Guildhall staff.

The same hand is to be found copying more or less all the entries on fols 1–5v and 8–12v at the beginning of Letter Book I, which was begun in 1399 at the accession of Henry IV.

---

[18] Parkes, 'Richard Frampton', p. 115.

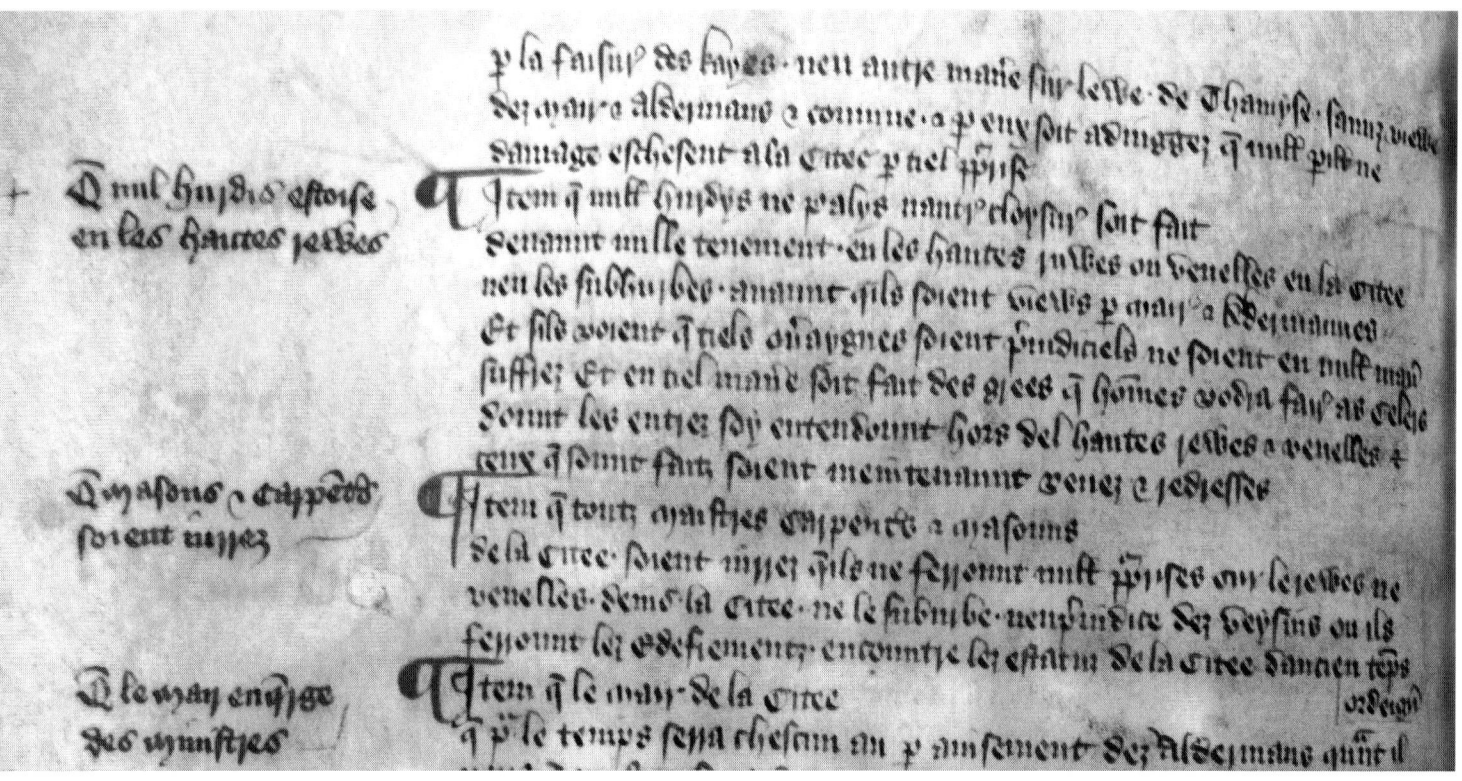

John Marchaunt, Chamber Clerk, 1380–99, Common Clerk, 1399–1417

Fig. 3.13 London Metropolitan Archives, COL/CS/01/012, *Liber Albus*, fol. 233v (extract): illustrating the hand of John Marchaunt

Fig. 3.14 London Metropolitan Archives, COL/AD/01/009, Letter Book I, fol. 5r (extract): illustrating the hand of John Marchaunt, common clerk, *c*. 1400

This hand records the appointment of the new mayor and sheriffs, new commercial agreements for merchants, the granting of a tenement within the Guildhall close to Richard Osbarn, the new chamber clerk, and the first Statute of Westminster of Henry's reign. On fol. 5r the hand makes a copy of a writ issued at Westminster relating to the Port of London (fig. 3.14). We believe this also to be the hand of Scribe D. The formality of the writing, the spacing and aspect of the whole is, of all the samples we have examined, the closest in appearance to Scribe D's literary texts. Typical letter-forms include a variety of his upper-case **A**s (line 2, 'Anno', line 12, 'Angl*ie*'); final kidney-shaped **s** (line 7, 'magis'); **g** with

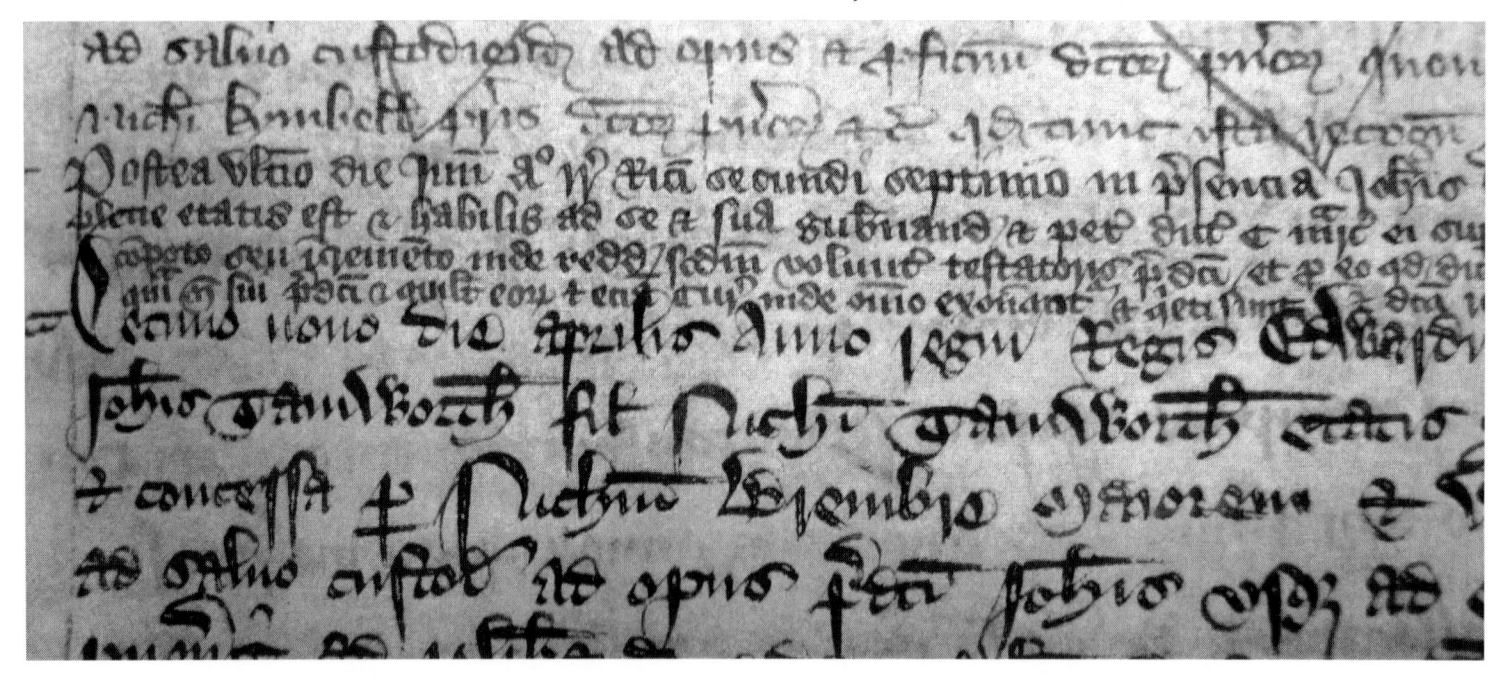

Fig. 3.15 London Metropolitan Archives, COL/AD/01/008, Letter Book H, fol. 52r (extracts, enlarged): illustrating an addition (lines 3–6) in the hand of John Marchaunt: (*above*) left half of extracted lines; (*opposite*) right half of extracted lines

squashed lower compartment and horizontal splay (line 3, 'regni'); three-quarter curved stroke within **P** and **C** (line 3, '*P*roclamacio', line 4, '*C*iuis'); the usual uneven level of minims at the base line; tags on **s**, **t**, and **d** (line 6, 'f*u*erit'); upper-case **I** with single protuberance (line 3 and last line, 'Iunii'); and upper-case **T** with double parallel line decoration (initial last line). These letter-forms, as well as the aspect of the whole, mark these folios as the work of Scribe D.

This copying of a large segment of text at the beginning of a new Letter Book helped us identify this as the hand of John Marchaunt. At the end of the fourteenth century the upkeep of the Letter Books was becoming the joint responsibility of the common clerk and the chamber clerk. They would have worked closely together, making decisions about what needed to be recorded. At the beginning of a new Letter Book the copying of important material such as this would be carried out by one of these men principally responsible for the content. In 1399–1400, when Letter Book I was begun, the chamber clerk was Richard Osbarn and the common clerk was John Marchaunt. This is not the hand of Osbarn, so it is probably that of Marchaunt. In a similar situation, John Carpenter, common clerk, wrote a significant portion at the beginning of Letter Book K.[19]

Some twenty years before becoming common clerk, John Marchaunt's appointment as chamber clerk of the Guildhall is recorded in Letter Book H for the year 1380.[20] As with Osbarn, one might expect to find certain entries in the Letter Books which would correspond with his clerkly duties. When we examined Letter Books G, H and I for examples of Marchaunt's hand, entries relating to the city's accounts and to the business of the city with regard to orphans produced several examples of a hand that was remarkably close to that of Scribe D. In the illustrated examples (fig. 3.15a and b) the top item (here only its last two lines) was entered in the fiftieth year of the reign of Edward III, 1376, by a hand we have not identified elsewhere. It registers the joint responsibility of two drapers for the 200 marks left

---

[19] See Chapter 5 below.

[20] 'The same day, in the presence of the said Common Council, Marchaunt was sworn and admitted clerk of the chamber, receiving yearly 100*s*. for his services from Michaelmas [29 September], 4 Richard II. [AD 1380].' *Calendar of Letter-Books*, VIII, fol. 131b (cxxxi b).

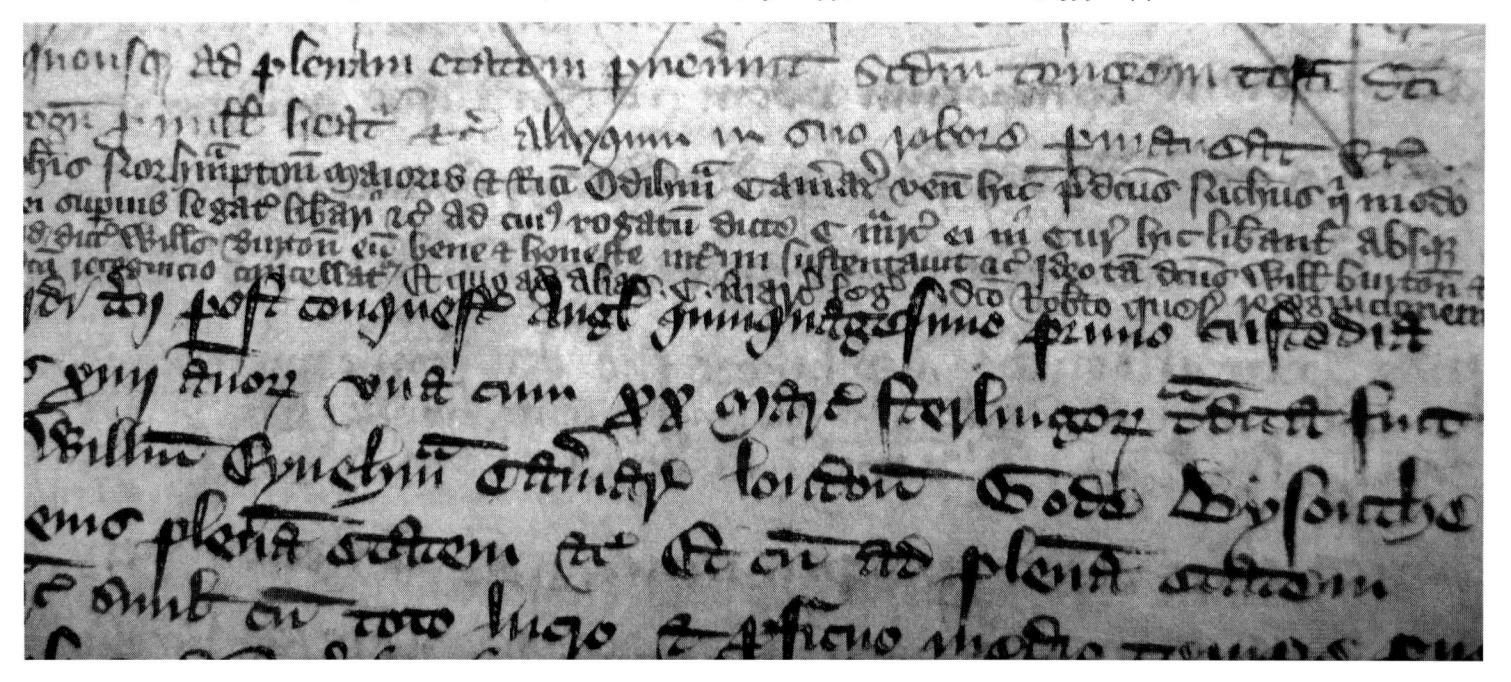

John Marchaunt, Chamber Clerk, 1380–99, Common Clerk, 1399–1417

to Nicholas and Robert Kymbell, whose father had died while they were minors. The second entry (beginning at line 3 in fig. 3.15) was copied in 1383 in a hand which we would identify as that of John Marchaunt. It records that Nicholas Kymbell presented himself before John of Northampton, the mayor, and Richard Odiham, the chamberlain, to request the 100 marks owing to him now that he had come of age. Although a very squashed example, the aspect of the hand is very similar to Marchaunt's, as are letter-forms such as the smooth-sided **w** with a taller middle stalk in the abbreviated form of 'Will*emus*' (fig. 3.15b, line 5); the three-quarter curved stroke in the 'O' of 'Odih*am*' and the 'C' of 'Cam*erarii*' (both fig. 3.15b, line 3); **g** with horizontal splay of the lower lobe in 'legat*us*' (fig. 3.15b, line 4), and 'gub*ernandum*' (fig. 3.15a, line 4); straight-sided **e** descending below the level of the following graph in '*p*resencia' (fig. 3.15a, line 3); and also his typical **N** in 'Norh*amptoun*' and 'Nich*olus*' (both in fig. 3.15b, line 3).[21] As chamber clerk working under Odiham as chamberlain and Northampton as mayor, both of whom are named in this document, Marchaunt would have been the person most likely to have entered the account of the release of funds to Nicholas Kymbell into the Letter Book.

From Caroline Barron's list of the officers of the Guildhall, it appears that John Marchaunt served as chamber clerk only in 1380–1, and that a John Dunstone, or Dustone, replaced him in 1382.[22] The record naming Dunstone (spelled 'Dustone') as chamber clerk occurs in Letter Book H, fol. 154r, dated 15 August, the sixth regnal year of Richard II (1382); the text reads:

> On Saturday the morrow of the Assumption B. M. [15 Aug.], the Common Council having met, a petition to similar effect was again presented, and the said Nicholas having failed to attend on summons by John Dustone, Clerk of the Chamber, it was agreed that the said Nicholas should be discharged.[23]

---

[21] The ink colour also marks it out as a contribution from the office of the chamberlain, since many such entries relating to the that office in Letter Book H are in a lighter, browner ink, suggesting perhaps, that each office of the Guildhall had its own ink recipe or supplier.

[22] Barron, *London in the Later Middle Ages*, p. 383.

[23] *Calendar of Letter-Books*, VIII, fol. 154 (cliv).

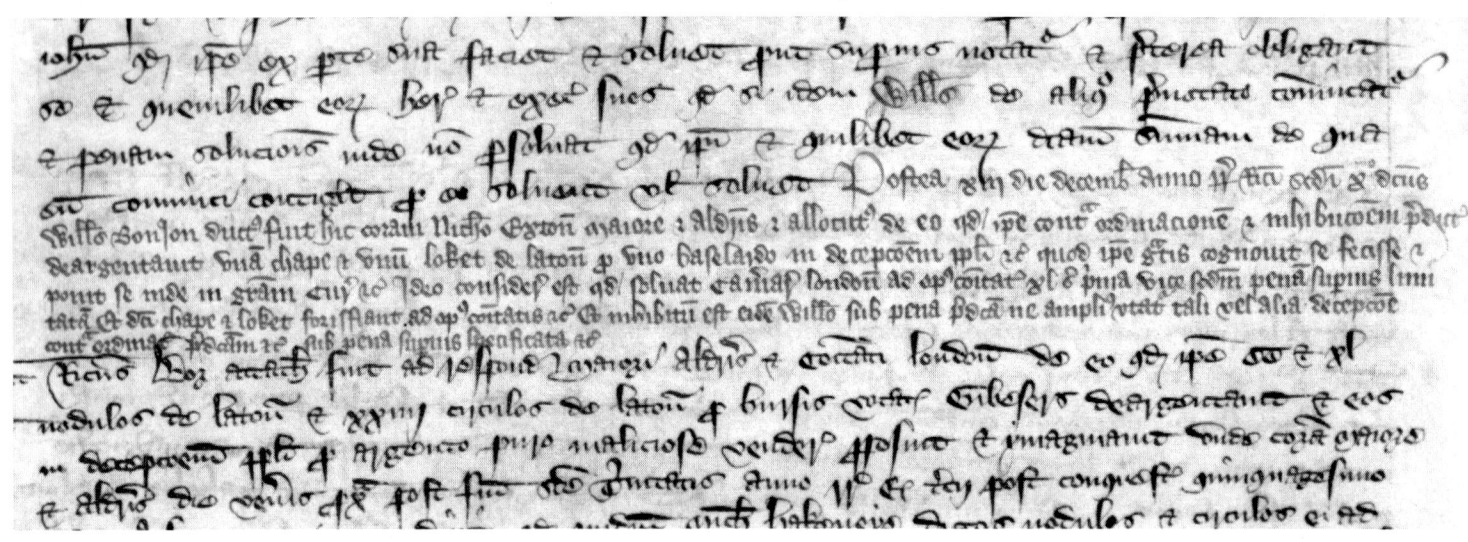

Fig. 3.16 London Metropolitan Archives, COL/AD/01/008, Letter Book H, fol. 42v (extract, reduced): lines 4 (beginning 'Postea') to 9 written in the hand of John Marchaunt in 1387

However, on 26 January 1383 John Dustone is described as 'Sergeant to the Mayor' in another document:

> 26 Jan., 6 Richard II. [AD 1382–3], grants by the Mayor, Aldermen, and good men of the misteries elected as a Common Council to John Dustone, Sergeant to the Mayor, of the gate on London Bridge and the custody thereof, so long as he remain in office.[24]

Therefore it appears that Dustone's tenure in the office of chamber clerk was brief, perhaps a temporary replacement for Marchaunt. The addition to the Kymbell document in Marchaunt's hand (fig. 3.15a and b), dated the last day of June, the seventh regnal year of Richard II (30 June 1383) suggests that Marchaunt returned to the office of chamber clerk after Dustone's brief tenure.[25]

According to Penny Tucker, Marchaunt served as an attorney in the city's courts from 1380 to 1393.[26] Sometimes judgements of the city courts were entered in the Letter Books, perhaps as precedents for carrying out city justice. One example in Letter Book H illustrates Marchaunt making such an entry in 1387 (fig. 3.16). A citizen named William Bonjohn had broken one of the ordinances of the city guild of the Girdlers for a second time and was fined accordingly in the court. The entry appears on fol. 42v of Letter Book H, following on from an entry dated 1376 when the same Bonjohn had also been accused of acting against the ordinances of his mistery. Features of the hand in this record mark it out as the work of Scribe D: the typical **w** in 'Will*elmu*s (fig. 3.16, line 5) rounded **d** in 'Alder*manni*s' and 'de' (fig. 3.16, line 5), **g** with almost triangular lower compartment in 'gratis' (fig. 3.16, line 6) and tags on final **d** and **t**. In Marchaunt's position as chamber clerk at the Guildhall, as one of the persons with responsibility for material entered into the Letter Books, and as an attorney in the courts where he may have witnessed the proceedings, he would have been aware of

---

[24] Ibid., fol. 162b (clxii b).

[25] Marchaunt must have remained at the Guildhall at the very least, for he continued to endorse deeds when they were read and enrolled in the Court of Husting. One record in which he did so is the copy of a deed entered into the Mercers' Account Book in 1396–7, where they also copied into their record the endorsement including copying Marchaunt's signature: See *The Medieval Account Books of the Mercers of London: An Edition and Translation*, ed. Lisa Jefferson, 2 vols. (Aldershot, 2009), pp. 120–1. Jefferson notes (p. 121, n. 45) 'John Marchaunt was clerk of the Chamber at the Guildhall, sworn and admitted to this office from Michaelmas 1380.'

[26] Tucker, *Law Courts and Lawyers*, app. 8.2, p. 386.

John Marchaunt, Chamber Clerk, 1380–99, Common Clerk, 1399–1417

Fig. 3.17 Kew, National Archives, E 40/2360, dorse: showing three of lines of text at the top, and a signature at end of line 4 in the hand of John Marchaunt

the previous record regarding Bonjohn's contravention of the ordinances of the guild of Girdlers, and so been able to update the existing record rather than entering a new one at the later date.

We also have a signature in Marchaunt's hand which may be compared with the hand of Scribe D (fig. 3.17). The hand is more formal and angular than the hand of most of his literary manuscripts, but although the document is in Latin, the general aspect and the range and selection of certain letter-forms even in this short passage are comparable to Marchaunt's. The portion written by Marchaunt is at the top of the dorse of this document, lines 1–3, and the signature at the end of line 4. The text that takes up most of line 4 and the remaining writing on lines 5–6 is not that of Marchaunt, and given that it runs over his signature, it must have been written after his entry. Features typical of Marchaunt's hand are the **h** of 'hustengo' (fig. 3.17, line 1) in which the tail is neatly tucked away under the letter; upper-case **A** in 'Anno' (fig. 3.17, line 2), which is the exact replica of the final example of upper-case **A** in fig. 3.6, with curved and leaning down-stroke; the **W** of 'Wulfstani' (fig. 3.17, line 2), which has a taller middle stalk; both round **e** (fig. 3.17, line 1, 'terre'), and the more angular **e** with straight stroke on the lower left side of the bowl are used (fig. 3.17, line 2, 'die'). The level of minims at the baseline is uneven, as in 'conquestum' (fig. 3.17, line 3) and 'hustengo' (fig. 3.17, line 1); and the **d** in 'London', 'de' (fig. 3.17, line 1) and 'die' (fig. 3.17, line 2) are typical of Marchaunt's more angular formation of the **d** graph. Doyle and Parkes remark on the difference in the degree of formality in Scribe D's hand in some of his manuscripts, and we should expect to see those same degrees of difference in his documentary work.

The Marchaunt signature is on the dorse of a document granting two tenements to John Castre and John Marchaunt. The document itself, on the front side, was copied in 1405 by the chamber clerk, Richard Osbarn, on behalf of William Castre, ironmonger. Castre was Marchaunt's brother-in-law, married to his sister Alice, who was selling these parcels to two relatives. The signature on the dorse shows that this memorandum was enrolled at the Husting Pleas of Land by Marchaunt himself, perhaps specifically because of his personal interest.[27]

An entry in Letter Book G, on fol. 232v (fig. 3.18), may be further evidence for identifying

---

[27] Kew, National Archives, E 40/2360. See 'Deeds: A.2301–A.2400', in *Descriptive Catalogue of Ancient Deeds*, II, 61–74.

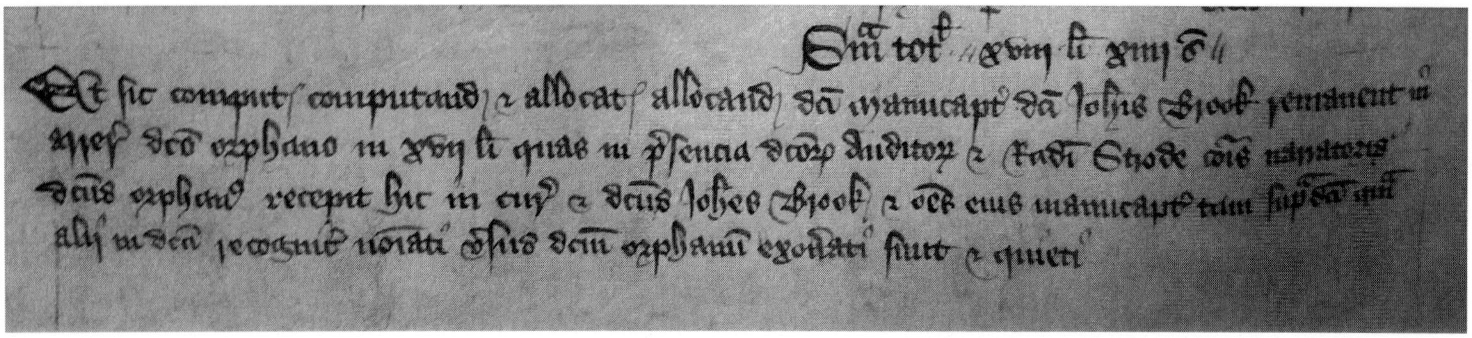

Fig. 3.18 London Metropolitan Archives, COL/AD/01/007, Letter Book G, fol. 232v (extract): illustrating the hand of John Marchaunt in an entry written in 1381

Scribe D with John Marchaunt. It deals with the case of John Spaldynge, who had become an orphan of the city in 1369, and records the final payment of the account in 1381 in the presence of Richard Odiham, the chamberlain, and Ralph Strode the common serjeant. Like the similar Osbarn example discussed in Chapter 2, this later entry appears beneath the original record of arrangements. Since the chamberlain had responsibility for looking after the interests of city orphans, it would presumably have been his clerk (i.e. John Marchaunt) who made the entry. The handwriting of this entry has the same angular aspect as the document with Marchaunt's signature (fig. 3.17).

Compare the shape of modern **r** in 'carta' of the signature document (fig. 3.17, line 1) with that of 'recepit' in the orphan document (fig. 3.18, line 4), and of 'siluer' in Marchaunt's manuscript of Trevisa (fig. 3.1, line 16); the angular **e** in both documents (figs 3.17 and 3.18) with those on almost every line of the Trevisa manuscript (fig. 3.1); the angular heads to **l** in 'london' in the signature document (fig. 3.17, line 1) with 'allocand*um*' in the orphan document (fig. 3.18, line 2); the **x** of 'sexto' (fig. 3.17, line 3) with 'exo*n*erati' (fig. 3.18, line 5) and 'xpm' in the *Piers Plowman* manuscript, London MS SL V.88 (fig. 3.2, line 14); the unusually long **r** in 'regni' (fig. 3.17, line 2) with 'arrer*e*' (fig. 3.18, line 3) and the 'r' of 'under' in one of his *Canterbury Tales* manuscripts (fig. 3.10, line 12); and the shape of the macron over 'london' (fig. 3.17, line 1) and 'co*m*u*n*is' (fig. 3.18, line 3). We also see the same abbreviation mark extending from a final 't' at the end of 'ten*ementis*' (fig. 3.17, line 2) and 'manucapt*ii*' (fig. 3.18, line 4). There are differences, of course. The 1381 entry relating to Spaldynge (fig. 3.18) uses secretary **a** alongside anglicana **a**, and the only example of **g** in this document is a secretary **g** (fig. 3.18, line 5). But the similarity of aspect is still striking. The match shows that Scribe D was the chamber clerk in 1381, i.e. that he was John Marchaunt.

As an attorney in the city's courts, Marchaunt made occasional entries in the Plea and Memoranda Rolls and recorded copies of deeds, wills and charters for the citizens of London in the Court of Husting.[28] The deed of 1390 illustrated in fig. 3.19 may also be in Marchaunt's document hand. Typical letter-forms include final kidney-shaped **s** (fig. 3.19, line 1, 'filius', 'heres'), upper-case **I** in two versions (fig. 3.19, line 7, 'Ioh*ann*i' [Shadworth] and 'Ioh*ann*i' [Wodecok]), several of his forms of **A** (fig. 3.19, lines 4 and 9, 'Auu*n*c*u*li', and line 9, 'Ade'), tags on **d**, **k** (fig. 3.19, line 2, 'Wodecok'), **t** (fig. 3.19, line 1, 'Doget') and **e** (fig. 3.19, line 4, 'Wisbeche'), smooth-sided **w** (fig. 3.19, line 5, 'Westchepe'), and **e** with angled left side (fig. 3.19, line 10, 'ex'). The script is slightly different, since the anglicana **a** which is so much a part of his literary script is absent, and the whole aspect is much spikier than in his literary manuscripts. However, this deed deals with the transfer of property from a family of le

---

[28] London Metropolitan Archives, CLA 023/DW/01/117, mem. 10v, item 96. For Marchaunt serving as attorney in the city's courts, 1380–93, see Tucker, *Law Courts and Lawyers*, app. 8.2, p. 386.

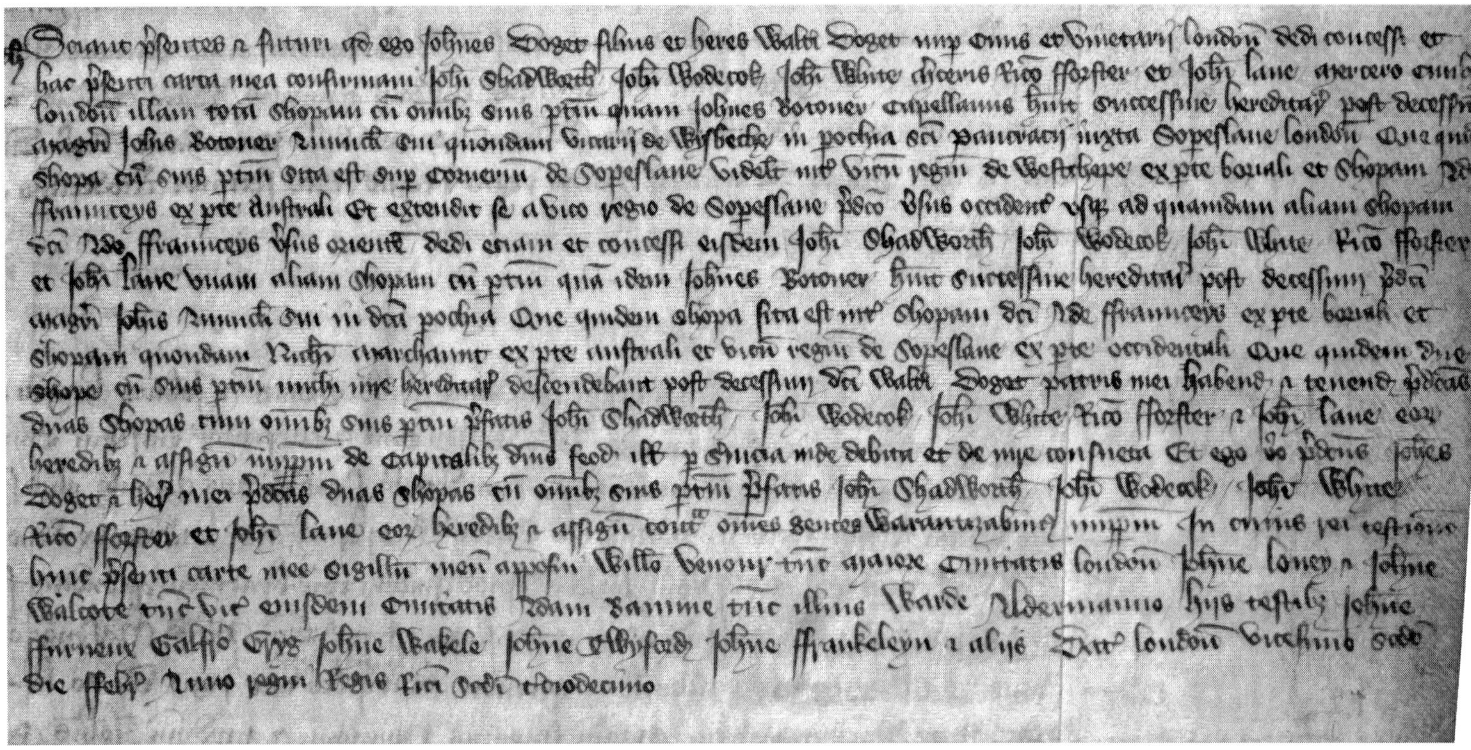

John Marchaunt, Chamber Clerk, 1380–99, Common Clerk, 1399–1417

Fig. 3.19 London Metropolitan Archives, CLA 023/DW/01/117, mem. 10v, item 96 (extract): illustrating the hand of John Marchaunt

Botoners in the fourteenth century, and the le Botoners were ancestors of the Marchaunts.[29] Marchaunt's father Nicholas is named in this deed as owning shops on the southern side of the le Botoners' property. A family interest may have been one of the reasons why Marchaunt copied this particular deed, and thus would support an identification.

The final piece of evidence for our identification of John Marchaunt as Scribe D was first noted by Manly and Rickert. The name 'Jhon Marcant' appears in the margin of one of Scribe D's copies of Chaucer's *Canterbury Tales* (fol. 180r of London, British Library, MS Harley 7334; fig. 3.20). Manly and Rickert thought that the name had probably been added in the sixteenth century, but we think it more likely to be written in a fifteenth-century hand.[30] It is not the signature of John Marchaunt himself, but may have been added by a later

---

[29] Marchaunt's will names the Le Botoners: see Kew, National Archives, E 40/12349. It was enrolled in 10 Henry V (1422) in the Court of Hustings. *Descriptive Catalogue of Ancient Deeds*, V, 291–2. For information on the Le Botoners and the ancestral connections of John Marchaunt, see A. F. Sutton, 'The Mercery Trade and the Mercers' Company of London from the 1130s to 1348' (unpublished PhD dissertation, University of London 1995), p. 295. The family connections given in a table on this page are somewhat tortuous, but there is a clear descent from a John Le Botoner, senior, who died in 1302 to Nicholas Marchaunt, son of Lettice le Botoner and a Christian Marchaunt. One of Nicholas Marchaunt's aunts, Amicia, married a Richard Mallyng and named Nicholas Marchaunt as her heir (c. 1360–84). A second aunt, Juliana, married a Henry le Chaucer, vintner, and received a property in Soper Lane from her father. This may be a property that descended in family ownership. Sutton remarks (p. 295) that 'Nicholas was the heir of the Le Botoners and a long tradition of mercery.'

[30] *Text of 'The Canterbury Tales'*, ed. Manly and Rickert, I, 226. Manly and Rickert report two occurrences of the name, one on fol. 144r which they read as 'Jhon Marcant', and the other on fol. 180r, which they read as 'Jhon Marka' (unfinished). In fact the folio references should be reversed, with 'Jhon Marcant' on fol. 180r as in fig. 3.20. A. I. Doyle agrees with us that this is an informal fifteenth-century hand, rather than sixteenth, calling attention to the long 'r' (private correspondence, January 2012).

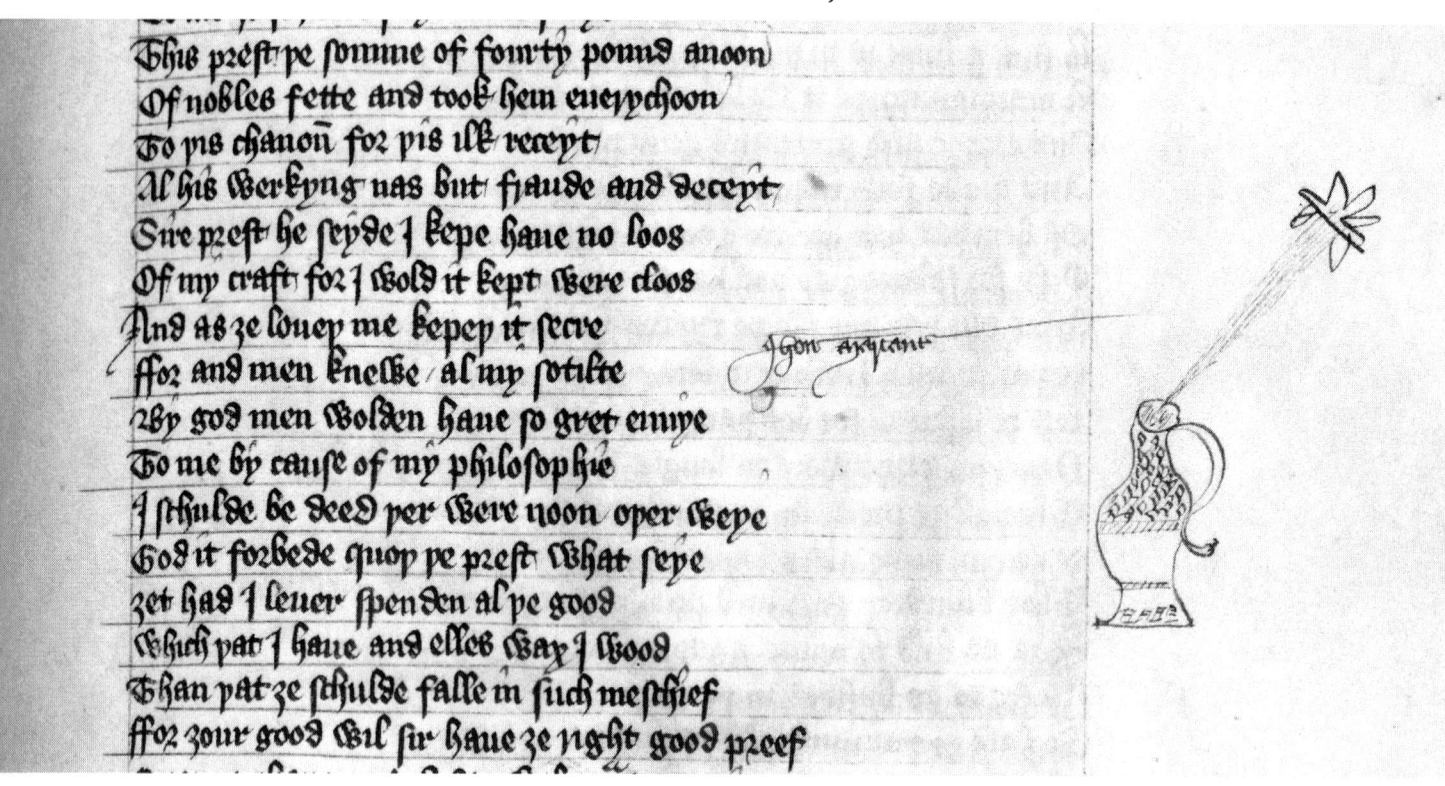

Fig. 3.20 London, British Library MS Harley 7334, fol. 180r (extract, reduced slightly): a manuscript of Geoffrey Chaucer, *The Canterbury Tales* copied by John Marchaunt, showing the name 'Jhon Marcant' scribbled into the margin

owner or user who knew the manuscript's provenance. A notation in a manuscript's border may be a mere scribble, but when it is a name it usually relates to the user, owner or to someone known to the owner. Here, the signature appears next to a line which reads, 'And as ȝe loueþ me kepeþ it secre'. This may relate to the common clerk's need to keep the city's affairs private. Marchaunt's name in the margin of a manuscript we believe to be copied by him must be more than coincidence.

Like Richard Osbarn, John Marchaunt must have spent a number of years working in a lesser role at the Guildhall to give him the required apprenticeship experience before being elevated to the position of chamber clerk in 1380. Tucker records Richard Osbarn serving as an attorney in the city's courts as early as 1390, ten years before his elevation to the office of chamber clerk: it is probable that Marchaunt was similarly apprenticed from *c.* 1370. We have discovered an early record that may refer to him: in Letter Book G, an entry for 1369 names a John Marchaunt as one of the armed men in the vintaine of Hugh Brenge, sent by the mayor and aldermen of the City of London to defend Calais at the king's request.[31] It is not clear whether the men were assembled from the wards, or whether they were specifically chosen by the mayor and aldermen, but the John Marchaunt who went on this campaign was clearly a citizen of London. Our John Marchaunt may have been in his late teens or early twenties at that time. War with France resumed in July 1369 when John of Gaunt led an expedition to Artois, Picardy and Normandy, an expedition in which Geoffrey Chaucer also participated as a young man.[32]

It is possible that Marchaunt acquired some qualification in law in the 1370s, since by 1380

---

[31] Sharpe, *Calendar of Letter-Books*, VII, fol. 226 (ccxxvi).

[32] *Chaucer-Life Records*, ed. Crow and Olson, pp. 31–2, note in the accounts of the king's wardrobe that Chaucer's name is included among others of the king's household travelling abroad in connection with Gaunt's campaign in the autumn of 1369, though his participation may not have involved combat.

he was acting as an attorney in the city's courts.[33] In the rubric to her appendix listing city attorneys Tucker makes the point that she excludes the names of those who only appeared jointly with others; those she lists were qualified to act as attorney alone.[34] Marchaunt is one of the latter class. That he was not obliged to act with another attorney suggests that he had higher legal qualifications.

Marchaunt's name also appears in *The Appeal of Thomas Usk against John Northampton* (1384). This document implies that a clerk named 'Marchaund' was closely associated with John of Northampton, at least from 1381 to 1383 when Northampton served two terms as Mayor of London. Usk wrote:

> At every council meeting was John More, Richard Norbury, and William Essex, and at some Adam Bame. But otherwise the mayor made his own decisions; one Willyngham, a scrivener, and one ... Marchaund clerk made a record of many matters in my absence, and on occasion were more privy [to information] than I.[35]

Since we know that John Marchaunt was sworn in as chamber clerk in 1380, it is probable that the 'Marchaund' named by Usk was our John Marchaunt, chamber clerk, who would have attended meetings of the mayor's council in the inner chamber of the Guildhall. He was perhaps taking the notes which would later be formed into declarations of policy, or read aloud to the citizens, but he may also have been present in the role of attorney or adviser.[36]

In his position as chamber clerk, Marchaunt was the controller, or the chief financial officer, for the city. An entry in the Memoranda and Enrolment Rolls of the Exchequer for 1382–3 shows that a John Marchaunt was presented by John of Northampton, the mayor, to be appointed attorney for the City of London to render the collectors' customs accounts.[37] As a legal officer for the city he would have been involved with all facets of its government, and must have acquired a thorough understanding of its laws and customs. This would have provided precisely the kind of experience required to qualify him for service as common clerk.

If John Marchaunt began his apprenticeship at the Guildhall *c.* 1370 at around twenty years of age, he would have been about fifty at the turn of the century, and in his seventies when he died. Thus if his copying of literary manuscripts extended over his entire career (rather than being concentrated at the end), then perhaps the estimated dates for his copies of Middle English literature need to be reviewed. This would apply in particular to manuscripts of works known to have been composed before 1400, to manuscripts made up of material

---

[33] Tucker, *Law Courts and Lawyers*, app. 8.2, p. 386. Given Marchaunt's association with the conventual church of Holy Trinity, Aldgate, which is mentioned in his will, he may have begun his education at the school there, perhaps with an early exposure to canon law as taught by the Augustinian canons, or perhaps graduating from that school to the inns of court.

[34] Ibid.

[35] R. Chambers and M. A. Daunt, *A Book of London English, 1384–1425* (Oxford, 1931), p. 24.

[36] For further discussion, see pp. 118–19, 134–9 below.

[37] Kew, National Archives, E 159/159. Michaelmas, 6 Richard II 1382. The early membranes are not numbered, but the Marchaunt entry is on the fourth membrane, almost at the bottom. Marchaunt was appointed by the city to act as attorney to render the customs accounts for the ports. The accounts he kept would have gathered together information from all the first-hand accounts of collection of duties from ports in England including those of Geoffrey Chaucer as controller at the Wool Quay. One such account, National Archives E 356/14 appears to be written by the hand of Scribe D.

which has obviously been copied at different times, or manuscripts which indicate alteration or addition.

This raises the question of what significance our identification of Scribe D as John Marchaunt has for our understanding of the production of some of the most important literary manuscripts of the late fourteenth and early fifteenth centuries. The sheer number of manuscripts he copied demonstrates his centrality to the literary copying we have located among clerks either working for, or connected with, the Guildhall. The earliest of Marchaunt's known manuscripts may be his copy of *Piers Plowman*, the so-called Ilchester manuscript (now London, University Library, MS SL V.88), dated to the 1390s by Doyle and Parkes.[38] Doyle later explained that this dating was based on the style of illumination.[39] Skeat was the first scholar to suggest that the Ilchester manuscript contained an important version of the 'C' text of the poem, perhaps an 'earlier draught'; but Derek Pearsall dismissed that notion, describing the conflated Prologue as the result of 'extensive editorialisation'.[40] Pearsall concluded that some of the interpolations of the 'C' prologue represent intelligent revision but that there is also 'bungling', which might be the result of 'memorial reconstruction'.[41] He felt that the blame for this might not necessarily reside with the scribe but could be the result of his attempt to reconstruct the text from a number of unreliable sources. This situation is, of course, mirrored by Osbarn's attempts to reconstruct a comprehensive copy of *Piers* more than a decade later; the same comments about multiple exemplars available, not always of the best versions, also apply.[42] It seems therefore that multiple exemplars of some texts, like *Piers Plowman*, were accessible to clerks at the Guildhall for a considerable period.

Pearsall concludes that the scribe/editor of the Ilchester manuscript may have been a Langland enthusiast. Langland was certainly in London when John Marchaunt was at the Guildhall as a young man, possibly from the late 1360s.[43] Since Langland's 'extensive knowledge of legal terminology' might point to some kind of legal or clerical employment, whether only at Westminster or also in the royal courts at the Guildhall, it is possible that Marchaunt (Scribe D) and Langland knew each other, as suggested by Kerby-Fulton.[44] Marchaunt's inclinations in those earlier years may well have been in tune with those of Langland. Pearsall acknowledges the scribe's Lollard leanings in the *Piers* manuscript, as well as his pretensions as an alliterative poet.[45] John Bowers also believes that Scribe D (Marchaunt) was at least 'willing to engage in ongoing contests over Lollard terminology',

---

[38] Doyle and Parkes, 'Production of Copies', p. 196 (repr. p. 234). The Manchester Rylands 'Brut', identified by Simon Horobin as having been copied by Marchaunt, also dates from early in his career, but as this identification is only recent, no scholars have as yet commented on its place in Scribe D's œuvre.

[39] A. I. Doyle, 'Remarks on Surviving Manuscripts of *Piers Plowman*', in *Medieval English Religious and Ethical Literature: Essays in Honour of G. H. Russell*, ed. G. Kratzmann and J. Simpson (Cambridge, 1986), pp. 35–48 (p. 45).

[40] *The Vision of William concerning Piers the Plowman*, ed. Skeat, II, lxxi; D. Pearsall, 'The "Ilchester" Manuscript of *Piers Plowman*', *Neuphilologische Mitteilungen* 82 (1981), 181–93 (p. 181 and nn. 3, 4).

[41] Pearsall, 'The "Ilchester" Manuscript', p. 188.

[42] See Chapter 2 above.

[43] Pearsall, 'The "Ilchester" Manuscript', p. 193.

[44] Kerby-Fulton, 'Professional Readers of Langland', p. 106.

[45] D. Pearsall, 'The Manuscripts and Illustrations of Gower's Works', in *A Companion to Gower*, ed. S. Echard (Cambridge, 2004), pp. 73–97 (p. 97). Pearsall flags up the prominence of the Lollard reference in the *Confessio* manuscript, Bodley 902, also with Marchaunt connections, at V.1802.

suggesting that in his early career he was perfectly happy to participate in 'Lollard/Wycliffite controversies'.[46] The fact that the Lollard references in the Oxford, Corpus Christi College, MS 198 manuscript of the *Canterbury Tales* could be from a remnant of an earlier version might lend support to this theory. The Man of Law's endlink, where the 'Lollere' references appear, is the last text of the portion of the *Tales* which in Harley 7334, Marchaunt's second manuscript of the *Tales*, underwent revision, according to Tatlock.[47] Kerby-Fulton has assessed some of these revisions and suggests lexical improvements in Harley 7334 which she sees as moving away from Lollard jargon.[48] This might suggest that Marchaunt realized that a 'cleansing' of some texts was politically judicious and undertook to do so when copying the *Tales* for a second time.

Certainly Marchaunt was a man of conventional piety, as may be seen when, in 1398, he applied for permission to have a portable altar in his home.[49] Marchaunt's strict piety is also evinced in his will when he requests that his executors should have the 'power to dismiss a dishonest chaplain and to appoint a fit and honest one in his place'.[50]

Kerby-Fulton and Justice also argue that in Scribe D's copying of Langland, he uses 'legal and parliamentary terminology in embryonic and alliterative "interventions"'.[51] Their article was written assuming a Westminster connection for Scribe D, but in line with our identification of his profession as a lawyer, attorney, chamber clerk and common clerk at the Guildhall, it is now clear that Marchaunt was simply drawing on his knowledge of the law.

Marchaunt also collaborated with two other scribes in a copy of Trevisa's *De proprietatibus rerum*. Ralph Hanna suggests that Sir Thomas Berkeley, a frequent visitor to London to attend Parliament from his native Gloucestershire, may have taken his London visits as an opportunity to disseminate the 'literary works he had patronised'.[52] Hanna also remarks that the copy used to create Additional MS 27944 must have derived directly from Trevisa's

---

[46] Bowers, 'Two Professional Readers of Chaucer and Langland', pp. 117, 119. To support his argument Bowers cites the two lines in the Corpus Christi College *Canterbury Tales* manuscript which retain the reference to Lollards (at II:73 and 77) and argues that Chaucer himself probably censored these references after the Lollard crisis of 1395.

[47] J. S. P. Tatlock, *The Harleian Manuscript 7334 and Revision of the 'Canterbury Tales'*, Chaucer Society 2nd series 41 (London, 1909), p. 11. Although Jeremy Smith and Charles Owen argued that Harley 7334 preceded Corpus 198, Horobin and Mosser suggest that, in fact, the order may be the other way around. See J. Smith, 'Studies in the Language of Some Manuscripts of Gower's *Confessio Amantis*' (unpublished PhD dissertation, University of Glasgow, 1985), p. 251; C. A. Owen, *The Manuscripts of 'The Canterbury Tales'* (Cambridge, 1991), p. 8, n. 1; S. Horobin and D. W. Mosser, 'Scribe D's SW Midlands Roots: A Reconsideration', *Neuphilologische Mitteilungen* 106 (2005), 289–305 (p. 302, n. 15). The linguistic evidence is supported by the codicological evidence described in E. Stubbs, *A Study of the Codicology of Four Early Manuscripts of the Canterbury Tales; Aberystwyth, National Library of Wales MS. Peniarth 392D (Hengwrt), Oxford, Corpus Christi College, MS. 198 (Corpus), London, British Library MS. Harley 7334 (Harley 4), and California, San Marino, Huntington Library MS. El. 26 C 9 (Ellesmere)*, The Norman Blake Editions of *The Canterbury Tales*, HRI Online, University of Sheffield (forthcoming).

[48] K. Kerby-Fulton, 'Langland in his Working Clothes', in *Middle English Poetry: Texts and Traditions, Essays in Honour of Derek Pearsall*, ed. A. J. Minnis (York, 2001), pp. 139–61 (pp. 146–7).

[49] 'Lateran Regesta 68: 1398–1399', in *Calendar of Entries in the Papal Registers Relating to Great Britain and Ireland*, vol. 5: 1398–1404, ed. W. H. Bliss (London, 1904), pp. 210–38.

[50] *Descriptive Catalogue of Ancient Deeds*, V, 292.

[51] Kerby-Fulton and Justice, 'Marketing Ricardian Literature', p. 218.

[52] R. Hanna, 'Sir Thomas Berkeley and his Patronage', *Speculum* 64 (1989), 878–916 (p. 909).

holograph in 'a reasonably direct route from author and patron to London scribes'.[53] This exemplar, or one very like it, remained available in London for more than thirty years, providing the copy for at least two further manuscripts. Given the identification of Scribe D as Marchaunt, it is possible that the exemplar copies were brought to the Guildhall's community of clerks, and remained with them.

Marchaunt also copied a *Brut* manuscript, which, like Osbarn's copy of the *Brut* in Lambeth Palace MS 491, contained what Lister Matheson described as the 'Common Version' of the text to 1377; both manuscripts belong to Matheson's 'Stage 1' development of the text thereafter, with Marchaunt's copy probably having the full continuation (the manuscript is imperfect at the end), and Lambeth 491 a shortened version of the same text.[54] Marchaunt's *Brut* looks early, the hand resembling the looser, slightly less formal hand of the Langland Ilchester manuscript much more than the more formal hand of the *Confessio Amantis* and *Canterbury Tales* manuscripts. Altogether the presentation is less deliberate and structured than his later work. Hanna, citing John Taylor, suggests that the text 'appears to emanate from clerical and administrative writing teams, perhaps more specifically royal Chancery clerks'.[55] It is possible that at an early date the Guildhall established itself as the repository for the collection and dissemination of material used in *Brut* texts, with the charters, documents and custumals of the ancient rights and laws of the city held and copied at the Guildhall. Since one of the tasks of the Guildhall clerks was to record matter relevant to London in the Letter Books, and later in the Journals, and another was to produce copies of custumals summarizing the history of the city, much of the historical matter found in *Brut* texts would have been available in the scribes' heads as well as in documentary form.[56]

Kerby-Fulton and Justice's analysis of Princeton Taylor 5, copied by Marchaunt, suggests that Scribes D and Delta 'were involved in a common or even competitive pursuit of an appropriate and distinctive mode of presentation, a "look" for vernacular English poetry'.[57] The two scribes' concern with 'textual integrity' and the 'careful, conservative, good' texts which they achieved, suggested to Kerby-Fulton and Justice that they made a conscious effort to direct and shape their copies of vernacular texts for the 'cognoscenti of Ricardian writing'.[58] These conclusions accord with Pearsall's summary of what he perceives to be a 'standard' look characterizing the twenty-eight manuscripts of the *Confessio* which have survived from the first quarter of the fifteenth century.[59] They were mainly produced by scribes whose professionalism was indisputable, quality products in terms of the materials used and the work of the miniaturists and border artists who contributed to the volumes.

---

[53] Ibid., p. 910. Hanna suggests collaboration of Scribe D with the two other scribes within Berkeley's lifetime. He also draws attention to the number of copies of the *Polychronicon* copied by Doyle and Parkes' Scribe Delta. We have identified yet another copy of the *Polychronicon* by Delta (Aberdeen University Library, MS 21) and it would appear that Delta's 'specialization' in *Polychronicon* manuscripts mirrors that of Marchaunt's Gowers and Pinkhurst's Chaucers.

[54] L. M. Matheson, *The Prose 'Brut': The Development of a Middle English Chronicle* (Tempe, 1998), pp. 81, 89 (Rylands), 91, 93 (Lambeth).

[55] Hanna, *London Literature*, p. 127, citing J. Taylor, *English Historical Literature in the Fourteenth Century* (Oxford, 1987), pp. 110–32, 146–7.

[56] See Hanna, *London Literature*, pp. 44–103, which has great significance for the Guildhall as a copying and distribution centre.

[57] Kerby-Fulton and Justice, 'Marketing Ricardian Literature', p. 223.

[58] Ibid.

[59] Pearsall, 'Manuscripts and Illustrations of Gower', pp. 80, 89.

John Marchaunt, Chamber Clerk, 1380–99, Common Clerk, 1399–1417

Pearsall describes the eight-folio quire as the 'standard', with the texts almost always copied in double columns mainly of forty-six lines. Hanna's survey of the work of Andrew Horn, a section of whose work appears alongside that of Marchaunt, Carpenter and Osbarn in the *Liber Albus*, takes Pearsall's argument about the 'standard' look a step further by describing the type of law books and custumals prepared at the Guildhall in relation to the literary manuscripts.[60] He sees the books prepared by Horn, the Guildhall chamberlain in the 1320s, as 'important models for London book-making', involving 'various compilational processes', and requiring 'choices' to be made about the contents which allowed for a 'subsequent flexibility in using exemplars'.[61] He observes that the layout of texts employed for those massive volumes is remarkably similar to the *ordinatio* found in some fifteenth-century copies of the *Confessio Amantis*.[62] Thus, in choosing the double column layout for his Gower and Trevisa manuscripts, Marchaunt may have been influenced by the layout of London custumals like Horn's.

According to Pearsall, the 'standard' *Confessio* manuscripts have two miniatures and display the same kind of decorative hierarchy: four- and three-sided borders, decorated and pen-flourished initials of varying sizes, as well as both decorated and undecorated paraphs.[63] The preconceived hierarchical structure of the decoration appears to be designed to allow an easier passage through the text for the reader. In summary, Pearsall sees 'a production programme or even campaign, associated with and contributing significantly to the great expansion in the commercial production of large manuscripts of secular vernacular poetry and prose in the early decades of the fifteenth century.'[64] He sees a possible 'political motive' behind the production and points to the ownership of several of these early copies by members of the Lancastrian royal family,[65] a point we shall consider in Chapter 7.

Pearsall refers to the two 'standard' pictures which he believes 'may be presumed to have been authorised by Gower'.[66] Since many of the early manuscripts with miniatures are written by Marchaunt, it seems possible that he consulted Gower himself about their inclusion. The quality of some of the miniatures and the fine illumination demonstrate that Marchaunt was producing manuscripts for the wealthiest clients, who could afford to have them completed in the workshops of Herman Scheerre and John Sifrewas, two of the most skilled artists of the period. Two manuscripts, Cambridge, Pembroke College, MS 307, also copied by a scribe working in the vicinity of the Guildhall,[67] and Oxford, Bodleian Library, MS Bodley 902, a manuscript whose first two quires were copied by Marchaunt, both have an image of the lover as an old man, which Pearsall considers an 'unusual' choice.[68] Pearsall cites Garbaty, who argues that this particular picture of Amans represents Gower in 'the

---

[60] Hanna, *London Literature*, pp. 74, 75. Hanna describes the Guildhall custumals as written in double columns and between forty and forty-four lines per column.

[61] Ibid., p. 74.

[62] Ibid.

[63] Pearsall, 'Manuscripts and Illustrations of Gower', p. 80.

[64] Ibid.

[65] Ibid., p. 95.

[66] Ibid., p. 86.

[67] See Chapter 6 below.

[68] Pearsall, 'Manuscripts and Illustrations of Gower', p. 89.

long gown of his tomb effigy'.[69] It may be significant that this picture appears at I.203 of the *Confessio*, in the first quire of Bodley 902 which was copied by Marchaunt. These two quires may provide us with evidence of Marchaunt updating an earlier copy of the *Confessio* manuscript near the end of Gower's life, or after his death.

In similar fashion, Kerby-Fulton and Justice describe the situation on the first, recopied bifolium of Princeton Taylor 5. The entire manuscript, apart from the first quire, was copied by Marchaunt. However, the first quire is a contribution by two more scribes, the outer bifolium by one scribe and the inner six folios by a second. On the first folio is a picture of an aged, bearded Gower set in the margin of the Nebuchadnezzar miniature. A second portrait of the author, writing, appears in the first initial 'O' of the first line of English text on the same folio.[70] Similarly an older bearded author portrait appears in Philadelphia, Rosenbach Museum and Library, MS 1083/29, which we have now identified as written by the hand of John Carpenter when he was Marchaunt's under-clerk.[71] Pearsall also suggests that in British Library, MS Egerton 1991, a manuscript copied entirely by Marchaunt, there is a single miniature with space left for two more, one of which he postulates as ready for an author portrait similar to those in Rosenbach and Taylor. Since Marchaunt and Carpenter were working together at the Guildhall at the time when these manuscripts were copied, the changes may be evidence of their deliberate updating of the *Confessio*, not only its text but also its decoration, reflecting both temporal and political changes.[72] It could equally well be, as Joel Fredell argues, that the manuscripts were merely being 'recycled' for new owners, a situation which must have occurred with remarkable frequency given the mortality rate and the rise and fall of fortunes in the political climate of the late fourteenth and early fifteenth centuries.[73]

The text of the *Confessio* is, as Pearsall comments, 'remarkably stable'.[74] He suggests a variety of reasons for this: all copies derive from excellent exemplars; the copying of Latin may have influenced the care the scribes exercised; the early copies were of a professional nature; and such a lengthy work would not be passed over to amateur scribes to copy. He is sceptical about Macaulay's 'recensions', stating that there is obviously some authorial revision but doubting that any evidence about the stages of these revisions would be recoverable. The discovery that scribes of the Guildhall working in close proximity to the author, and probably known personally to him, were among the professional copyists of Gower's text may assist Gower scholars in further evaluation of what Fredell calls 'the old creation story of the *Confessio*'s multiple recensions'.[75]

---

[69] Ibid., p. 89, n. 31; T. J. Garbáty, 'A Description of the Confession Miniatures for Gower's *Confessio Amantis* with Special Reference to the Illustrator's Role as Reader and Critic', *Mediaevalia* 19 (1996), 319–43.

[70] Kerby-Fulton and Justice, 'Marketing Ricardian Literature', p. 218; Pearsall, 'Manuscripts and Illustrations of Gower', p. 88. Pearsall sees the 'author' picture as 'a throwback to a tradition of English text illustration as old as Laȝamon'.

[71] See Chapter 4 below.

[72] The question arises of who might have commissioned the possible 'updating' of text and image, and who paid for the work. It seems not unreasonable to suggest that clients deferred to the skills of Marchaunt himself to arrange this, a suggestion mooted by Kerby-Fulton and Justice (citing Jeremy Griffiths), in 'Marketing Ricardian Literature', p. 228.

[73] J. Fredell, 'The Gower Manuscripts: Some Inconvenient Truths', *Viator* 41:1 (2010), 231–50.

[74] Pearsall, 'Manuscripts and Illustrations of Gower', p. 94.

[75] Fredell, 'The Gower Manuscripts', p. 250.

John Marchaunt, Chamber Clerk, 1380–99, Common Clerk, 1399–1417

Marchaunt's work in preparing two of the earliest manuscripts of the *Canterbury Tales* offers parallels in terms of these scribes refashioning manuscripts of Middle English literature. Stubbs has conducted close folio-by-folio codicological analysis of both Oxford, Corpus Christi College, MS 198 (Corpus) and British Library, MS Harley 7334 (Harley).[76] In the opinion of Manly and Rickert, as Corpus was 'the least altered copy of a very early manuscript of high quality, it is of some authority; but … it is not a major tradition'.[77] Their pronouncement reflects the opinion of scholars of the *Tales* from Furnivall's time to the present day, and their account of the manuscript is still the benchmark description by which Corpus is judged. The text of some tales in Huntington Library MS EL 26 C9 (Ellesmere) and National Library of Wales, MS Peniarth 392D (Hengwrt), the manuscripts copied by Adam Pinkhurst, are considered superior to those represented in Marchaunt's copies. However, with an awareness of Marchaunt's work at the Guildhall and his possible acquaintance with Chaucer, a review of the state of scholarship on these two codices might be worth while.

In the 1980s Norman Blake described Corpus as 'a manuscript which has organized the poem in accordance with a different principle, namely by dividing it into chapters rather than prologues and tales', a feature he felt was 'significant for the position of Corpus in the hierarchy of manuscripts'.[78] The numbering of tales as chapters might reflect a different, early concept of Chaucer's collection of tales, perhaps without the frame narrative, to be chosen for reading individually rather than as a whole.

In 1987 Corpus was disbound, and Linda Lee, the former Librarian of Corpus Christi College, deposited with the manuscript the notes she took at the time. These include information about a different kind of vellum used at particular points in the manuscript. Stubbs analysed the physical 'abnormalities' in the manuscript as described by Lee, in correlation with the development of the text, and concluded that Manly and Rickert's assertion that Corpus is the 'least altered copy' of the *Canterbury Tales* can be refuted. The vellum substitutions in Corpus show Marchaunt to have altered the text and order of the *Tales* just as he later altered manuscripts of the *Confessio* to update that text.[79]

---

[76] See Stubbs, *A Study of the Codicology*, pp. 94–135, 136–78.

[77] *Text of 'The Canterbury Tales'*, ed. Manly and Rickert, I, 96. Two other *Canterbury Tales* manuscripts, British Library, MS Lansdowne 851 and British Library, Sloane MS 1686, were copied using the same exemplars which were available for Corpus 198 (copied by Marchaunt). Given that there are family connections between the owners of the Corpus and Lansdowne manuscripts and that both manuscripts were copied within a few years of each other, it is possible that at that early date the exemplars themselves were in family ownership and scribes were commissioned privately to make further copies, perhaps for other family members. This could be one reason why no further copies of the same set of exemplars appear until the single example in Sloane 1686. As noted at the end of Chapter 2 above, Osbarn's manuscripts also do not appear to have been made available for further copying, even though his manuscripts are cheaply produced paper-and-parchment compilations probably written for personal use.

[78] N. F. Blake, *The Textual Tradition of the 'Canterbury Tales'* (London, 1985), p. 72.

[79] The thicker vellum in Corpus was used mainly in the middle portion of the manuscript to enable additions to some tales or to reposition them. All the instances of vellum substitution occur at fault lines in the *Tales* which highlight the major areas of textual disruption and the differences between the manuscript orders. Most of the folios of substituted vellum coincide with places where, in the Hengwrt manuscript copied by Pinkhurst, there is a change in the colour of the ink. Six individual folios, one of which is the first folio, are also missing in Corpus and again the six 'losses' occur at crucial tale conjunctions. Linking passages, originally lacking or never acquired for Hengwrt, are also missing in Corpus. The first quire of Corpus with the text of the General Prologue up to line 578, but with decorative anomalies after line 541 where the descriptions of

Scribes and the City

If John Marchaunt were reordering or revising the Corpus manuscript in line with the changes effected in Hengwrt by his colleague in the Guildhall, Adam Pinkhurst, then it seems probable that some parts of Corpus were already in existence, as earlier copies of individual tales or groups of tales. There may have been an earlier version of the General Prologue, for example, in a single quire which was later extended to accommodate the addition of the last five pilgrims (Reeve, Miller, Pardoner, Summoner, Manciple), tales which are thought to have been composed late in Chaucer's life.[80] It is difficult to understand why Marchaunt and Pinkhurst, who were both working at or near the Guildhall, did not confer on the development of the texts and the construction, or alteration, of manuscripts of the *Tales*.

Analysis of the physical make-up of Marchaunt's two copies of the *Tales* as well as the two copied by Adam Pinkhurst led Stubbs to conclude that Marchaunt copied some Chaucer texts from earlier exemplars whilst the author was still alive.[81] Stubbs's conclusions might shed light on the state of Chaucer's text for some tales, the dating of the latest linking passages, and the possibility that copies of the *Tales* were circulating both in London and in the provinces during his lifetime. In their palaeographical analysis of the Hengwrt manuscript, Doyle and Parkes argue that in Hengwrt 'more than one section may have been in progress, or suspense, at the same time and [that] some of the present sections may be survivors of parallel copies made by the same scribe'.[82] They illustrate this diagrammatically.[83] The same situation exists in both Corpus 198 and Harley 7334, copied by Marchaunt, and in Pinkhurst's other manuscript of the *Tales*, the Ellesmere manuscript, and may reflect the working practices of busy scribes trying to fit manuscript-copying around their day jobs.[84]

The Harley 7334 manuscript is something of an enigma. Nineteenth-century editors considered its text to be the most authoritative, despite the puzzling textual variants. J. S. P. Tatlock attempted to analyse the variant readings and was baffled as to why three-quarters of them occurred in the first third of the manuscript, which included half of the Squire's Tale.[85] No attempt has ever been made to relate the textual and dialectal anomalies of Harley 7334 to its codicological structure, which may be defined in a number of ways using the following criteria: the use or non-use of red ink; the five or six different hands supplying the running titles; the changes in script style of John Marchaunt; and the changes in decorative

---

the Reeve, Miller, Summoner, Pardoner and Manciple are introduced, shows evidence of several layers of preparation and alteration. See E. Stubbs, '"Here's One I Prepared Earlier": The Work of Scribe D on Oxford, Corpus Christi College MS 198', *Review of English Studies* NS 58 (2007), 133–53.

[80] D. Pearsall, *The Canterbury Tales* (London, 1985), p. 53. Pearsall argues that in these tales the 'fit of pilgrim to tale is consistently close and well-worked out' which might suggest that 'the group was added late, when Chaucer had developed more fully his ideas about the strategy of the *Tales*'.

[81] Stubbs, 'A Study of the Codicology', pp. 231–4. See also *Hengwrt Chaucer Digital Facsimile*, ed. Stubbs.

[82] A. I. Doyle and M. B. Parkes, 'Palaeographical Introduction', in *The Canterbury Tales: A Facsimile and Transcription of the Hengwrt Manuscript, with Variants from the Ellesmere Manuscript*, ed. P. G. Ruggiers (Norman OK, 1979), pp. xix–xlix (p. xxvi).

[83] Doyle and Parkes, 'Palaeographical Introduction', p. xxxi; see also *Hengwrt Chaucer Digital Facsimile*, ed. Stubbs.

[84] See also the conclusion to Chapter 5 below.

[85] Tatlock, *The Harleian Manuscript 7334 and Revision of the 'Canterbury Tales'*, p. 11. The Squire's Tale was copied at the same time as the first group.

features. What is quite clear from such an analysis is that the first third of the manuscript (with the variant readings) was produced at a different time and under different influences or instructions from the rest.[86] It is also clear that for some tales in the Harley manuscript, Marchaunt had access to a different set of exemplars from those used for Corpus, mainly in the later part of the manuscript, and that multiple exemplars of single tales or groups of tales must have been available to him. Harley 7334 could have been produced in at least four different stages. Given that Marchaunt was working at the Guildhall in the 1380s, that he was working for a considerable time with Ralph Strode, and that he and Chaucer had other acquaintances in common, it is possible that he had access to early copies of some tales during Chaucer's lifetime.[87]

The identification of this important scribe of Gower and Chaucer as John Marchaunt reinforces our argument for the centrality of the Guildhall in the copying and dissemination of Middle English literature in the last few decades of the fourteenth century and the first quarter of the fifteenth. Marchaunt preceded both Carpenter and Osbarn by a generation, and it is probable that both clerks worked under his direction. He was both chamber clerk and common clerk for the City of London through a period of 'discursive "turbulence"' extending over almost forty years, a period which, according to Sheila Lindenbaum, witnessed the convergence of cultural and institutional influences on writing in England.[88] Much remains to be discovered about the role of highly placed Guildhall clerks and about their relationships with the authors of whose work they produced some of the finest manuscripts surviving from that period.

---

[86] See also Horobin and Mosser, 'Scribe D's SW Midlands Roots', p. 300. According to Horobin and Mosser, the majority of the South West Midlands dialectal forms also cohere in the first third of the manuscript, suggesting that a separate exemplar existed for that part.

[87] For further suggestions, see discussion of the puy in Chapter 6.

[88] S. Lindenbaum, 'London Texts and Literate Practice', in *The Cambridge History of Medieval English Literature*, ed. D. Wallace (Cambridge, 2002), pp. 204–309 (pp. 288, 284). See also Barron, 'Political Culture of Medieval London', pp. 110–33; M. Turner, 'Conflict', in *Middle English*, ed. P. Strohm, Oxford Twenty-First Century Approaches to Literature (Oxford, 2007), pp. 258–73; M. Turner, 'Usk and the Goldsmiths', *New Medieval Literatures* 9 (2007), 139–77.

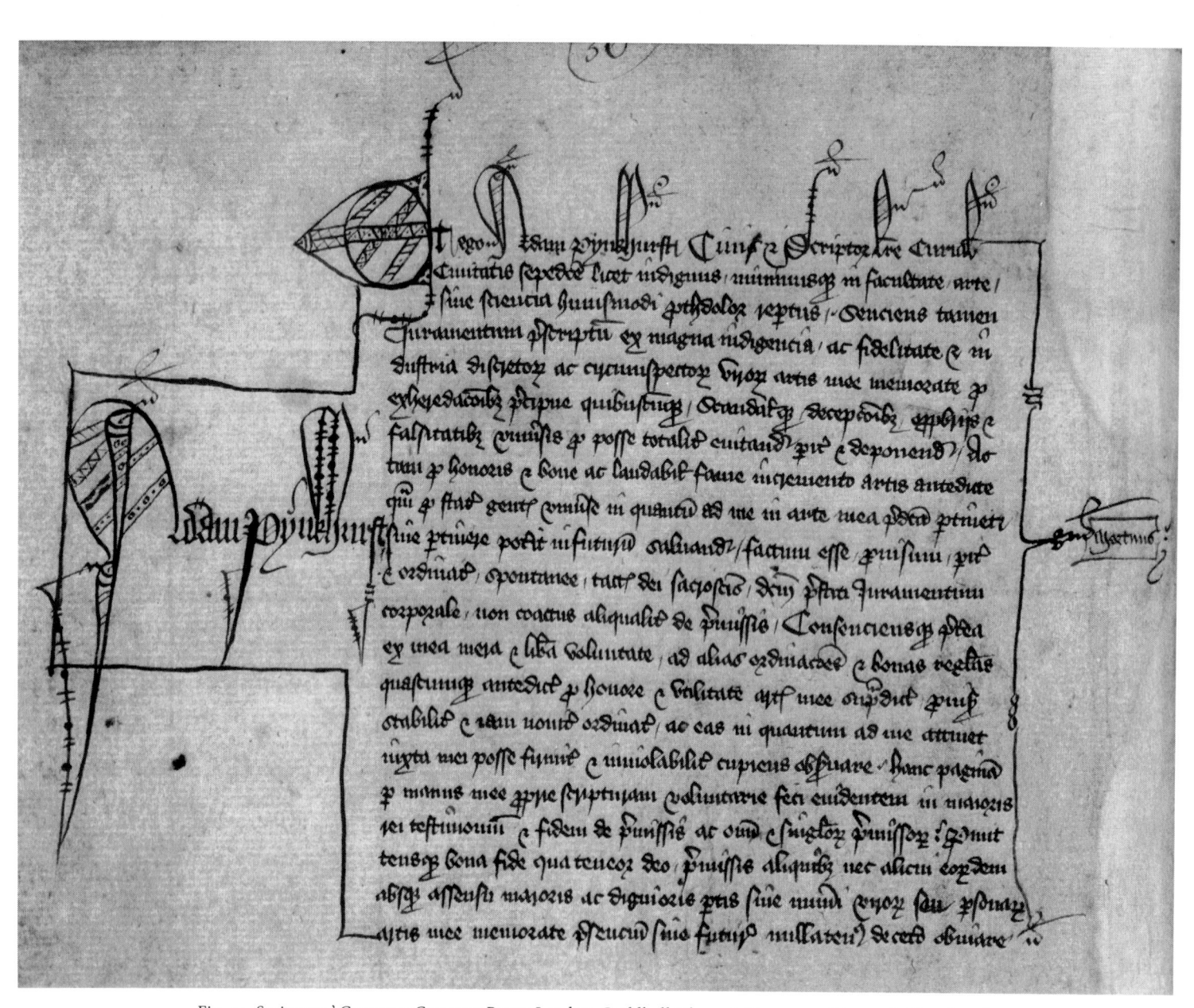

Fig. 4.1 Scriveners' Company Common Paper, London, Guildhall Library MS 5370, p. 56 (upper half, reduced), showing Adam Pinkhurst's signature and oath taken as a member of the company, *c.* 1391–2

4

Adam Pinkhurst, Scrivener and Clerk of the Guildhall, *c.* 1378–1410

THE HAND of the scrivener Adam Pinkhurst can be found in Guildhall documents, so in addition to work he performed as a scrivener of London (a member of the company then calling itself the Craft of the Writers of Court Letter), keeping records for the Mercers' Company and taking on copying work for Geoffrey Chaucer, he may also have had an affiliation to the London Guildhall.

In an article published in 2006 Linne Mooney identified the hand that wrote two of the oldest and the most authoritative copies of Chaucer's *Canterbury Tales* as that of the scrivener Adam Pinkhurst, and linked his name to a poem Chaucer had written to the scribe who was making the first copies of his works in the 1380s.[1] The two *Canterbury Tales* manuscripts, Aberystwyth, National Library of Wales, MS Peniarth 392D (Hengwrt) and San Marino, CA, Huntington Library, MS EL 26 C.9 (Ellesmere), had long been accepted to be written by the same hand, and there had been significant speculation about the identity of this scribe.[2] Mooney matched the hand of these two Chaucer manuscripts (also used in four other literary manuscripts), with an oath written and signed by Pinkhurst around 1391 in the Scriveners' Company Common Paper, now on deposit in the Guildhall Library, MS 5370. Pinkhurst may well have been a member of the Scriveners' Company before 1391, since he is so called ('Adam Pynkhurst, scriptor et civis Londonie') in two deeds of transfer of property in 1385.[3] Since in late 1387 or early 1388 he wrote a petition on behalf of the Mercers' Company, appealing Nicholas Brembre, former mayor, of treason, and also wrote the Mercers' wardens' accounts for 1391–2, Mooney also speculated that he might have been employed directly by the Mercers' Company and therefore might have his workplace in their hall, at that time a portion of the Hospital of St Thomas of Acon on Cheapside.[4] Following from that, Mooney

---

[1] Mooney, 'Chaucer's Scribe', pp. 97–138.

[2] For original argument that these two manuscripts were written by the same hand, see Tatlock, 'The *Canterbury Tales* in 1400', pp. 128, 133. Further support was lent by later publications including *Text of 'The Canterbury Tales'*, ed. Manly and Rickert, I, 23, 268; and Doyle and Parkes, 'Production of Copies', pp. 170–4, 185–92 (repr. pp. 208–12, 223–30). Publications speculating on the identity of the 'Adam' addressed in Chaucer's poem are summarized in Mooney, 'Chaucer's Scribe', p. 99, n. 11.

[3] London, CLRO, Husting Rolls of Deeds and Wills, roll 113, documents 97 and 98, dated 12 April 1385 and 20 April 1385. These are further discussed in Mooney, 'Chaucer's Scribe', p. 101, n. 15, and pp. 109–10. The Scriveners' Company Common Paper contains the oaths of members beginning on p. 53, where a contemporary hand in the upper margin has dated the entries to the regnal year 14 Richard II (22 June 1390 – 21 June 1391). Pinkhurst's is the eighth, but as there were almost certainly eight members, he would be signing with the others at the start of the book, not as an indicator that he had just become a member.

[4] Mooney, 'Chaucer's Scribe', pp. 106–12. With more time for examining the hands in the Mercers' account book, Mooney is less certain of the hand either before or after the folios on which John Organ's account were recorded, which she previously suggested might be written by Pinkhurst, and would agree with Lisa Jefferson that it is more probable that only the 1391–2 accounts for

had imagined that it was through his work for the Mercers that he could have gained access to exemplars of literary texts; but the research findings outlined in this book suggest that scribes directly employed by the Guildhall had access to significant numbers of vernacular literary texts. Finding that Pinkhurst had an affiliation with the Guildhall leads us to reconsider his workplace and source for exemplars.

We identify Pinkhurst's hand in eight literary manuscripts, listed here in the order of their probable date of copying:[5]

> Aberystwyth, National Library of Wales, MS Peniarth 393D: Chaucer, *Boece*, possibly *c.* 1385[6]
>
> Cambridge, Trinity College, MS B.15.17 (353): Langland, *Piers Plowman*, B-version, Richard Rolle, *Form of Living*; and an anonymous poem on Christ's love, 1390s[7]
>
> London, British Library, Additional MS 35287: extensive correction to a copy of Langland, *Piers Plowman*, B-version, written by another scribe, 1390s[8]
>
> Aberystwyth, National Library of Wales, MS Peniarth 392D: Chaucer, *Canterbury Tales*, the so-called Hengwrt manuscript, *c.* 1399[9]
>
> Hatfield House, Herts., Cecil Papers, Box S/1: Chaucer, *Troilus and Criseyde*, a fragment, two sides of a narrow strip used in binding, 1400s[10]

John Organ are copied by Pinkhurst. See *Medieval Account Books of the Mercers*, ed. and trans. Jefferson, I, 10–12, 24; cited by Jane Roberts in her argument against some of the attributions of manuscripts to Pinkhurst, 'On Giving Scribe B a Name and a Clutch of London Manuscripts from *c.* 1400', *Medium Aevum* 80:2 (2011), 247–70 (pp. 256–7). See also n. 51 below.

[5] For relative dates or sequence of writing, see M. L. Samuels, 'The Scribe of the Hengwrt and Ellesmere Manuscripts of the *Canterbury Tales*', *Studies in the Age of Chaucer* 5 (1983), 49–65; repr. in *The English of Chaucer and his Contemporaries*, ed. J. J. Smith (Aberdeen, 1988), pp. 38–50 (p. 46); Horobin and Mooney, 'A *Piers Plowman* Manuscript', pp. 86–91, n. 54. In 2007 A. J. Fletcher, 'The Criteria for Scribal Attribution: Dublin, Trinity College, MS 244, Some Early Copies of the Works of Geoffrey Chaucer, and the Canon of Adam Pynkhurst Manuscripts', *Review of English Studies* 58 (2007), 597–632, proposed adding another manuscript to this list, Dublin, Trinity College MS 244, but we have not included it here because we have not examined it at first hand and find it difficult to make a secure identification from the images attached to Fletcher's article. S. Horobin has questioned this identification, in 'The Criteria for Scribal Attribution: Dublin, Trinity College MS 244 Reconsidered', *Review of English Studies* 60 (2009), pp. 371–81.

[6] E. Stubbs, 'A New Manuscript by the Hengwrt/Ellesmere Scribe? Aberystwyth, National Library of Wales, MS Peniarth 393D', *Journal of the Early Book Society* 5 (2002), 161–8.

[7] Horobin and Mooney, 'A *Piers Plowman* Manuscript', esp. pp. 65–92.

[8] S. Horobin, 'Adam Pinkhurst and the Copying of British Library MS Additional 35287 of the B Text of *Piers Plowman*', *Yearbook of Langland Studies* 23 (2009), 61–83.

[9] For the hand common to this and other manuscripts as 'Scribe B' or the 'Hengwrt/Ellesmere scribe' see Tatlock, Manly and Rickert, Doyle and Parkes as in n. 2 above; and as Adam Pinkhurst, Mooney, 'Chaucer's Scribe', p. 113.

[10] For the hand common to this and other manuscripts as 'Scribe B' or the 'Hengwrt/Ellesmere scribe' see Doyle and Parkes, 'Production of Copies', p. 170 (repr. p. 208); and as Adam Pinkhurst, Mooney, 'Chaucer's Scribe', p. 113.

San Marino, CA, Huntington Library, MS EL 26 C.9: Chaucer, *Canterbury Tales*, the so-called Ellesmere manuscript, 1400s[11]

Cambridge, Trinity College, MS R.3.2 (581): Gower, *Confessio Amantis*, a stint of three quires, fols 9r–32v, probably after 1408[12]

Cambridge, University Library, MS Kk.1.3, pt. 20 (XX): Chaucer, *Canterbury Tales*, fragment, a single leaf containing the end of the Prioress' Prologue and beginning of her tale, possibly written later than the preceding manuscript[13]

Judging from this list of manuscripts by Pinkhurst's hand, it is clear that in terms of his literary output he was principally a copyist of works by Chaucer: he wrote all or parts of five manuscripts of the writings of Chaucer, two of Langland and one of Gower. Mooney argued that identification of the scribe as 'Adam Pinkhurst, scrivener' also connected him directly with the author, Geoffrey Chaucer, based on the single-stanza poem, 'Chaucer's Words unto Adam his own Scriveyn', which survives in only one manuscript, written by John Shirley many years after Chaucer's death, *c.* 1430–2.[14] She cited as a connection between the scribe Adam Pinkhurst and the scribe addressed in the poem the facts that they have the same relatively unusual given name of Adam and the same occupational descriptor of scrivener; and she noted that most scholars accept John Shirley's attribution of the single-stanza poem as canonical.[15]

---

[11] For the hand common to this and other manuscripts as 'Scribe B' or the 'Hengwrt/Ellesmere scribe' see Tatlock, Manly and Rickert, Doyle and Parkes as in n. 2 above; and as Adam Pinkhurst, Mooney, 'Chaucer's Scribe', p. 113.

[12] Doyle and Parkes, 'Production of Copies', esp. p. 170 (repr. p. 208).

[13] That this was written by the same scribe as Hengwrt and Ellesmere was suggested tentatively by A. I. Doyle, 'The Copyist of the Ellesmere *Canterbury Tales*', in *The Ellesmere Chaucer: Essays in Interpretation*, ed. M. Stevens and D. Woodward (San Marino CA, 1995; repr. 1997), pp. 49–67 (pp. 64–5). It was accepted as Pinkhurst's hand by Horobin and Mooney, 'A *Piers Plowman* Manuscript', pp. 86–91, n. 54. Scholars beginning with Doyle and including Horobin and Mooney have dated it late in the scribe's career, around the same time as the Ellesmere *Canterbury Tales*. However, these arguments had been based principally on palaeographical grounds because of the greater frequency of secretary forms in this piece of writing. Given the use of secretary forms in Pinkhurst's writings as early as the 1390s, that might no longer be a determining factor for date. Horobin notes that the sample is so brief that dating on linguistic grounds is difficult: see Horobin and Mooney, '*Piers Plowman* Manuscript', p. 91, n. 54.

[14] Mooney, 'Chaucer's Scribe', pp. 98, 101–3; for date of Shirley's manuscript see M. Connolly, *John Shirley: Book Production and the Noble Household in Fifteenth-Century England* (Aldershot, 1998), pp. 77–80.

[15] The poem survives in John Shirley's miscellany of works by Chaucer and other contemporary vernacular writers, now Cambridge, Trinity College, MS R.3.20, p. 367, the only manuscript survival of the poem; John Stowe also printed it in his edition of Chaucer's works in 1561 (STC 5075), sig. Rrr3v. The poem is generally accepted as having been Chaucer's composition: see Brusendorf, *The Chaucer Tradition*, pp. 57–8; E. P. Hammond, *Chaucer: A Bibliographical Manual* (New York, 1933), p. 405; G. Chaucer, *A Variorum Edition of the Works of Geoffrey Chaucer*, vol. 5: *The Minor Poems*, ed. G. B. Pace and A. David (Norman OK, 1982), pp. 133–7; and its inclusion in *The Riverside Chaucer*, ed. Benson, p. 650. For an opposing view, see A. Gillespie, 'Reading Chaucer's Words to Adam', *Chaucer Review* 42 (2008), 269–83.

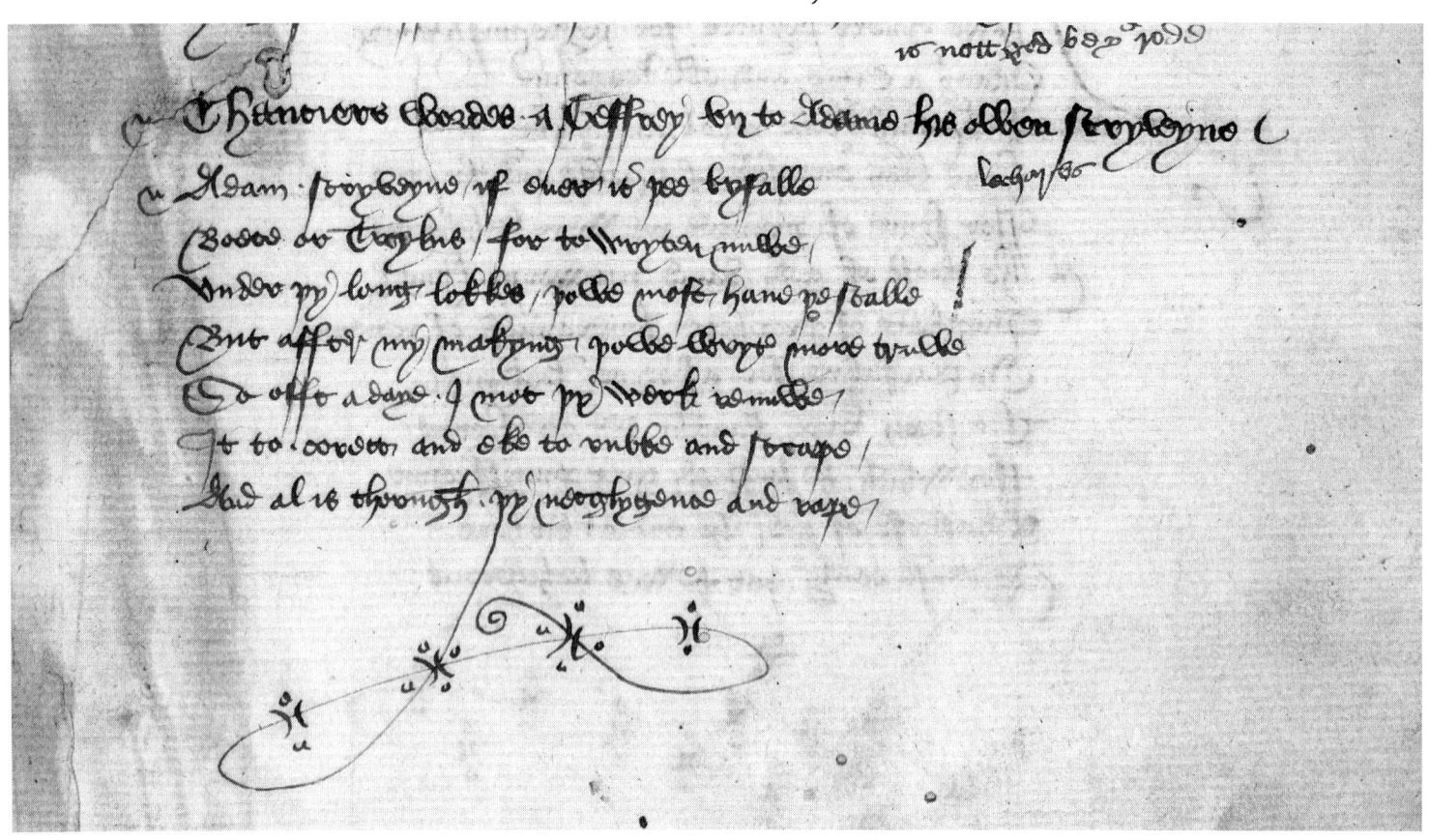

Fig. 4.2 Cambridge, Trinity College, MS R.3.20, p. 367 (lower third): 'Chaucer's Words unto Adam his own Scriveyn' copied by John Shirley *c.* 1430

> *Chauciers Wordes, a Geffrey un to Adame his owen scryveyne*
> Adam scryveyne if ever it þee byfalle
> Boece or Troylus for to wryten nuwe,
> Under þy long lokkes þowe most have the scalle
> But affter my makyng þowe wryte more truwe,
> So offt a daye I mot þy werk renuwe
> It to corect and eke to rubbe and scrape,
> And al is thorugh þy necglygence and rape.[16]

In this poem Chaucer chastises Adam for mistakes made through carelessness and haste, which have required the author himself to make numerous corrections to the manuscripts of *Troilus and Criseyde* and *Boece* copied by Adam.[17] Such a poem indicates a close working relationship between Chaucer and Pinkhurst in the 1380s when these works were written, since an author would correct only the first copies made from authorial drafts, not later ones made by scribes.[18]

The connection between Chaucer and Pinkhurst in this poem has been challenged by Alexandra Gillespie, who argues that the poem is a fictitious construct, that the heading of the poem in Shirley's manuscript was not authorial but scribal, and that John Shirley, writing decades later, was our only source for attributing the poem to

---

[16] Text transcribed from Cambridge, Trinity College, MS R.3.20, p. 367, written by John Shirley. The letters *u* and *v* have been regularized, as have punctuation and capitalization, according to modern practice. See also Mooney, 'Chaucer's Scribe', pp. 101–2 and n. 17.

[17] For further study of whether Pinkhurst was a careful or careless copyist, see J. Sánchez-Martí, 'Adam Pynkhurst's "Necglygence and Rape" Reconsidered', *English Studies* 92:4 (2011), 360–74.

[18] Mooney, 'Chaucer's Scribe', p. 102.

Chaucer.[19] We would argue that Chaucer himself names his scribe as 'Adame scryveyne' in the poem (line 1), and as Chaucer was living and working in London in the 1380s, he would presumably have hired a scrivener of London (rather than a scrivener of another city) to do his copying. The records of the Scriveners show no other Adam as a member of the company, even looking ahead as far as Robert Wade, who on p. 66 dated his oath in the fifth year of Henry VI (1427–8). In addition, since Mooney's publication, Simon Horobin has found evidence of another connection between Pinkhurst and Chaucer in the 1380s besides the poem whose authorship Gillespie has questioned. Chaucer was employed by Richard II from 1374 to 1386 as controller of the wool custom for the City of London, and at times also as controller of petty customs, but toward the end of this period he frequently requested leave to appoint deputies to carry out day-to-day tasks at the Customs House.[20] Horobin has identified Chaucer's petition to the king requesting that a permanent deputy be appointed to take his place as controller of the wool custom, dated 17 February 1385, as being written in Pinkhurst's hand (fig. 4.3). This demonstrates 'a concrete link between poet and scribe in 1385, a date that coincides closely with the period in which Chaucer was working on *Troilus* and *Boece*'.[21]

As Horobin points out, another hand has added the words, 'le Roy lad grante' to the top, and 'oxen[ford]' to the bottom, to note that permission was duly granted. He also notes that the aspect of this piece of Pinkhurst's writing is more similar to that in the Cambridge University Library MS Kk.1.3 fragment of the *Canterbury Tales* than to other manuscripts written by Pinkhurst (see fig. 4.8). Although the haste with which the petition is written makes it difficult to be certain of its writer, characteristics of Pinkhurst's letter-forms that are identifiable here are the anglicana **g** formed of three strokes instead of four, with the result that the strokes forming the lower lobe do not always meet on the right side, or they cross one another forming a spike on the right side of the lower lobe (fig. 4.3, line 2, 'granter'); **y** often dotted with the left branch upright rather than slanted, and the crossing of left and right branches occurring below the base line (fig. 4.3, line 2, 'Geffroy'); final long **r** with its shoulder slightly wavy (fig. 4.3, line 3, 'respounder'); **w** with tall top of the main stalks, of equal height, arched but not looping (fig. 4.3, line 2, 'Wolkee').[22]

Horobin concluded that:

[Derek] Pearsall suggests that the frequent requests for deputies during this period were driven by the need to free up more time to work on *Troilus*, and it would be natural for Chaucer to employ the scribe who was copying his literary work to draft the petition that would allow him to devote more time to his work. So ... I do not see any reason to

---

[19] Gillespie, 'Reading Chaucer's Words to Adam'. She does not explain why John Shirley would have assigned these names to an anonymous poem and its addressee.

[20] *Chaucer Life-Records*, ed. Crow and Olson, pp. 148–270, with the petitions to appoint deputies, and their appointments, pp. 162–9.

[21] Horobin, 'Adam Pinkhurst, Geoffrey Chaucer, and the Hengwrt Manuscript', p. 356. The document, Kew, National Archives, C 81/1394/87, is illustrated as fig. 1 on p. 354. We reproduce it here, in two halves, because the figure accompanying Horobin's article was so small as to make it difficult to see the details of that identification. The text of the petition is given in *Chaucer Life-Records*, ed. Crow and Olson, p. 168. See also K. A. Rand Schmidt, *The Authorship of 'The Equatorie of the Planetis'* (Cambridge, 1993), pp. 29–30, plate C on p. 32.

[22] These characteristics of Pinkhurst's handwriting are described in detail in Mooney, 'Chaucer's Scribe', pp. 123–35.

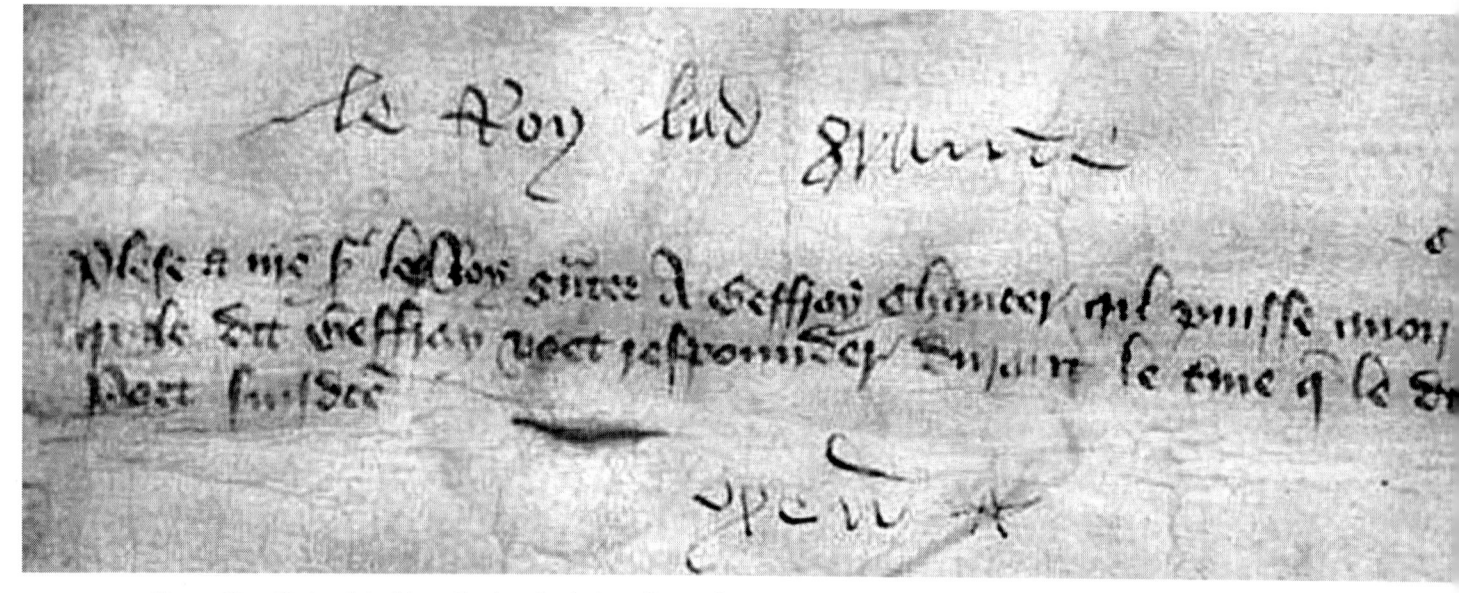

Fig. 4.3 Kew, National Archives, C 81/1394/87 (enlarged): Geoffrey Chaucer's petition requesting permission to name a permanent deputy in 1385, written in the hand of Adam Pinkhurst (identified by Simon Horobin)

doubt what the text seems to be telling us: that Adam Pinkhurst produced fair copies of *Troilus* and *Boece* for Chaucer while he was composing these texts in the 1380s.[23]

The next question is whether the connection between author and scribe continued up to the poet's death in 1400, which would lend greater authority to the copies of the unfinished *Canterbury Tales* that are written by Pinkhurst's hand, the Hengwrt and Ellesmere manuscripts.[24] Several scholars have taken up this question since Mooney's publication in 2006. Analysis of the arrangement, gaps, and errors in Pinkhurst's copying of the Hengwrt manuscript led Daniel Mosser to conclude (as other scholars had done before, without knowledge of the scribe's identity) that Pinkhurst was receiving blocks of text without understanding the whole picture as he wrote this early copy of the *Tales*, so he was probably working at a distance from Chaucer. However, Mosser left open the possibility that a connection remained between Pinkhurst and Chaucer, because he found evidence in the text to suggest that Pinkhurst was deliberately leaving gaps in the expectation of filling them at a later time. This suggested to him that Pinkhurst began the work while Chaucer was alive and still writing, receiving the text piecemeal until Chaucer's death in October 1400, and afterwards completed it from the remaining foul papers.[25] Apart from its odd ordering of the tales and links, scholars agree that the actual wording of Pinkhurst's copies of the *Tales* are the closest we have to the author's own words, so he evidently did have privileged access to authoritative or even authorial exemplars.[26]

After a similar analysis of the gaps and errors in the text of the Hengwrt manuscript Horobin concluded that Pinkhurst prepared it either at some remove from Chaucer or after Chaucer's death, citing in favour of the latter interpretation the evidence that other scribes,

---

[23] Horobin, 'Adam Pinkhurst, Geoffrey Chaucer, and the Hengwrt Manuscript', p. 356. Pearsall's suggestion that the requests for deputies related to Chaucer's writing of *Troilus and Criseyde* comes from Pearsall, *The Life of Geoffrey Chaucer*, p. 129.

[24] Mooney, 'Chaucer's Scribe', pp. 119–20, concludes with this argument.

[25] D. W. Mosser, '"Chaucer's Scribe", Adam and the Hengwrt Project', in *Design and Distribution of Late Medieval Manuscripts in England*, ed. M. Connolly and L. R. Mooney (York, 2008), pp. 11–40.

[26] *Text of 'The Canterbury Tales'*, ed. Manly and Rickert, I, 276; S. Horobin, *The Language of the Chaucer Tradition* (Cambridge, 2003).

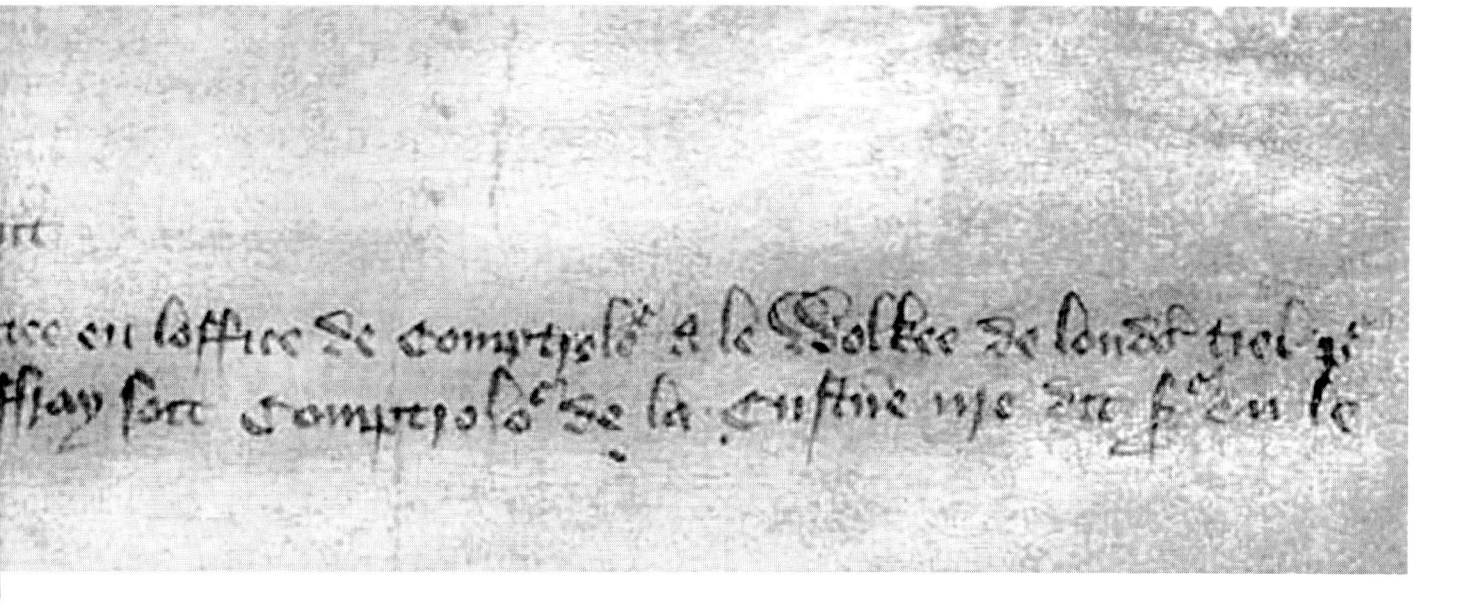

like Doyle and Parkes's Scribe D (now identified as John Marchaunt), show signs of having received the portions of the *Canterbury Tales* in similar pieces.[27] Whereas Mosser argues that Pinkhurst was writing at least partly while Chaucer was still composing, Horobin leans toward Pinkhurst's writing (along with other scribes of early copies) from the foul papers left in his study after Chaucer's death. In support of his preference for interpreting the Hengwrt manuscript as Pinkhurst's post-1400 attempt to unscramble the available portions of the *Tales*, Horobin argues that Scribe D appears to have assembled one of his copies of the *Tales*, Oxford, Corpus Christi College, MS 198, similarly ignorant of Chaucer's intentions for their order.[28]

Both these articles were written before we revealed Scribe D's identification as John Marchaunt and Pinkhurst's connection with the Guildhall, which brings these two scribes into close working relationship. Since there is evidence that some tales were circulating in London before Chaucer's death, Marchaunt, Pinkhurst and others would presumably have accessed the tales in fragments even during Chaucer's lifetime.[29] Their accessing portions of Chaucer's unfinished text in pieces after the author's death would not preclude their copying the first portions of the *Tales* while Chaucer was still alive and composing them.[30] After his death, they and others each assembled the incomplete *Tales* in separate attempts to create an appearance of completeness and order. As to the foul papers left behind after Chaucer's death, there is no reason why these incomplete fragments in Chaucer's own hand should have remained in the poet's house at Westminster. On the contrary, there is much more evidence that they passed to some other locale central to these scribes.[31] Identical problems encountered by Pinkhurst and Scribe D in copying the Monk's Tale and Merchant's Tale,

---

[27] Horobin, 'Adam Pinkhurst, Geoffrey Chaucer, and the Hengwrt Manuscript', pp. 357–67.

[28] Ibid., pp. 360, 365.

[29] For instance Chaucer's 'Envoy to Bukton' refers to his Prologue and Tales of the Wife of Bath, which must therefore have been known to Bukton and others of its original audience.

[30] See Stubbs, *A Study of the Codicology*, pp. 231–4.

[31] For the former suggestion that the tenement in Westminster became the centre of production for Chaucer's works after his death, see Bowers, 'House of Chaucer & Son', 133–43. Even Bowers admits that 'These speculations focusing upon the Westminster tenement as the original "Center for Chaucerian Studies" are perhaps ... fanciful' (p. 140).

among others, show that they were working from the same defective exemplars at least for those portions of the *Tales*.[32]

Thomas Chaucer, to whom John Bowers attributed the dissemination of his father's works after 1400, held the office of coroner for the City of London almost uninterrupted from 1402 to 1418 and again briefly in 1421–2.[33] The office of coroner did not entail regular presence at the Guildhall, since until 1483 coroners were appointed by the king and usually concurrently held some office in the king's household, such as chamberlain or butler (as in the case of Thomas Chaucer).[34] Most of the work of the coroner was carried out by a deputy, but Barron notes that the coroner himself was sometimes called on to preside over the possessory assizes and occasionally also the inquests.[35] Thus the clerks of the Guildhall were not unknown to Thomas Chaucer, and his affiliation with the civic secretariat during the reigns of Henry IV and Henry V might be reason enough for him to place the manuscripts of his father's works in their safekeeping, or, if holding the manuscripts himself, to hire them to carry out the dissemination Bowers envisages.

Horobin cites Ralph Hanna's conclusions from analysis of the early copies of Chaucer's *Troilus and Criseyde* that the 'shifts in affiliation from one textual tradition to another … coincid[ing] with codicological boundaries in the manuscripts themselves, [suggest] that these manuscripts were copied from physical units containing parts of the poem, which were circulating within the London book trade.'[36] Hanna posited a '*Troilus* clearing house' that could lend portions to scribes preparing simultaneous copies, and Horobin suggests a similar scenario for circulation of portions of the *Canterbury Tales* around the time of Chaucer's death and after, arguing further that 'Adam Pinkhurst was clearly a pivotal figure in the organization of this process, with access to authoritative exemplars but with no privileged insight into how these should be organized and arranged.'[37] In the light of the evidence we are about to present linking Pinkhurst to the Guildhall alongside Marchaunt

---

[32] *Text of 'The Canterbury Tales'*, ed. Manly and Rickert, I and II, *passim*. In these volumes of the eight-text edition Manly and Rickert make complicated assessments of the textual affiliations of the manuscripts copied by Adam Pinkhurst and Scribe D. Among other things, they suggest that when copying Harley 7334, Scribe D had access to the same exemplars used by Pinkhurst for the Hengwrt manuscript in at least some parts of The Merchant's Tale (vol. 2, pp. 268–83), Sir Thopas (pp. 361–8), Melibeus (pp. 371–92) and The Parson's Tale (pp.454–70). They also suggest that in Harley 7334, copied by Scribe D, all the tales in Fragment I (Knight's Tale to Man of Law's Tale) and the tales of the Squire, Wife of Bath, Summoner and Nun's Priest show the influence of Pinkhurst's Hengwrt copying. For the early part of the General Prologue, some of The Knight's Tale, for the linking passage between Friar and Summoner, The Second Nun's Tale and the prologues of the Nun's Priest's and the Manciple's tales, Scribe D had access to the same exemplars used by Pinkhurst when he copied Ellesmere. See also Horobin, 'Adam Pinkhurst, Geoffrey Chaucer, and the Hengwrt Manuscript', pp. 363–5.

[33] Bowers, 'House of Chaucer & Son', pp. 138–41; Barron, *London in the Later Middle Ages*, p. 371. Sir John Tiptoft held this office briefly for a portion of the year in 1407.

[34] Barron, *London in the Later Middle Ages*, pp. 194–5.

[35] Ibid., p. 195.

[36] R. Hanna, 'The Manuscripts and Transmission of Chaucer's *Troilus*', in his *Pursuing History: Middle English Manuscripts and their Texts* (Stanford, 1996), pp. 115–29 (p. 125).

[37] Horobin, 'Adam Pinkhurst, Geoffrey Chaucer, and the Hengwrt Manuscript', pp. 366–7; Hanna's suggestion of the *Troilus* clearing house is from *Pursuing History*, p. 125. For a similar suggestion regarding a pool of *Canterbury Tales* exemplars in London, accessible in particular to the scribes of Hengwrt, Ellesmere and Cambridge University Library, MS Dd.4.24, see Owen, *The Manuscripts of 'The Canterbury Tales'*, pp. 12–13, 98.

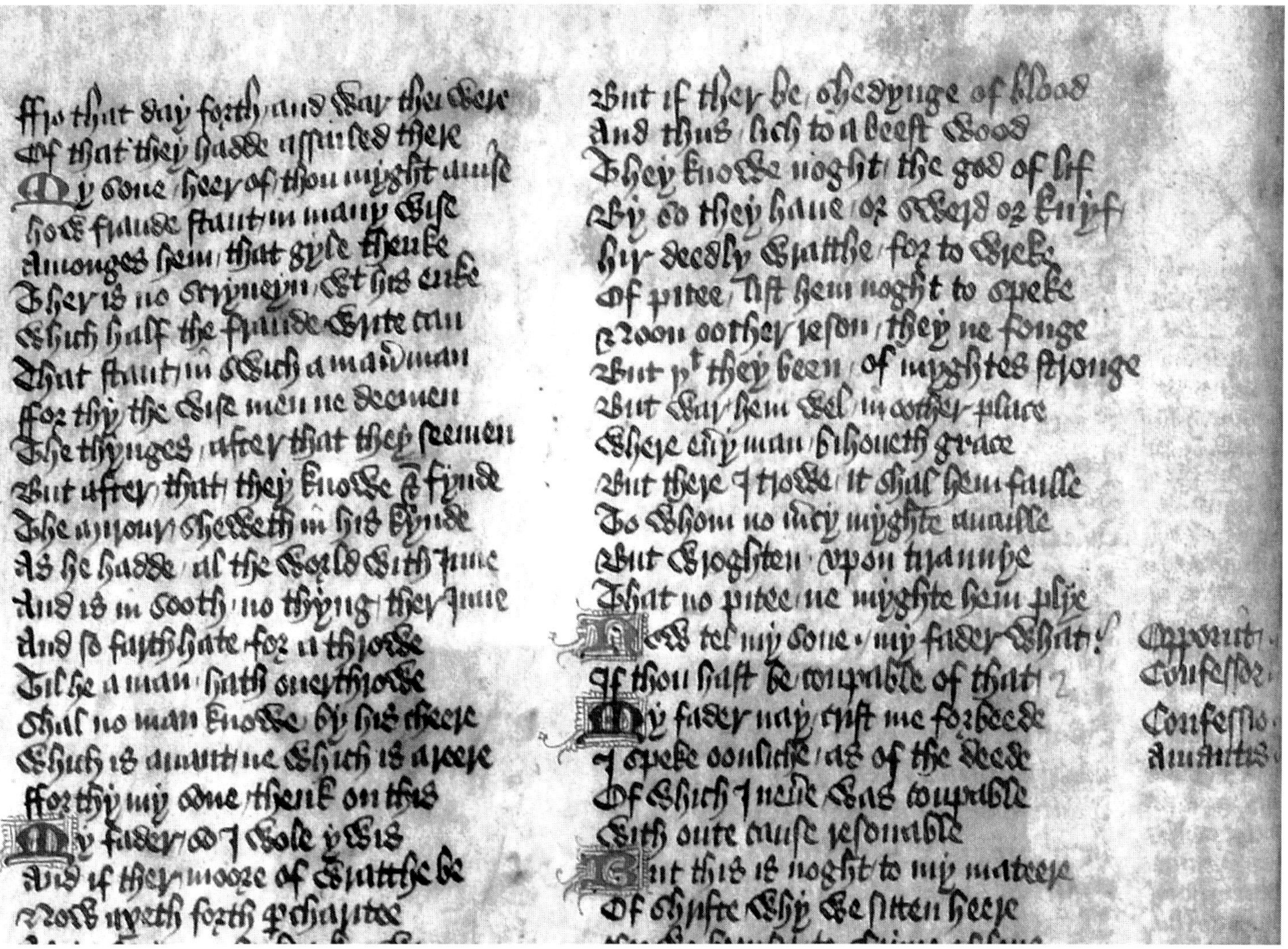

Fig. 4.4 Cambridge, Trinity College, MS R.3.2, fol. 11v (extract), illustrating the hand of
Adam Pinkhurst in his stint at copying a manuscript of Gower's *Confessio Amantis*

and Osbarn, it seems that the 'clearing house' for Middle English vernacular texts, not only the *Tales* but other Middle English texts as well, might have existed within the precinct of the Guildhall itself.

We have found Adam Pinkhurst's hand in a number of London Guildhall documents, showing that he held some clerkly position at the Guildhall at least during the reign of Henry IV and possibly earlier. His last entry in the Letter Books occurs in September 1410, where he recorded results of the election of sheriffs for the coming year, in Letter Book I (fol. 98r).[38]

Fig. 4.5 shows how Adam Pinkhurst has entered the results of the mayoral election on the feast of the Translation of St Edward King and Martir (13 October), the eleventh year of the reign of Henry IV (1409). In the light of the importance of this entry in the Letter Book, he writes in a formal secretary script, similar to the one he used for headings in his manuscripts of literary texts, like the Hengwrt manuscript of Chaucer's *Canterbury Tales*, or in entering his oath into the Scriveners' Common Paper (fig. 4.1). In spite of the differences caused by the greater formality of this script (which he may have considered appropriate to the content and use of Latin), some features of his handwriting and some letter-forms reveal this to be written

---

[38] London Metropolitan Archives, COL/AD/01/009 (Letter Book I), fol. 98r, dated the feast of St Matthew the apostle (21 September) in 11 Henry IV (30 September 1409 – 29 September 1410). He also records the election of sheriffs on fol. 62v.

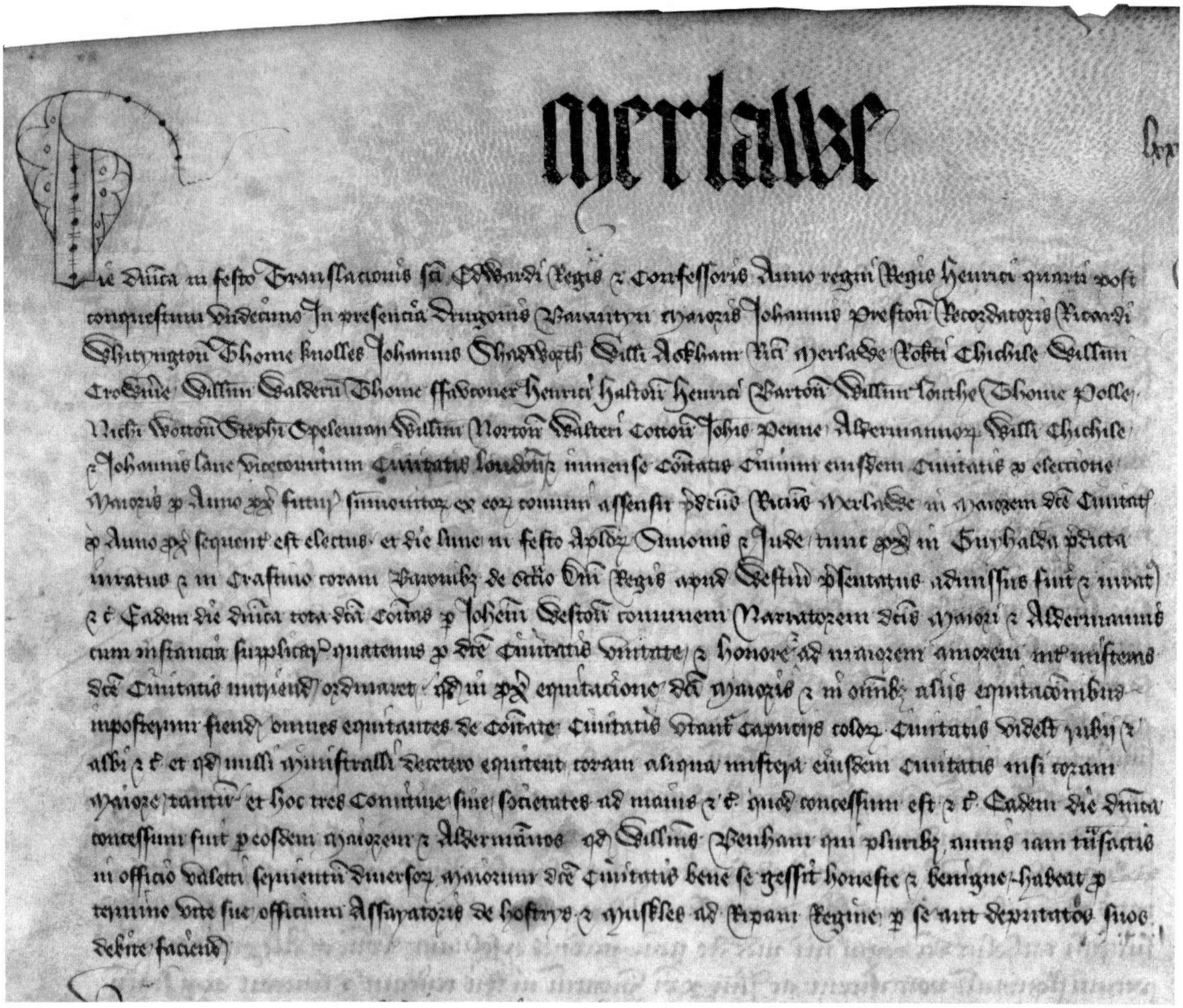

Fig. 4.5 London Metropolitan Archives, COL/AD/01/009, Letter Book I, fol. 87r (top half, slightly reduced): illustrating the hand of Adam Pinkhurst in 1409

by his hand. First, the decorated initial displays the tendency to over-elaboration also to be seen in his signature and oath in the Scriveners' Common Paper (fig. 4.1). This decoration includes the double-slash-and-dot motif that Pinkhurst used on sweeping extensions and on vertical strokes set within large initials, as here.[39] Second, the letter **w** has two wide arched strokes at the tops of the two main stalks, interlocked but neither of them closing the loop (fig. 4.5, line 1, 'Edwardi'). Third, the letter **y** has a vertical left branch, and the crossing of left and right branches is set below the base line (fig. 4.5, penultimate line, 'assayatoris'). Fourth, the enlarged initial form of **d** has a wide loop at the top of its ascender which returns to the stalk in a straight line (fig. 4.5, line 1, 'dom*ini*ca'). Fifth, even while adopting secretary forms of letters **a** and **g** in this piece of writing, the scribe still shows a preference for the usual, non-rounded form of **e** and for the two-compartment 8-shaped **s**, even in terminal position. Sixth, the top bar of upper-case **T** is waving and slopes downward left to right (fig. 4.5, line 1, 'Translacionis'; compare fig. 4.4, col. b, beginnings of lines 3, 12, 14). The dot, or tick, above

[39] Mooney, 'Chaucer's Scribe', pp. 137–8, fig. 10 on p. 135.

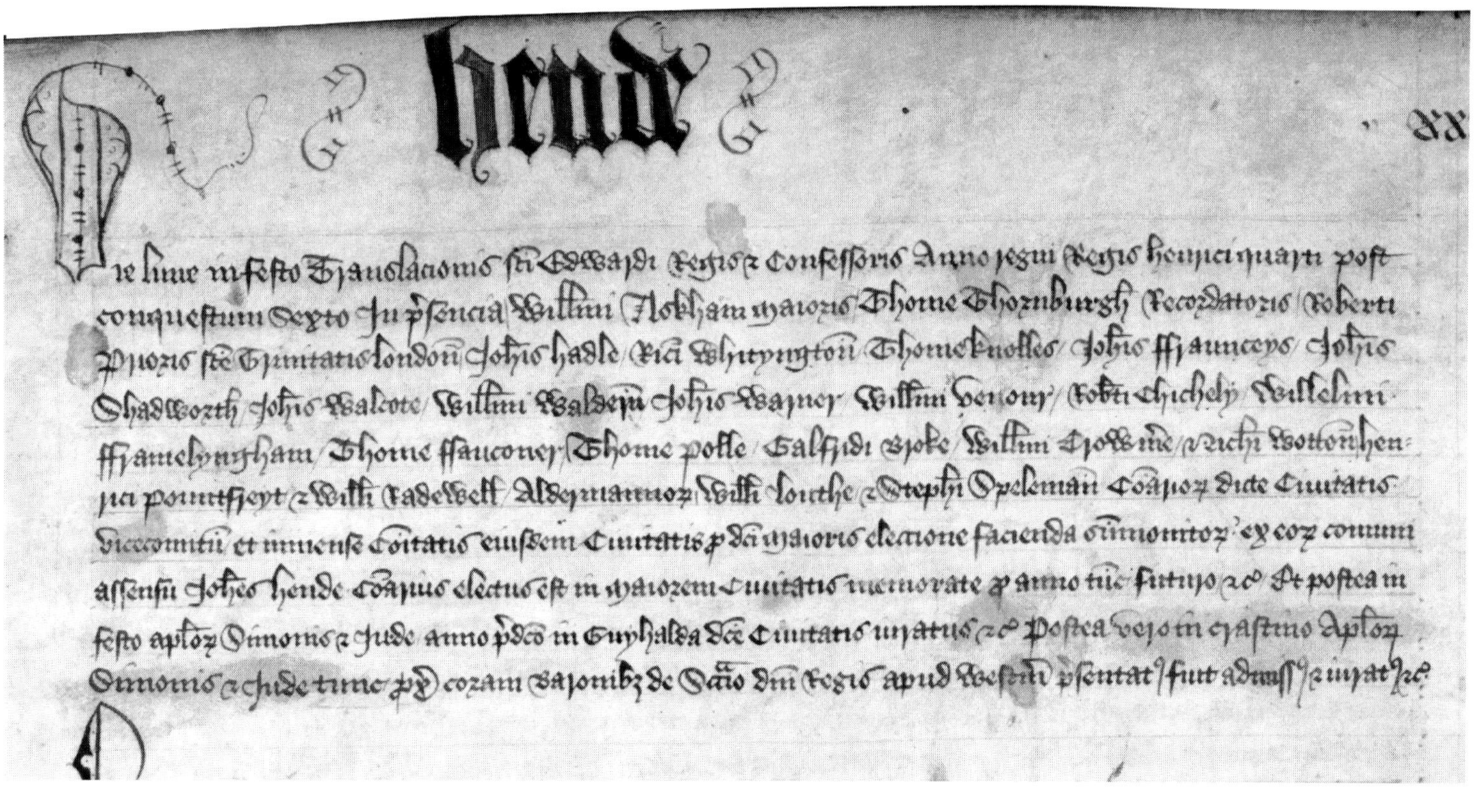

Fig. 4.6 London Metropolitan Archives, COL/AD/01/009, Letter Book I, fol. 36r (top half, slightly reduced): illustrating the hand of Adam Pinkhurst in 1406

letter **i** is often crescent-shaped, opened to the right, like an upside-down comma (fig. 4.5, line 1, 'Regis'; compare fig. 4.4, col. b, line 9, 'in').

The entries illustrated in figs 4.5 and 4.6 are typical of those Adam Pinkhurst makes to the Letter Books, relating to decisions of the mayor's court and to elections, which suggests that he may have been a clerk for the recorder of the city, who was responsible for these aspects of city government. The recorder himself was the highest-ranking civil servant at the Guildhall, receiving an annual wage of £66 13s. 4d. by the early fifteenth century.[40] Recorders wore the livery of the court of aldermen and were seen as allies of the aldermen, pleading on behalf of the city in the courts; Caroline Barron notes that as an additional sign of their prestige, 'Not only did the recorder wear the alderman's livery but he also had a clerk who was entitled to wear the same livery as the serjeants who served the chamberlain.'[41] Her lists of civic office holders includes a list of the recorders but does not include a list of the clerks of the recorder, so we do not know whether Pinkhurst ever served in this capacity.[42] Such a position would place him on a par with the chamber clerk and just below the common clerk in the civic hierarchy, and would bring him into daily contact with Richard Osbarn and John Marchaunt. It is clear at least that he served at some time in some capacity at the Guildhall, since those not employed in an official capacity would not enter material into the Letter

---

[40] For this description of the recorder's status and responsibilities, see Barron, *London in the Later Middle Ages*, pp. 173–4.

[41] Barron, *London in the Later Middle Ages*, p. 174; she cites *Liber Albus*, fols 42–3.

[42] Barron, *London in the Later Middle Ages*, pp. 356–74, lists civic office holders c. 1300–1500, including recorders, undersheriffs, common serjeants-at-law, chamberlains, chamber clerks/ controllers, common clerks, mayor's esquires/swordbearers, common serjeants-at-arms/common criers, waterbailiffs, common hunts, serjeants of the channel, coroners and deputy coroners. A search for the names of clerks serving under the recorders is an area for further study. Barron's list, p. 356, shows that the recorder changed frequently, every two to four years, so the clerk might be the bureaucrat parallel with controller and common clerk who held their jobs over a longer period.

Scribes and the City

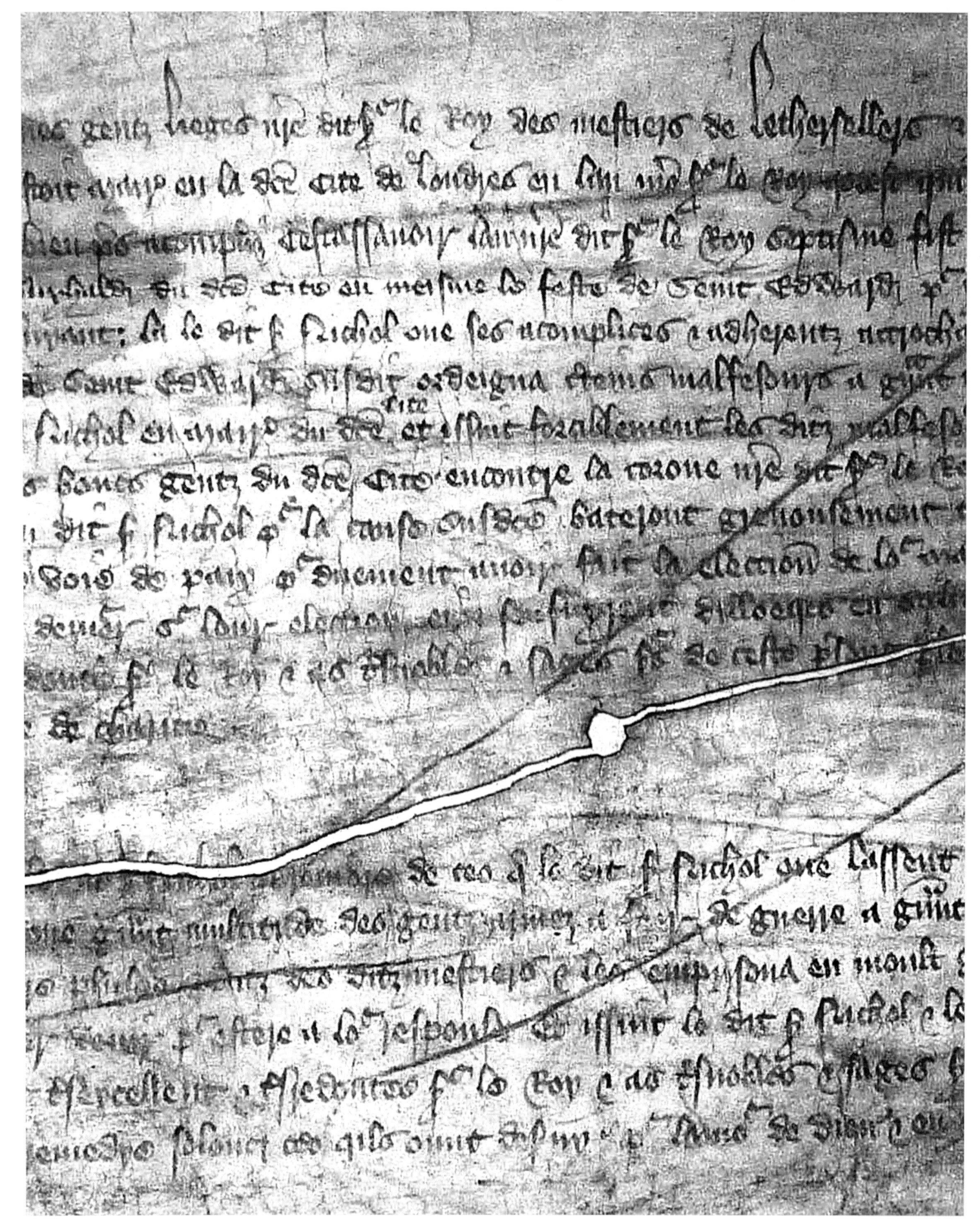

Fig. 4.7 Kew, National Archives, SC 8/21/1001B, Ancient Petitions (extract, enlarged):
the badly damaged copy of the Leathersellers' and White Tawiers' petition to the King's Council
appealing Nicholas Brembre of treason, 1388, written in the hand of Adam Pinkhurst

Books, especially not such important entries as those relating to city elections. However, this need not have been a long-standing appointment as Osbarn's, Marchaunt's and Carpenter's appear to have been: Barron's lists of office holders show that some men came and went in short spaces of time, and sometimes returned to serve a second or third term.

Chaucer scholars accord Pinkhurst an exalted position as Chaucer's scribe, the scrivener to whom he turned to write out the first clean copies of his texts from authorial drafts. We might interpret his large script and frequent decorative flourishes as signs of an inflated ego, but in his day he was probably only one of many civil servants, scriveners trained in the law, and literate scribes who made up the learned middle class of London and royal bureaucracy, just one with an unusually florid style. Placing him now in the context of others who were copying Middle English literary texts at the Guildhall allows us to see him in perspective, and to associate him with these literate bureaucrats. He had the best or first access to Chaucer and Chaucer's authorial drafts, but Scribe D, John Marchaunt, might be seen to have held a similar relationship to John Gower and even appears to have had access to early drafts of some of Chaucer's *Tales*.[43] The identification of Pinkhurst's hand in Guildhall documents means that we can now add him to the body of writers and copyists in the civic bureaucracy who appear to have held and shared exemplars of many of the late fourteenth- and early fifteenth-century texts in Middle English. Hanna's clearing house is coming into focus.

Besides Horobin's identification of Pinkhurst's hand writing Chaucer's petition to Richard II to be allowed a permanent deputy at the wool customs in 1385, we have identified a number of further documents either naming Pinkhurst or written in his hand that help to flesh out his affiliations and activities. The earliest of these is another of the petitions of twelve livery companies of London appealing Nicholas Brembre of treason in late 1387 or more likely early 1388. Mooney had already identified him as the copyist of the Mercers' petition, the earliest corporate petition to the king written in the English language (Kew, TNA, Ancient Petitions, SC 8/20/997).[44] At least eleven other companies filed appeals at the same time, of which the petition of the Leathersellers and White Tawiers (TNA, SC 8/21/1001B) appears also to have been written by Pinkhurst (fig. 4.7).[45] The Leathersellers' petition is written in French, the most common language of petitions at this period. The parchment is so badly damaged through damp that it is barely legible over most of its surface, but where clear it shows all the signs of being written by the same hand as that of the Mercers' petition.

The script employed in writing this petition is Pinkhurst's less formal, more hasty script, employing secretary single-compartment **a** and terminal sigma **s**, and thus its aspect matches other less formal examples of his writing in the Mercers' Petition, the Hatfield House fragment of Chaucer's *Troilus and Criseyde*[46] or the fragment of the *Canterbury Tales* now in Cambridge University Library MS Kk.1.3, part XX (fig. 4.8). Characteristic of Pinkhurst's hand in the petition is the overall aspect, involving the spacing between letters (which in Pinkhurst's hand are seldom connected), the spacing between words, and the relative height of minims in the line to ascenders and descenders, the space left between lines, and so forth.

---

[43] See pp. 62–5 above, 135–6 below.

[44] Mooney, 'Chaucer's Scribe', pp. 106–8.

[45] The twelve petitions, or appeals, are listed by Mooney, 'Chaucer's Scribe', p. 106, n. 37. The others were presented on behalf of the Cordwainers, Saddlers, Embroiderers, Founderers, Pinners, Armourers, and Cutlers plus minor cutlery crafts (Kew, National Archives, SC 8/20/998–1000 and SC 8/21/1001B–1006), the Drapers (SC 8/94/4664), and the Tailors (C 49/10/3).

[46] Hatfield House (Berkshire), Cecil Papers, Box S/1, illustrated in Mooney, 'Chaucer's Scribe', figs. 2A and 2B on p. 127.

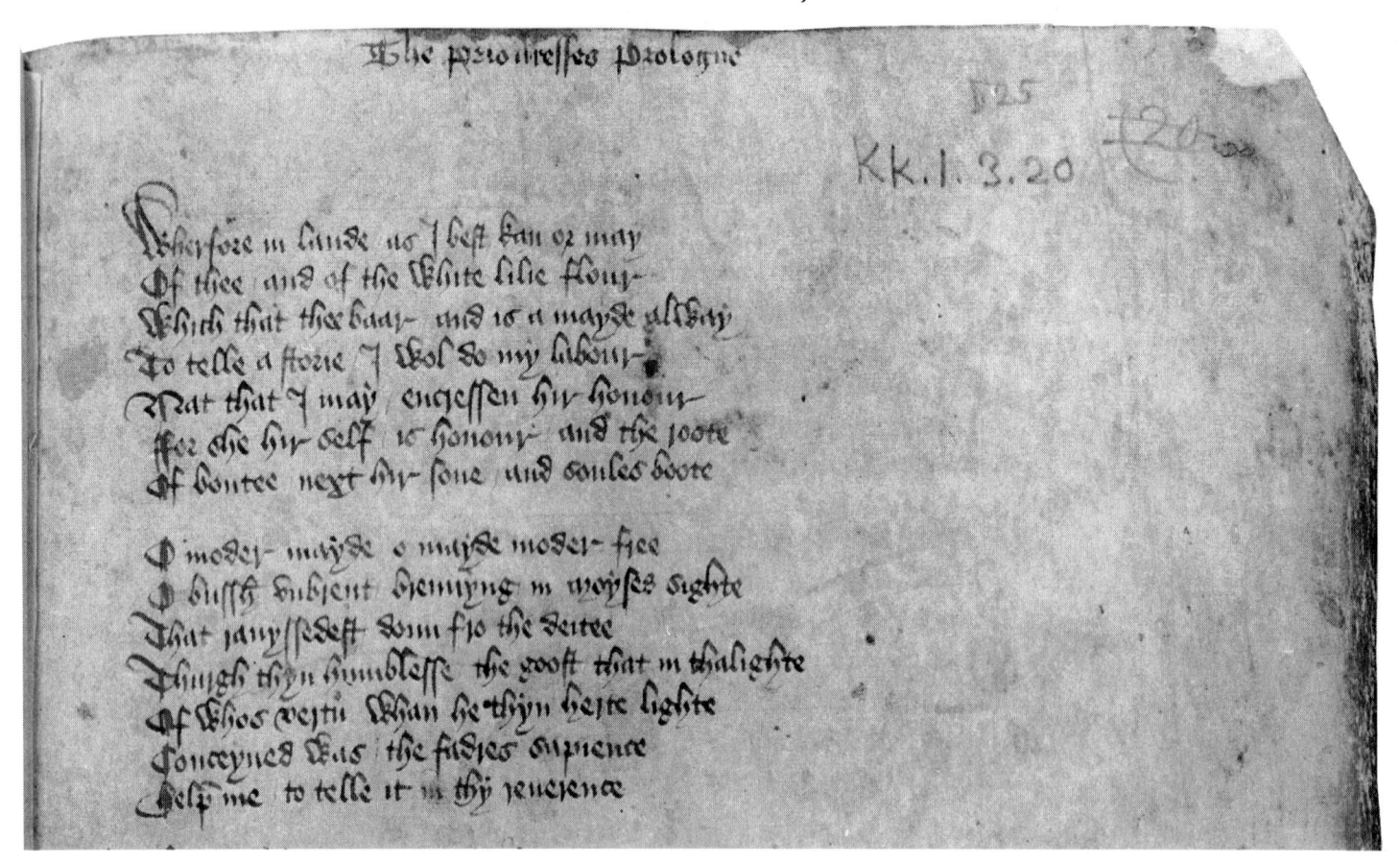

Fig. 4.8 Cambridge University Library MS Kk.1.3, Part XX, fol. 1r (top half): a fragment of Geoffrey Chaucer's *Canterbury Tales* written in the hand of Adam Pinkhurst

Letter-forms characteristic of this scribe are the very tall ascenders in the first line of text; long **r** extending well below the line and in terminal position having a waving shoulder (fig. 4.7, line 3, 'Cestassavoir'; line 11, 'lour'); anglicana **g** with strokes crossing at the right side of the lower lobe, creating a spike to the right (fig. 4.7, line 8, 'gentz'; line 15, 'guerre' and 'graunt'); letter **y** with vertical left branch and the crossing set below the base line (fig. 4.7, line 1, 'Roy'); and the dot or tick above **i** sometimes having a crescent shape, opening right (fig. 4.7, line 6, 'susdit').

This discovery shows that Pinkhurst took on work from other livery companies as well as the Mercers, even at that busy time of preparing petitions appealing Brembre while king and parliament waited for them. This suggests that he may not have been a direct employee of the company, as Mooney had surmised, but a freelance scrivener in London in the 1380s. If by then he was also an employee of the Guildhall below the rank of recorder, he would have been permitted to accept commissions from persons or organizations besides the city itself, just as Richard Osbarn did in copying the book of the Goldsmiths' charters thirty years later (1418).

The next document relates to a transfer of property, and shows Pinkhurst's hand again in his role as a scrivener, trained in the correct wording of legal documents and available for hire to write them. In the sample we have found he writes on behalf of John of Northampton, former mayor of London and the principal of one of the factions in London in the 1370s and 1380s.[47] John of Northampton and his followers had caused so much strife in London in

---

[47] The events summarized in this paragraph are described in greater detail in R. Bird, *The Turbulent London of Richard II* (London, 1949); P. Nightingale, 'Capitalists, Crafts and Constitutional Change in Late Fourteenth-Century London', *Past and Present* 124 (1989), 3–35 (p. 31); P. Nightingale, *A Medieval Mercantile Community: The Grocers' Company and the Politics and Trade of London*,

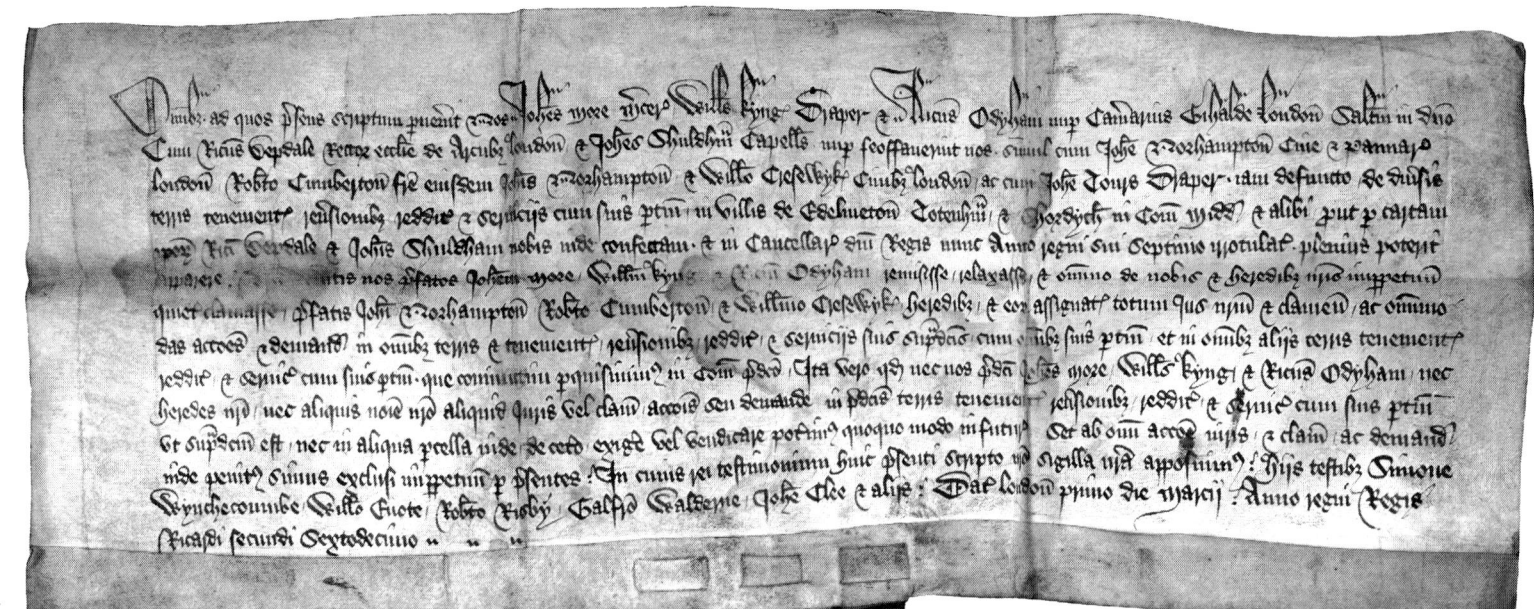

Fig. 4.9 London, British Library, Additional Charter 40542 (reduced): petition on behalf of John of Northampton written by Adam Pinkhurst in March 1393

the months following the 1383 mayoral election (which he lost) that he was brought before Richard II accused of treason in 1384, but, in response to the pleas of Queen Anne, offered a reduced sentence of exile from London and loss of all his possessions. He was eventually pardoned through the efforts of John of Gaunt, and returned to his former status as a freeman of London in 1391–2. This deed (fig. 4.9) records the transfer of property back to the pardoned and reinstated Northampton (and his brother and a third man) from men who had held it during his exile, some of them former members of his faction in London politics.

The deed, dated at London the first day of March, the sixteenth year of the reign of Richard II (1393), records the transfer of Northampton's largest and most important properties in Edmonton, Tottenham and Shoreditch in the county of Middlesex. The four men to whom they had been enfeoffed (together with another since deceased) in the seventh year of the reign (1383–4) are here returning the properties to John of Northampton and Robert Comberton, his brother, together with William Cresswyck, citizen of London.[48]

1000–1485 (New Haven, 1995), p. 312; and summarized in relation to Pinkhurst and the Mercers in Mooney, 'Chaucer's Scribe', pp. 106–9.

[48] Cresswyck had served as undersheriff of London, 1383–91: see Barron, *London in the Later Middle Ages*, app. 2(ii). He would thus have risen to this office just as Northampton ceased to be mayor, and left it just as Northampton was permitted to return to the city. These are the first properties Northampton mentions in his will, enrolled in the Husting Rolls, London, Metropolitan Archives, CLA 023/DW/01/126, item 117, membranes 26–8. Estelle Stubbs made this discovery, having been

Characteristics of Pinkhurst's hand include the extended ascenders in the top line with double oblique lines inside the loops and tremolos to the right of them (fig. 4.9, line 1, 'Om*nibus*', 'Joh*annes*', 'Kyng', 'Ric*ardus*', 'Odyham', 'Gihalde', 'London', Salut*em*'; compare fig. 4.1, top line of text); the decorative **D** with ascender turning to the right over the letter, in this instance also decorated with the double-slash-and-dot decoration that Pinkhurst often used (fig 4.9, line 1, 'Draper'); upper-case **N** with a dot or vertical line and dot in the centre (fig. 4.9, line 7, 'Norhampton'); **w** with tall arches at the tops of the stalks, not closed to form loops (fig. 4.9, line 1, 'Will*elmus*'); **y**, often dotted, whose left branch is vertical and whose crossing is below the base line (fig. 4.9, line 1, 'Odyham'); terminal anglicana long **r** with waving shoulder (fig. 4.9, line 1, 'Draper'); **g** with spike to the right extending from the lower lobe (fig. 4.9, line 5, 'Regis'); and preference for the 8-shaped **s** even in terminal position. This document of 1393 shows Pinkhurst in his role as scrivener, but it also connects him with the London faction of John of Northampton, as did the petitions of the Mercers and Leathersellers appealing Nicholas Brembre (leader of the other faction) in 1387–8.

From the documents now identified as written by Pinkhurst's hand we can piece together a probable career for Chaucer's scribe: he was a member of the Scriveners' Company of London by 1385 and entered his oath into the company's Common Paper in 1391–2; in this period he may have been working as a freelance scrivener in the city, taking work from the Mercers' and Leathersellers' companies in 1387–8 and writing up the wardens' accounts for the Mercers' Company in 1391–2, when John Organ was one of the wardens. His knowledge of transfer of property would come with being a scrivener, and in this capacity he may have been hired for writing up deeds, like the one of 1393 relating to the properties of John of Northampton. As his entries into Letter Book I often relate to the elections of mayors and sheriffs, he may have found work after 1400 as a clerk in the office of the recorder, or the chief clerk for the recorder, whose responsibilities included overseeing these elections. The latest entry we find for him in Letter Book I is dated 1410: if this date marks Pinkhurst's retirement from office at the Guildhall, or his death, it would offer only a narrow window for writing his stint in Trinity College MS R.3.2, which most Gower scholars date after Gower's death in 1408.[49]

Given this new timeline for the scribe, we might reconsider the evidence for there being either one or two persons by the name of Adam Pinkhurst, and for the period in which he worked for the Mercers' Company, which Mooney outlined in her article.[50] Having identified documents relating to land transactions in Surrey as early as 1355 involving an Adam Pinkhurst and his wife Joanna, Mooney speculated that there were two men of this name, probably father and son, each connected with Chaucer in some way. Until the discovery of the documents we have described in this chapter, the latest document (not literary manuscript) certainly written in Pinkhurst's hand, as identified by Mooney in 2006, were the 1391–3 accounts entered into the Mercers' Company account book. Thereafter, the

---

directed to these charters relating to Tottenham at the British Library by Andrew Prescott, whom we thank for the tip.

[49] Mooney reported Jane Roberts's suggestion that the manuscript need not have been written after 1408 if one assumes that Gower himself changed the 'Quia unusquisque' in revising the *Confessio Amantis* to read 'dum vixit' anticipating his own death and the poem's being read by posterity: see Mooney, 'Chaucer's Scribe', p. 115, n. 69. Roberts has changed her opinion on this since 2004–5 discussions with Mooney: see Roberts, 'On Giving Scribe B a Name', p. 252, n. 16.

[50] Mooney, 'Chaucer's Scribe', pp. 116–19.

Mercers' accounts are written in a hand that is similar to his, but which on close inspection we have decided is more likely to have been that of the principal clerk of the company.[51] Thus the 1410 entry in Letter Book I is the latest datable document in his hand.

At the other end of the timeline, the earliest document Mooney had found referring to a man named 'Adam Pinkhurst' comes from the Feet of Fines for Surrey, dated 25 June 1355, recording that Adam Pynkhurst and his wife Johanna, together with Adam Geffray de Horsham and his wife Letitia, had sold a piece or pieces of property in Dorking and Betchworth, Surrey. The fact that the Adam Pinkhurst named here was already married by 1355 led Mooney to speculate that this could be the father (or uncle or other member of an older generation) in the same family as the scribe. This still seems the most likely account of the Adam Pinkhurst documents, though the possibility remains that he had a very long career.

The legal transactions involving an Adam Pinkhurst, purchasing property with his wife Joanna (1355) and acknowledging a debt (1356),[52] suggest that that man had reached legal maturity by then, so he might have been born in the 1330s. If he were twenty years of age in 1355, he would be around seventy-five when writing the 1410 entry in Letter Book I. Could a scribe continue writing, even part time, until such an age? Our research into others who served the Guildhall for long terms makes this seem not altogether unlikely.

Richard Osbarn was named to the important post of chamber clerk or controller for the city in 1400 and held it until his retirement in 1437. (He died in 1438.) He must have served for a considerable number of years before 1400, since young apprentices were not appointed to such a post, so we may assume that he was at least thirty in 1400, sixty-seven at retirement. These dates are comparable to the length of service for John Marchaunt, who was named to the important post of chamber clerk in 1380 and retired from the Guildhall thirty-seven years later; like Osbarn, he must have served for a considerable period before being appointed chamber clerk in 1380, so he would have been born around 1350, and been sixty-seven at retirement and seventy-two when he died in 1422. Finally there is the example of John Shirley, who died 21 October 1456 at the age of ninety (if his tomb inscription as reported by John Stow is to be believed), having copied in 1447–9, when over the age of eighty, his final anthology of Middle English verse, Oxford, Bodleian Library, MS Ashmole 59.[53]

---

[51] This change in attribution of the hand after 1393 is in accord with Anne Sutton, Lisa Jefferson and Jane Roberts. Mooney had noted that the scripts of both the ordinances at the beginning of the volume and the accounts after 1393 were less certainly written by the hand of the 1391-3 accounts, or Adam Pinkhurst. See A. F. Sutton, *The Mercery of London: Trade, Goods and People, 1130–1578* (Aldershot, 2005), p. 179; *The Medieval Account Books of the Mercers*, ed. and trans. Jefferson, I, 10–12, 24; Roberts, 'On Giving Scribe B a Name', p. 256. None of these sources for the identity of Martin Kelom as scribe of the ordinances or later accounts were known to Mooney, the only one completed in 2004-5 when she was writing 'Chaucer's Scribe' being H. J. Creaton, 'The Warden's Accounts of the Mercers' Company of London, 1347, 1391–1464', 2 vols. (unpublished MPhil dissertation, University of London, 1976), I, 19–22.

[52] Mooney, 'Chaucer's Scribe', pp. 116–17.

[53] Connolly, *John Shirley*, summarized his biography, pp. 10–11; but the most in-depth study was written by A. I. Doyle, 'More Light on John Shirley', *Medium Aevum* 30 (1961), 93–101. See John Stow, *Survey of London*, STC 23341 (London, 1598). Doyle could find no reference to him earlier than 1414, so some scholars have questioned Stow's reading of the tomb: it would have been easy to mistake by twenty years, since dates would be written in scores, iiii^{xx} is 80, iii^{xx} is 60. This would still show Shirley compiling his manuscript when over the age of sixty.

If the Adam Pinkhurst who was named in legal transactions in Surrey were to be identified as the scribe and we could estimate his age to be at least twenty in 1355, he would have been around fifty in 1385 when involved in land transactions in which he is called 'scrivener', copying *Boece* and *Troilus* and on the receiving end of a jocular poem by Chaucer; fifty-two when writing the Mercers' and Leathersellers' petitions in 1387–8; sixty-five when writing the Hengwrt manuscript around the time of Chaucer's death in 1400; at least seventy-three when copying his stint in Trinity College MS R.3.2 in 1408 or later; and seventy-five when his hand last appears in the Letter Books (1410).[54] This seems a long career, or series of careers, from King's Archer and member of Edward III's household in youth, to becoming a scrivener of London and possibly an employee of the London Guildhall toward the end of his life. However, such shifts of career or position were not unheard of: consider the case of Geoffrey Chaucer, who served as soldier, then king's esquire and member of Edward III's household until around the age of thirty-four, then controller of customs for twelve years to age forty-six, and holder of other offices in the gift of the king until his death in 1400.[55] Given these comparisons, it does not seem impossible that there was but one Adam Pinkhurst, who served Edward III in the household alongside Geoffrey Chaucer and later changed career to work as a scrivener, Guildhall employee and copyist; however, the balance still seems tipped in favour of there having been two men of this name, one with land holdings in Surrey and serving Edward III as King's Archer until 1377, while the other was always a writer of one sort or another, perhaps this first Adam's son or nephew, introduced to Geoffrey Chaucer by his elder relative who had served alongside him in Edward III's household.[56]

Our closer examination of documents already named in Mooney's article help to flesh out the Adam Pinkhurst who served as the King's Archer, who was probably an older relative of the Adam Pinkhurst, scrivener. The first document is the lease of a farm near Guildford, Surrey in 1370 by Adam Pinkhurst, which Mooney wrote about in her 2006 article.[57] We have examined the original copy of this document, which provides more detail than the summary in the published *Feet of Fines*. It is dated the octave of St Martin (18 November), in the forty-fifth year of the reign of Edward III (1370), and records the lease by Adam Pinkhurst and his wife Joanna of a large property in Bromleigh (now Bramley), a few miles south of Guildford. The property is described as 'uno mesuagio uno molendino Centum acris terre quinque acris parti sexaginta acris', that is, a manor and a mill on three parcels of

---

[54] The transfer of Pinkhurst the royal archer's annuity for collection from the sheriffs of Surrey and Sussex need not have signaled retirement and exit from London since such transfers were made for accounting reasons within the King's Exchequer: money to pay this annuity may have been more abundant, and therefore easier to collect on time, in the counties than in the city. His ownership of property in Surrey need not mean that he lived there throughout the year, since many Londoners, including clerks like Carpenter, owned properties outside London, some as income property rather than personal accommodation.

[55] On this timeline he would have been forty in 1377 at the end of Edward III's reign, after which the references to him in records of the payment of his annuity refer to him as *'nuper'*, formerly, king's archer.

[56] If they are two men, there is no reference anywhere to a wife of the scrivener Pinkhurst, but we believe we have by no means identified all the surviving documents relating to him, so one may yet be named. There is a John Pinkhurst named in documents in London in the next generation, perhaps a son or nephew of the scrivener, named for his grandfather or great-grandfather.

[57] Mooney, 'Chaucer's Scribe', pp. 117–18; the transaction is summarized in *Pedes Finium, or Fines Relating to the County of Surrey*, ed. F. B. Lewis, Surrey Archaeological Society extra vol. 1 (Guildford, 1894), pp. 110, 126, 140, 220.

land of 100 acres, 5 acres, and 60 acres, which Adam Pinkhurst and his wife Joanna already occupied ('tenendum') presumably awaiting the court date for formalizing this agreement.[58] This document also records Adam Pinkhurst as the son of John Pinkhurst, so we have probably the name of the scribe's grandfather.

In January 1378 Adam Pinkhurst, named as having been one of the archers of Edward III, was granted custody of the manor and park of Ashurst, near Thursley in Surrey, with 3*d.* per day as his wages for managing this property on behalf of the king.[59] The Ashurst property included a fishery and a large meadow called 'Frithinghurstmead'. This assignment would have come shortly after Pinkhurst retired from active service, probably at the death of Edward III. The uncertainty of the times, or insecurity of receiving such an award from the competing uncles of the young Richard, is shown in the fact that only six months later, in June 1378, another man, Philip Walwayn the elder, was granted custody of Ashurst in lieu of his £10 annuity. Ownership of land outside London, and managing a manor in Surrey on behalf of the king, need not rule out identity with the scrivener, since many men, including John Gower, owned properties in the counties surrounding London.

We hope that further research may reveal more details of Adam Pinkhurst, the scrivener, which might help to establish whether he was the same man who served as King's Archer or, if not, how the two were related. For us, the identification of scrivener with the Adam who copied manuscripts for Chaucer in the 1380s and who wrote the manuscripts heretofore attributed to 'Scribe B' is without question, but much more remains to be done to establish his place within the London cultural environment of clerks and authors. His appearance in Letter Book I, discussed and illustrated above, helps us now to connect him with Scribe D, John Marchaunt, who wrote another two of the five earliest *Canterbury Tales* manuscripts and so many copies of Gower's *Confessio Amantis*, and with the other clerks working for the city and its livery companies who copied literary manuscripts. In this community of clerks copying Middle English literature, probably in their spare time, we now have a cultural context for this important scribe of Chaucer.

---

[58] The mill pond can still be seen beside a narrow road through the countryside within the boundaries of the present village of Bramley. Owners of the property named in the lease of 1370 were John Puttuk and his wife Margaret, and Emerus Puttuk and his wife Isabella.

[59] Mooney, 'Chaucer's Scribe', p. 118; *Calendar of the Patent Rolls Preserved in the Public Record Office: Richard II*, vol. 1: *1377–1381*, ed. H. C. Maxwell Lyte et al. (London, 1895), p. 104. Details of the grant of Ashurst to Pinkhurst, the reassignment of it and the raid are all taken from *The Victoria History of the County of Surrey*, vol. 3, ed. H. E. Malden (London, 1911), pp. 10–16. For grant to Pinkhurst, see *Calendar of Patent Rolls, 1377–1381*, p. 104. Thursley, Surrey, is less than 10 miles south-west of Bramley where Pinkhurst's farm and mill lay; the modern village of Witley, Surrey, presumably named for the manor, is 2 miles east of Thursley (so closer to Bramley), with a large pond (the fishery?) lying half-way between Thursley and Witley.

5

John Carpenter, Common Clerk, 1417–37

JOHN MARCHAUNT was succeeded in the office of common clerk by John Carpenter, the best known of these clerks of the Guildhall. Among historians Carpenter is known for having compiled the *Liber Albus*; among literary scholars and art historians for having overseen the painting of the 'Dance of Macabre', with John Lydgate's text, onto the walls of the cloister at St Paul's Cathedral;[1] and among scholars of the history of the book for having devoted part of Richard Whittington's legacy to the building of the Guildhall library and at his death having left the bulk of his extensive personal library to it. Several of these initiatives are associated with the four-time mayor of London Richard Whittington, who named Carpenter as chief executor of his will: it was in Whittington's fourth mayoralty, 1419–20, that the *Liber Albus* was completed, and both the paintings in St Paul's and the building of the library were paid for in part by Whittington's legacy.[2] Carpenter's interest in vernacular literature is seen not only in his knowledge of Lydgate's 'Dance of Macabre' but also, as we have discovered, in his copying of manuscripts of major pieces of Middle English literature. We shall here make the case for his having been the copyist of the following Middle English manuscripts, not previously even identified as having been written by the same hand:

New York, Pierpont Morgan Library, MS M.817: Chaucer, *Troilus and Criseyde* (the so-called Campsall manuscript)

Philadelphia, Rosenbach Museum and Library, MS 1083/29: Gower, *Confessio Amantis*

Cambridge, University Library, MS Dd.8.19: Gower, *Confessio Amantis*

As a copyist of vernacular literature, he demonstrates that even the busiest and wealthiest of the clerks of the Guildhall in this period found time for copying Middle English manuscripts.

Whereas with our other clerks of the Guildhall we began with a group of literary manuscripts already attributed to a single scribe and then connected the handwriting of that scribe to the same hand in documents in the archives of the city, we here reverse the process by moving from a known clerk of the Guildhall to show that his handwriting in documents of the city matches that of three manuscripts not previously connected with each other or with him. Two examples of John Carpenter's handwriting offer a base for comparison with other documents and manuscripts that we have identified as being written by his hand. The first (fig. 5.1) is a note written on the dorse of John Marchaunt's will, which Carpenter

---

[1] 'Dance of Macabre' by John Lydgate, *The Index of Middle English Verse*, ed. C. Brown and R. H. Robbins (New York, 1943), no. 2590/2591; sometimes titled 'The dance of Poules' in the manuscripts, ed. F. Warren and B. White, *The Dance of Death*, EETS OS 181 (1931), pp. 7–77; *The Digital Index of Middle English Verse*, ed. L. R. Mooney, et al. (www.DIMEV.net), no. 4105/4107.

[2] For more on Whittington and his charities, see C. M. Barron, 'Richard Whittington: The Man Behind the Myth', in *Studies in London History Presented to Philip Edmund Jones*, ed. A. E. J. Hollaender and W. Kellaway (London, 1969), pp. 197–248. Also A. F. Sutton, 'Whittington, Richard', in *Oxford Dictionary of National Biography* (Oxford, 2004).

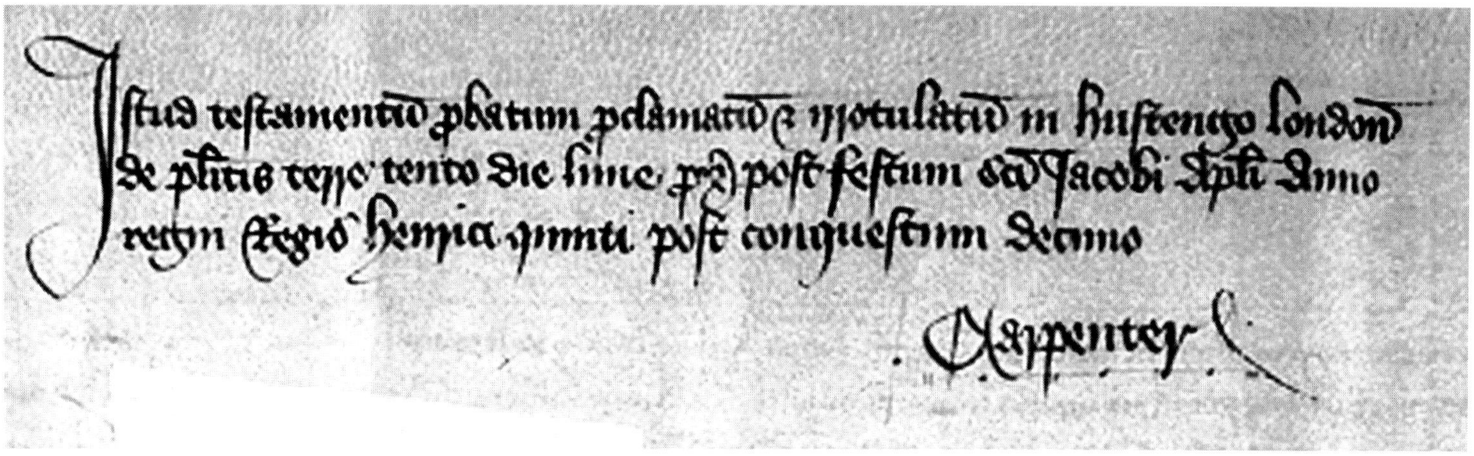

Fig. 5.1 Kew, National Archives, E 40/12349: the dorse of John Marchaunt's will, a note of its entry in the Husting Rolls written and signed by John Carpenter

would have annotated and signed as one of the two executors.[3] He notes that the will has been proved, proclaimed in the court of Husting and enrolled in the Husting rolls on the first Monday after the feast of St James the Apostle (25 July) in the tenth year of the reign of Henry V (1422).

Kellaway writes that 'The signing of public documents by the common clerk seems to have been initiated by Carpenter. The name "Carpenter" without "John" or "J" was the form used.'[4] As common clerk, his responsibilities included overseeing the keeping of the Letter Books, including recording important items in them himself. Just as Marchaunt wrote several folios at the beginning of Letter Book I, Carpenter wrote the beginning of Letter Book K. He sometimes signed important entries in the Letter Books, including two on fol. 212v of Letter Book I which will serve as our second example of his hand (fig. 5.2). The first paragraph on this page is the conclusion of an entry relating to a malefactor, one Thomas of Forde of Canterbury, sawyer, who was to be punished in the pillory for defrauding members of the public with false promises, claiming to be a soothsayer; as Brewer notes, it was considered an important document since it is titled a 'proclamation' and entered into the Letter Book. It is unusual, too, both in that it is signed by the common clerk in the Letter Book copy, and that it is written in English.[5] The next two, the first in French, the second in English, reproduce a request from the king that Londoners should assist with ships, men and supplies to furnish food and drink for his campaign in France.[6] As one of these entries specifically mentions Rouen, and the next entry after these is dated 2 December 1419, they must be royal requests

---

[3] See p. 10 n. 20 and p. 55 n. 29 above. The will is Kew, National Archives, E 40/12349. The will was enrolled on 10 Henry V (1422) in the Court of Husting; see *Descriptive Catalogue of Ancient Deeds*, V, 291–2. We would like to thank Caroline Barron for drawing our attention to this will. A. I. Doyle has called our attention to another will, that of Thomas Knolles, citizen and grocer, 15 Henry VI, that is similarly endorsed by Carpenter, illustrated in *The Register of Henry Chichele Archbishop of Canterbury, 1414–1443*, vol. 2: *Wills Proved before the Archbishop or his Commisaries*, ed. E. F. Jacob and H. C. Johnson, Canterbury and York Society 42 (Oxford, 1937), frontispiece.

[4] Kellaway, 'John Carpenter's *Liber Albus*', p. 67, n. 5.

[5] T. Brewer, *Memoir of the Life and Times of John Carpenter* (London, 1856), pp. 14–15, where he gives a modernized transcription. His explanation for its being written in English is that it was 'no doubt read or exhibited to the populace assembled to witness the punishment of the offender' (p. 14).

[6] The second entry may also have been written in English because it was meant to be proclaimed to the populace.

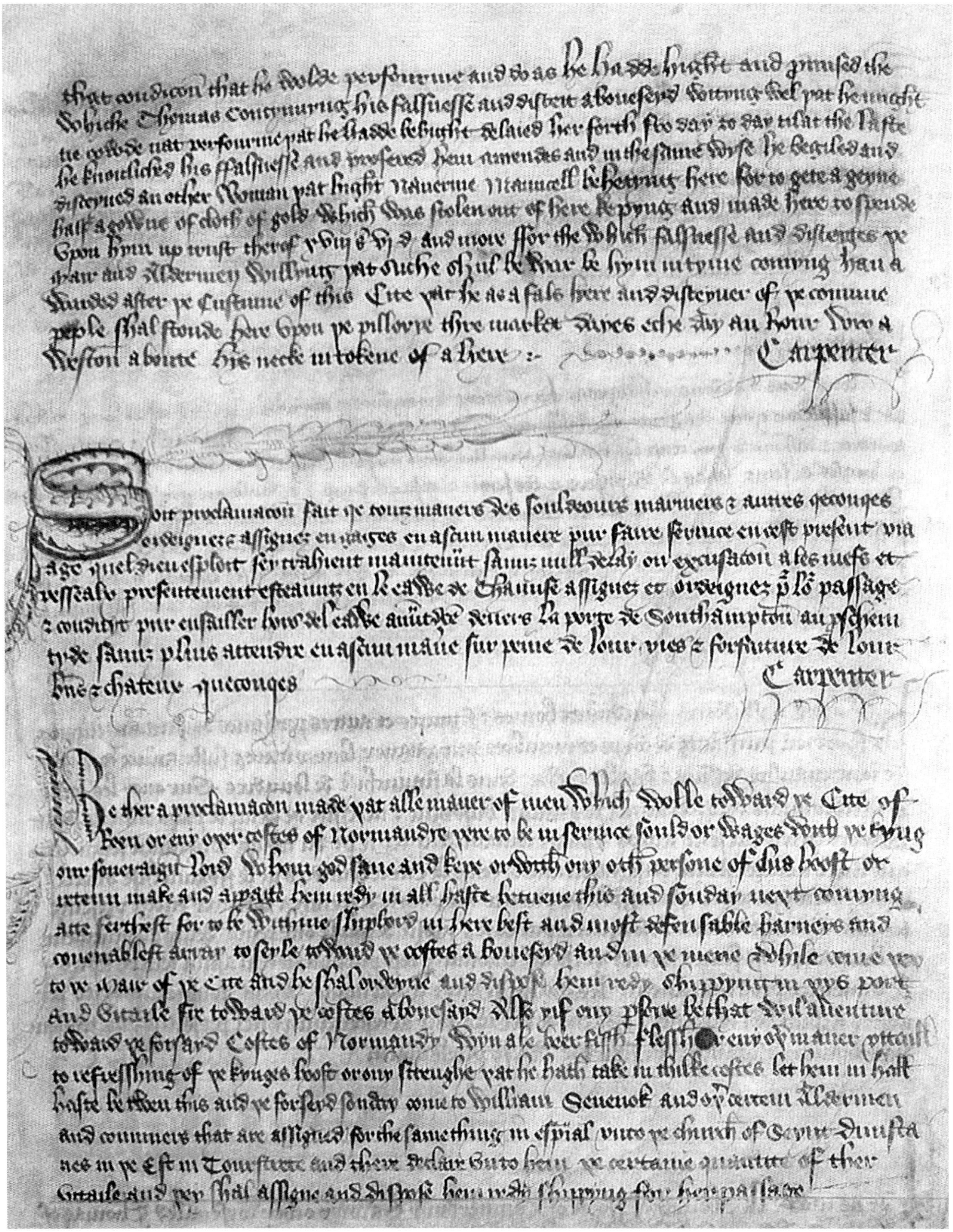

Fig. 5.2 London Metropolitan Archives, COL/AD/01/009, Letter Book I, fol. 212v (extract): illustrating entries written and signed by John Carpenter, common clerk

for assistance for the siege of Rouen.[7] The use of English for the second of these documents and for the entry relating to Thomas of Forde probably relates to their being proclamations originally written to be read aloud to London citizens: English would reach the widest segment of that population.

The characteristics of John Carpenter's handwriting as seen in these two samples are an angular form of *anglicana formata*, sometimes with a slant toward the right, using a thick nib which causes the script to have a bold or blackletter appearance. The writer exhibits good control over the script, with letters lined up very straight along the base line, and with very regular divisions between letters and words; in more formal writing the letter-forms are consistent throughout a piece of writing. Of course, he could write both hastily, as he does in some of the Letter Book entries, or in a very formal manner, as he does in his literary manuscripts, so letter-forms characteristic of both secretary and anglicana scripts appear in his writing, depending on the context. As with John Marchaunt, the wide range of contexts in which he was required to write make it difficult to identify his hand, as does the range of styles he was capable of writing. Idiosyncrasies of Carpenter's handwriting across the various styles include a tendency, even in informal writing, to square off the bowls of letters, producing angular shapes where curves should be: see for example letter **o** of 'irrotulatu*m*' (fig. 5.1, line 1); the **a** and first **d** of 'hadde' (fig. 5.2, line 1); the **q** of 'queconques' (fig. 5.2, line 18); the **a** of 'Carpenter' in both signatures of fig. 5.2. Similarly, the tops of ascenders are sometimes squared rather than arched, as in the **s** of 'souldeours' (fig. 5.2, line 12) and the **s** of 'seruice' (fig. 5.2, line 13). This tendency to angularity occasionally becomes extreme in his more formal writing, where the graph of the letter sometimes becomes quite distorted: see, for example, the squared form of **A** in 'Aldermen' (fig. 5.2, line 8) and 'Also' (fig. 5.2, line 26), an unusual form of the graph that occurs commonly in Carpenter's handwriting, though always mixed with other **A** graphs. Initial or upper-case **w** often has two straight, closely set and parallel lines as the main stalks, as in 'whiche' (fig. 5.2, line 2); but there is wide variation in this graph, as illustrated by the more curved and footed **w** of 'wolle' (fig. 5.2, line 19), or the variant graph he sometimes employed with the left stalk bent to the left as an approach stroke (fig. 5.2, line 24, 'while'). The descenders of long **s**, **f**, **p** and **q** are normally straight, or only slightly curving to the left, and taper to a point, as for example fig. 5.2, line 17, the **s** of 'sur' and **p** of 'peine'. The shape of **I** in fig. 5.1, line 1, with curved approach forming a completed lobe and with a stalk that splits into two strands but joins up again at the top, is repeated in several of the pieces of writing we have identified as Carpenter's. As with our other identifications, we recognize that other scribes may use similar individual graphs, but it is the combination of these forms that supports the identification.

In formal writing or display script Carpenter is an early user of cadels in England, that is, the embellishment of capital letters with geometric patterns and parallel lines. An example of this is in the beginning of the entry we have illustrated in fig. 5.2, where the top paragraph illustrated the signed conclusion of an entry that began on fol. 212r of Letter Book I. The recto side of this folio, showing the beginning of the entry, is illustrated in fig. 5.3. Both of the entries in this illustration are written by Carpenter, the first signed simply 'C' and the second signed on the verso (see fig. 5.2) with his full surname.

---

[7] Brewer, *John Carpenter*, pp. 16–17, describes another request from the king during this campaign, dated 19 August 1418, to which the city sent its reply on 8 September, sending wine, ale, and 500 cups.

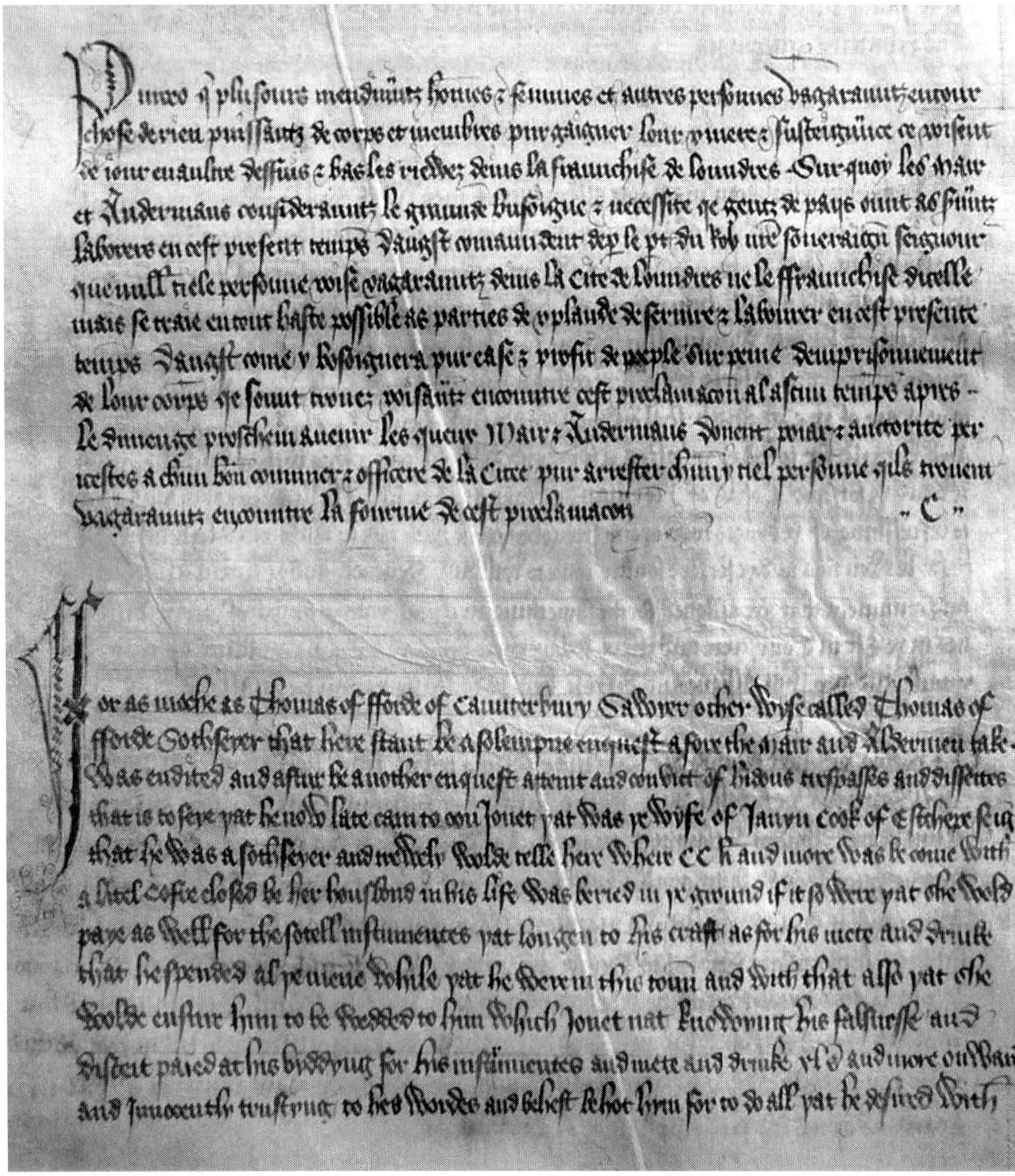

Fig. 5.3 London Metropolitan Archives, COL/AD/01/009, Letter Book I, fol. 212r (extract): illustrating entries written and signed by John Carpenter, common clerk

The early and simple form of cadels used here are the four diamond shapes that break the stalk of the initial F of the second entry (fig. 5.3, line 13, 'ffor') and the lozenge shape attached to the top of the ascender of the same letter. Another decorative trick is the zig-zag in the lobe of **P** in the entry above, signed by Carpenter only with his initial **C**; and the zig-zag in the left stalk of the **F** of the lower entry, where cadels decorate the right stalk. Such decorative features are found in all three of the literary manuscripts we have identified as written by Carpenter, and in all cases it is clear from ink colour and style of script that the scribe was writing the engrossed initials himself. These entries were made in Letter Book I in 1419, and Carpenter thus precedes the common use of cadels in England by a few decades. He may have encountered this technique in French documents delivered to London, since similar early use of cadels is found, for example, in the script on the frontispiece

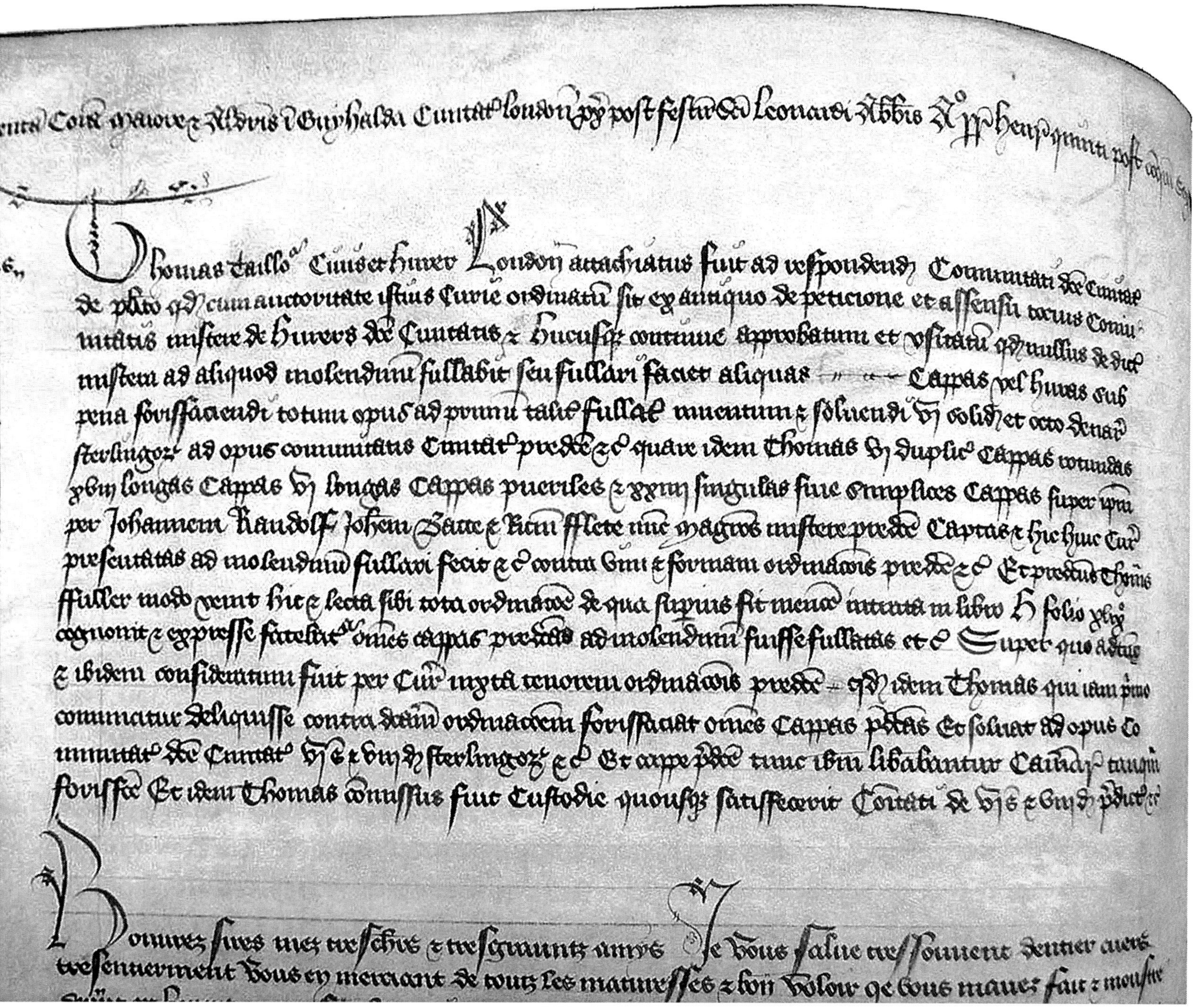

Fig. 5.4 London Metropolitan Archives, COL/AD/01/009, Letter Book I, fol. 222v: illustrating entries written and signed by John Carpenter, common clerk

of the *Grandes Heures de Jean de Berry*, written *c.* 1409 by the duke's secretary, Jean Flamel.[8]

Another example from Letter Book I can be seen in fig. 5.4, a copy of a letter from the king to the commons, mayor and aldermen of the city, in which the first line after the heading includes a **T** in 'Thomas' and an **L** in 'London' with similar primitive cadels breaking the long strokes of the crossing of **T**, and the ascender and loop of **L**. The zig-zag pattern decorates the stalk of **T**.

---

[8] Paris, Bibliothèque nationale de France MS Lat. 919, frontispiece. Illustrated in M. Drogin, *Medieval Calligraphy: Its History and Technique* (New York, 1980), p. 71, plate 67. The term 'strapwork' is also used to describe these decorative features.

Fig. 5.5 London Metropolitan Archives, COL/CS/01/012, *Liber Albus*, fol. 1v:
John Carpenter's large and elaborate signature at the front of the *Liber Albus*

Carpenter's use of full-blown cadels (or strapwork) is shown again in his signature on the verso of the first leaf of the *Liber Albus* (fig. 5.5), a signature which Kellaway had dated to the sixteenth century because of the florid style of its cadels, but which was almost certainly written in the fifteenth century, and by Carpenter himself.[9]

A. I. Doyle called our attention to the similarity between the script in these signed entries in Letter Book I and that in Pierpont Morgan M.817, the Campsall manuscript of Chaucer's *Troilus and Criseyde* which may have belonged to Henry V.[10] The rubric explicit and incipit use primitive cadels, as in Letter Book I. Here the tendency to angularity has been given free rein, but is particularly evident in the squared tops of ascenders, such as we saw in Letter Book I. The closely set, parallel straight stalks of **w** are evident here (fig. 5.6, line 7, 'which' and 'who'; line 10, 'while'). The descenders of long **s, f, p** and **q** are straight or slightly concave, tapering to a point (fig. 5.6, line 16, the **s** of 'deuyse'). The upper-case **A** is here distorted still further than in the Letter Books (fig. 5.6, line 10, the **A** of 'LAy'; line 13, 'And'). We also see in this example Carpenter's tendency to place a punctus at the end of each line of verse.

We have commented that Carpenter appears to be less the compiler than the instigator of the *Liber Albus*, but where he addresses the reader in Books I and IV (fols 5r–18r, 268r) we have no doubt the work was written in his own hand. Kellaway and Barron both speak of these portions of the *Liber Albus* as being written by Carpenter himself: Kellaway writes of the beginning of Book I that this 'is an original composition and neither a transcript nor an abstract', and Barron describes the titles and duties of officers of the Guildhall as having been written by Carpenter.[11] These folios give us a less angular sample of his handwriting, with greater horizontal spread than the more formal examples of his hand (fig. 5.7).

The aspect of the script is similar here to that in the two other literary manuscripts we would assign to John Carpenter: Philadelphia, Rosenbach Museum and Library, MS 1083/29, and Cambridge University Library, MS Dd.8.19, both manuscripts of John Gower's *Confessio Amantis*.

The leaf from the Rosenbach manuscript of Gower's *Confessio Amantis* illustrated as fig. 5.8 shows the characteristics we associate with Carpenter's handwriting: the use of primitive cadels in the top line (the **h** of 'hebes' and the **s** of 'scola'); the form of **w** with straight parallel stalks (fig. 5.8, col. a, line 17, 'write'); the **A** distorted by an angular top (fig. 5.8, col. a, line 7, 'Absit'; col. b, line 1, 'As'; line 13, 'Amonges'); the straight or slightly concave descenders of **f**, long **s**, **q**, **p**, etc. (fig. 5.8, col. a, line 7, 'Absit'; line 13, 'of'); and, as we saw in fig. 5.6, the tendency to place a punctus at the end of each line of verse.

---

[9] *Liber Albus*, London Metropolitan Archives, CLRO COL/CS/01/012, fol. 1v in the newer foliation. See Kellaway, 'John Carpenter's *Liber Albus*', p. 70. Brewer, *John Carpenter*, pp. 19–20, believed it to be Carpenter's signature.

[10] Personal communication, 2002 and again 2012, clarifying that he had noted this in a letter to Michael Benskin in 1997; Doyle had previously suggested that MS M.817 might be '[a product] from Westminster rather than London', see Doyle, 'English Books in and out of Court from Edward III to Henry VI', in *English Court Culture in the Later Middle Ages*, ed. V. J. Scattergood and J. W. Sherborne (London, 1983), pp. 163–81 (p. 172). See also p. 100 n. 31 below.

[11] Kellaway, 'John Carpenter's *Liber Albus*', p. 75, in his table of the sources for the *Liber Albus*, Book I, fols 15r–19r; Barron, *London in the Later Middle Ages*, p. 186, writes of his descriptions of officers and their oaths on those folios: 'Carpenter wrote that the common clerk, like the chamberlain and common serjeant-at-law, was elected by common council.'

Scribes and the City

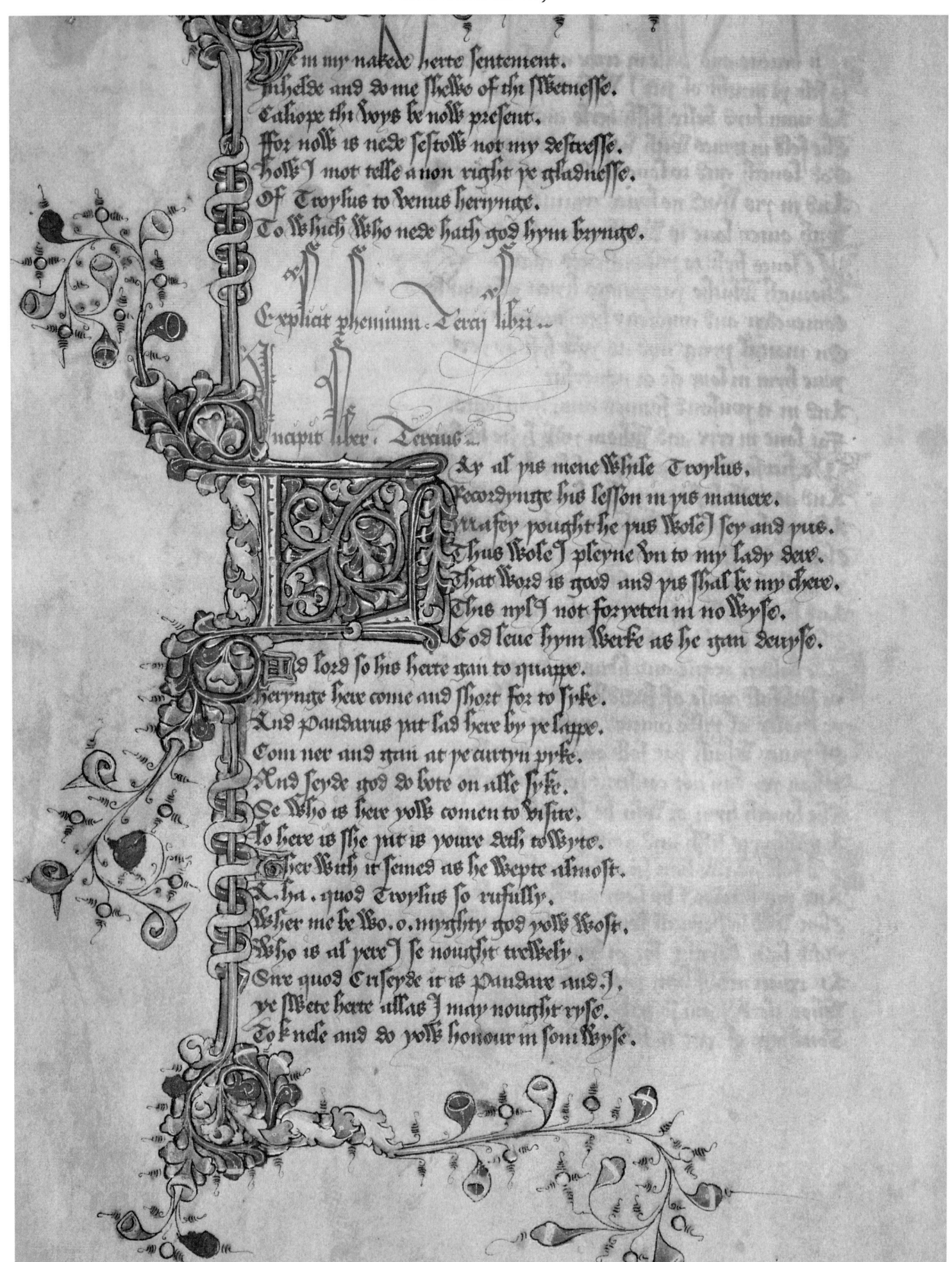

Be in my nakede herte sentement.
Inhelde and do me shewe of thi swetnesse.
Caliope thi voys be now present.
ffor now is nede sestow not my destresse.
How I mot telle a non right þe gladnesse.
Of Troylus to Venus herynge.
To which who nede hath god hym brynge.

Explicit phemium. Tercij libri.

Incipit liber. Tercius.

Lay al þis mene while Troylus.
Recordynge his lesson in þis manere.
ffra sey þought he þus wole I sey and þus.
Thus wole I pleyne vn to my lady dere.
That word is good and þis shal be my chere.
This nyl I not foryeten in no wyse.
God leue hym werke as he can deuyse.

And lord so his herte gan to quape.
Herynge here come and short for to syke.
And Pandarus put lad here by þe lappe.
Com ner and gan at þe curtyn pyke.
And seyde god do bote on alle syke.
Se who is here yow comen to visite.
Lo here is she þat is youre deth to wryte.
Therwith it semed as he wepte almost.
A. ha. quod Troylus so rufully.
Wher me be wo. o. myghty god yow wost.
Who is al þere I se nought trewely.
Sire quod Criseyde it is Pandare and I.
ye swete herte allas I may nought ryse.
To knele and do yow honour in som wyse.

Fig. 5.6 New York, Pierpont Morgan Library & Museum, MS M.817, fol. 43v
Geoffrey Chaucer's *Troilus and Criseyde* written in the hand of John Carpenter

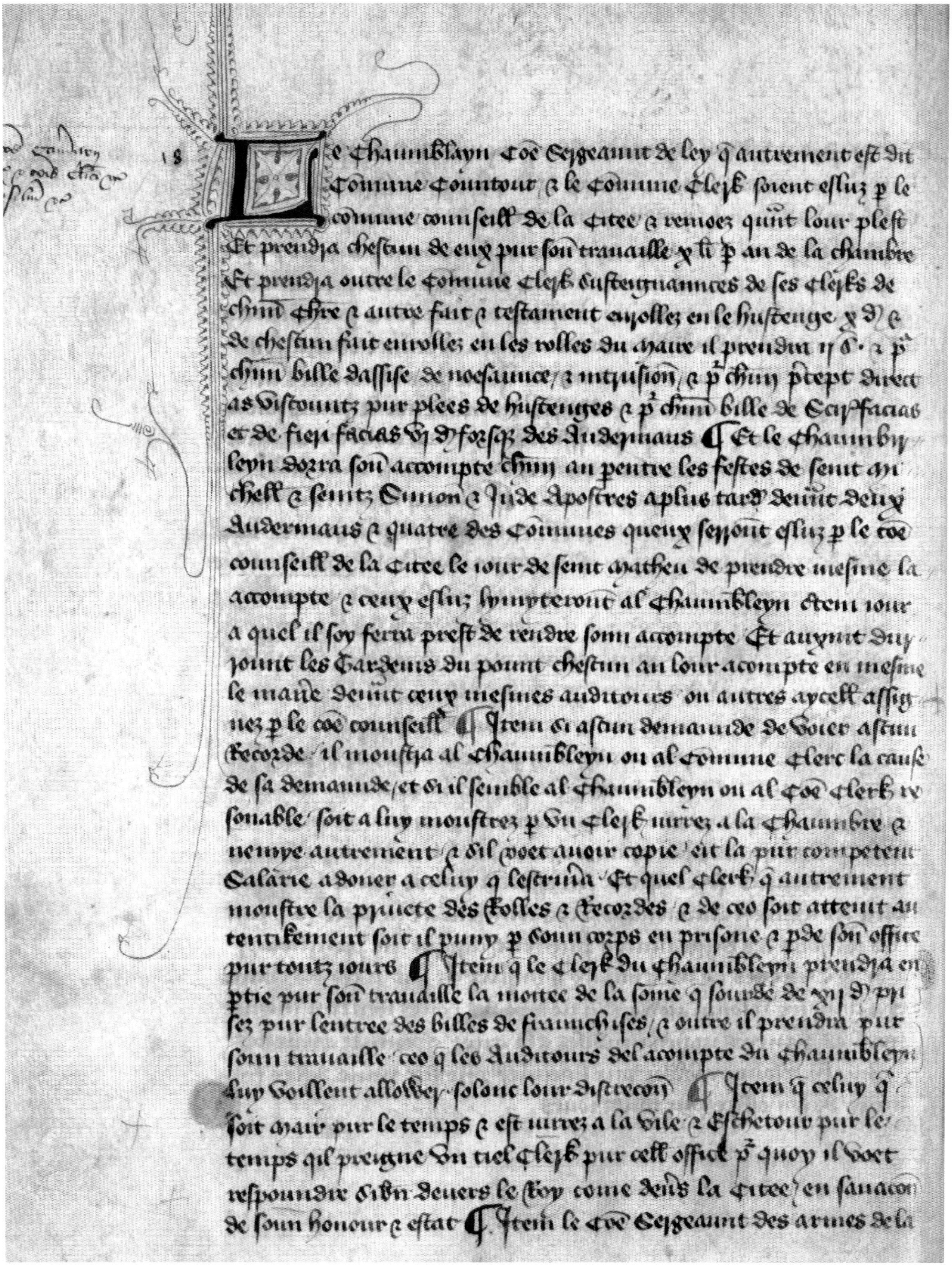

Fig. 5.7 London Metropolitan Archives, COL/CS/01/012, *Liber Albus*, Book I, fol. 17v: illustrating the hand John Carpenter, here describing the officers of the Guildhall

Fig. 5.8 Philadelphia, Rosenbach Museum and Library, MS 1083/29, fol. 1r (extract): John Gower's *Confessio Amantis* written in the hand of John Carpenter

We have also identified Carpenter's hand in another incomplete copy of Gower's *Confessio Amantis*, now Cambridge, University Library, MS Dd.8.19 (fig. 5.9). This sample of Carpenter's handwriting shows us the primitive cadels in the rubric explicit and incipit; the form of **w** with straight parallel stalks (fig. 5.9, col. a, line 3, 'which'); the **A** distorted by angular top (fig. 5.9, col. a, last line, 'And'; col. b, line 2, 'And'); the straight or slightly concave descenders of **f**, long **s**, **p** and **q** (fig. 5.9, col. a, line 2, the **s** and **p** of 'speke', and the **f** of 'of'; line 5, the **p** of 'Incipit'). The top of **I** in the rubric 'Incipit' (fig. 5.9, line 5) has a solid lozenge like the one in Letter Book I at the top of the initial **F** (fig. 5.3). The initial **E** of 'Explicit' (fig. 5.9, line 4) has the zig-zag decorative feature on its left side, as do the **I** of 'Incipit' and the **l** of 'liber' in the following line.

Like Marchaunt and Osbarn, John Carpenter appears to have spent his entire career at the Guildhall. His nineteenth-century biographer, Thomas Brewer, said he had found sufficient evidence to date his birth to *c.* 1377.[12] The earliest records of his activities are as an attorney

---

[12] Brewer, *John Carpenter*, p. 3, writes, 'From some facts ... which are well ascertained, it may be inferred that he was born somewhere about the close of the long reign of Edward the Third, or the beginning of the disastrous career of his ill-fated successor Richard the Second.' Brewer (p. 3) also identified his parents (through his wife Katherine's will) as Richard and Christina Carpenter, whose bodies (from John's will) were buried in the church of St Martin Outwich, in Bishopsgate Street. He also notes (pp. 3–4) that Richard may be the Richard Carpenter named in a pardon dated 1381 who lived in Billiter Lane, and/or the Richard Carpenter named in relation to the

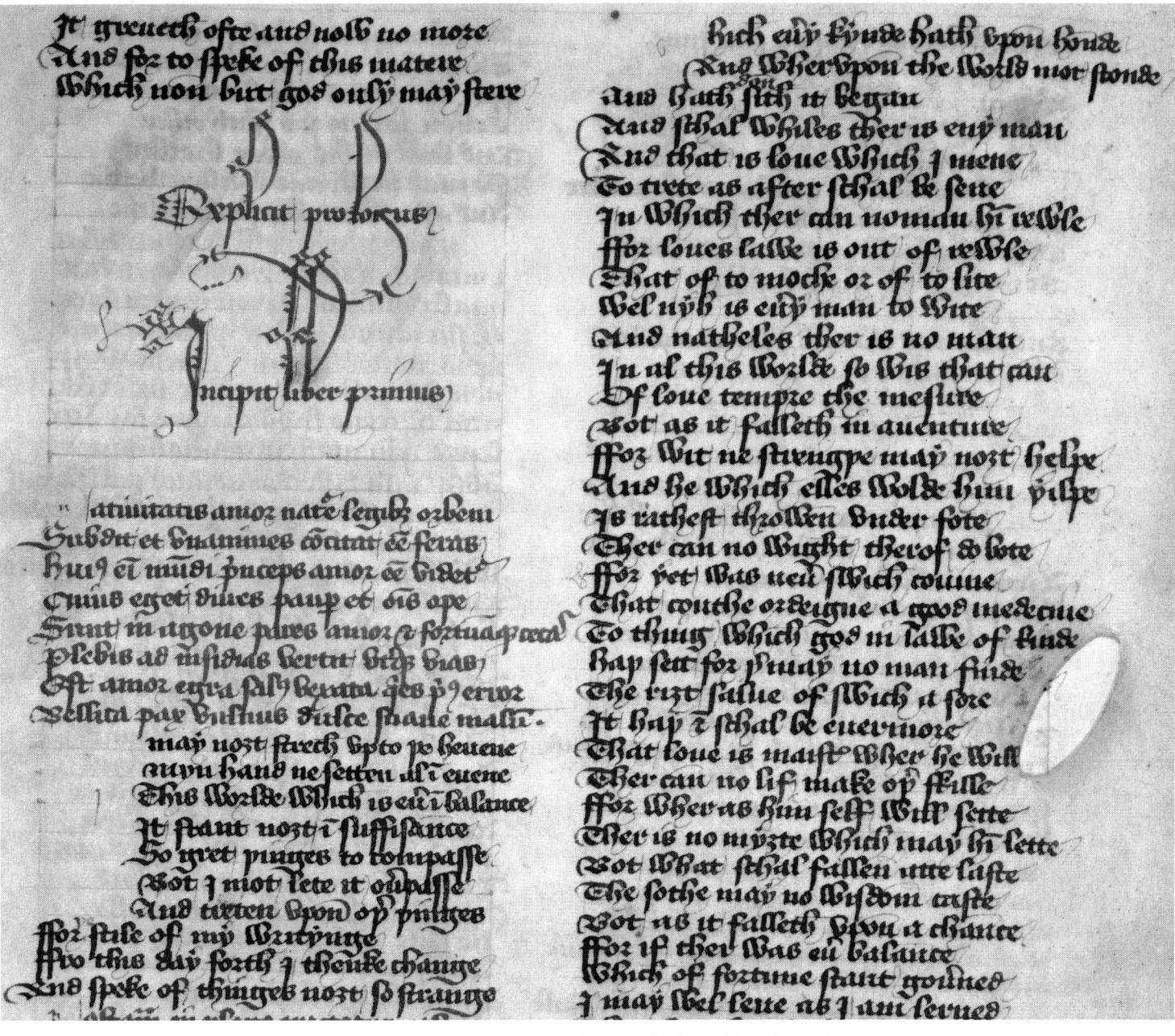

Fig. 5.9 Cambridge, University Library, MS Dd.8.19, fol. 7v (extract):
John Gower's *Confessio Amantis* written in the hand of John Carpenter

in the city's courts at the very beginning of the fifteenth century.[13] When he succeeded Marchaunt as common clerk in 1417 he stated that he had served under Marchaunt as his clerk, though we have been unable to discover whether this was for the entire period of Marchaunt's service in that office.[14] The common clerk was entitled to a £10 annuity and

> guardianship of a warden in 1410, who was a Chandler; but as Richard was a common given name and Carpenter a common surname, these identifications are only speculative.

[13] Tucker, *Law Courts and Lawyers*, app. 8.3, 'John Carpenter, [Mayor's Court Attorney], 1403–1415'. Kellaway, 'John Carpenter's *Liber Albus*', p. 67, n. 4, cites for this information *London Assize of Nuisance, 1301–1431: A Calendar*, ed. H. M. Chew and W. Kellaway, London Record Society 10 (London, 1973), nos. 658–9. He also notes that Carpenter acted as sheriff's clerk in 1421, citing *Calendar of Plea and Memoranda Rolls: Preserved Among the Archives of the Corporation of the City of London at the Guildhall*, ed. A. H. Thomas, 6 vols. (London, 1943), IV, but this would have been while serving as common clerk.

[14] Kellaway, 'John Carpenter's *Liber Albus*', mistakenly cites Letter Book I, fols 179v–190r, for the terms of Carpenter's replacing Marchaunt in 1417; it should be Letter Book I, fols 179v–180r. Brewer, *John Carpenter*, p. 12, cites the folio as 194v, and gives a modernized transcript, pp. 12–13.

a lodging over the middle gate to the Guildhall precinct; however, Carpenter waived those entitlements in favour of Marchaunt for the lifetime of his predecessor (as recorded in the entry of 20 April 1417 in Letter Book I dealing with Carpenter's appointment).[15] Caroline Barron explains that this waiving of fee and lodging in favour of a living predecessor was common practice in the civic secretariat.[16] Without the annuity Carpenter would still find means of support in his position as common clerk through collecting the fees attached to the office: '10*d*. for every deed or will enrolled in the Hustings, 2*s*. for every deed enrolled in the mayor's court rolls, and 6*d*. for every writ drawn up for assizes of nuisance and freshforce',[17] besides fees collected for special services offered to livery companies.[18] Barron notes that in Carpenter's time, 'an average of seventy-two deeds and wills were enrolled yearly in the Husting', yielding the common clerk an annual income of 60*s*. (£3) from just this one source; she also notes as an example of the common clerk's receipt of fees from livery companies an instance of Carpenter's receiving 20*s*. from the Brewers in 1420 'for offering counsel, and for other services'.[19] We have also found him being remunerated by the Mercers' Company for services that presumably only the common clerk could render: in the company's medieval accounts book, under a heading for 'foreign costs' relating to a weaver, John van Neweden, 'Ducheman', for writing three letters to Ghent, Bruges and Ypres 33*s*. and 4*d*. (£1 plus 1 mark) and for writing a letter of discharge from his franchise in relation to Neweden an additional 2*s*.[20] This amounted to almost £2 for a single service of writing four letters on behalf of the Mercers. Barron cites many other examples of the common clerk receiving *douceurs* from the companies.[21] Carpenter would not have long to wait for the annuity either, since Marchaunt enjoyed his retirement for only five years, dying in 1422. Carpenter served as one of the executors of Marchaunt's will (Richard Osbarn was the other), and in his own will of

---

[15] Letter Book I, fols 179v–180r. Barron notes these details, too, *London in the Later Middle Ages*, p. 186, in which she interprets the Letter Book I reference to lodging as referring to 'a house over the middle gate of Guildhall'.

[16] Barron, personal communication, 28 April 2011. Similar waiving of the annuity, lodging and robes took place when William Chedworth replaced Richard Osbarn as chamber clerk in 1437; see pp. 28–9 above. For royal clerks the equivalent award of additional income was the grant of a wealthy parish incumbency by the king, or at least of a corrody like the one that Thomas Hoccleve received toward the end of his life; but the royal clerks were expected to be in at least minor orders, and those receiving the greater benefices, major orders. However, there was no such expectation for civic clerks, so they would not necessarily have been eligible for such rewards even where the city had the incumbency in its gift. For Hoccleve, see J. A. Burrow, *Thomas Hoccleve*, Authors of the Middle Ages 4 (Aldershot, 1994), pp. 29–30, 48.

[17] Barron, *London in the Later Middle Ages*, p. 185, citing Carpenter's own description of the office of common clerk in *Liber Albus*, fols 47v–48r.

[18] Barron, *London in the Later Middle Ages*, p. 186. It should be noted that he was not required to pay his clerks out of this income, since they were to be provided for from the Chamber: see Barron, *London in the Later Middle Ages*, p. 188, citing (n. 111), *Liber Albus*, fol. 48r.

[19] Barron, *London in the Later Middle Ages*, p. 186. This payment or 'gift' as he terms it, is also invoked by Kellaway, 'John Carpenter's *Liber Albus*', pp. 68–9, and had been previously cited by Barron, 'Richard Whittington', pp. 213–4, and previously by *Book of London English*, ed. Chambers and Daunt, p. 172.

[20] London, Mercers' Company Archives, Account Book of 1347, 1391–1464, fol. 81r.

[21] See Barron, *London in the Later Middle Ages*, p. 186, n. 92, for the term *douceurs*, and C. M. Barron, 'The Government of London and its Relations with the Crown, 1400–1450' (unpublished PhD dissertation, University of London, 1970), pp. 127–8 for others.

1442 noted that one of the books he bequeathed had been given to him by his predecessor.[22] Carpenter completes the triumvirate of high-level clerks of the Guildhall who clearly knew one another very well and worked together over a number of decades. They shaped London government through their long careers, and through their selection of material to be incorporated into the *Liber Albus* to serve as the manual for future generations. All three also displayed an interest in books, including works of vernacular literature.

John Carpenter achieved a level of esteem unmatched by any of his predecessors. As William Kellaway notes, he assumed responsibilities normally the preserve of aldermen: 'He signed proclamations in the name of the mayor and aldermen, and occasionally acted as an arbitrator, a duty normally performed by aldermen.'[23] The prestigious Mercers' Company granted him the right to wear its livery in 1426–7.[24] In addition to the £10 annuity he received as common clerk after the death of Marchaunt, the city granted him in 1430 an annual rent of £10, and in the following year he and his wife Katherine were granted 'a lease of land and shops in St Peter Cornhill for eighty years, paying a rose yearly for thirty years and 20s. yearly thereafter.'[25] In 1436 the city granted him exemption from serving on watches, assizes, or juries, or being burdened with any work other than that attached to his office as common clerk.[26] The document granting these exemptions refers to Carpenter as the city's 'beloved' secretary; Kellaway comments that 'the endearment "beloved" is sufficiently unusual to testify to the esteem in which Carpenter was held.'[27] Unlike any common clerk before or since, he was elected to represent the city as MP in 1437 and again in 1439.[28] He retired in or before October 1438, when his successor, Richard Barnet, was named to the office, but he remained active in serving the city for several years, as its MP in 1439, and serving on commissions of enquiry into kidells as late as 1440.[29] In 1439 the king granted Carpenter

---

[22] John Marchaunt's will is in the National Archives, E 40/12349; John Carpenter's is the National Archives, C 146/9532.

[23] Kellaway, 'John Carpenter's *Liber Albus*', pp. 67–8, citing Letter Book I, fols 196–8, and *London Possessory Assizes: A Calendar*, ed. H. M. Chew, London Record Society I (London, 1965), no. 232 for signing proclamations; and for acting as arbitrator, *Calendar of Plea and Memoranda Rolls*, III, 262; Journal of the Court of Common Council 3, fol. 80r (these references are from Kellaway, p. 67, nn. 5, 6).

[24] Kellaway, 'John Carpenter's *Liber Albus*', p. 68, citing J. M. Imray, '"Les Bones Gents de la Mercerye de Londres": A Study of the Membership of the Medieval Mercers' Company', in *Studies in London History Presented to Philip Edmund Jones*, ed. A. E. J. Hollaender and W. Kellaway (London, 1969), pp. 155–78 (p. 175). Brewer, *John Carpenter*, p. 29, tells of Carpenter and the other executors of Whittington's will obtaining from the king in 1425 a charter confirming a grant of Richard II allowing the Mercers' Company to be created a brotherhood for the relief of members who met with misfortune, with its own seal and legal rights not granted to any other company: he speculates that it was in gratitude for his efforts in this matter that the company 'solicited [Carpenter] to become a member'.

[25] Kellaway, '*Liber Albus*', p. 68, n. 20. Brewer, *John Carpenter*, p. 38. Kellaway neglects to mention Katherine in this transaction.

[26] Kellaway, 'John Carpenter's *Liber Albus*' p. 68, citing (n. 11) *Calendar of Letter-Books*, X, fol. 210.

[27] Kellaway, 'John Carpenter's *Liber Albus*', p. 68.

[28] Kellaway, 'John Carpenter's *Liber Albus*', p. 68, citing *Calendar of Letter-Books*, X, 211; B. R. Masters, 'The Town Clerk', *Guildhall Miscellany* 3 (1969–70), 55–74.

[29] Ibid., citing (nn. 15, 17, 19) London CLRO, Journal 3, fol. 172r; *Calendar of Letter-Books*, X, 232, n. 21; and *Calendar of Patent Rolls, 1436–1441*, pp. 371, 453.

exemption from serving in any office, civil or military, from serving in parliament, or from receiving a knighthood.[30]

John Carpenter was clearly a very busy man once he took office as common clerk. The additional burdens of representing the city in petitions to the king and parliament, serving on inquisitions, and executing the final wishes of several prominent and wealthy Londoners had clearly become too much for him by 1436, when the city granted the various exemptions detailed above; the 1439 royal grant of immunity from service further lightened his load. As early as 1419, in the preface to the calendar that makes up Book IV of the *Liber Albus*, he had noted that he did not feel he could take the time required to assemble a complete collection of copies of important documents for the *Liber Albus*, given the demands of his other work for the city as common clerk. It appears that the three manuscripts we have attributed to his hand were written before he took on this office, while serving as clerk under John Marchaunt, another prolific copyist of Middle English literary manuscripts.

The Campsall manuscript of *Troilus and Criseyde*, Pierpont Morgan M. 817, belonged to and was perhaps commissioned by Henry V while he was Prince of Wales (1399–1413), so it was clearly copied in this period. Ian Doyle commented that the arms of Henry V as prince of Wales were *added* in a space left for them in the border.[31] This could indicate speculative copying, with the arms left blank for any noble recipient, but it might equally well suggest that the manuscript was commissioned to be given to Henry in his latter years as Prince of Wales, and the arms were left to be added once the manuscript was completed, in case Henry's status changed.[32] The Rosenbach MS 1083/29 copy of John Gower's *Confessio Amantis* is highly decorated and illuminated but has no indications of its earliest owners; however, details of the border decoration would, according to Kathleen Scott, probably date it before 1413.[33] Cambridge, University Library, MS Dd.8.19 likewise has no indication of early owners' names, and though beautifully written on good-quality parchment with wide margins and extensive rubric for Latin, its planned scheme of decoration was never completed: spaces are left for decorated or illuminated initials that were never filled. The text of Books V, VII and VIII includes several major gaps, and some folios are placed out of order and transposed. Both Rosenbach and Cambridge are copies of the first recension of Gower's *Confessio Amantis*; Carpenter may have known of the second recension and left

---

[30] Kellaway, 'John Carpenter's *Liber Albus*', p. 68, citing (n. 18) *Calendar of the Patent Rolls Preserved in the Public Record Office: Henry VI*, vol. 3: *1436–1441*, ed. H. C. Maxwell Lyte *et al.* (London, 1901), p. 356. Brewer, *John Carpenter*, p. 46, notes that there is a copy of this letter patent in British Library, MS Cotton Vespasian C. XIV, fol. 277r, from which he made his modern translation, pp. 46–9. It was dated 3 December, 18 Henry VI. If Brewer is right about his date of birth, he would have been sixty in this year.

[31] Doyle, 'English Books in and out of Court', p. 172. He notes further, 'the even showier writing of [Morgan M.817] has no precise parallel, probably because it was a tour de force by someone who normally followed a plainer mode, not necessarily in books. As with the Ellesmere Gower, here we may have exceptional products from Westminster rather than London.'

[32] This would date the copying to any time from 1410, when for a time the Prince of Wales ruled as head of the king's council during his father's illness, until 1413, when he succeeded to the throne upon his father's death.

[33] The border decoration includes gold balls from which emanate black ink squiggles: according to Scott, these squiggles were usually washed with green after 1413. See K. L. Scott, *Dated and Datable English Manuscript Borders, c. 1395–1499* (London, 2002), p. 12.

John Carpenter, Common Clerk, 1417–37

portions of the text to complete with second-recension lines when he could gain access to an appropriate exemplar.[34]

The dating of these manuscripts shows that Carpenter was probably doing his literary copying before 1417 while working as a clerk under John Marchaunt. Since he would have been a relative unknown then, it seems unlikely that Henry himself would have commissioned him to prepare the Campsall manuscript. Richard Whittington or another wealthy London merchant might have commissioned it as a gift for Henry, asking Marchaunt, the literary clerk they knew best, to prepare it or give the work to his protégé Carpenter. After 1417, once he had become common clerk, Carpenter may have had dealings with Henry himself, and we find him signing messages from Henry to the city pleading for support for the war in 1419, as recorded in Letter Book I (see fig. 5.2). After Henry's death he seems to have had a reputation for dealing with king and council, leading others to seek him out to intercede for them. He was requested to plead with king and council on behalf of the Mercers' Company in 1425 (and was rewarded by the Mercers with an invitation to wear their livery when this suit was successful).[35] Again in 1437 he was requested to intercede with the king's council on behalf of the citizens of Norwich, who had had their liberties withdrawn by the king, and he was then named together with the archbishop of York to decide the terms under which the king would restore their rights.[36]

Once Carpenter was in position as common clerk, the demands on his time would not allow for the copying of literary books; moreover, that position made him a wealthy man, so he would have been able to delegate such copying to others. In his will Carpenter left gifts to no fewer than nine men named as his clerks or former clerks, so whether in his official position as common clerk of the Guildhall, or in his household, he had a number of people to take on writing tasks for him.[37] His wealth by then would have enabled him to commission books that he wished to present as gifts, too, so the kinds of books he wrote before becoming common clerk he might now commission other scribes to write for him.

John and Katherine Carpenter appear to have had no children, not even any who died in infancy, since none are named in their wills among requests for prayers to be said for their souls and those of family members. However, they did leave bequests to a number

---

[34] There is more work to be done in a thorough study of this manuscript of the *Confessio*; and one might also fruitfully examine whether the corrected readings of *Troilus* which Richard Osbarn added to his copy in Huntington Library MS HM 114 came from the same archetype as was used for Carpenter's copy of the poem in Morgan MS M.817.

[35] Brewer, *John Carpenter*, pp. 28–9, describes this incident as if it followed from Carpenter's efforts as Whittington's executor. He notes that Carpenter was requested only to obtain confirmation of a charter granted the Mercers by Richard II, but obtained still more: a charter that made the Mercers 'a corporate body, with perpetual succession and other legal incidents' (p. 29). He then suggests that the Mercers rewarded him with membership in the company.

[36] Ibid., pp. 42–3.

[37] Of these nine, seven were listed as 'late my clerk': Robert Langford, John Crouton, Richard Mordan, John Brown, Richard de Lafeld, Richard Lovell, and Robert Blount, and each was left books, or in Richard Mordan's case, a book plus money; the last of these, Robert Blount, was clearly a clerk working within the Guildhall since he was left a book of forms for documents relating to law and custom of the city, to be deposited on Blount's death in the Chamber at the Guildhall for the use of the clerks there. In addition to these seven, there are two men, Nicholas Mason and John Elys, listed as currently his clerks at the time of writing the will (1441), so presumably in his household: these were left a significant sum of money (5 marks) to split between them, plus any other books that the executors chose to give them.

of other family members:[38] to John's older brother who was also named John, who must therefore have outlived him; to his brother Robert; to his nephew Richard, son of Robert; to his nephew John, son of his brother John; to his niece Margery, daughter of his brother John; to his niece Joan, daughter of Robert; and to his niece Katherine, daughter of Robert who had lived with him and his wife from her youth.[39] Carpenter left gifts of money to his household servants, and to his cousin John Reynold, who was later more particularly named as an executor in Katherine's will.[40] Further, he left a book to another man of the name of John Carpenter who was then (1441) warden of St Anthony's hospital in Threadneedle Street.[41] As Brewer notes, this John Carpenter is not named as a relative in the bequest in the will, but there seems to have been some connection between them: they are both named, together with the chancellor of the Exchequer, in a grant from the king of property to be kept for the benefit of St Anthony's hospital, so our John Carpenter, named in the grant as the former common clerk of the city, was in some way connected with the hospital, perhaps as a trustee.[42] The John Carpenter who was warden of St Anthony's cannot be either the brother or nephew of our John Carpenter, since he is named separately in the will. He had been provost of Oriel College, Oxford, since 1425, was warden of St Anthony's hospital 1433–44, and was appointed bishop of Worcester in 1444, where he remained until his death in 1476.[43] He was also named, together with Carpenter's brothers John and Robert, as overseers and coadjutors of the executors of Carpenter's will, which suggests a family tie.[44]

Carpenter's other bequests follow the pattern of alms given by most wealthy men of the later Middle Ages: he left money to the Charterhouse and the Fraternity of Sixty Priests of London (of both of which he was a lay member), and to many other religious houses in and around London, to hospitals and to lepers, recluses and prisoners. His major benefactions during his lifetime were made in the names of other men who had assigned him as executor in their wills, and with their wealth. The chief of these was Richard Whittington, whose wealth enabled Carpenter to carry out many good deeds for the sake of Whittington's soul: to tear down and rebuild the Newgate, including rebuilding and modernizing its prison; to build conduits for delivering fresh water to several parts of the city; to repair St Bartholomew's hospital in Smithfield; to found a chantry for one priest at St Paul's cathedral; to have the walls of the cloister at St Paul's painted with the Dance of Macabre together with Lydgate's verses (this paid for by Whittington's legacy together with moneys from other men's legacies over which Carpenter had control as executor); to complete the rebuilding work begun on

---

[38] For these family members and Reynold, see Carpenter's will in Brewer, *John Carpenter*, pp. 131–44; for Katherine's wills, see pp. 145–65.

[39] Ibid., pp. 58, 136–7; original will, TNA, C 146/9532. Since John Carpenter, Common Clerk, had an older brother also named John, he is often referred to as 'John Carpenter junior', or 'Jenkin' even in official records.

[40] Brewer, *John Carpenter*, pp. 145–50, 151–65 (pp. 146–7).

[41] Ibid., p. 137; original will, Kew, National Archives, C 146/9532. For more on this John Carpenter, see R. M. Haines, 'Carpenter, John (c. 1395–1476)', in *Oxford Dictionary of National Biography* (Oxford, 2004).

[42] Brewer, *John Carpenter*, p. 52.

[43] Ibid., pp. 52–3. See A. B. Emden, *A Biographical Register of the University of Oxford, to AD 1500*, 3 vols. (Oxford, 1957–9), s.v. 'Carpenter, John (d. 1476), bishop of Worcester.'

[44] Brewer, *John Carpenter*, p. 101; original will, Kew, National Archives, C 146/9532. However, Brewer, p. 53, argues that he was not a Londoner but a native of Westbury upon Trin, near Bristol, where he was buried, so the common name and associations may only be a coincidence.

the Guildhall itself and, together with a legacy from William of Bury, to build and furnish with books the library at the Guildhall.[45]

John Carpenter named twenty-six books in his will, which he left to various people and institutions. While many men must have owned books, they seldom listed them separately in their wills as Carpenter does, so this shows the high value that he placed upon books as the best gifts he could leave as tokens of remembrance to members of his family, former clerks at the Guildhall, and associates. Many others before us have studied the will, with its lists of books, as an indication of the reading interests of a man in Carpenter's position. But it must be noted that he only names the twenty-six books specifically so that the right book will be given to the right person, whereas all the remainder of his books he need not name because they were all to go either to the two clerks in his employ at the time of his death (at the discretion of his executors) or into the Guildhall library which he had helped to build with Whittington's legacy. Some books he identified by their provenance: an abbreviated bible that John Sudbury had given him; a book containing the ten commandments, twelve articles of faith, etc. in French, that had belonged to Sir Thomas Pykworth; a book on architecture given him by William Cleve; and a copy of the *Secretum Secretorum* attributed to Aristotle, given him by 'my master', John Marchaunt.[46]

One major benefaction dating from his lifetime may relate to the couple's childlessness, but also demonstrates Carpenter's keen interest in education: it is his donation of land to support and educate four sons of Londoners, to be called 'Carpenter's children', who were to be housed and fed in the Guildhall college of priests and provided with an education including university, until they should receive a benefice.[47] The foundation was handed over to the city in 1417; by 1847 its value had increased so much that it was one of the founding endowments of the City of London School.[48]

Throughout his life John Carpenter seems to have had a particular interest in books, and access to books and education. His foundation for the training of four sons of Londoners is matched by his decision to spend part of Whittington's legacy to build a library within the Guildhall close, endowing it with the remainder of his own collection at his death, at his executors' discretion.[49] The executors who were to choose which of his books would be suitable for this purpose were themselves advocates of greater education for the clergy and common people alike: William Lichfield, Rector of All Hallows Church, and Reginald Pecock, then rector of St Michael Paternoster and master of its associated college in the Riola, or Royal district of London, that is, Whittington's Hospital.[50] Wendy Scase comments

---

[45] Brewer, *John Carpenter*, pp. 28–30.

[46] Ibid., pp. 93–100, summarizes the will, and supplies a list of the books named in it, together with bibliographical notes (pp. 121–30) and a translation of the will itself (pp. 131–44). He identifies each of these men, pp. 60–7.

[47] Matthew Davies describes these four boys as the core of a 'choir school' but says that 'the choristers were to receive schooling at a convenient place', which suggests that there was not a school within the Guildhall close itself. See Davies, 'Carpenter, John'.

[48] According to Brewer, the document by which Carpenter made this bequest is lost, but John Stow describes it in his *Survey of London* and accounts of the city list the properties and the income derived from them. See Brewer, *John Carpenter*, pp. 72–90. See also Davies, 'Carpenter, John '.

[49] Davies, 'Carpenter, John ', suggests that the Guildhall Library 'may well have been Carpenter's own idea' and also that 'it is possible that it was he who administered the library from 1425 [until his death].'

[50] Scase, 'Reginald Pecock, John Carpenter and John Colop's "Common-Profit" Books', p. 269.

that the terms by which Carpenter left his books are suggestive of those in common profit books, which were given to an individual or institution in return for prayers for the soul of the deceased, with the additional proviso that the books be passed on to some other devout person at the death of the first, for the same purpose, adding the first's name to those whose souls should be prayed for, and so on until the book fell apart.[51] She shows that John Colop, to whom Carpenter left 20s. in his will,[52] can be connected with the production of at least four common profit books, three during his lifetime in relation to serving as executor for other men of like mind, and one produced from his own legacy.[53] Carpenter was connected with Colop and other like-minded men, William Lichfield and Reginald Pecock, through several links that suggest he shared their concerns for making reading matter accessible to more people. Carpenter owned a book given to him by the Grocer John Sudbury, whose goods Colop had been assigned in 1430 (with one John Gamalin) to dispose of when he died intestate;[54] a Richard Morden, probably Carpenter's clerk to whom he left not only a book (as to other clerks) but also 13s. 4d. (1 mark), may be the 'Morden' who wrote a common-profit memorandum at the front of a book Colop had caused to be made from the goods of John Killum, Grocer, whose executor he was. (Richard Morden also served as one of the executors of Katherine Carpenter's will in 1458.)[55] In addition, Carpenter was probably responsible for appointing Colop to assist in distributing Whittington's wealth for alms and for allowing him accommodation for life in a messuage within the parish of St Michael Paternoster in Riola, where Whittington's Hospital was located. It might also have been Carpenter who appointed Pecock as Rector of St Michael Paternoster in Riola and master of Whittington's Hospital.[56] Carpenter's common-profit bequests in turn included a book, *De meditationibus et orationibus Sancti Anselmi*, which he left to Sir William Taillour, his private chaplain, with the proviso that it should be passed at his death to some other devout person.[57] He left to one of his former clerks at the Guildhall, Robert Blount, besides other books, a bequest for his lifetime of all his small booklets illustrating 'the modes of entry and engrossing of the acts and records as well according to the common law of the realm as the custom of the city of London', to be given at his death to the city, to be kept in the chamber of the Guildhall 'for the information of the clerks there'.[58] Scase draws particular attention to his bequest of books to the Guildhall library, which Brewer translates as follows:

> Provided always, that if any good or rare books shall be found amongst the said residue of my goods, which, by the discretion of the aforesaid Master William Lichfield and Reginald Pecok, may seem necessary to the common library at Guildhall, for the profit of the students there, and those discoursing to the common people, then I will and bequeath that those books be placed by my executors and chained in that library, under

---

[51] Ibid., pp. 261–2, 267–70.

[52] Brewer, *John Carpenter*, pp. 100, 141.

[53] Scase, 'Reginald Pecock, John Carpenter and John Colop's "Common-Profit" Books', pp. 261–2.

[54] Ibid., p. 262; Brewer, *John Carpenter*, pp. 139–40.

[55] Scase, 'Reginald Pecock, John Carpenter and John Colop's "Common-Profit" Books', pp. 262, 273, n. 49.

[56] Ibid., p. 267.

[57] Brewer, *John Carpenter*, p. 139.

[58] Ibid., p. 141.

such form that the visitors and students thereof may be the sooner admonished to pray for my soul.[59]

As Scase points out, like the common-profit books, these are to be given to the library for use by persons unnamed and indefinitely, with the request that they should pray for the donor's soul when using them.[60]

Scase further suggests that some of Carpenter's books might not have met with church authorities' approval for donation to a library where their messages would be widespread; this is her interpretation of the clause which precedes the donation of the books, at the discretion of his executors, to the Guildhall library, in which he gives 20s. to the 'lord ordinary to whom the insinuation and proof of my present will shall belong' in order that he not make an inventory of the goods but allow them to be distributed without listing.[61] Noting that he also gave 20s. (£1) to each of his executors, Pecock and Lichfield, Scase concludes:

> By means of this extraordinary arrangement, Carpenter seems to have calculated to arrange for the disposal of his books in a way that would benefit his own soul and the new city library, and to evade – with the collaboration of the two city rectors Pecock and Lichfield – the intervention of the ecclesiastical authorities, into whose hands, perhaps, or just to whose notice, simply, he did not wish his books to pass.[62]

What she is suggesting here is that John Carpenter may have had sympathy for the Lollard cause, and that some of the books he intended for the Guildhall library may have spread Lollard ideas. We should therefore consider Carpenter's orthodoxy. First of all, Pecock was in good odour with the authorities until well after Carpenter's death. During Carpenter's lifetime, as Scase herself notes, Pecock was only proposing to make didactic reading material more generally available in order to *combat* heretical movements like that of the Lollards.[63] Carpenter employed a chaplain in his house, Sir William Taillour, who was remembered in his will, and had the accoutrements for private services as well: a great missal, a silver-gilt cup and *paraxium*, two silver phials or cruets, and a white damask chasuble, which he left to the church of St Martin Outwich where his parents were buried.[64] These do not suggest unorthodoxy, but rather wealth, devoutness, and perhaps physical incapacity, since many wealthy landowners, merchants and members of the English court had petitioned to have a private altar in their homes.[65] If we consider the books he names, his reading material seems to have been highly orthodox, even including a copy of Roger Dymok's treatise *Contra duodecim errores et hereses Lollardorum*.[66]

---

[59] Ibid., pp. 143–4.

[60] Scase, 'Reginald Pecock, John Carpenter and John Colop's "Common-Profit" Books', p. 269.

[61] Brewer, *John Carpenter*, p. 143; Scase, 'Reginald Pecock, John Carpenter and John Colop's "Common-Profit" Books', p. 169.

[62] Scase, 'Reginald Pecock, John Carpenter and John Colop's "Common-Profit" Books', p. 169.

[63] Ibid., p. 266. See also A. Hudson, *Studies in the Transmission of Wyclif's Writings* (Aldershot, 2008), 1–18.

[64] Brewer, *John Carpenter*, pp. 57, 133–4.

[65] C. Richmond, 'Religion and the Fifteenth-Century English Gentleman', in *The Church, Politics and Patronage in the Fifteenth Century*, ed. R. B. Dobson (Gloucester, 1984), pp. 193–208 (p. 199), notes that, besides many others, there were private chapels at Paston, Mautby, and Caister (Suffolk); Ightham Mote (Kent); Stonor (Bucks.); Stanton Harcourt (Oxon.); and Cotele (Cornwall).

[66] Brewer, *John Carpenter*, pp. 121–30, lists and identifies the books named in Carpenter's will. Dymok's treatise is number 13 in that list, given to Master William Byngham, rector of the church

Scase focuses on the bequest to the Guildhall library. After the allocation of the twenty-six volumes named in Carpenter's will, the remainder of his books were to be deposited, at the discretion of his executors, in the Guildhall library 'for the profit of the students there, and those discoursing to the common people'.[67] Did his books include volumes of Middle English literature such as he copied many years before? We cannot know what constituted the collection of the Guildhall library, since no book list survives from the brief period before it was dispersed in the sixteenth century. It would not have included books pertaining to London government, laws, customs and forms, since those were kept separately in the chamber at the Guildhall even after the new library was built, as evidenced by the booklets John Carpenter left to Robert Blount, which were to be given at Blount's death to the chamber at the Guildhall for the benefit of the clerks there.

Given our discovery that clerks at the Guildhall were involved in copying Middle English secular literary texts, it might be that the remaining books from which Masters Lichfield and Pecock were to choose volumes suitable for deposit in the Guildhall library included such texts of vernacular literary writing. One fragment of evidence that the collection did include such texts, and that Lichfield and Pecock deemed them suitable for the library, is the fragment of Chaucer's *Troilus and Criseyde*, copied by Adam Pinkhurst, that survives in the collection that belonged in the sixteenth century to William Cecil.[68] Cecil, secretary to Lord Protector Somerset, was the official who, following the dissolution of the Guildhall chapel, college and its library, before January 1549 removed the books remaining in the Guildhall library and never returned them, although the city had requested him to do so.[69] A fragment of Pinkhurst's copy of *Troilus and Criseyde* was used as material for binding and later discovered when the book was rebound; it is now stored separately at Hatfield House, Cecil Papers, Box S/1.[70] However, this evidence suggests only one possible means by which the scrap used for binding came into Cecil's possession, since Cecil's forebears might have acquired a copy of *Troilus and Criseyde* written by Pinkhurst before Cecil cleared the shelves of the dissolved library, or, indeed, the scrap might have been inserted by an independent bookbinder to whom the book of accounts was given for binding.

---

of St John Zachary in London, founder of God's House in Cambridge for the education of twenty-four youths who were intended to become grammar school masters to improve education in the country (ibid., pp. 66-7, 139).

[67] Ibid., p. 143. For a useful summary of the history of the Guildhall library, see *Corpus of British Medieval Library Catalogues*, vol. 14: *Hospitals, Towns, and the Professions*, ed. N. Ramsey and J. M. W. Willoughby (London, 2009), pp. 156-65. These editors had identified only two surviving books from the library (p. 161).

[68] Doyle and Parkes, 'Production of Copies', p. 170 (repr. p. 208).

[69] Bowsher, *et al.*, *London Guildhall*, I, 210, tells of the dismantling of the library following the Chantries Act of 1548, and of Cecil's removing 'all such books of St Augustine's works and other as he now desireth that remain in Guildhall chapel with this gentle request to be made to him upon delivery of the same, but this house trusteth that he, having perused them, will return them to the said library there to remain to such use as they were provided for', quoting CLRO, Repertory 12(1), fols 40v-41r, and citing J. Stow, *Survey of London* (London, 1603), I, 275, for non-return of the books. They note that the twenty books identified as surviving from the medieval Guildhall by N. Ker, *Medieval Libraries of Great Britain* (London, 1964), pp. 126-7, 'were probably stored elsewhere in the Guildhall, perhaps in the Alderman's Court, and may not have been books from the new library' (Bowsher, I, 210).

[70] See p. 68 below.

6

Other Scribes Associated with the Guildhall or its Clerks

BESIDES THE SCRIBES who were most closely affiliated with the Guildhall, other scribes who copied Middle English literature can also be tied more loosely to this centre of production. Some may have been employed at some time during their careers by the Guildhall, while others were employed by the major livery companies whose halls stood a short distance away.

RICHARD FRAMPTON

THE FIRST is the Lancastrian scribe Richard Frampton. Malcolm Parkes identifies him as 'a freelance commercial scribe' and lists seven books copied by his hand, only three of them collections of works of literature, numbered 2, 3 and 6 in Parkes's list.[1] They are as follows (in the probable order of their writing, according to Parkes):

> London, British Library, MS Cotton Claudius D.ii, fols 139r–268v, and London, Corporation of London Record Office, Cust. 8, fols 137r–290v: *Statutes*, the last copied by Frampton dated 14 Richard II (1391)
>
> Glasgow, University Library, MS Hunterian T.4.1 (84): Guido delle Colonne, *Historia destructionis Troiae*; *Liber magni Alexandri*; Archbishop Turpin's *Itinerarium*; Marco Polo, *De Oriente*; Odoricus, *Itinerarium*; and Mandeville's *Travels*. This manuscript is signed, *Nomen scriptoris Ricardus plenus amoris Framptoun* on fol. 126v, by which we know the name of this scribe.
>
> Paris, Bibliothèque nationale de France, MS lat. 3603: Heinrich Suso, *Horologium sapientiae divinae*. This manuscript was subsequently owned by Charles d'Orléans during and after his captivity in England, 1415–40.[2] However, its place in Parkes's chronological ordering of Frampton's *œuvre* suggests that it was commissioned long before Charles was captured: it was presumably given to him by a member of the English nobility who had originally owned it.
>
> San Marino, CA, Huntington Library, MS HM 19920: *Statuta*. Both M. B. Parkes and K. L. Scott[3] note that this manuscript was copied in two stages, the first

---

[1] Parkes, 'Richard Frampton'. As he notes (p. 114, n. 2), Doyle had previously identified all but two of these in 'The Manuscripts', p. 144, n. 19, and most had been been identified in R. Somerville, 'The Cowcher Books of the Duchy of Lancaster', *English Historical Review* 51 (1936), 598–615.

[2] See F. Avril and P. D. Stirnemann, *Manuscrits enluminés d'origine insulaire, VIIe–XXe siècle* (Paris, 1987), no. 209.

[3] K. L. Scott, *Survey of Manuscripts Illuminated in the British Isles*, vol. 6: *Later Gothic Manuscripts, 1390–1490*, 2 vols. (London, 1996), cat. no. 20 (2.84-5) describing Huntington Library MS HM 19920; vol. 2, plates 80, 82, 83. Scott suggests that Frampton worked together with a second scribe in writing both parts of the manuscript, based on Parkes's notes about the manuscript kept with it at the Huntington Library; but Parkes himself makes no mention of a second scribe in his

(fols 1r–226v) for statutes ending 21 Richard II (1398), and the second (fols 227r–254v) continuing from these and ending 7 Henry IV (1405–6). A calendar for the use of York was added to fol. 92v *c.* 1413, possibly when the manuscript was purchased by or given to the Yorkshire family of John Holme (d. 1438) of Paull Holme, Yorkshire; the coats of arms for this family may have been added at the same time.[4]

Kew, National Archives, DL 42/1–2: Great Cowcher Books of the Duchy of Lancaster, in two volumes, for writing which Frampton was paid between 1402/3 and 1406/7, according to accounts of the Receiver General for the Duchy. These may have been commissioned soon after Henry IV became king in 1399, to record what portion of his wealth resided in his Lancastrian estates, so it would date from about the same time as the *Inspeximus*. (See fig. 6.4.)

Cambridge University Library, MS Mm.5.14: Guido delle Colonne, *Historia destructionis Troiae*; *Liber magni Alexandri*; Middle English *Siege of Jerusalem*.

Kew, National Archives, DL 42/192–3: A second copy of the Great Cowcher Books, also in two volumes, for writing which Frampton was paid between 1412/13 and 1415/16. This may have been commissioned at the time of Henry V's accession.

In this group are two sets of the Great Cowcher Books of the Duchy of Lancaster, a first copy written between 1402/3 and 1406/7 and a second copy written in less formal script between 1412/13 and 1415/16. The accounts of the Receiver General for the Duchy of Lancaster also record that Frampton was paid for producing a two-volume 'portehos', probably a breviary, for Henry IV.[5] R. Somerville also noted that Frampton's hand appears in other documents of the Receiver General's office, that in 1406/7 he ordered six oak chests for the office in which to keep original charters, and that he is referred to as *clericus* in Duchy accounts.[6] Parkes argues that Frampton began working as a freelance scribe or in some government office in London or Westminster – Ian Doyle described his hand as similar to that of chancery scribes – and then that, after working for the Duchy of Lancaster on a piece-by-piece basis, he was taken in as a clerk in the Receiver General's Office, thus working for the Lancastrian monarchs Henry IV and Henry V.[7] We have discovered several new pieces of Frampton's handwriting, including the *Inspeximus* of Henry IV confirming charters granted to the City of London, probably written in 1399 or 1400, and a second copy of this same document inserted into London's *Liber Albus*, as described in Chapter 1. These two finds suggest that the government office where Frampton had been employed before he was taken on permanently by the Lancastrian chancery was in fact the London

---

article, 'Richard Frampton', written some ten years later than Scott's *Survey*, and we could not detect a second hand on the folios Scott lists as written by her Hand A.

[4] Dutschke, *Guide to Medieval and Renaissance Manuscripts in the Huntington Library*, II, 617.

[5] Somerville, 'The Cowcher Books of the Duchy of Lancaster'; the reference to the 'portehos' is at p. 600. Hanna and Lawton call it 'a two-volume breviary for Henry IV (now lost)', in their description of the copy of *The Siege of Jerusalem* copied by Frampton in Cambridge, University Library, MS Mm.5.14, in *Siege of Jerusalem*, ed. Hanna and Lawton, p. xx.

[6] Somerville, 'Cowcher Books of the Duchy of Lancaster', pp. 599, 600, n. 1.

[7] Doyle, 'The Manuscripts', p. 93: Doyle described him as 'a scribe known to have worked in Westminster or London from at least 1402 to 1416 for Henry IV and V.'

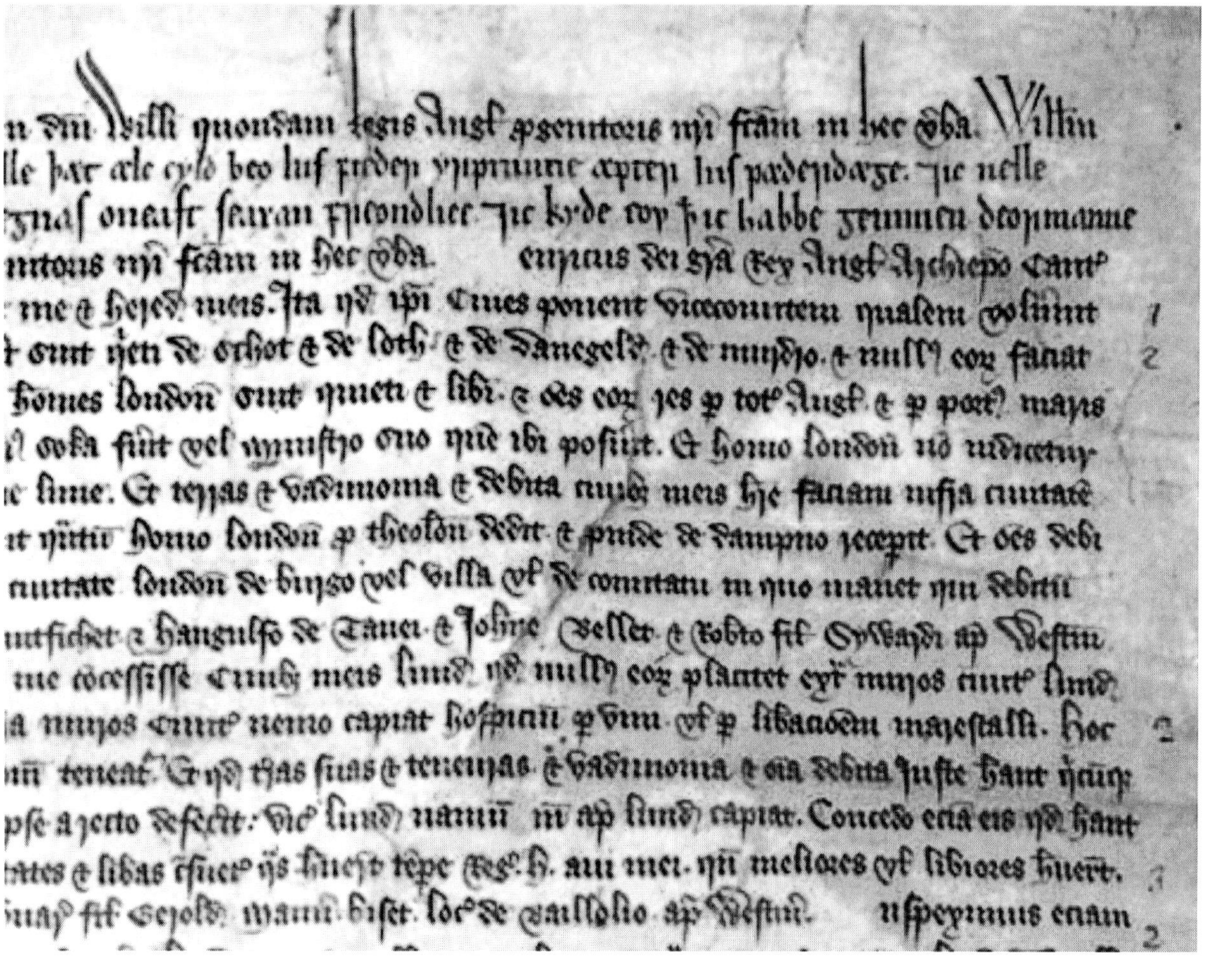

Fig. 6.1 London Metropolitan Archives, charter 50, m. 12 (upper right corner; beginning of text, as the charter is bound with the first membrane outermost): the hand of Richard Frampton copying Henry IV's *Inspeximus* of the City of London Charters and Privileges, c. 1399–1400

Guildhall.[8] Since Parkes dates his career as a writer from 1390 to 1420, this suggests that at least the first third of his career may have been spent at the Guildhall.

The first newly discovered piece of handwriting by Frampton is Corporation of London Record Office, Charter 50, the *Inspeximus* of Henry IV relating to grants and charters awarded to the City of London by previous monarchs; its very nature demands that it should have been written in the first year of Henry's reign, 1399–1400. It is written on twelve large membranes, the first ten of these measuring approx. 890 mm wide by 670 mm in height, the eleventh approx. 890×660 mm, the twelfth approx 890×340 mm. The text is written centred on each membrane, so they appear never to have been joined in a roll, but there is extra space left at the bottom of all twelve membranes for the approx. 10 cm turn-up along the bottom edge. The membranes are gathered in reverse order in the usual fashion, the beginning of the document on the bottom, the three-quarter-sized next to the top and the half-sized one on top (or inside when rolled up). Strings knotted through the turn-up attach the still-intact seal of Henry IV, now enclosed in a protective box. Space is left for a large initial at the beginning (upper left corner of the first, bottom-most membrane), and spaces are left for decorated or illuminated initials at other major breaks in the text, but the charter

---

[8] For a description of the make-up of the *Liber Albus* see Chapter 1 above; Kellaway, 'John Carpenter's *Liber Albus*', pp. 67–84. Parkes says rightly that 'a determined search for other manuscripts [by Frampton's hand] would be like looking for the proverbial needle in the widely scattered remains of a demolished haystack' ('Richard Frampton', p. 124), so new examples of manuscripts by his hand will probably come to light one by one as scholars who recognize his hand happen upon it, as on this occasion.

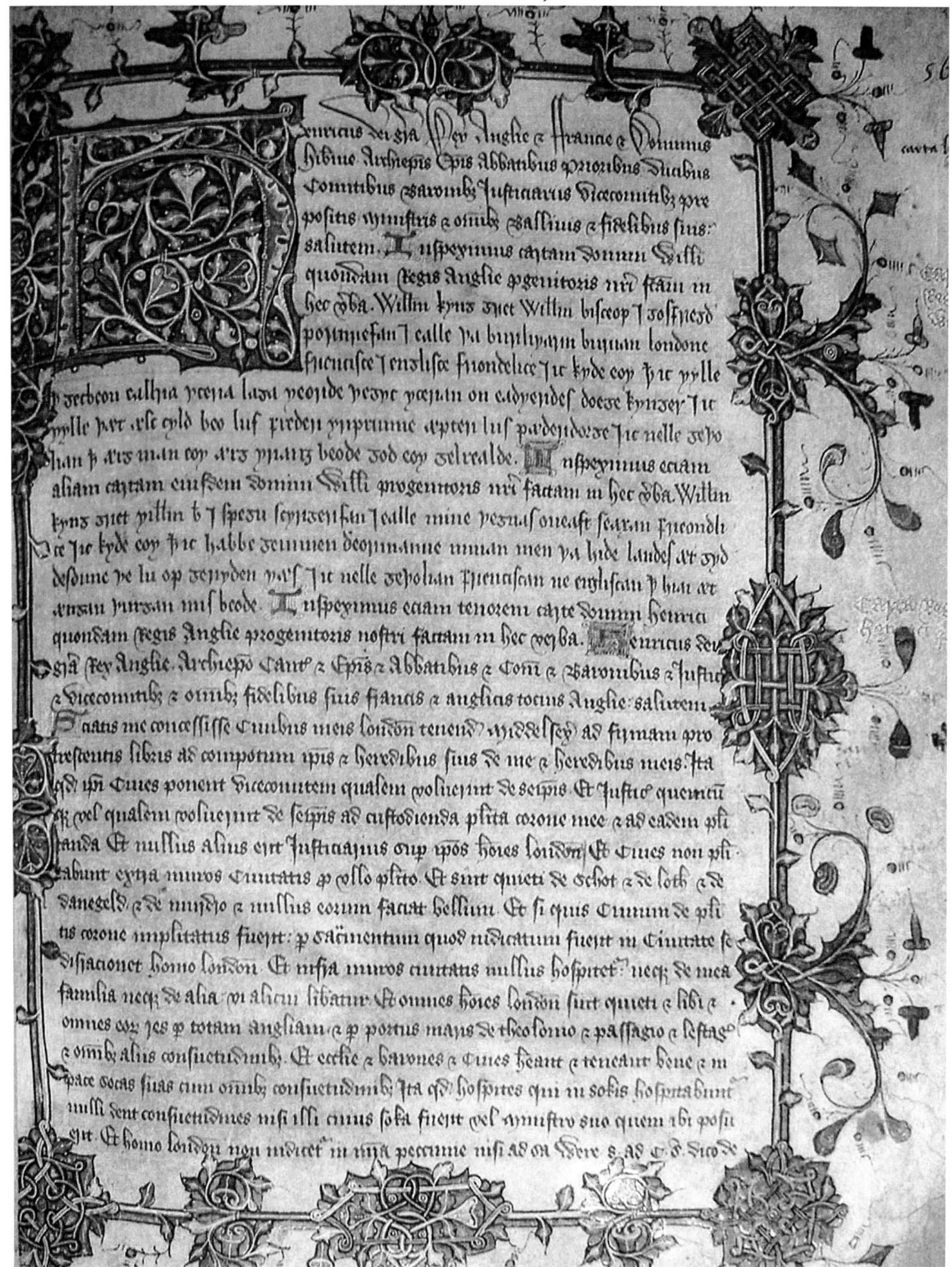

Fig. 6.2 London Metropolitan Archives, COL/CS/01/012, *Liber Albus*, fol. 6or (reduced): the hand of Richard Frampton copying Henry IV's *Inspeximus* of the City of London Charters and Privileges written in codex format between 1399 and 1419

was never decorated. Kellaway and others writing on the *Liber Albus* had not sought out the original Charter 50 that would have enabled them to see that the same scribe had written both it and the copy inserted into the *Liber Albus*.

It may be that Henry IV, or more likely the city, commissioned Frampton to write the second copy of this *Inspeximus* at the same time, in quires of folio size; Kellaway only noted that it must have been copied 'before the grant of Henry V's charter of 12 July 1414', since if written in 1417–19 the scribe would have used the latest charter. The fact that the *Liber Albus* uses Henry IV's *Inspeximus* charter instead of Henry V's is further evidence that the *Liber Albus* was conceived well before 1419. While the original Charter 50 was left undecorated, this second copy of the *Inspeximus* was meant for presentation or for show, since it is elaborately decorated, with a large illuminated initial at its beginning (see fig. 6.2). This second copy was subsequently bound into Book II of the *Liber Albus*, becoming what are now fols 60r–105v,[9] probably at the time of its compilation in 1417–19; but as it seems likely that the *Liber Albus* was a work in progress from at least the beginning of the reign, this second copy may have been commissioned by the city in 1399–1400.[10]

All these folios, gathered into six quires, were written by Richard Frampton except the last nine lines on fol. 105v, which begin the additions to Henry's document, recording grants made by subsequent kings up to Henry VIII, which fill added leaves of Book II, fols 106r–120v.[11]

In his article 'John Carpenter's Liber Albus' William Kellaway described this portion of the *Liber Albus* as 'the work of a skilled scribe'.[12] It seems likely that Richard Frampton's six quires were originally prepared as a separate piece, a separate booklet, perhaps specifically commissioned for insertion in the *Liber Albus*. As noted above, the *Inspeximus* begins with an illuminated initial by an artist different from that of the other illuminated initials in the *Liber Albus*. The other illuminated portion of the *Liber Albus* that was also prepared separately, is the extract from the *Liber Custumarum* of Andrew Horn that now appears as fols 20r–43v of the *Liber Albus*. At its completion in 1419 the *Liber Albus* itself was decorated with illuminated initials and borders at the beginnings of each book, by a different artist from that of the *Liber Horn* or *Inspeximus* booklets. In order to have written the *Inspeximus*, Frampton needed access to the archives where the city's charters were stored. It therefore seems clear that he was at that time a clerk of the Guildhall. It may be that his production of the *Inspeximus* for Henry IV to sign was the commission which brought his skills to the notice of the new king.

As Parkes points out, only three of the manuscripts copied by Frampton (those now in Paris, Glasgow and Cambridge) contain literary texts. All the rest, including our two new finds, are copies of the statutes or other collections of documents. The four volumes of the Cowcher Books record the charters relating to the estates of the Duchy of Lancaster, and,

---

[9] These are fols 6r–101v by the old numbering used by Kellaway, 'John Carpenter's *Liber Albus*', p. 76. Throughout our description of the manuscript, we use the newer foliation, marked in pencil in the centre of lower margin of rectos.

[10] See Chapter 1 above.

[11] Fol. 105 is equivalent to fol. 101 in old numbering used by Kellaway; fol. 120 equivalent to fol. 116 in the old numbering. It is clear that the booklet in which Henry's *Inspeximus* is written originally ended at fol. 105, because the oldest, that is, medieval arabic foliation ends here with '46' and further arabic foliation through the end of Book II is added by another hand in a darker ink, matching that of the added texts of fols 106–20.

[12] Kellaway, 'John Carpenter's *Liber Albus*', p. 76.

according to Parkes, may have taken up as much as six or seven years of Frampton's active career as a scribe. The statutes, with portraits of the kings, and the second copy of them (item 4 above) may have been produced originally for either the city or the Lancastrians, but whoever its original commissioner, the earlier copy (item 1 above) seems likely to have belonged to the city, for it was the city that lent it to Rate and Cotton and it is the city that still owns the second half, Corporation of London Record Office, Cust. 8, fols 137r–290v.[13] Thus the earliest piece of Frampton's writing, completed in 1391 according to Parkes, may be associated with the Guildhall. This supports the idea of his original employment by the Guildhall (whether as a full-time clerk or for bespoke pieces of writing as a freelance scribe) and subsequent employment by the Duchy of Lancaster and/or Henry IV.

It may be that the double copying of the *Inspeximus* in Henry's first year as monarch marked the change in Frampton's employment from Guildhall to royal service. He was clearly working for the Lancastrian chancery only a few years later, when the Lancastrian Receiver General, John Leventhorp, was assembling the Duchy holdings, charters, grants, etc. for the Cowcher Books, the fair copy of which was made by Frampton.[14]

As we would expect, the handwriting Frampton employs in writing the *Inspeximus* most closely resembles his handwriting in the first portion of the Huntington Library HM 19920 copy of the *Statutes* (fols 1r–226v), which were written in 1398 or soon after. Parkes describes the changes in Frampton's handwriting over the period when he was writing the seven books he lists, and this placement fits well with the characteristics of the hand in the *Inspeximus*, of which the original copy at least, and probably the second, illuminated, copy in quires, would have been written in 1399–1400.

According to Parkes, Frampton's hand is characterized by its distinctive aspect, by its curving approach strokes to **m**, **n**, **i** and long **r**, and by its formation of anglicana two-compartment **g**.[15] Parkes points to the curved and often elongated approach stroke to initial letters **m**, **n**, **i** and long **r**. This feature of his handwriting does not appear in its exaggerated form in the manuscripts and documents illustrated here, but something like this approach stroke can be seen in the Huntington Library copy of the *Statutes* (fig. 6.3, col. b, line 4, 'iustice', line 20, 'nul', etc.). A similar feature can also be seen in the original *Inspeximus* of Henry IV (fig. 6.1, line 1, 'nostri', line 6, 'nullus'); and in the *Inspeximus* inserted into the *Liber Albus* (fig. 6.2, line 6, 'nostri' and 'in'). The second characteristic Parkes points to is Frampton's formation of 8-shaped anglicana **g**. He writes:

> The hallmark of Frampton's **g** is the way he traced the strokes forming the bottom compartment of the letter. This was constructed with a diagonal hairline stroke descending from the point where the lobe joins the stem of the letter to the point where it was broken into the tail. The tail was completed by a short, shallow double curve (a broad stroke traced with a clockwise movement reversed into a shorter anti-clockwise movement) which rejoined the stem. The characteristic feature of Frampton's **g** is that the point where the hairline diagonal stroke was broken into the tail, is close to (and

---

[13] The first portion was borrowed and not returned by Cotton, who was notorious for such practices. See *Memorials of London and London Life*, ed. and trans. Riley, p. vii.

[14] Doyle and Parkes, 'Production of Copies', p. 192 (repr. p. 230), discuss Leventhorpe's compilation of the Cowcher Books and employment of Frampton to copy them, citing Somerville, 'The Cowcher Books of the Duchy of Lancaster', pp. 598–615, and Somerville, *History of the Duchy of Lancaster*, vol. 1 (London, 1953).

[15] Parkes, 'Richard Frampton', pp. 115–16.

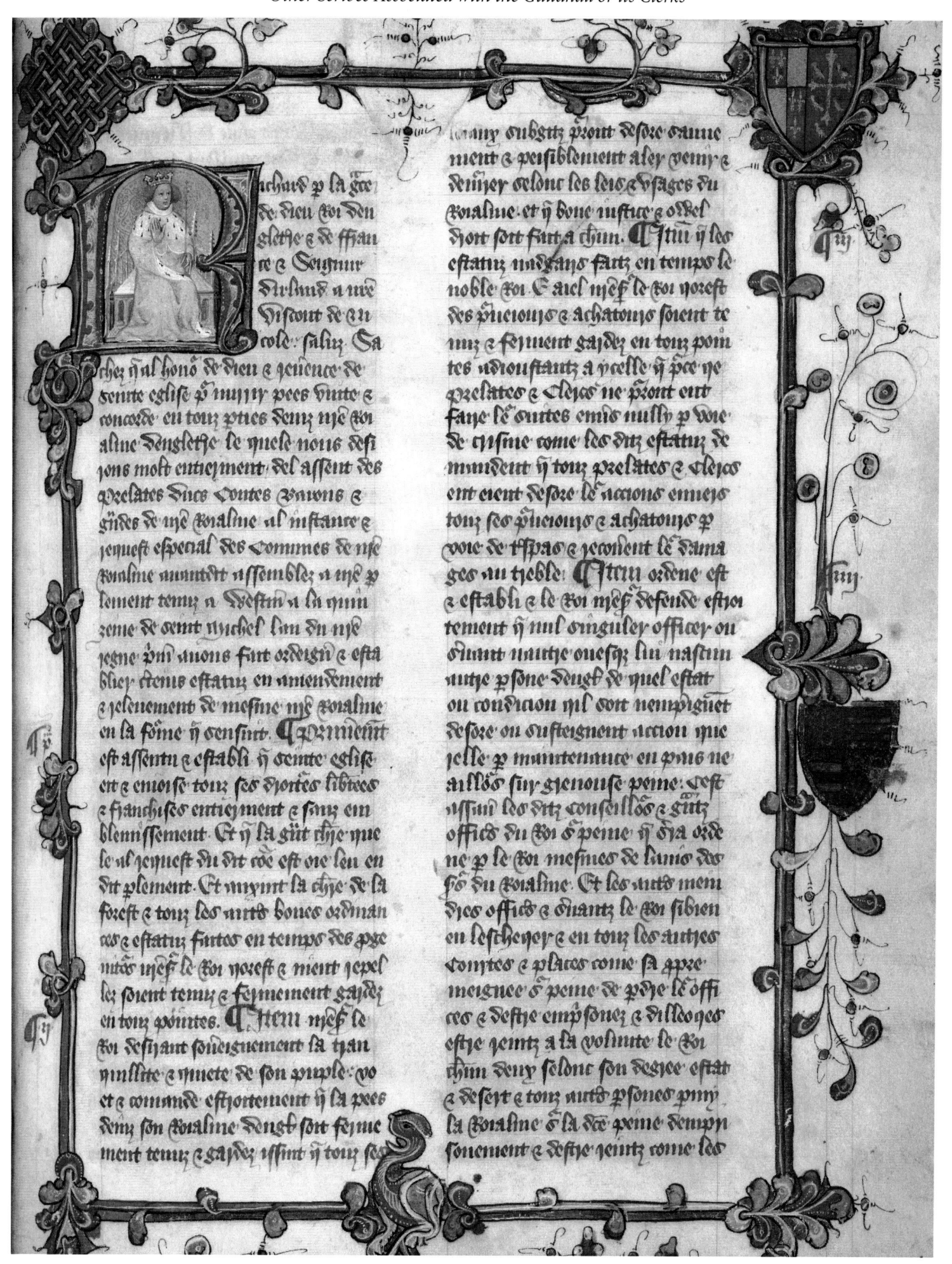

Fig. 6.3 San Marino, CA, Huntington Library, MS HM 19920, p. 173 (reduced): a copy of the *Statutes* written in the hand of Richard Frampton

Fig. 6.4 Kew, National Archives, DL 42/1, fol. 1r (reduced): First Great Cowcher Book of the Duchy of Lancaster, copied by Richard Frampton, 1402–3.

often beneath) the preceding letter, giving the false impression that the **g** is leaning backwards.

This characteristic **g** is illustrated in Frampton's copy of the *Statutes* (fig. 6.3, col. b, line 3, 'vsages', line 20, 'singuler'); in the original *Inspeximus* (fig. 6.1, line 6, 'danegeld'); and in the *Liber Albus* copy of the *Inspeximus* (fig. 6.2, fifth line from bottom, 'Angliam').

Another letter-form that is consistent across all samples of Frampton's handwriting is his lower-case **d**, whose upper part is formed of a broad straight line extending from the point where the top of the lobe meets the stem of the letter, angled back over the letter and beyond, often well to the left of the lobe, and then turns sharply to form an arched hairline curving back over the letter, running back to the point where the broad stroke joined the stem and lobe. The lobe itself is also often pointed toward the left rather than rounded. This **d** is illustrated in Frampton's copy of the *Statutes* (fig. 6.3, col. a, line 5, 'dirland'); in the original *Inspeximus* (fig. 6.1, line 6, 'de' several times in this line); and in the *Liber Albus* copy of the *Inspeximus* (fig. 6.2, line 5, 'domini').

Frampton shows a preference for sigma-shaped final **s** for terminal position; as well as occasionally using kidney-shaped **s** in this position, he also employs the two-compartment, 8-shaped anglicana **s**, especially in the earlier pieces of his writing. This 8-shaped **s** has the appearance of leaning forward because each of the lobes is ovoid with the top leaning to the right. This letter-form is illustrated in Frampton's *Statutes* (fig. 6.3, col. a, line 13, 'Barons'); in the original *Inspeximus* (fig. 6.1, line 1, 'progenitoris'); and in the *Liber Albus* copy of the *Inspeximus* (fig. 6.2, third line from bottom, 'hospites' and 'sokis'). Finally, we note an idiosyncratic combination of graphs in the Latin 'Et' in which the **t** is so close to the **E** that it almost sits inside the curve of the main stroke of **E**, and a single stroke serves for the crossing of both **E** and **t**: in the *Statutes* (fig. 6.3, col. b, line 30, 'Et'); in the original *Inspeximus* (fig. 6.1, line 10, 'Et'); and in the *Liber Albus* copy (fig. 6.2, four lines from bottom and seven lines from the bottom, 'Et').

Fig. 6.2, illustrating the first page of the *Liber Albus* copy of the *Inspeximus*, also shows Frampton using an archaizing hand to quote portions of two charters granted to the City of London by William the Conqueror. He uses this hand in lines 7–12, beginning with the words, 'William kyng', and again in lines 13–17 to quote from the second charter. Frampton is here repeating the archaizing of script that he had employed for these same passages in the original Charter 50 (see fig. 6.1, the last word of line 1 through line 3). In both cases Frampton copies not only the aspect and ductus of the older documents but the archaic Anglo-Saxon letter-forms as well. Parkes, who has written on the purposes for which scribes employed archaizing scripts, would probably describe Frampton here as one of those 'Scribes [who] employed hybrid archaizing hands when copying documents, in order to emphasize the authenticity of the copy by indicating that the originals contained letter forms appropriate to their purported dates.'[16] In other words, Frampton is trying to legitimize Henry IV's *Inspeximus* of the Conqueror's charters by writing these brief passages from the originals in the script they employed, to show that he was copying them directly. Frampton must have had access to the city's archives that preserved charters or copies of charters to have had the original charter of William the Conqueror before him, to enable him to copy the script. Thus he must have held some office at the Guildhall by 1399, at the beginning of the reign.

---

[16] M. B. Parkes, 'Archaizing Hands in English Manuscripts', in *Books and Collectors, 1200–1700: Essays Presented to Andrew Watson*, ed. J. P. Carley and C. G. C. Tite (London, 1997), pp. 101–41 (p. 102).

When Richard Frampton's copy of the *Inspeximus* was incorporated into the *Liber Albus* it was named in the introduction for Book II and listed in its index. It was further incorporated into the *Liber Albus* by the addition of running titles and marginal glosses in the hand of Richard Osbarn, the scribe who was responsible for assembling the *Liber Albus* from its constituent parts. Osbarn wrote the indices, running titles and marginal glosses as finding aids virtually throughout the *Liber Albus*, including portions incorporated from earlier sources, like the sixty-folio booklet of Henry IV's *Inspeximus*.

As we have discussed above, Osbarn was also a copyist of literary manuscripts, including Huntington Library HM 114 and Lambeth Palace Library MS 491.[17] This latter manuscript contains Osbarn's copy of the *Siege of Jerusalem* (Lambeth 491, fols 217r–227v), which is textually closest to that of Richard Frampton's *Siege* in Cambridge University Library MS Mm.5.14. These two copies of the *Siege* are members of the *delta* group of *Siege* manuscripts as defined by J. R. Hulbert and Mabel Day and refined by Hanna and Lawton. In this group Osbarn's copy and Frampton's copy are linked with a fragment of the *Siege* now in Exeter, Devon Record Office, MS 2507, copied half a century later, and British Library, MS Cotton Caligula A.ii, part 1, also copied in the second half of the fifteenth century and switching to conflate with another exemplar belonging to the *gamma* group of manuscripts part-way through.[18] Thus although neither Osbarn's nor Frampton's copies were made from each other, they did share an archetype. This makes them the most closely affiliated manuscripts of the *delta* group, circulating in the southern part of England in the early fifteenth century. Hanna and Lawton further suggest that they represent a deliberate distribution of the *Siege of Jerusalem* text in London, perhaps by a wealthy Yorkshire patron:

> The group *delta* reflects the most southerly dispersal of *The Siege*. Both our copies U [Cambridge Univ. Library Mm.5.14] and D [Lambeth 491, part 1, fols 217r–27v] represent London work of the period *c.* 1410–25, and testify to a relatively early movement out of the poet's home locale [in West Yorkshire], in which *beta* had circulated. Here we may be dealing with some variety of patronal distribution, in which the fruits of a provincial culture have been marketed by that patron within the ambit of a developing national capital-based culture.[19]

At least two possible mechanisms for such distribution suggest themselves. On the one hand, if one imagines *The Siege* as having been composed at Bolton Abbey, the poem might have been distributed by the abbey's patrons, the Clifford earls of Skipton. Thomas, the sixth lord, a knight of the King's Chamber under Richard II, could well have been the medium by which the text came south to the capital. On the other hand, Richard Frampton, the scribe of U, did most of his identifiable copying for the Duchy of Lancaster; the text could have been available to him through Duchy sources, and might have come south with other materials from Duchy headquarters near Pontefract (West Yorks.).[20]

---

[17] He has been called 'the HM 114 Scribe' in articles by scholars including R. Hanna, L. R. Mooney and J. Bowers. For his identification as Richard Osbarn see Chapter 2 above.

[18] J. R. Hulbert, 'The Text of *The Siege of Jerusalem*', *Studies in Philology* 28 (1930), 602–12; *The Siege of Jerusalem*, ed. E. Kölbing and M. Day, EETS OS 188 (1932; repr. 2001), with analysis of manuscripts in Day's introduction (see esp. pp. ix–xi); *Siege of Jerusalem*, ed. Hanna and Lawton, pp. lv–lxxiv.

[19] Compare Hanna, 'Thomas Berkeley and his Patronage', pp. 909–13.

[20] *Siege of Jerusalem*, ed. Hanna and Lawton, pp. lxviii–lxix.

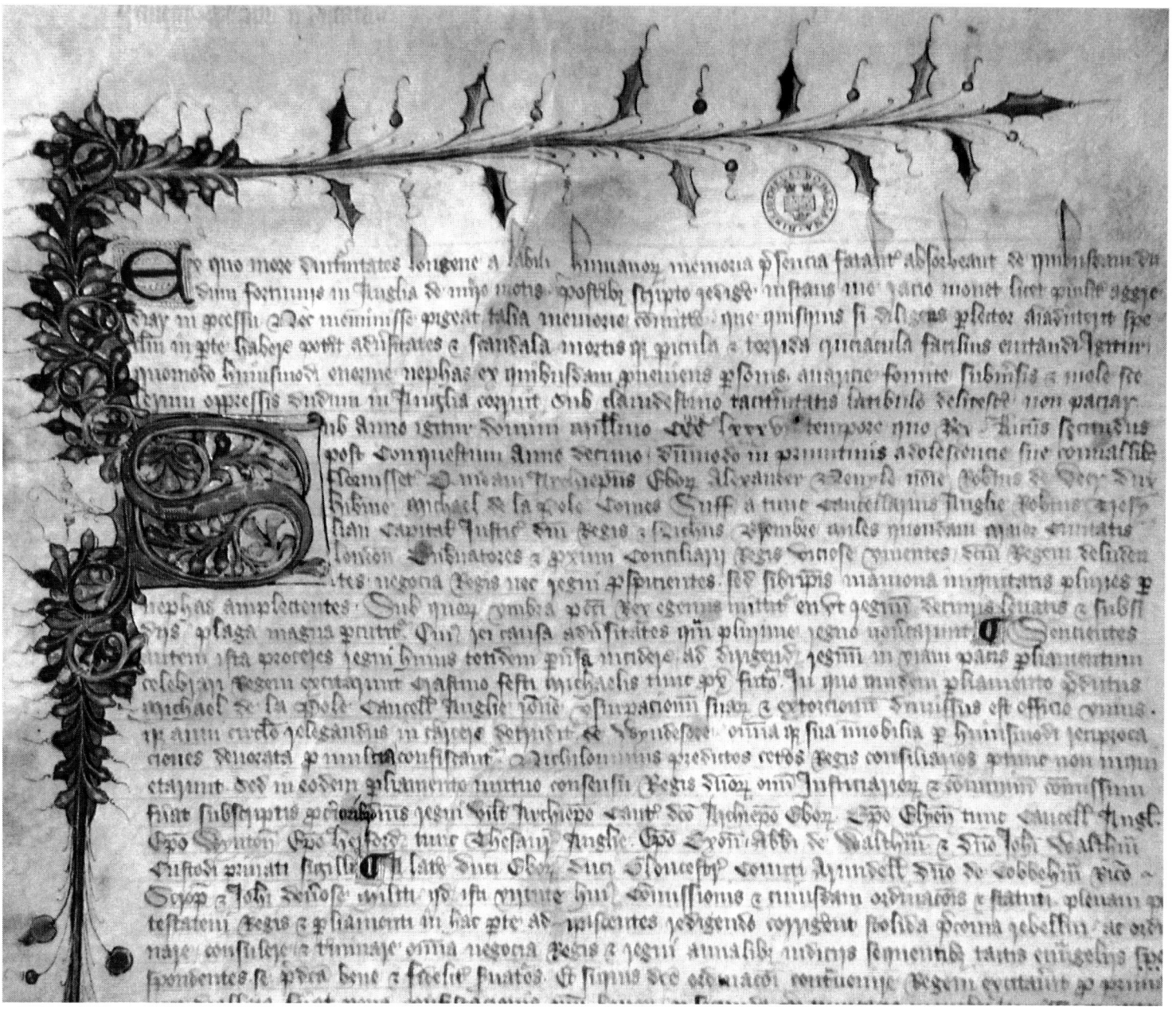

Other Scribes Associated with the Guildhall or its Clerks

Fig. 6.5 Oxford, Bodleian Library, Bodley misc. 2963, or Rolls 9, m. 1 (top):
Thomas Favent's *Historia sive narracio de modo et forma mirabilis parliamenti apud Westmonasterium*, copied by Richard Frampton

Another similarity between the literary productions of these two men is that both appear to have produced their copies of literary texts in booklets which were later bound together: Osbarn's HM 114 is composed of three booklets, his Lambeth 491 of two booklets; while Frampton's Glasgow Hunterian T.4.1 is composed of two booklets. From the evidence of the close textual affiliation of copies of *The Siege* by these two scribes it appears that Frampton had some kind of link to the Guildhall clerical staff, or perhaps may have served in its office in the 1390s before becoming a full-time Lancastrian employee.

We have discovered another document written by Frampton that connects him still further with the house of Lancaster, and with the same London political faction around John of Northampton with which Marchaunt and Pinkhurst were connected: his is the hand of one of only two surviving manuscripts of Thomas Favent's *Historia*, recording events of the Merciless Parliament of 1388 (fig. 6.5).[21]

---

[21] Oxford, Bodleian Library, Bodley misc. 2963, or Rolls 9; T. Favent, *Historia sive narracio de modo et forma mirabilis parliamenti apud Westmonasterium*, ed. M. McKisack, in *Camden*

Favent's *Historia* is a partisan account of the Merciless Parliament at which the Lords Appellant tried and executed several of Richard II's favourites, including Nicholas Brembre: the petitions of the Mercers, Leathersellers and White Tawiers, and ten other livery companies of London were addressed to the Lords Appellant in this parliament. Gwilym Dodd, to whom we owe our initial view of this document, comments that although historians had previously speculated that the then single known surviving manuscript was written by Favent's own hand, we cannot know whether Bodley misc. 2963 was the original fair copy (in which case Favent and Frampton may have been 'closely acquainted and directly collaborated to produce the *Historia*') or whether it was merely Frampton's copy of another, earlier manuscript of the *Historia*.[22] Dodd acknowledges that both Favent and the copyist Frampton may have been commissioned to write and copy the *Historia*, or might have written it or copied the surviving manuscript 'for the same reasons that Thomas Usk wrote the *Testament of Love*, as an unsolicited gift intended to curry favour with London's oligarchy in the hope that lucrative office or employment would follow.'[23] In either case, both men's careers seem not to have been harmed by the *Historia*, since Favent subsequently held the position of Collector of Tunnage and Poundage in the Port of London, 1391–5, and Frampton subsequently found permanent employment in the Lancastrian chancery.[24]

THOMAS USK & JOHN BRYNCHLEY

THE SECOND CLERK associated with those we have identified at the Guildhall who showed an interest in Middle English literature was the poet Thomas Usk. In 2004 Caroline Barron identified the clerk of the Goldsmiths' Company, named in their accounts before 1384, as the poet Thomas Usk: his name had previously been mistranscribed, so his identity as the clerk for the company had not been known.[25] Usk had written an appeal (in English) against the former mayor John of Northampton in 1384, when he was himself imprisoned for his collusion with Northampton's faction. He was subsequently released and promoted to the position of serjeant-at-arms by Richard II, and then fell again when he was tried and executed by the Merciless Parliament in 1388.[26] He is known to literary scholars as the author of *The Testament of Love*, written between his release and death. Usk was the son of a Londoner; his father was a member of the craft of cap makers.[27]

Miscellany XIV, Camden Society 3rd series 37 (1926); T. Favent, *History or Narration Concerning the Manner and Form of the Miraculous Parliament at Westminster*, trans. A. Galloway, in *The Letter of the Law: Legal Practice and Literary Production in Medieval England*, ed. E. Steiner and C. Barrington (Ithaca NY, 2002), pp. 231–52; J. Taylor, 'Favent, Thomas', in *Oxford Dictionary of National Biography* (Oxford, 2004). The only other known surviving copy is in private hands in New York City; we thank Gwilym Dodd for this reference and for allowing us to see an image of this manuscript, which we conclude is *not* written by the hand of Richard Frampton.

[22] G. Dodd, 'Was Thomas Favent a Political Pamphleteer? Faction And Politics in Later Fourteenth-Century London', *Journal of Medieval History* 30 (2011), 1–22.

[23] Ibid.

[24] Ibid.; Taylor, 'Favent, Thomas'.

[25] C. M. Barron, 'Review of Lisa Jefferson (ed.), *Wardens' Accounts and Court Minute Books of the Goldsmiths' Mistery of London, 1334–1446*', *Urban History* 32 (2005), 173–5.

[26] Usk's appeal was published as an early example of London English in *Book of London English*, ed. Chambers and Daunt, pp. 18–31.

[27] J. Leyerle, 'Thomas Usk', in *Dictionary of the Middle Ages*, ed. J. R. Strayer, vol. 12 (New York, 1989), pp. 333–5 (p. 333).

Other Scribes Associated with the Guildhall or its Clerks

Usk worked as clerk of the Goldsmiths' Company in 1380-3, and supported the faction in London politics led by John of Northampton in which prominent Goldsmiths such as Adam Bamme were also involved.[28] When the tides turned against the Northampton faction Usk was imprisoned. Presumably to gain his freedom and win favour he wrote his appeal, or accusation, against John of Northampton and his three confederates, John More, Richard Norbury and William Essex, confessing his own part in Northampton's activities. He also named others who had been involved, including Adam Bamme, fellow Goldsmith, and John Marchaunt, who had been chamber clerk of London in 1380-3 as we have noted above.[29]

In her article 'Usk and the Goldsmiths' Marion Turner examined the cultural environment in which Usk worked – the social, commercial and material world of London livery companies – and Usk's own reliance on the truths of that mercantile culture.[30] She concluded that 'The literary activities of the scribes employed by the Goldsmiths and their fellow great livery companies [Pinkhurst by the Mercers, Brynchley by the Tailors] reveal to us a new aspect of late-fourteenth-century literary culture: these clerks formed a conduit between the livery companies and the writings of men such as Chaucer and Gower.'[31] Usk's *Testament of Love*, written in 1385-7, is frequently cited as a witness to the earliest readers of the writings of Geoffrey Chaucer, in particular of his *Troilus and Criseyde* which was written in the years immediately preceding.[32] As both poet and clerk, Usk illustrates that the clerks of the London livery companies not only read and responded to the writings of men such as Chaucer and Gower, but emulated them by composing their own literary pieces. The clerks of the London Guildhall and/or of the livery companies may themselves be responsible for some of the anonymous Middle English writings surviving in late medieval manuscripts produced in London.

John Brynchley, clerk of the Tailors' Company, offers early evidence of ownership of a manuscript of Chaucer's *Canterbury Tales*, which he left in his will of July 1420 to William Holgrave, another Tailor.[33] As Manly and Rickert note, he also bequeathed both a Latin and an English copy of Boethius's *Consolation of Philosophy*, the English one presumably Chaucer's *Boece*.[34] Matthew Davies and Ann Saunders point out that Brynchley was not a

---

[28] For the factions in London politics in the 1370s and 1380s, and beyond, see Bird, *Turbulent London*. For the history of the Goldsmiths' Company, see T. F. Reddaway, *The Early History of The Goldsmiths' Company, 1327-1509*, bound with *The Book of Ordinances, 1478-83*, ed. L. E. M. Walker (London, 1975).

[29] For studies of Usk's involvement in the factions, and of his appeal, see P. Strohm, 'Politics and Poetics: Usk and Chaucer in the 1380s', in *Literary Practice and Social Change in Britain, 1380-1530*, ed. L. Patterson (Berkeley 1990), pp. 83-112. For the naming of Marchaunt see Chapter 3 above.

[30] M. Turner, 'Usk and the Goldsmiths', *New Medieval Literatures* 9 (2007), pp. 139-77.

[31] Turner, 'Usk and the Goldsmiths', p. 176.

[32] For discussion of the earliest readers of Chaucer, including Usk, see P. Strohm, *Social Chaucer* (Cambridge MA, 1989), pp. 24-83, and Pearsall, *The Life of Geoffrey Chaucer*, pp. 181-5; M. Turner, *Chaucerian Conflict: Languages of Antagonism in Late Fourteenth-Century London* (Oxford, 2006), chap. 4. For an edition of his *Testament*, see T. Usk, *The Testament of Love*, ed. R. A. Shoaf, TEAMS Middle English Texts series (Kalamazoo MI, 1998).

[33] *Text of 'The Canterbury Tales'*, ed. Manly and Rickert, I, 607; for text of the will, C. F. E. Spurgeon, *Five Hundred Years of Chaucer Criticism and Allusion, 1357-1900*, 8 vols., Chaucer Society 2nd series 48-50 and 52-6 (Cambridge, 1908-17), I, 25-6; *The Fifty Earliest English Wills, 1387-1439*, ed. F. J. Furnivall, EETS OS 78 (1882), p. 136.

[34] *Text of 'The Canterbury Tales'*, Manly and Rickert, I, 607.

professional scribe but a tailor who later took on the role of clerk for the company.[35] His will is one more piece of evidence that clerks of London livery companies either wrote or purchased manuscripts of Middle English literature.

THE PETWORTH SCRIBE

MANY YEARS AGO Jeremy Griffiths identified a scribe of four Middle English literary manuscripts as the clerk of the Skinners' Company of London in 1441, the so-called Petworth scribe.[36] The manuscripts he identified as written by this hand were London, British Library, MS Arundel 119; Cambridge, Pembroke College Library, MS 307; Tokyo, Takamiya Collection, MS 54; and Oslo and London, Schøyen Collection, MS 615. These, Griffiths argued, matched the hand that wrote fols 2r–19r of the Guild Book of the Fraternity of Our Lady's Assumption (one of the religious guilds that formed the Skinners' Company of London), copying (probably all at one time) the ordinances of the company and lists of wardens and members from 21 Richard II to 19 Henry VI (1398–1441). Other scholars have added to the list of manuscripts proposed as written by this hand, though Ian Doyle considered that some were copied by another hand of similar training.[37] If all the manuscripts proposed are by a single hand, his literary manuscripts include the following:

Cambridge, Pembroke College, MS 307
   John Gower, *Confessio Amantis*

Edinburgh, National Library of Scotland, MS Advocates 18.1.7, fols 6r–23v
   Nicholas Love, *Mirror of the Blessed Life of Jesus Christ*

Lichfield, Cathedral Library, MS 29, fols 196v–293v
   Geoffrey Chaucer, *Canterbury Tales*

London, British Library, MS Arundel 119
   John Lydgate, *Siege of Thebes*

London, British Library, MS Sloane 3501
   Master of Game

Oslo & London, Schøyen Collection, MS 615 [*olim* H. C. Pratt]
   John Walton, *Boethius*

Petworth House, Sussex (The National Trust), MS 7, fols 9r–307v
   Geoffrey Chaucer, *Canterbury Tales*

Tokyo, Takamiya Collection, MS 45, single leaf
   Gilte Legend fragment

---

[35] M. Davies with A. Saunders, *The History of the Merchant Taylors' Company* (Leeds, 2004), pp. 43, 275.

[36] J. Griffiths, 'Thomas Hingham, Monk of Bury and the Macro Plays Manuscript', *English Manuscript Studies* 5 (1995), 214–19 (p. 214). The four he identified then were Schøyen Collection MS 615, Pembroke College MS 307, British Library, MS Arundel 119, and the second hand of Takamiya Collection MS 54. See also Scott, *Survey: Later Gothic Manuscripts*, II, 343.

[37] A. I. Doyle, 'The Study of Nicholas Love's *Mirror*: Retrospect and Prospect', in *Nicholas Love at Waseda: Proceedings of the International Conference, 20–26 July 1995*, ed. S. Oguro et al. (Cambridge, 1997), pp. 163–74 (pp. 172–3).

Tokyo, Takamiya Collection, MS 54, fols 17r–194v
   South English Legendary

Tokyo, Waseda University, NE 3691
   Nicholas Love, *Mirror of the Blessed Life of Jesus Christ*

Whether all of these or only the four originally identified by Griffiths are by the clerk of the Skinners' Company, his copying of several manuscripts of literary texts illustrates yet another clerk of a livery company in and around the Guildhall who was engaged in this activity, though a generation after the clerks we have been describing.[38]

A BREWER'S COMPANY SCRIBE

STILL MORE EVIDENCE has recently emerged of literary copying in and around the Guildhall. Simon Horobin has recently identified the hand of Oxford, Bodleian Library, MS Digby 102 as the second clerk in the Brewers' Company accounts for the first few decades of the fifteenth century.[39] This manuscript (Digby 102) contains a copy of the C text of William Langland's *Piers Plowman* together with Richard Maidstone's *Seven Penitential Psalms* and the anonymous *Debate between the Body and the Soul*.[40] As Horobin points out, Digby 102 preserves 'one of the best manuscripts of the C text'[41] which is very closely affiliated with two other copies of the C text, San Marino, CA, Huntington Library, HM 143, and London, University of London Library MS SL V.88, the so-called Ilchester manuscript, written by John Marchaunt. Horobin identified this hand in the Memorandum Book of the London Brewers' Guild, writing some entries among those by the main hand, that of Brewers' Company clerk William Porland (d. 1441), for instance on fol. 50r.[42] He offered a probable identification of this clerk as Robert Lynford, who was a junior clerk working with William Porland, member of the Brewers' Company (he is named in a list submitted to the mayor in 1420) and resident in the Brewers' Hall itself.[43] His entries to the Memorandum Book can be dated 1418–41, but Horobin argued for copying of Digby 102 in the first quarter of the fifteenth century, toward the earlier part of his employment as an apprentice under William Porland.[44]

Horobin pointed to evidence of the sharing of exemplars of texts such as *Piers Plowman* among clerks of the Guildhall and those of the livery companies, particularly those with halls near the Guildhall: the Brewers, Bowyers, Barbers, Pinners, Curriers and Girdlers.[45] His suggestion that the Guildhall itself served as a focus for the sharing of exemplars of

---

[38] More work needs to be done to clarify whether all or only some of these manuscripts are written by the hand of the Skinners' Company clerk.

[39] S. Horobin, 'The Scribe of Bodleian Library, MS Digby 102 and the Circulation of the C Text of *Piers Plowman*', *Yearbook of Langland Studies* 24 (2010), 89–112.

[40] Langland's *Piers Plowman* is *Index of Middle English Verse* number 1459 (the C-text is number 2460 in the online *DIMEV*); Maidstone's *Seven Penitential Psalms* is numbered 1961 (print), and 3207 (online). The *Debate* is numbered 351 (print), and 605 (online).

[41] Horobin, 'The Scribe of MS Digby 102', p. 89.

[42] Ibid., pp. 94–6, fig. 3 (illustrating fol. 50r). The memorandum book is London Metropolitan Archives, CLC/L/BF/A/021, or Brewers' Company Memorandum Book, Guildhall MS 05440.

[43] Horobin, 'The Scribe of MS Digby 102', pp. 96–7.

[44] Ibid., pp. 97–8.

[45] Ibid., pp. 99–101.

vernacular literary manuscripts is further supported by our identification of the HM 114 Scribe as Richard Osbarn, by our new evidence of Pinkhurst's probable employment at the Guildhall, and in particular by our identification of Scribe D as John Marchaunt, copyist of one of the other two manuscripts of *Piers Plowman* whose text is closest to that of Digby 102.[46]

THOMAS URSEWYKE & RICHARD SOTHEWORTH

ANOTHER CLERK OF THE GUILDHALL who demonstrated an interest in Middle English literature was Thomas Ursewyke, who was first serjeant, then recorder of London 1453–71, and then Chief Baron of the Exchequer from 1471 until his death in 1479. An inventory of his goods in 1479 included books kept in his chapel, including a manuscript of Chaucer's *Canterbury Tales* which Manly and Rickert thought most likely to be the Hengwrt manuscript, National Library of Wales, MS Peniarth 392D, copied by Adam Pinkhurst.[47] Ursewyke may also have owned the copy of John Gower's *Confessio Amantis* in Cambridge, Trinity College, MS R.3.2, in which Marchaunt, Pinkhurst and Thomas Hoccleve each had a part, since Doyle and Parkes read his name in drypoint in the upper corner of fol. 120r, 'Thomas Wrswyk', as the probable owner.[48] Scholars have tried to connect the manuscript with Westminster and royal clerks through Ursewyke,[49] but our identifications of Marchaunt and Pinkhurst as employees at the Guildhall, and of the literary copying and dissemination that appears to have been centred there, suggest instead that Ursewyke's acquisition of Hengwrt and MS R.3.2 could date from his years as recorder of London instead.

Another recorder of London could also have owned a *Canterbury Tales* manuscript. Manly and Rickert noted that the earliest mention of a manuscript of the *Tales* was in the will of Richard Sotheworth (d. 1419), who left 'quendam librum meum de Canterbury Tales' to John Stopyndon (*fl.* 1447/8); they further suggest that Richard may have been the son of Matthew Sotheworth (or Matthew de Southworth), who was recorder of London in 1401.[50] They were unable to identify the manuscript named in the will with any now surviving, there being so few that had been written before 1420. Thus the two earliest records naming manuscripts of *The Canterbury Tales* may be connected with officers of the Guildhall.

---

[46] Ibid., pp. 100–1. Further work is called for to identify the scribe who copied the third manuscript closely affiliated with these two, Huntington Library MS HM 143.

[47] *Text of 'The Canterbury Tales'*, ed. Manly and Rickert, I, 616–17.

[48] Doyle and Parkes, 'Production of Copies', p. 209 (repr. p. 247).

[49] See K. Kerby-Fulton and S. Justice, 'Langlandian Reading Circles and the Civil Service in London and Dublin, 1380–1427', *New Medieval Literatures* 1 (1997), 59–83. Doyle and Parkes, 'Production of Copies', p. 209 (repr. p. 247), suggests that the 'Ursewyke' whose name appears in Trinity College MS R.3.2 may have been 'an earlier namesake of Urswick [the Recorder of London], Receiver of the County Palatine of Lancaster, and perhaps Sir Thomas's father or kinsman although he may not have frequented the capital until the 1420s.'

[50] *Text of 'The Canterbury Tales'*, ed. Manly and Rickert, I, 606. Barron, *London in the Later Middle Ages*, p. 356, shows that he was recorder also in 1398, citing Letter Book H, fol. 444; her next recorder on ths list is Thomas Thornburgh in 1404, so the period of Sotheworth's tenure was at least 1398–1401, and possibly until 1404.

THOMAS HOCCLEVE & THE CLERKS OF THE GUILDHALL

BOTH Adam Pinkhurst and John Marchaunt contributed to the writing of the Trinity College MS R.3.2 copy of John Gower's *Confessio Amantis*. This manuscript was the focus of an article by Doyle and Parkes[51] in which Pinkhurst and Marchaunt are designated scribes B and D respectively, because theirs are the second and fourth hands in the manuscript. The identification of scribe E, the fifth scribe of the manuscript, as Thomas Hoccleve places its production in London or Westminster.[52] Our further identifications of Pinkhurst and Marchaunt help to pinpoint its production in London, near or within the Guildhall close. How, then, does the poet and Privy Seal clerk, Thomas Hoccleve, become involved as the fifth hand in this multiple-scribe manuscript?

Thomas Hoccleve's contribution to the manuscript is quite small, consisting of less than three folios (82r–84r) at the beginning of quire 11 and a catchword on the singleton leaf inserted between quires 4 and 5. Scribe A wrote the preceding quire (quire 10) and went on to complete Hoccleve's quire (quire 11), but forty-six lines (one column) are left out of the text, corresponding to a blank column on fol. 84rb, between Hoccleve's and Scribe A's copying. Doyle and Parkes offered two possible explanations for this hiatus.[53] Their first is that Scribe A's exemplar for quire 10 had more text than would fit into his copy (perhaps revisions written into the margins, since this is one of the places where Gower added material for his second recension). That quire of the exemplar passed from his hands before he was given the next to copy, so he left five sides blank at the beginning of his next quire (quire 11) to accommodate this overflow material later. They then surmise that Hoccleve set out to fill the gap, but either omitted forty-six lines because of *homoioteleuton* (the word *con* occurs both at the beginning of the omitted passage and in the first line of Scribe A's continuation of the quire) or because the exemplar he was using lacked those lines. Their second explanation is that Hoccleve began copying quire 11 as his stint in the manuscript but abandoned his work after nine columns (possibly because his exemplar was incomplete), and Scribe A completed it, leaving a blank column either because his exemplar was deficient or for another reason (including *homoioiteleuton*, as above). They do not offer an explanation why Hoccleve should have begun but not finished the quire, or, in the former possibility, why he should have been the one to fill in the gap.[54]

Doyle and Parkes conclude from the additional singleton added between quires 4 and 5 that the scribes were copying line for line and page for page from their exemplar (otherwise Scribe C would not have needed an extra sheet, and could have simply written the sixty-four lines that Pinkhurst omitted because of misruling at the beginning of quire 5.[55] On the other hand, it seems clear that the scribes were not working in this way by the point in the

---

[51] Doyle and Parkes, 'Production of Copies', pp. 164–82 (repr. pp. 202–20).

[52] Ibid., pp. 182–5 (repr. pp. 220–3).

[53] Ibid., pp. 204–6 (repr. pp. 242–4).

[54] Ibid., pp. 166–7, 185 (repr. pp. 204–5, 223), where Doyle and Parkes conclude that there was no central figure overseeing the production of this manuscript, but by 'supervisor' we mean the person who was distributing quires to the various scribes for copying.

[55] Ibid., p. 165 (repr. p. 203). Pinkhurst had ruled his third quire with forty-four instead of the usual forty-six lines per column, so when he finished his stint, there were sixty-four lines remaining (two per column, four per side for sixteen sides) that he had not written in quire 4: thus the need for Scribe C to write them onto a singleton leaf to be inserted between the end of Pinkhurst's stint (quires 2–4) and the beginning of his (quires 5–6).

Table 6.1 Scribal contributions to Trinity College MS R.3.2

Quire	Extent	Scribe
I	8 leaves	C? or D?
II	8 leaves	C? or D?
III	8 leaves	C? or D?
IV	8 leaves	A? or D?
V	8 leaves	A? or D?
1	fols 1–8	A
2	fols 9–16	B
3	fols 17–24	B
4	fols 25–32	B
added leaf	fol. 33ra–va	C
catchword	fol. 33va	E
5	fols 34–41	C
6	fols 42–49	C
7	fols 50–57	A
8	fols 58–65	C
9	fols 66–73	D
10	fols 74–81	A
11	fols 82–84ra	E
	fols 84rb–89vb	A
12	fols 90–97	C
13	fols 98–105	A
14	fols 106–113rb	A
	fols 133rb–113vb	D
15	fols 114–121	D
16	fols 122–129	D
17	fols 130–137	D
18	fols 138–145	D
19	fols 146–153	D

copying where Hoccleve's hand begins (quires 11–12), for although there had been overflow from quire 10 causing problems for the copying of quire 11, the following quire 12 shows no indecision about where to begin the text: thus Scribe C must have copied quire 12 only after Scribe A had completed quire 11.

Table 6.1 shows the quires and folios copied by each of the five scribes who contributed to writing Trinity College MS R.3.2, also accounting for the missing five quires that would once have stood at the beginning of the manuscript. The supervisor may have begun by assigning three quires per stint to the scribes (assigning them simultaneously for line-for-line copying), but then reduced the numbers of quires to one or two after the problems encountered in quire 10, allowing time for each scribe (with the possible exception of Hoccleve) to complete his stint before the next took over. It seems likely that Gower's revisions are to blame for this change in the plan of production, since his additions (added to margins or inserted as extra leaves) would throw off the line-for-line copying from the exemplar. Doyle and Parkes noted that Gower made revisions in this way in explaining why Scribe A ran into difficulties in quire 10:

> If these extra lines had already been incorporated within the pattern of regular eight-leaf quires and forty-six-line columns in his exemplar, Scribe A would not have been faced with a problem. However, if the extra lines had been written in the margins or on

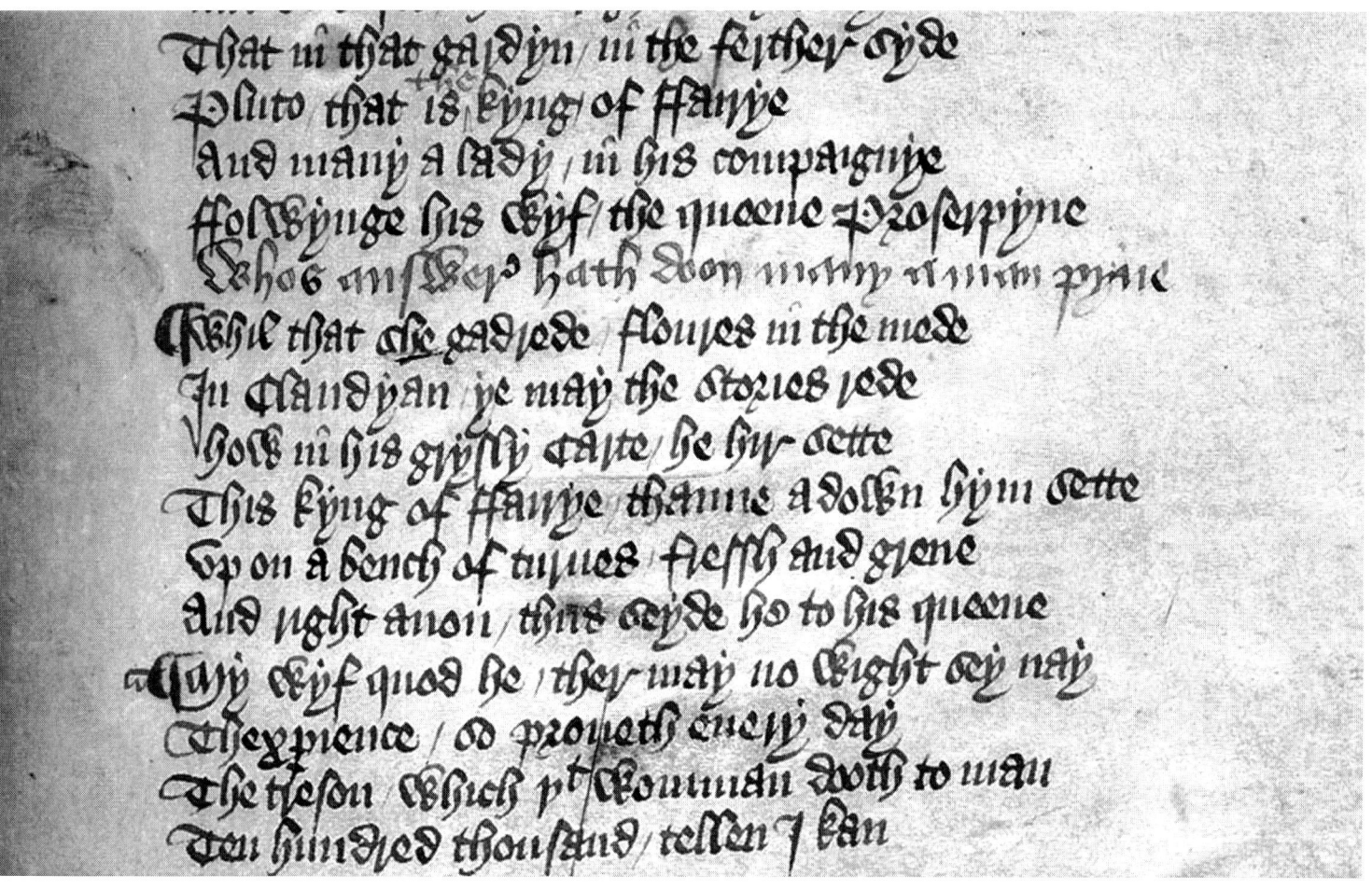

Fig. 6.6 Aberystwyth, National Library of Wales, MS Peniarth 392D, fol. 150r (extract): showing where a hand probably identifiable as that of Thomas Hoccleve inserted the missing line (the fifth line of the image)

inserted leaves (and it seems likely that this was Gower's procedure when revising), the copyist would have found himself with an overflow of material at the end of his own regular quire.[56]

They did not carry this analysis to its logical conclusion, that this copy of the *Confessio Amantis* must have been made from an exemplar copy to which Gower himself had made revisions.

Hoccleve may also have supplied the catchword to the bottom of fol. 33va where Scribe C completed the sixty-four lines left out by Pinkhurst's misruling.[57] Supplying a catchword when the scribe does not do so is usually the task of the supervisor of a manuscript's production, but Hoccleve's very limited contribution to this manuscript seems (at first) to counter any conclusion that he served in this capacity for the Trinity College MS R.3.2 copy of *Confessio Amantis*.[58] However, it was he who had access to the exemplar for quire 10 after it had been removed from Scribe A's possession, and this would seem to suggest some role as the one who distributed quires to the various scribes who contributed to the volume, his own contributions coming only to finish the material at the two trouble spots.

Hoccleve also may have intervened to finish incomplete lines in the Hengwrt manuscript of the *Canterbury Tales* copied by Pinkhurst (fig. 6.6).[59] Doyle and Parkes noted (tentatively)

---

[56] Ibid., p. 204 (repr. p. 242).

[57] Ibid., p. 166 (repr. p. 204), suggests that this catchword was 'probably E's hand'.

[58] Ibid., pp. 166–7 (repr. pp. 204–5) makes this point too.

[59] The hands of Hoccleve and Pinkhurst are thus linked in these two manuscripts which may later have been owned by Thomas Ursewyck; see p. 122 above.

Hoccleve's completion of lines or half-lines in the text of the Hengwrt manuscript that Pinkhurst had left blank, presumably because they were missing from the exemplar he was copying (an exemplar presumably written in Chaucer's own hand) or because he could not read the exemplar at this point because it was smudged or partially erased.[60] Hoccleve completed lines on fols 88v, 138v, and 150r, as follows (with words written by Hoccleve's hand in boldface):

Fol. 88v:
(*CT* D.2048: Summoner's Tale, part of the friar's sermon)

> Seyde on a day bitwix hem two right thus
> A lord is **lost if he be vicious**
> And dronkenesse is eek a foul record

Fol. 138v:
(*CT* D.1305–6: Merchant's Tale, January's encomium of marriage)

> And if thow take a wyf **she wole destroye**
> **Thy good substance and thy body annoye**
> This sentence and an hundred thynges worse

Fol. 150r:
(*CT* E.2230: Merchant's Tale, Pluto and Proserpina in the garden)

> ffolynge his wyf the queene Proserpyne
> **Whos answere hath doon many a man pyne**
> Whil that she gadrede floures in the mede

These incomplete lines may indicate that Pinkhurst was copying from a very rough draft or wax tablets that might easily be rubbed by accident to obscure the text. As Daniel Mosser points out, leaving the lines blank rather than completing them himself shows that Pinkhurst was a careful and non-intrusive copyist.[61]

Hoccleve may have completed the lines some time after the initial copying of the Hengwrt manuscript: he need not have been present in an editorial capacity when Pinkhurst was copying it, or even immediately thereafter. He may have had access to the finished copy of Hengwrt and felt compelled to complete these lines from another exemplar, or he may have owned the manuscript himself. Yet another possibility, if we assume that Chaucer was still living at least during part of Pinkhurst's copying, is that Hoccleve carried the finished quires between London and Westminster (a journey he made almost daily), and filled in these spaces that Pinkhurst could not read in the foul papers from Chaucer's dictation.

This shows Hoccleve as a perfectionist where copies of Chaucer's works were concerned, wanting to fill any small gaps left by the scribes. He may have been just as fastidious when it came to manuscripts of other Middle English authors. If he had similar access to the completed copy of the Trinity College MS R.3.2 *Confessio Amantis* and noticed that the quire signature was missing on the added singleton leaf, he may have felt he should add it to fol. 33v, even well after its original copying.

---

[60] Doyle and Parkes, 'Palaeographical Introduction', p. xlvi.

[61] Mosser, 'Adam and the Hengwrt Project', pp. 29–33. Mosser also quotes Norman Blake with regard to the smaller gaps in the text in the Hengwrt manuscript, 'This behaviour suggests that the scribe of Hg [the Hengwrt manuscript] did not add anything to the text on his own initiative.' Blake, *Textual Tradition of the 'Canterbury Tales'*, p. 65.

Other Scribes Associated with the Guildhall or its Clerks

How did Hoccleve become involved in the copying of Trinity College MS R.3.2 at all? Our recent discovery that Hoccleve's father was William Hoccleve (or Occleve), Draper of London, gives the poet a family connection with the city, but not necessarily with the clerks of the Guildhall.[62] Was it through the connection with Chaucer that he was acquainted with Pinkhurst and thus with the textwriter-clerks in and around the Guildhall? Linne Mooney has shown that Hoccleve was in fact acquainted with Chaucer by demonstrating that he wrote the 9 November 1399 Privy Seal document acknowledging Henry IV's renewal of Chaucer's annuity and commanding the exchequer to pay him the £10 he was owed in arrears.[63] Her discovery of Privy Seal documents written by Hoccleve's hand as early as 1383, probably during his apprenticeship under Guy de Rouclif, shows that he could have known John Gower too, since he may have already been working at the Office of the Privy Seal by 1382, when de Rouclif sold Gower two properties.[64] Thus Hoccleve may have known not only Chaucer but Pinkhurst and Gower as well.[65] In regard to the catchword on fol. 33v of the Trinity *Confessio Amantis*, an additional speculative explanation would be that if Hoccleve had access to the Pinkhurst quires before they were put together with the stints of other scribes, it may have been he who noticed the gap left as a result of Pinkhurst's misruling, and saw to it that his error was made good. Rather than write the singleton leaf himself, which would have introduced a different hand for a very short stint, he perhaps asked Scribe C to write it, since a reader would encounter his hand anyway in the next quire. Hoccleve could then have added the catchword himself.

Hoccleve may have known the clerks at the Guildhall not only through Chaucer and Gower but generally through acquaintance with the circle of literate clerks in London and Westminster. His minor poems include three addressed to Sir Henry Somer, who served as a clerk of the Exchequer (parallel with Hoccleve's position in the Privy Seal) until 1405, when Somer was promoted to Keeper of the Privy Wardrobe, then further promoted to baron of the Exchequer (1408), and chancellor of the Exchequer (1410). Hoccleve addressed a begging poem to him in 1408, soon after his elevation to baron of the Exchequer, or 'Soustresorer', hoping that the clerks of the Privy Seal might receive their annuities in a more timely fashion now that they had a friend in such an exalted position.[66] In Hoccleve's holograph manuscript, Huntington Library MS HM 111, the begging poem is immediately followed by another (a roundel) addressed to Somer and apparently thanking him for some bounty in the approach to Christmas.[67] Although these two poems are usually linked, it seems possible that the roundel was written to thank and praise Somer after the success of the first poem. M. C. Seymour argues that if the first poem had been written in December 1408, shortly after Somer's appointment as a baron of the Exchequer on 8 November, then the poetic plea was unsuccessful, since Hoccleve did not receive the next instalment of his annuity until

---

[62] E. Stubbs and L. R. Mooney, 'A Record Identifying Thomas Hoccleve's Father', *Journal of the Early Book Society* 14 (2011), 233–7.

[63] Mooney, 'Some New Light on Thomas Hoccleve', p. 312.

[64] Ibid., pp. 310–11 and esp. n. 45.

[65] Doyle and Parkes, 'Production of Copies', pp. 198–9 (repr. pp. 236–7), discusses the possibility that Hoccleve was acquainted with Chaucer and Gower.

[66] San Marino, CA, Huntington Library, MS 111, fols 38v–39v; *Hoccleve's Works*, vol. 1: *The Minor Poems*, ed. F. J. Furnivall and I. Gollancz, EETS ES 61 (1892); rev. ed. J. Mitchell and A. I. Doyle (1970), pp. 59–60.

[67] Huntington Library, MS 111, fol. 39v; *Hoccleve's Works: Minor Poems*, p. 60.

13 February 1409.[68] However, it seems possible that the following roundel praising Somer might have been written as a separate piece, and thus in response to the receipt of some other gift instead. This was also around the time of Hoccleve's marriage, so Somer may, as an acquaintance, have taken his cue from the general begging poem to offer Hoccleve a gift in view of his changed circumstances.

Hoccleve's third poem to Somer connects them both with a group of government clerks who met on a regular basis to dine.[69] This poem Hoccleve wrote to Somer on behalf of 'La Court de Bone Conpaignie', the Court of Good Company,[70] accepting both Somer's proposal that their regular feasts be started up again at the Temple on the following Thursday, 1 May, and his proposal to contribute more than his share to provide adequate funds for the occasion. 1 May was a Thursday in 1410 and 1421. If the poem was written in 1410 the impetus for Somer's proposal was presumably a wish to celebrate with his friends his forthcoming elevation to chancellor, and that group of friends, the Court de Bone Conpaignie, included Hoccleve, as Hoccleve says he is 'un de la dicte Court'.[71] His poetic response to Somer on the group's behalf suggests that part of their entertainment had consisted of literary works recited after the dinners.[72] While Hoccleve's addresses to kings and dukes do not necessarily suggest personal acquaintance, his addresses to fellow clerks or former clerks, like Somer, do suggest by their tone that he knew them personally. Such a regular gathering of clerk-administrators with literary inclinations may have included members of the civic secretariat as well as royal clerks.

The Court de Bone Conpaignie, at which the clerks of royal (and perhaps civic) government entertained one another with reciting verse of their own creation, recalls the London *puy* or *pui*, which appears to have been a regular gathering of the London literati and their patrons for feasts combined with poetic competitions, held in the Guildhall chapel.[73] The London puy was initiated by merchants in the thirteenth century in imitation of its namesake, fraternities called *puys* in Valenciennes and other towns and cities of northern France and

---

[68] M. C. Seymour, *Selections from Hoccleve* (Oxford, 1981), p. 110; see also Burrow, *Thomas Hoccleve*, p. 16. For the marriage in 1408 see Mooney and Stubbs, 'A Record Identifying Thomas Hoccleve's Father', p. 235.

[69] Furnivall and Gollancz, followed by Seymour, took the date to be 1410, when Somer was not yet chancellor, Seymour further suggesting that Somer knew before his appointment that it was imminent, celebrating with his friends on 1 May an appointment that would not take place until 20 June: Seymour, *Selections from Hoccleve*, p. 111. Burrow, *Thomas Hoccleve*, p. 29 and n. 114, puts the date at 1 May 1421, noting that the only two possible years when 1 May fell on a Thursday were 1410 and 1421 and that Somer had not yet been appointed chancellor (as Hoccleve addresses him in the heading of the poem in HM 111, fol. 41v). It may also be that Hoccleve has forgotten the relative dates of Somer's appointment and the feast, both in 1410, when, years later, he writes the explanatory heading into HM 111.

[70] Huntington Library, MS 111, fols 41v–43r, *Hoccleve's Works: Minor Poems*, pp. 64–6.

[71] Quoted from the heading Hoccleve provided in MS HM 111, fol. 41v. Seymour, *Selections from Hoccleve*, p. 111, suggests the forthcoming promotion as a reason for Somer's desire to revive the feasts and contribute generously to the one on 1 May 1410.

[72] Seymour, *Selections from Hoccleve*, pp. 111–12, comments, 'Undoubtedly the *balade* added to the pleasure of the feast', and draws attention to the regulations governing the puy which are recorded in Horn's *Liber Custumarum*.

[73] One possible reason for the change of venue for the poetic competitions, and thus perhaps for a change in name that meant that further dinners were not referred to by the name 'puy' may be the dilapidation of the Guildhall chapel toward the end of the fourteenth century.

Flanders.[74] The statutes governing the London puy were recorded by Andrew Horn in his *Liber Custumarum* in the early fourteenth century, but not in the portion inserted into the *Liber Albus*.[75] As Helen Cooper points out, Horn's statutes use the word *conpaignie* to describe the fraternity gathered for the puy, as do Chaucer to describe his pilgrims, and Hoccleve to describe his 'Court de Bone Conpaignie'.[76] While acknowledging that the puy itself probably did not continue to Chaucer's day, Derek Pearsall argues that there must have been gatherings of 'merchants and lawyers' in London at which Chaucer and other authors read their work and perhaps competed for the prize of a free dinner or being named the master of the feast.[77] He cites the example of Henry Scogan who, according to John Shirley in his rubric introduction to a copy of Scogan's *Moral Balade*, delivered the balade by reading it aloud to the sons of Henry IV in attendance at a dinner held in the Vintry ward of London around 1407.[78] Shirley actually calls the dinner 'a souper of feorthe merchande', suggesting that it was the fourth meeting of the year for a company of merchants, so according to him the royal princes had been invited to a regular meeting of merchants, this one held in the home of Lewis John.[79] Thus there is evidence, though scant, that there were meetings where literature was read aloud, both in the city among merchants and in the inns of court among royal clerks. As the training and job descriptions of royal clerks, civic clerks, attorneys and lawyers overlapped, and some men stepped over these boundaries in the course of their careers, the royal *conpaignie* of clerks to which Hoccleve belonged need not have excluded their compeers at the Guildhall, or vice versa.[80]

Another of Hoccleve's begging poems, his 'Balade to my maister Carpenter' offers a more direct link to the Guildhall clerks. Using a similar tone of familiarity, he asks his addressee to stand between him and his creditors who are demanding immediate payment

---

[74] See H. Cooper, 'London and Southwark Poetic Companies: "Si tost c'amis" and the *Canterbury Tales*', in *Chaucer and the City*, ed. A. Butterfield (Cambridge, 2006), pp. 109–24 (pp. 109–10), citing (n. 1) A. Butterfield, 'Puy', in *Medieval France: An Encyclopedia*, ed. W. W. Kibler and G. A. Zinn (New York, 1995). See also A. F. Sutton, 'Merchants, Music and Social Harmony: The London Puy and its French and London Contexts, circa 1300', *London Journal* 17 (1992), 1–17.

[75] See *Munimenta Gildhallae Londoniensis*, I, 216; London Metropolitan Archives, COL/CS/01/006 (*Liber Custumarum*), fol. 216, where it is called *le feste de puy*. Influence of the puy on John Gower was discussed by Fisher, *John Gower*, pp. 78–3; its influence on Chaucer's frame of the story-telling competition in the *Canterbury Tales* is discussed by H. Cooper, 'Sources and Analogues of Chaucer's *Canterbury Tales*: Reviewing the Work', *Studies in the Age of Chaucer* 19 (1997), 183–210 (pp. 204–9); repr. 'The Frame', in *Sources and Analogues of the Canterbury Tales*, ed. R. M. Correale and M. Hamel, vol. 1 (Cambridge, 2002), pp. 1–22.

[76] Cooper, 'Poetic Companies', p. 111.

[77] D. Pearsall, 'The *Canterbury Tales* and London Club Culture', in *Chaucer and the City*, ed. A. Butterfield (Cambridge, 2006), pp. 95–108 (p. 107).

[78] Ibid., p. 105. As Pearsall points out, Henry Scogan is assumed on the basis of this didactic poem to have been tutor to the princes in the 1390s; if this were not the case, to address in such a way the princes would be presumptuous.

[79] Pearsall points out (ibid., p. 106) that Lewis John was 'deputy butler to the royal household from 1402 to 1407 when the chief butler was Thomas Chaucer.'

[80] J. Coleman, *Public Reading and the Reading Public in Late Medieval England and France* (Cambridge, 1996), p. 195, also cites the example of the poem, 'Crowned King', dating from 1415, in which a group of royal clerks combine reading of romances and revelling when journeying to Southampton. (Also cited by Pearsall, 'London Club Culture', p. 107.)

and threatening him with imprisonment (*duresse*).[81] As common clerk of the city, Carpenter could perhaps not help in his official capacity since that would hinder due process of law, but he could ask Hoccleve's creditors to grant him more time to repay, as John Burrow suggests, or he could help as a wealthy friend or acquaintance by paying the debts or assuming the debt himself – thus becoming either Hoccleve's benefactor or his new creditor.[82] Toward the end of his life Hoccleve entered this begging poem into fol. 41r of his holograph anthology, Huntington Library HM 111, and by way of illustrating the notes that had originally accompanied the poem, he wrote into the right margin, 'A d B & C d D &c', that is, so much is demanded from creditor B and so much from creditor D, etc.[83] Surely there would be no reason to give the amounts, only the names of the creditors, if he wished Carpenter only to obtain respite in regard to the due date. Below the list of debts Hoccleve added in MS HM 111, 'Ceste balade feust tendrement considere & bonement execute', which we interpret as him recording, years later, the generosity of the addressee by stating that the balade was sympathetically received and read, and its pleas well answered, that is, the debts were paid. If so, Carpenter or the original addressee thus demonstrated his friendship and concern for Hoccleve by paying the debts on his behalf.

The name of the addressee, 'Carpenter', is written over an erasure in the first line of the holograph copy of this poem written in the 1420s, MS HM 111, and scholars have suggested several reasons for this. F. J. Furnivall and I. Gollancz noted in their Early English Text Society edition, '"Carpenter" is written over an erasure, the original having probably another name, to whose owner it had been sent, as it was doubtless afterwards sent to other moneyful folk.'[84] Seymour also noted the erasure and Furnivall's suggestion that it shows the poem was sent to more than one possible benefactor, but commented that there seemed no logical explanation 'why Hoccleve should alter [the addressee's name in] his own fair copy'.[85] For even if he had sent this begging poem to more than one person, there would be no reason to first record one of their names, and then erase it to replace it with another in his holograph copy written years later in the 1420s. John Burrow suggested that 'the poem was first addressed to some other likely mediator, for the name Carpenter is squeezed in over an erasure in HM 111, and the metre of the line in which it occurs requires not three but two syllables'.[86]

Given our recognition of Carpenter and his predecessor Marchaunt as copyists of Middle English literature, and our identification of Marchaunt as scribe D, who worked with Hoccleve on the production of Trinity College MS R.3.2, we think it highly likely that the two-syllable name that originally stood in HM 111, and the original addressee of the begging poem, was 'Marchaunt'. John Marchaunt would have been common clerk in

---

[81] Huntington Library, MS HM 111, fol. 41r-v; *Hoccleve's Works: Minor Poems*, pp. 63-4. Seymour also notes the familiar tone: 'Its tone is decidedly friendly, like the *Balades to Sir Henry Somer*, and suggests an acquaintance formed in earlier days, perhaps at the Court de Bone Conpaignie.' Seymour, *Selections from Hoccleve*, p. 110.

[82] Burrow, *Thomas Hoccleve*, p. 16.

[83] For illustration of this balade, see *Thomas Hoccleve: Facsimile*, HM 111, fol. 41r-v.

[84] *Hoccleve's Works: Minor Poems*, p. 63, n. 1.

[85] Seymour, *Selections from Hoccleve*, p. 110.

[86] Burrow, *Thomas Hoccleve*, p. 16. We would have the same objection regarding the changing of the name in the holograph, denoting multiple recipients, as Seymour raises with regard to Bower's suggestion.

Other Scribes Associated with the Guildhall or its Clerks

the period 1408–9 to which Burrow dates the balade.[87] Hoccleve would have recorded the poem in HM 111 in the period 1422–6, when he wrote all three of his surviving holograph manuscripts (two are deposited in the Huntingdon Library, and one in Durham University Library); Doyle and Burrow assign an earlier date to the two Huntington manuscripts than to the Durham one, so perhaps the balade was written down in the earlier part of that span.[88] Evidence of references to dedicatees of the poems in the headings of HM 111 suggest a date of 1422 for the holograph, after the death of Henry V in August of that year (since four headings offer prayers for his soul), and soon after John Duke of Bedford's elevation to Regent of France in September, since the heading to a balade addressed to John speaks of his now ('ore') holding both those titles.[89] The date, suggesting copying HM 111 probably over several months in 1422, offers an explanation for the change of addressee in the begging poem copied into the holograph manuscript. Hoccleve may have written the poem and addressed it to Marchaunt before the latter's death in July 1422, but afterwards returned to his draft, and out of respect for his recently deceased benefactor, changed the name to that of Marchaunt's successor, John Carpenter.[90]

Whether the original recipient was Marchaunt or not, even the record of Carpenter's name in Hoccleve's copy of this begging poem demonstrates his acquaintance with the clerks at the Guildhall who had an interest in Middle English literature. Since the tone of the poem itself, and the marginal notes Hoccleve recorded in his holograph both suggest his gratitude to the addressee, he would only have substituted Carpenter's name if he (Carpenter) could be considered as generous a friend as the original addressee.

Thomas Hoccleve provides clues to the social intermingling of literary-minded clerks in London and Westminster. His 'Dialogue with a Friend', though fictional, also illustrates the kinds of interaction that would occur among them, the emotional and material support to be gained through such interaction. For instance, his fictitious friend offers suggestions about what to write next and what kinds of writing would please the patron Hoccleve is seeking; he then lends Hoccleve his book of the *Gesta Romanorum* from which Hoccleve could extract and translate the Tale of Jereslaus' Wife.[91] Gatherings like the 'Court de Bone Conpaignie' offered opportunities for writers to meet one another and read and receive feedback on their latest writings. The royal and civic clerks of London and Westminster clearly formed a hub for both the composition and the copying and dissemination of Middle English literature, and in the reigns of Henry IV and Henry V their interest in the use of English for both literature and government found support from the monarch.

---

[87] Ibid.

[88] *Thomas Hoccleve: Facsimile*, p. xx.

[89] Huntington Library, MS HM 111, fols 1r, 26r, 27r and 40r; fol. 37v. See *Thomas Hoccleve: Facsimile*, p. xx.

[90] Marchaunt's will, Kew, National Archives, E 40/12349, was probated and entered into the Hustings Roll on the Monday next after the feast of St James the Apostle (25 July) in 10 Henry V (21 March – 31 August 1422). This record of its probate was written onto the dorse of the will by John Carpenter, one of Marchaunt's executors. See fig. 4.1.

[91] *Thomas Hoccleve's Complaint and Dialogue*, ed. J. A. Burrow, EETS OS 313 (1999).

7

Conclusions

Numerous scholars of Middle English literature have proposed that there was a central repository for manuscripts of the writings of the London authors William Langland, Geoffrey Chaucer, and John Gower, to which the patrons of provincial authors such as John Trevisa or the anonymous author of *The Siege of Jerusalem* might bring exemplars of their works for copying and dissemination.[1] It seems clear now that the Guildhall close was just such a site. There is ample evidence pointing to it as a central London clearing house for Middle English literature. In this final chapter we shall consider briefly what difference it makes to know the identity of the scribes and where they were based.

Now that we have identified the clerks of the Guildhall as having been involved in the copying of medieval English literary manuscripts, it remains to consider both how they found the time to do this work and why they chose to do it.

Concerning the issue of time, we may note that, provided the scribe had an exemplar for long-term loan, a work space and materials ready to hand, copying was an activity that could be picked up and worked on for short periods between or after other work. Attorneys in the city's courts would be very busy when the courts were in session, but would have long periods when they were not in session, when they could devote all their energies to other scribal activity. Penny Tucker explains that even the most common city courts, the Husting courts, met irregularly, with a long break in summer, 'between late July (sometimes even late June) and mid-October or even November', and a month's break at Christmas.[2]

Studies of manuscripts written by Continental scribes who dated the beginning and ending of their work on a manuscript allow us to estimate the speed of professional scribes. The time it took a scribe to copy a leaf would vary depending on the difficulty of the script, the size of the page, whether it was in single or double columns, and whether the text was prose or verse, but based on the Continental studies, a professional could write between two and four folios per day, and thus between twelve and twenty-four folios per week.[3] Writing *anglicana formata* in double columns for Gower's *Confessio Amantis* might be relatively time-consuming, so Hoccleve's contribution to the Trinity College MS R.3.2 copy of Gower's *Confessio Amantis* (fols 82, 83, and one column on fol. 84r) might represent

---

[1] E.g. Owen, *Manuscripts of 'The Canterbury Tales'*, p. 98; *English Works of John Gower*, ed. Macaulay, I, xlvii, echoed by Fisher, *John Gower*, pp. 66, 116–17, 124–7, 303–6; and R. F. Green, *Poets and Princepleasers: Literature and the English Court in the Late Middle Ages* (Toronto, 1980), pp. 179–83; Hanna, 'Thomas Berkeley and his Patronage', pp. 909–16; Hanna, *Pursuing History*, p. 125; Bowers, 'The House of Chaucer & Son', p. 137; Kerby-Fulton and Justice, 'Marketing Ricardian Literture', p. 225.

[2] P. Tucker, *Law Courts and Lawyers*, p. 136.

[3] P. Gumbert, 'The Speed of Scribes', in *Scribi e colofoni: Le sottoscrizioni di copisti dalle origini all'avvento della stampa: Atti del seminario di Erice X Colloquio del Comité International de Paleographie Latine (23–8 Ottobre 1993)*, ed. E. Condello and G. De Gregorio (Spoleto, 1995), pp. 57–69; D. Wakelin, 'Writing the Words', in *The Production of Books in England, 1350–1500*, ed. A. Gillespie and D. L. Wakelin (Cambridge, 2011), pp. 34–58 (p. 35); J. Le Goff, *Time, Work and Culture in the Middle Ages*, trans. A. Goldhammer (Chicago, 1980), pp. 35, 37, 41, 45–7, 49. All these figures assume a six-day working week.

Conclusions

a single day's work. Pinkhurst's three quires (twenty-four leaves) might have taken ten to twelve days to complete, equivalent to two weeks of full-time work. Writing single columns of verse for Langland's *Piers Plowman*, Hoccleve's *Regiment of Princes* or Chaucer's *Troilus and Criseyde,* a professional scribe might accomplish four folios a day, completing an eight-leaf quire in two days. If he were working full time, one of our scribes could complete an eighty-folio manuscript of *Piers Plowman* in twenty days, or just over three weeks; he could finish a hundred-folio manuscript of Hoccleve's *Regiment* in twenty-five days, approximately a month's work; the 120-folio *Troilus* would take him thirty days, or five weeks. A more difficult script such as the one Carpenter used in writing the Pierpont Morgan M. 817 copy of *Troilus* would take longer, perhaps forty days at three folios per day. If he wrote an entire copy of the *Confessio Amantis*, approximately 200 folios in double columns, at two and a half folios per day, it would take eighty days, or a little over thirteen weeks.[4] Even at the slowest rate of two folios per day, it would have taken John Marchaunt only four years of full-time copying to complete all his portions of the fourteen literary manuscripts attributed to him.[5] Even if scribes could not find time during the court recesses to devote to full-time copying, long summer evenings would provide them time for part-time copying, if they chose to spend them in this way and if their hands and eyes could bear the additional strain.[6] All the literary copying that has been attributed to these scribes would account for a very small proportion of their working careers.

There are many reasons why the clerks of the Guildhall might devote time to copying English literary manuscripts, and we shall consider them here under four headings.

Special commission The City of London, that is, the mayor and aldermen, or the mayor himself, might wish to have a copy of Middle English writings for presentation to the king or another influential member of his court, so the clerks might be asked to prepare a volume that could then be beautifully illuminated at an atelier in Paternoster Row and bound as a gift, for instance for New Year or to mark a special occasion like a wedding. The clerks would then be copying these manuscripts as part of their work for the city. We have already noted that the beautiful copy of *Troilus and Criseyde* prepared for Henry, Prince of Wales, *c.* 1410–13 might have been commissioned by the mayor or by one of the aldermen in this way.

---

[4] We have used average folios for these texts from manuscripts copied by clerks of the Guildhall; for *Confessio Amantis* we have used the average of 200 folios based on some of John Marchaunt's manuscripts, 207 folios of 42–3 lines per column for Oxford, Christ Church MS 148 and Corpus Christi College MS 67; 201 folios for Bodley 294 with 42–6 lines per column; 183 folios of 46 lines per column for Bodley 902.

[5] These calculations assume a six-day week and forty-eight weeks in the year, allowing four weeks for holidays and illness. The manuscripts are Trinity R.3.2 (*Confessio Amantis*), 8+42 = 50 folios (25 days); Additional MS 27944 (*De Proprietatibus Rerum*), 6+139 = 145 folios (73 days); Egerton 1991 (*Confessio Amantis*), 214 folios (107 days); Harley 7334 (*Canterbury Tales*), 286 folios (143 days); London University Library V.88 (*Piers Plowman*), 126 folios (63 days); Columbia University Library Plimpton 265 (*Confessio Amantis*), approx. 200 folios (100 days); Manchester Rylands Eng 103 (*Brut*), 126 folios (53 days); Bodley 294 (*Confessio Amantis*), 201 folios (100 days); Bodley 902 (*Confessio Amantis*), 14 folios (7 days); Christ Church 148 (*Confessio Amantis*), 207 folios (104 days); Corpus Christi 67 (*Confessio Amantis*), 207 folios (104 days); Corpus Christi 198 (*Canterbury Tales*), 265 folios (133 days); Princeton Taylor 5 (*Confessio Amantis*), 184 folios (92 days); total 1,104 days, divided by 288 working days per year, approximately four years. This does not, of course, take into account manuscripts he may have written which no longer survive.

[6] By way of comparison, we note that Geoffrey Chaucer found time for composing literary texts after hours working at the Customs Wharf: see Chaucer's *House of Fame*, lines 629–34, 652–8.

Financial In the earlier part of their careers, taking on extra copying of any kind would increase the scribes' income. (Once they were earning the salaries of chamber clerk or common clerk, with the opportunities for copying documents related to the city's business that came with those positions, they would have sufficient income from other sources to forego literary copying, unless they had a particular interest in the content.) Osbarn's manuscripts have all been dated to the first quarter of the fifteenth century, when he was serving as chamber clerk, but with the exception of the incomplete Harley manuscript of *Troilus* they appear to have been manuscripts he prepared for his own or his community's use. Carpenter's literary manuscripts date from the period before he formally took on the position of common clerk, when serving as Marchaunt's under-clerk, and the fact that we have not been able to find manuscripts datable after 1417 may be due to the increased pressures on his time once in office. We are not certain about what position Pinkhurst may have held at the Guildhall, but if he had been a clerk serving the recorder's office he might have found time for copying during the courts' summer recess, and may have needed the income. Two of Frampton's three literary manuscripts date from early in his career, so he too may have been writing these for extra income aside from his duties as a clerk. Hoccleve seems to have copied mostly manuscripts of his own works, and even those were written mainly in the last years of his life when there is less evidence of his copying for the Privy Seal.[7] John Marchaunt is the anomaly here, with fourteen manuscripts attributed to his hand. He could well have had time for copying literary manuscripts in the 1380s and 1390s, when he served as chamber clerk 1380–99, as an attorney in the city's court 1380–93, and probably as Henry Perot's clerk up to 1394.[8] As we have noted, he probably fulfilled the responsibilities of the common clerk after Perot's death in 1394, although he was not formally appointed as common clerk until 1399. The years of service as a court attorney or under-clerk with Perot might have afforded him time for literary copying, but only a few of his literary manuscripts have been dated to this period: the *Brut* chronicle in Manchester, John Rylands Library, MS Eng. 103, and the Ilchester *Piers Plowman* which is now London University Library MS SL V.88. Stubbs has argued that the two *Canterbury Tales* manuscripts written by his hand could contain portions completed before Chaucer's death in October 1400, but even that would run over to the period when he was serving as common clerk.[9] We believe his involvement in copying literary texts must have stemmed from personal interest or political motivation.

Personal acquaintance The major London authors were known to the Guildhall clerks. Chaucer apparently employed Pinkhurst to make the first copies of his poetic works in the 1380s.[10] Thomas Usk was clerk of the Goldsmiths' Company and knew Marchaunt well enough to accuse him of confederacy with John of Northampton's faction in his appeal of 1384. When Chaucer went abroad in 1378 he gave power of attorney to Gower and Richard Forster (or Forester), the latter an attorney in the city courts from 1367 to 1408, who took over the tenancy of Chaucer's apartment over Aldgate after he vacated it in October 1386.[11]

---

[7] *Thomas Hoccleve Facsimile*, intro. Burrow and Doyle, pp. xx–xxi; Mooney, 'A Holograph of Hoccleve's *Regiment of Princes*', pp. 263–96.

[8] Tucker, *Law Courts and Lawyers*, p. 299, notes this possibility given that Marchaunt received a legacy under Perot's will, Kew, National Archives, PCC PROB11/1/9, fols 68v–69r.

[9] Stubbs, 'The Work of Scribe D on Oxford, Corpus Christi College MS 198', pp. 133, 139–43, 153.

[10] Mooney, 'Chaucer's Scribe'.

[11] *Chaucer Life-Records*, ed. Crow and Olson, pp. 54, 145–6; Tucker, *Law Courts and Lawyers*, p. 385.

Conclusions

In 1385 Chaucer had named 'moral' John Gower and 'philosophical' Ralph Strode to correct any errors in his *Troilus and Criseyde*: Strode was common serjeant at the Guildhall from 1373 to 1382 and an attorney in its courts from then until his death in 1387; he occupied an apartment over Aldersgate during this period, in the gift of the city as were Chaucer's rooms over Aldgate.[12]

Gower himself may have served in some capacity at the Guildhall in the 1360s and 1370s before he moved into lodgings within the priory of St Mary Overie in Southwark. His knowledge of the law and the training of lawyers led Fisher to conclude that he had served in some sort of legal capacity.[13] For instance, he could not have represented Chaucer as his attorney in 1378 unless he had some legal training. Macaulay had discovered references to a Gower in legal yearbooks for 1355 and 1356, where a man by the name of Gower is referred to as counsel or occasionally as a judge.[14] Macaulay had thought these too early to refer to the poet, but as we do not know the date of his birth, he may have been serving as a clerk-attorney at the beginning of his career.[15] If he were born in 1330, he would be twenty-five or twenty-six at this time, and parallels with Osbarn and Marchaunt who served in higher offices for nearly forty years after having been attorneys suggest that they might begin quite young.[16] Osbarn, for instance, was working as an attorney in the city's courts as early as 1390, forty-eight years before the date of his death, while 1355 would be fifty-three years before the date of Gower's death.

John Fisher argued that Gower identifies himself as associated with the law courts when he says, in *Le Mirour de l'omme*, that he wears a gown with striped sleeves:[17]

> je ne suy pas clers,
> Vestu de sanguin ne de pers,
> Ainz ai vestu la raye mance,
> Poy sai latin, poy sai romance. (lines 21772–5)

Translation: I am not a cleric, dressed in red or purple, rather I wear a gown with striped sleeves [lit. the striped sleeve]; I know a little Latin; I know a little French.

Gowns of red or purple signified a clerk in holy orders, while the wearing of striped gowns is associated with the serjeants, barristers and their apprentices in royal courts, and the men of the London city courts.[18] Fisher notes that John Stow had reported:

> I read that in the year 1516, it was agreed by a common council in the Guildhall that the sheriffs of London should (as they had been accustomed) give yearly rayed gowns to the recorder, chamberlain, common sergeant, and common clerk, the sword-bearer, common hunt, water-bailiff, common crier, like as to their own offices.[19]

---

[12] Fisher, *John Gower*, p. 62.

[13] Ibid., pp. 57–8.

[14] *The Complete Works of John Gower*, ed. G. C. Macaulay, 4 vols. (Oxford, 1899–1902; republished 1968), IV, ix; cited by Fisher, *John Gower*, p. 57.

[15] Fisher, *John Gower*, p. 57.

[16] Ibid., p. 59, suggests this date for Gower's birth.

[17] Ibid., p. 55. For the text, see *The Complete Works of John Gower*, I, 246, lines 21772–5. We note that judges also wore red gowns.

[18] Fisher, *John Gower*, frontispiece and p. 55.

[19] Ibid., p. 55; citing John Stow, *Survey of London* [1603 edition], ed. W. J. Thoms (London, 1876), p. 196.

Table 7.1 Manuscripts of Gower's *Confessio Amantis* written by Guildhall scribes and their associates

Manuscript	Scribe
Cambridge, Pembroke College, 307	Petworth scribe (Skinners' Clerk)
Cambridge, Trinity College, R.3.2	Marchaunt, Pinkhurst and Hoccleve
Cambridge, University Library, Dd.8.19	Carpenter
Glasgow, University Library, Hunterian S.1.7	Marchaunt or a scribe trained by him
London, British Library, Egerton 1991	Marchaunt
London, British Library, Royal 18 C.xxii	Scribe Delta*
London, University College, Frag. Angl. 1	Trevisa–Gower scribe
New York, Columbia University Library, Plimpton 265	Marchaunt
New York, Pierpont Morgan Library & Museum, M.125	Marchaunt or a scribe trained by him
Oxford, Bodleian Library, Bodley 294	Marchaunt
Oxford, Bodleian Library, Bodley 693	Trevisa–Gower scribe (see Bodley 902)
Oxford, Bodleian Library, Bodley 902	Trevisa–Gower scribe and Marchaunt
Oxford, Bodleian Library, Laud misc. 609	Trevisa–Gower scribe
Oxford, Christ Church, 148	Marchaunt
Oxford, Corpus Christi College, 67	Marchaunt
Philadelphia, Rosenbach Museum and Library, 1083/29	Carpenter
Princeton, University Library, Taylor 5	Marchaunt

* Although we have not yet found evidence of Delta's activity at the Guildhall, he is included here because Doyle and Parkes point to the similarity of his hand to that of Scribe D: Doyle and Parkes, 'Production of Copies', pp. 178, 206–8 (repr. pp. 216, 244–6).

The clerks of the seventeenth-century Guildhall wore parti-coloured gowns with one cloth rayed, or striped, in different colours, depending on whether they served the sheriffs or the mayor; Fisher speculated that the custom might have extended as far back as the fourteenth century, and concluded that Gower could equally have served the law at the Guildhall as in the royal courts.[20] The fact that the *Liber Albus* in 1419 also refers to members of the civic secretariat wearing livery appropriate to their offices suggests that this custom did extend as far back as the early fifteenth century.[21]

Fisher points out that Gower also wrote knowledgeably about 'the privileges of serjeancy' in the *Le Mirour de l'omme*, which might describe the serjeants of either the royal or the civic courts.[22] Chaucer's assigning of power of attorney to Gower and Forster in 1378 suggests that Chaucer associated the two men with each other, and knew that they could confer on any of his business that arose during his absence from the country; thus Gower is more likely to have been associated with the city courts than the royal ones. He may have served as an under-clerk to the recorder who, as we have noted above with respect to Pinkhurst, was allowed to wear the same (striped) livery as the serjeants who served the chamberlain.[23] Gower might also have served as chamber clerk before Marchaunt, where Barron's lists of officers of the Guildhall show a forty-five-year stretch from 1335 to 1380 with a single name, Richard de Waltham, attached to it: had Gower served in this position he would have been granted the gown with striped sleeves as well, and such a position would connect Marchaunt with Gower personally.[24]

[20] Fisher, *John Gower*, p. 56 and n. 65, again citing Stow, ed. Thoms, p. 196.

[21] *Liber Albus*, fols 42–3, as discussed at p. 77 n. 41 above.

[22] Fisher, *John Gower*, p. 57; *Mirour de l'omme*, line 24373.

[23] See p. 77 n. 41.

[24] Barron, *London in the Later Middle Ages*, p. 363.

Conclusions

If Gower was associated with the Guildhall and known to Marchaunt and Pinkhurst, it would explain why these Guildhall clerks are responsible for so many early manuscript copies of his *Confessio Amantis*: one-third of the surviving manuscripts are written by them or their associates, including almost all the earliest ones (table 7.1).

Political The preservation and dissemination of literature written in English was part of a wider movement toward the adoption of English as the language of government and commerce during the last decades of the fourteenth and first decades of the fifteenth centuries, exactly the period of these clerks' active careers. In London in the 1370s and 1380s the earliest documents written in English are associated with the faction of London politics led by John of Northampton: the Jubilee Book setting down precedents and rules for the governance of London, compiled in 1377–8 and burned during the mayoralty of Nicholas Exton in 1387; Thomas Usk's 1384 appeal against John of Northampton and others whose faction he had previously served; the appeal of the Mercers' Company against Nicholas Brembre in early 1388, written by Pinkhurst.[25] Northampton himself may have been a relatively small player in a wider movement toward the adoption of English, led by the aristocracy and royalty. When brought before Richard II accused of treason, John of Northampton claimed the support of John of Gaunt, who was also Chaucer's brother-in-law.[26] Henry IV as earl of Derby supported both Chaucer and Gower. He was the first English monarch since the Conquest to deliver his coronation oath in English, and both he and Henry V used the English language for proclamations they wished to reach the widest audience of their people. Henry V adopted it as the language to be used for royal government.[27]

Fisher described the connection between royal and literary language in his 1992 article, 'A Language Policy for Lancastrian England'.[28] As he notes, in the decades leading up to Henry Bolingbroke's usurpation Chaucer began to write literary pieces in English for John of Gaunt and the court of Richard II; John Gower wrote his *Confessio Amantis* in English dedicated first to Richard II and then to Henry IV when earl of Derby; in Oxford John Trevisa translated Higden's *Polychronicon* and Bartholomeus's *De proprietatibus rerum* into English prose, Thomas Usk wrote his *Testament of Love*, etc. Both Chaucer and Gower received rewards from John of Gaunt and his son Henry Bolingbroke, and Trevisa's patron Sir Thomas Berkeley was a supporter of Henry IV.[29] Fisher believed that there must be a connection between the emergence of English as a literary language and the rise of the Lancastrians, to whom Chaucer was related through Katherine Swynford and Phillipa Chaucer; whether that policy was spoken or simply understood, or arose from Henry Beaufort, tutor to Henry V, or from Henry IV, Fisher could not say, but he concluded:

> Hoccleve, no more than Lydgate, ever articulated for the Lancastrian rulers a policy of encouraging the development of English as a national language or of citing Chaucer as

---

[25] See Bird, *Turbulent London*, pp. 69–74, and Nightingale, *Medieval Mercantile Community*, p. 312; *Book of London English*, ed. Chambers and Daunt, pp. 33–7; Mooney, 'Chaucer's Scribe', pp. 106–10; Lindenbaum, 'London Texts and Literate Practice', pp. 286–93; Turner, 'Conflict', pp. 264–6. Barron, *London in the Later Middle Ages*, p. 127, calls the Jubilee book 'a similar attempt at constitution making' to the *Liber Albus*.

[26] Bird, *Turbulent London*, p. 27.

[27] *Book of London English*, ed. Chambers and Daunt, pp. 62–105, *passim*.

[28] J. H. Fisher, 'A Language Policy for Lancastrian England', *PMLA* 107 (1992), pp. 1168–80.

[29] *Chaucer Life-Records*, ed. Crow and Olson, pp. 271–5, 514–34; Fisher, *John Gower*, p. 68; Hanna, 'Thomas Berkeley and his Patronage', pp. 888–92.

the exemplar for such a policy. But we have the documentary and literary evidence of what happened. The linkage of praise for Prince Henry as a model ruler concerned about the use of English and of master Chaucer as the 'firste fyndere of our faire langage'; the sudden appearance of manuscripts of the *Canterbury Tales*, *Troylus and Criseyde*, and other English writings composed earlier but never before published; the conversion to English of the signet clerks of Henry V, the chancery clerks, and eventually the guild clerks; and the burgeoning of composition in English and the patronage of that literature by the Lancastrian court circle – these are concurrent historical events. The only question is whether the concurrence was coincidental or deliberate.[30]

We believe the movement toward the adoption of English goes back still further, into the late 1360s and 1370s, with John of Gaunt and men he supported or patronized as the enacters of that policy, all part of an attempt to reach the commons for support for himself and for his son Henry.[31]

The clerks we have identified at the London Guildhall – John Marchaunt, Adam Pinkhurst, John Carpenter and Richard Osbarn – appear to have been involved both with John of Northampton's faction and with John of Gaunt, Henry IV and Henry V. They may therefore have been participants in this movement, and involved on both the literary and the political sides. Marchaunt and Pinkhurst, a generation older than Osbarn and Carpenter, seem to have been closely affiliated with John of Northampton and his faction in the London politics of the 1370s and 1380s, as we have outlined above. Marchaunt was as much involved with the Northampton faction as Usk had been (by his own admission) in the early 1380s, since Usk names him in his appeal of 1384 as having been 'privier than I' to the plottings of John of Northampton and his associates.[32] Although the given name for the conspiring clerk, 'Marchaund', is illegible in Usk's appeal, the period Usk is describing is that in which John Marchaunt was chamber clerk while John of Northampton was mayor (1381–3), and their secret meetings were held, among other venues, in the chamber of the Guildhall. Usk tells us that he himself was involved in order to 'write thair billes' to be read or proclaimed to their supporters and the 'comunes' at large, and that the Marchaunt, clerk, who was present at secret meetings when Usk was absent, had 'writen many thynges' in his absence.[33] Pinkhurst seems to have been equally involved with Northampton's cause. As we have identified, he wrote not only the petition of the Mercers' Company but also that of the Leathersellers and White Tawiers appealing Nicholas Brembre of treason in early 1388.[34] Sheila Lindenbaum and Marion Turner agree that Pinkhurst probably composed the Mercers' Petition, whose choice of English may signal that it was the one among the twelve to be read aloud before the Lords Appellant and Merciless Parliament.[35] Even though she was writing before Mooney made the identification of its scribe as Pinkhurst, Lindenbaum picked out in the rhetoric of the Petition comparable strategies to those used by Middle English authors Chaucer, Gower and Langland, not only in the use of English and inclusion of anecdotes and puns but even in the 'cultivation of a professional and scribal

---

[30] Fisher, 'Language Policy for Lancastrian England', p. 1178.

[31] See also J. Catto, 'Written English: The Making of the Language, 1370–1400', *Past & Present* 179 (2003), 24–59.

[32] *Book of London English*, ed. Chambers and Daunt, p. 24.

[33] Ibid.; Turner, 'Conflict', pp. 264–5.

[34] See pp. 79–80, 82 above.

[35] Lindenbaum, 'London Texts and Literate Practice', p. 291; Turner, 'Conflict', p. 264.

obscurity'.[36] Turner identifies him with the cause, not just as a scrivener employed by a client to complete a task: she sees in the idiosyncrasy of the Petition some signs that Pinkhurst had 'employed his creative energies on it and that he was fully embedded in the politics of the piece'.[37] His use of English in the Mercers' Petition was simply in keeping with the group's overall strategy for reaching a wider segment of the population.

John Marchaunt's father, Nicholas Marchaunt, Mercer, was named as one of John of Northampton's supporters in the general pardon of 1384, so he at least adhered to that faction of London politics.[38] The companies with which clerks associated with writing in English are affiliated – the Mercers, Goldsmiths, Tailors, Skinners – all included large numbers of members who supported the Northampton faction.[39]

As Lynn Staley points out, however, the prime mover in the use of English propaganda for political gains may have been John of Northampton's patron, John of Gaunt.[40] Chaucer was of course bound to John of Gaunt through family connection and patronage, but he also received an annuity from Henry earl of Derby in the 1390s.[41] Gower received a collar of SSs, as an outward symbol of his affinity, from Henry earl of Derby, and this 'livery' of allegiance was so important to Gower that his tomb effigy is shown wearing it.[42] Fisher sees a connection between the dating of an entry in Henry's wardrobe accounts in autumn 1393 ordering a replacement collar for 'un Esquier John Gower' and the year in which [according to Fisher's dating] Gower replaced his original dedication of the *Confessio Amantis* to Richard II with a new one dedicating it to Henry earl of Derby.[43] After his accession Henry also granted Gower a two pipes of Gascony a year.[44]

The clerk Richard Frampton, whose work we have described above, may have worked for or been affiliated with the Guildhall secretariat in the 1380s and 1390s, since he wrote a manuscript of *Statutes* for the city, now one of the city's Custumals, before 1391.[45] Frampton's affiliation with London could have lasted until 1399/1400, when he wrote the *Inspeximus* of Henry IV in relation to charters granted to the City of London, and a second copy probably commissioned by the city in a size to fit into a volume of custumals. If the original charters were stored at the Guildhall rather than in the royal chancery (as it would be more normal for the recipient to store the original charters) then Frampton's access to them for recording

---

[36] Lindenbaum, 'London Texts and Literate Practice', p. 291; this point is also made by Turner, 'Conflict', p. 264, which also quotes Lindenbaum.

[37] Turner, 'Conflict', p. 265.

[38] 'Roll A 24: 1380–81', *Calendar of Plea and Memoranda Rolls*, II 275–302, or mem. 13–13v.

[39] Bird, *Turbulent London*, pp. 69, 73–4; Mooney, 'Chaucer's Scribe', pp. 106–7.

[40] L. Staley, 'Gower, Richard II, Henry of Derby, and the Business of Making Culture', *Speculum* 75 (2000), 68–96 (pp. 81–96).

[41] *Chaucer Life-Records*, ed. Crow and Olson, pp. 271–5.

[42] Fisher, *John Gower*, pp. 38, 68; he cites Kew, National Archives, Duchy of Lancaster Miscellanea, Bundle X, no. 43.

[43] Fisher, *John Gower*, p. 68; Fisher later cites *Complete Works of Gower*, IV, xvi, for evidence that 'Henry was … in the habit of impetuously giving his own or his retainers' collars away and then having to have duplicates made' (Fisher, pp. 341–2, n. 5).

[44] Fisher, *John Gower*, p. 68.

[45] See pp. 107, 112 above; the custumal is now split into two volumes, one London, Metropolitan Archives, CLRO, COL/CS/01/008, fols 137r–290v, and the other British Library, MS Cotton Claudius D.ii, fols 139r–268v; see Parkes, 'Richard Frampton', p. 114. As Parkes notes, the latest statute written by Frampton's hand is dated 1391.

the *Inspeximus* would depend upon affiliation with the Guildhall secretariat.[46] After 1400 he too appears to have been elevated to a full-time position in the Lancastrian chancery. Our discovery of his having written one of only two surviving copies of Thomas Favent's *Historia*, which describes the Merciless Parliament in which Nicholas Brembre and other favourites of Richard II were tried and executed, puts him in the same political circle as Marchaunt and Pinkhurst. His position vis-à-vis Favent's *Historia* is the same as Pinkhurst's with respect to the petitions of the Mercers and Leathersellers: whether Frampton helped to compose the *Historia* or was merely hired to write the elegant roll copy of it, his acquiescence in recording such a partisan account shows his affiliation with the faction of John of Northampton in London politics, and his subsequent employment as clerk for Henry IV further connects Gaunt and his son with that faction.

The clerks of the London Guildhall appear to have embraced English not only in their recording of the city's business but in their literature as well, and several of them seem to have composed work in English themselves. Generalizing from their focus on the scribes of Langland's *Piers Plowman*, whom they imagined centred on royal government in Westminster, Kathryn Kerby-Fulton and Stephen Justice commented that 'bureaucratic service in the English fourteenth and fifteenth centuries was a first home of the vernacular literary culture of Langland's and Chaucer's generation, and that the activities of those bureaucrats participating in it were substantially, not just accidentally, literary'.[47]

The clerks of the Guildhall – John Marchaunt, Adam Pinkhurst, Richard Osbarn, and John Carpenter – can be added to the names of those who, like the poets Thomas Usk, Geoffrey Chaucer, John Gower, and Thomas Hoccleve, bridged the gap between clerkship for government and writing in English. These four clerks who knew the London poets personally, attached themselves to – or possibly influenced – that faction of London politics, supported by John of Gaunt and his son Henry of Derby, that had recognized the usefulness of the English vernacular in winning the commons to its cause(s), just as the Lancastrians would do leading up to and after their rise to kingship. Men of many ranks and talents appear to have been involved: poets, lawyers, clerks, aldermen, mayors, earls, dukes, and kings.

Now that we have completed the circle of patrons, authors, and scribes by identifying these clerk-scribes, it seems clear that the London Guildhall itself was a centre for this activity. Furthermore, based on the copying that can be connected with it, from multiple exemplars accessible to the scribes over several decades, it is also clear that the Guildhall or some site within its close must have been a repository for works of vernacular literature from at least the very beginning of the fifteenth century, and probably earlier, in the last decades of Richard II's reign when these authors were actively writing and these city clerks were rising through the ranks at the Guildhall. In receiving, preserving and disseminating works of Middle English literature in the late fourteenth and early fifteenth centuries, the clerks of the London Guildhall preserved for us some of the greatest literature written in the English language.

---

[46] See pp. 108–9, 111–12 above.

[47] Kerby-Fulton and Justice, 'Langlandian Reading Circles', p. 59; see also Turner, 'Usk and the Goldsmiths', p. 141.

Epilogue

THE RESEARCH FOR THIS BOOK was conducted with funding from a major research grant from the Arts and Humanities Research Council, 'Identifying the Scribes Responsible for Copying Major Works of Middle English Literature', 2007–11, with Linne Mooney (Principal Investigator); Simon Horobin (Co-Investigator); and Estelle Stubbs (Research Associate). The scope of our research was partly limited by the bounds set for the project we had proposed for the grant and by time constraints. We have therefore set out our preliminary findings here to stimulate further research in this field: there is much still to be done.

First, the bounds we had set ourselves for the research project were the manuscripts of the English writings of five major authors of the late fourteenth and early fifteenth centuries: Geoffrey Chaucer, John Gower, John Trevisa, William Langland and Thomas Hoccleve. We have not had time to look for the hands of the Guildhall clerks in manuscripts of other Middle English literature, of other literature written in French or Latin (including works by Gower), or indeed, of bibles, prayer books, lectionaries, sermon collections, medical treatises, etc.

Second, we have not searched thoroughly for further manuscripts or documents written by hands that appear with, or are otherwise associated with, the Guildhall scribes we have described here: thus there is still work to be done on Scribe Delta, whose hand Doyle and Parkes argue is so similar to Scribe D's as to make them almost indistinguishable. Nor have we made a thorough search for the second hand in British Library, MS Harley 3943, who appears to be working under Osbarn's direction, nor for the contemporary hands that write British Library, Additional MS 27944 together with John Marchaunt. We have not made a thorough search for further literary manuscripts or documents written by the man we call the 'Trevisa–Gower scribe', who wrote a portion of Bodley 902 together with Marchaunt, and three other manuscripts of the *Confessio Amantis* (Bodleian Library, MSS Bodley 693 and Laud misc. 609, and a fragment, London, University College, Frag. Angl. 1), and one of Trevisa's *Polychronicon* (Tokyo, Senshu University Library, MS 1). Our Guildhall scribes may have copied works of Lydgate into manuscript, though we have not yet come across any such manuscripts in our searches. We *have* searched – though not thoroughly – for Hands A and C of Trinity College MS R.3.2 who wrote portions of that manuscript of the *Confessio Amantis* together with Marchaunt, Pinkhurst and Hoccleve; we think it likely that they were lesser clerks at the Guildhall.

We made some of these discoveries near the beginning of the four-year project, but delayed publishing the results because it soon became clear that each identification built on the others, and a book would better set out how all these men worked together over many decades at the Guildhall. Although we are not as certain of some identifications as of others, together they support one another, forming a substantial body of evidence for the copying of Middle English literature by clerks at the Guildhall. We therefore offer this book as a first step toward recognizing the importance of the Guildhall secretariat in the dissemination of Middle English literature and the introduction of English as the language of commerce and government, and we encourage other scholars in the field to take further steps to complete the journey of discovery.

Bibliography

Avril, F., and P. D. Stirnemann, *Manuscrits enluminés d'origine insulaire, VIIe–XXe siècle* (Paris, 1987)

Barron, C. M., 'Richard Whittington: The Man Behind the Myth', in *Studies in London History Presented to Philip Edmund Jones*, ed. A. E. J. Hollaender and W. Kellaway (London, 1969), pp. 197–248

—— 'The Government of London and its Relations with the Crown, 1400–1450' (unpublished PhD dissertation, University of London, 1970)

—— *The Medieval Guildhall of London* (London, 1974)

—— *London in the Later Middle Ages* (Oxford, 2004)

—— 'New Light on Thomas Usk', *Chaucer Newsletter* 26:2 (2004)

—— 'The Political Culture of Medieval London', in *Political Culture in Late Medieval Britain*, ed. L. Clark and C. Carpenter, The Fifteenth Century 4 (Cambridge, 2004), pp. 110–33

—— Review of Lisa Jefferson (ed.), *Wardens' Accounts and Court Minute Books of the Goldsmiths' Mistery of London, 1334–1446*, *Urban History* 32 (2005), 173–5

Bird, R., *The Turbulent London of Richard II* (London, 1949)

Blake, N. F., *The Textual Tradition of the 'Canterbury Tales'* (London, 1985)

Boffey, J., and C. Meale, 'Selecting the Text: Rawlinson C.86 and Some Other Books for London Readers', in *Regionalism in Late Medieval Manuscripts and Texts*, ed. F. Riddy (Cambridge, 1991), pp. 143–69

Bowers, J. M., 'The House of Chaucer & Son: The Business of Lancastrian Canon-Formation', *Medieval Perspectives* 6 (1991), 135–43

—— 'Two Professional Readers of Chaucer and Langland: Scribe D and the HM114 Scribe', *Studies in the Age of Chaucer* 26 (2004), 113–46

Bowsher, D., T. Dyson, N. Holder and I. Howell, *The London Guildhall: An Archaeological History of a Neighborhood from Early Medieval to Modern Times*, 2 vols. (London, 2007)

Brewer, T., *Memoir of the Life and Times of John Carpenter* (London, 1856)

Briquet, C.-M., *Les Filigranes* (Leipzig, 1923)

Brusendorff, A., *The Chaucer Tradition* (Oxford, 1925; repr. 1967)

Burrow, J. A., *Thomas Hoccleve*, Authors of the Middle Ages 4 (Aldershot, 1994)

Butterfield, A., 'Puy', in *Medieval France: An Encyclopedia*, ed. W. W. Kibler and G. A. Zinn (New York, 1995)

Calendar of Entries in the Papal Registers Relating to Great Britain and Ireland, vol. 5: *1398–1404*, ed. W. H. Bliss (London, 1904)

A Calendar to the Feet of Fines for London and Middlesex, vol. 1: *Richard I–Richard III*, ed. W. J. Hardy and W. Page (London, 1892)

Calendar of Letter-Books of the City of London, A–L, ed. R. R. Sharpe, 11 vols. (London, 1899–1912)

Calendar of the Patent Rolls Preserved in the Public Record Office: Henry VI, vol. 3: *1436–1441*, ed. H. C. Maxwell Lyte et al. (London, 1901)

Calendar of the Patent Rolls Preserved in the Public Record Office: Richard II, vol. 1: *1377–1381*, ed. H. C. Maxwell Lyte et al. (London, 1985)

Calendar of Plea and Memoranda Rolls: Preserved Among the Archives of the Corporation of the City of London at the Guildhall, ed. A. H. Thomas, 6 vols. (London, 1926–61)

Calendar of Wills Proved and Enrolled in the Court of Husting, London, 1258–1688, ed. R. R. Sharpe, 2 vols. (London, 1889–90)

Catto, J., 'Andrew Horn: Law and History in Fourteenth-Century England', in *The Writing of History in the Middle Ages: Essays Presented to Richard William Southern*, ed. R. H. C. Davies and J. M. Wallace-Hadrill (Oxford, 1981), pp. 367–91

—— 'Written English: The Making of the Language, 1370–1400', *Past & Present* 179 (2003), 24–59

Chambers, R. W., 'The Manuscripts of *Piers Plowman* in the Huntington Library and their Value for Fixing the Text of the Poem', *Huntington Library Bulletin* 8 (1935), 1–27

Chambers, R., and M. A. Daunt, ed., *A Book of London English, 1384–1425* (Oxford, 1931)

Chaucer, G., *The Text of 'The Canterbury Tales': Studied on the Basis of All Known Manuscripts*, ed. J. M. Manly and E. Rickert, 8 vols. (Chicago, 1940)

—— *A Variorum Edition of the Works of Geoffrey Chaucer*, vol. 5: *The Minor Poems*, ed. G. B. Pace and A. David (Norman OK, 1982)

—— *The Riverside Chaucer*, gen. ed. L. D. Benson (Oxford, 1987)

Coleman, J., *Public Reading and the Reading Public in Late Medieval England and France* (Cambridge, 1996)

Connolly, M., *John Shirley: Book Production and the Noble Household in Fifteenth-Century England* (Aldershot, 1998)

Cooper, H., 'Sources and Analogues of the *Canterbury Tales*: Reviewing the Work', *Studies in the Age of Chaucer* 19 (1997), 183–210; repr. 'The Frame', in *Sources and Analogues of the 'Canterbury Tales'*, ed. R. M. Correale and M. Hamel, vol. 1 (Cambridge, 2002), pp. 1–22

—— 'London and Southwark Poetic Companies: "Si tost c'amis" and the *Canterbury Tales*', in *Chaucer and the City*, ed. A. Butterfield (Cambridge, 2006), pp. 109–24

Creaton, H. J., 'The Warden's Accounts of the Mercers' Company of London, 1347, 1391–1464', 2 vols. (unpublished MPhil dissertation, University of London, 1976)

Crow, M. M., and C. C. Olson, ed., *Chaucer Life-Records* (Oxford, 1966)

Davies, M., 'Carpenter, John (d. 1442)', in *Oxford Dictionary of National Biography* (Oxford, 2004)

Davies, M., with A. Saunders, *The History of the Merchant Taylors' Company* (Leeds, 2004)

Dempster, G., 'Manly's Conception of the Early History of the *Canterbury Tales*', *PMLA* 61 (1946), 379–415

A Descriptive Catalogue of Ancient Deeds in the Public Record Office, ed. H. C. Maxwell Lyte, 6 vols. (London, 1890–1915)

The Digital Index of Middle English Verse, ed. L. R. Mooney *et al.*, www.DIMEV.net

Dodd, G., 'Was Thomas Favent a Political Pamphleteer? Faction and Politics in Later Fourteenth-Century London', *Journal of Medieval History* 30 (2011), 1–22

Doyle, A. I., 'More Light on John Shirley', *Medium Aevum* 30 (1961), 93–101

—— 'The Manuscripts', in *Middle English Alliterative Poetry and its Literary Background*, ed. D. A. Lawton (Cambridge, 1982), pp. 88–100, 142–7

—— 'English Books in and out of Court from Edward III to Henry VI', in *English Court Culture in the Later Middle Ages*, ed. V. J. Scattergood and J. W. Sherborne (London, 1983), pp. 163–81

—— 'Remarks on Surviving Manuscripts of *Piers Plowman*', in *Medieval English Religious and Ethical Literature: Essays in Honour of G. H. Russell*, ed. G. Kratzmann and J. Simpson (Cambridge, 1986), pp. 35–48

—— 'The Copyist of the Ellesmere *Canterbury Tales*', in *The Ellesmere Chaucer: Essays in Interpretation*, ed. M. Stevens and D. Woodward (San Marino CA, 1995; repr. 1997), pp. 49–67

—— 'The Study of Nicholas Love's *Mirror*: Retrospect and Prospect', in *Nicholas Love at Waseda: Proceedings of the International Conference, 20–26 July 1995*, ed. S. Oguro *et al.* (Cambridge, 1997), pp. 163–74

Doyle, A. I., and M. B. Parkes, 'The Production of Copies of the *Canterbury Tales* and the *Confessio Amantis* in the Early Fifteenth Century', in *Medieval Scribes, Manuscripts and Libraries: Essays Presented to N. R. Ker*, ed. M. B. Parkes and A. G. Watson (London, 1978), pp. 163–210; repr. in M. B. Parkes, *Scribes, Scripts and Readers: Studies in the Communication, Presentation and Dissemination of Medieval Texts* (London, 1991), pp. 201–48

—— 'Palaeographical Introduction', in *The Canterbury Tales: A Facsimile and Transcription of the Hengwrt Manuscript, with Variants from the Ellesmere Manuscript*, ed. P. G. Ruggiers (Norman OK, 1979), pp. xix–xlix

Drogin, M., *Medieval Calligraphy: Its History and Technique* (New York, 1980)

Dutschke, C. W., *Guide to the Medieval and Renaissance Manuscripts in the Huntington Library*, 2 vols. (San Marino CA, 1989)

Edwards, A. S. G., 'A Missing Leaf from the Plimpton *Fall of Princes*', *Manuscripta* 15 (1971), 29–30

Edwards, A. S. G., and D. Pearsall, 'The Manuscripts of the Major English Poetic Texts', in *Book Production and Publishing in Britain, 1375–1475*, ed. J. Griffiths and D. Pearsall (Cambridge, 1989), pp. 257–78

Emden, A. B., *A Biographical Register of the University of Oxford, to A.D. 1500*, 3 vols. (Oxford, 1957–9)

Favent, T., *Historia sive narracio de modo et forma mirabilis parliamenti apud Westmonasterium*, ed. M. McKisack, in *Camden Miscellany XIX*, Camden Society 3rd series 37 (1926)

—— *History or Narration Concerning the Manner and Form of the Miraculous Parliament at Westminster*, trans. A. Galloway, in *The Letter of the Law: Legal Practice and Literary Production in Medieval England*, ed. E. Steiner and C. Barrington (Ithaca NY, 2002), pp. 231–52

Fisher, J. H., *John Gower: Moral Philosopher and Friend of Chaucer* (New York, 1964)

—— '*Piers Plowman* and the Chancery Tradition', in *Medieval English Studies Presented to George Kane*, ed. E. D. Kennedy et al. (Cambridge, 1988), pp. 267–78

—— 'A Language Policy for Lancastrian England', *PMLA* 107 (1992), 1168–80

Fletcher, A. J., 'The Criteria for Scribal Attribution: Dublin, Trinity College, MA 244, Some Early Copies of the Works of Geoffrey Chaucer, and the Canon of Adam Pynkhurst Manuscripts', *Review of English Studies* 58 (2007), 597–632

Fredell, J., 'The Gower Manuscripts: Some Inconvenient Truths', *Viator* 41:1 (2010), 231–50

Furnivall, F. J., ed., *The Fifty Earliest English Wills, 1387–1439*, EETS OS 78 (1882)

Furnivall, F. J., and I. Gollancz, ed., *Hoccleve's Works*, vol. 1: *The Minor Poems*, EETS ES 61 (1892); rev. ed. J. Mitchell and A. I. Doyle (1970)

Garbáty, T. J., 'A Description of the Confession Miniatures for Gower's *Confessio Amantis* with Special Reference to the Illustrator's Role as Reader and Critic', *Mediaevalia* 19 (1996), 319–43

Gillespie, A., 'Reading Chaucer's Words to Adam', *Chaucer Review* 42 (2008), 269–83

Gower, John, *The English Works of John Gower*, ed. G. C. Macaulay, 2 vols., EETS ES 81 and 82 (1900–1)

—— *The Complete Works of John Gower*, ed. G. C. Macaulay, 4 vols. (Oxford, 1899–1902; republished 1968)

Green, R. F., *Poets and Princepleasers: Literature and the English Court in the Late Middle Ages* (Toronto, 1980)

Griffiths, J. J., '*Confessio Amantis*: The Poem and its Pictures', in *Gower's 'Confessio Amantis': Responses and Reassessments*, ed. A. J. Minnis (Cambridge, 1983), pp. 163–78

—— 'Thomas Hingham, Monk of Bury and the Macro Plays Manuscript', *English Manuscript Studies* 5 (1995), 214–19

Grindley, C., 'The Life of a Book: British Library Add. 35157 in Historical Context' (unpublished PhD dissertation, University of Glasgow, 1997)

Gumbert, P., 'The Speed of Scribes', in *Scribi e colofoni: Le sottoscrizioni di copisti dalle origini all'avvento della stampa: Atti del seminario di Erice X Colloquio del Comité International de Paleographie Latine (23–8 ottobre 1993)*, ed. E. Condello and G. De Gregorio (Spoleto, 1995), pp. 57–69

Haines, R. M., 'Carpenter, John (c. 1395–1476)', in *Oxford Dictionary of National Biography* (Oxford, 2004)

Hammond, E. P., *Chaucer: A Bibliographical Manual* (New York, 1933)

Hanna, R., 'Booklets in Medieval Manuscripts: Further Considerations', *Studies in Bibliography* 39 (1986), 100–11

—— 'The Scribe of Huntington HM 114', *Studies in Bibliography* 42 (1989), 120–33

—— 'Sir Thomas Berkeley and his Patronage', *Speculum* 64 (1989), 878–916

—— 'The Manuscripts and Transmission of Chaucer's *Troilus*', in *The Idea of Medieval Literature: New Essays on Chaucer and Medieval Culture in Honor of Donald R. Howard*, ed. J. M. Dean and C. K. Zacher (Newark, 1992), pp. 173–88; repr. in R. Hanna, *Pursuing History: Middle English Manuscripts and their Texts* (Stanford, 1996), pp. 115–29

—— *Pursuing History: Middle English Manuscripts and their Texts* (Stanford, 1996)

—— *London Literature, 1300–1380* (Cambridge, 2005)

Hanna, R., and D. Lawton, ed., *The Siege of Jerusalem*, EETS OS 320 (2003)

Hoccleve, T., *Thomas Hoccleve's Complaint and Dialogue*, ed. J. A. Burrow, EETS OS 313 (1999)

—— *Thomas Hoccleve: A Facsimile of the Autograph Verse Manuscripts*, intro. J. A. Burrow and A. I. Doyle, EETS SS 19 (2002)

Horobin, S., *The Language of the Chaucer Tradition* (Cambridge, 2003)

—— 'Adam Pinkhurst and the Copying of British Library MS Additional 35287 of the B Text of *Piers Plowman*', *Yearbook of Langland Studies* 23 (2009), 61–83

—— 'The Criteria for Scribal Attribution: Dublin, Trinity College MS 244 Reconsidered', *Review of English Studies* 60 (2009), 371–81

—— 'Adam Pinkhurst, Geoffrey Chaucer, and the Hengwrt Manuscript of the *Canterbury Tales*', *The Chaucer Review* 44 (2010), 351–67

—— 'The Scribe of Bodleian Library, MS Digby 102 and the Circulation of the C Text of *Piers Plowman*', *Yearbook of Langland Studies* 24 (2010), 89–112

Horobin, S., and L. R. Mooney, 'A *Piers Plowman* Manuscript by the Hengwrt/Ellesmere Scribe and its Implications for London Standard English', *Studies in the Age of Chaucer* 26 (2004), 65–112

Horobin, S., and D. W. Mosser, 'Scribe D's SW Midlands Roots: A Reconsideration', *Neuphilologische Mitteilungen* 106 (2005), 289–305

A. Hudson, *Studies in the Transmission of Wyclif's Writings* (Aldershot, 2008)

Hulbert, J. R., 'The Text of *The Siege of Jerusalem*', *Studies in Philology* 28 (1930), 602–12

Imray, J. M., '"Les Bones Gents de la Mercerye de Londres": A Study of the Membership of the Medieval Mercers' Company', in *Studies in London History Presented to Philip Edmund Jones*, ed. A. E. J. Hollaender and W. Kellaway (London, 1969), pp. 155–78

The Index of Middle English Verse, ed. C. Brown and R. H. Robbins (New York, 1943)

Irigoin, J., 'La Datation des filigranes du papier', *Codicologica* 5 (1980), 9–36

Jefferson, L., ed., *Wardens' Accounts and Court Minute Books of the Goldsmiths' Mistery of London, 1334–1446* (Woodbridge, 2003)

―, ed. and trans., *The Medieval Account Books of the Mercers of London: An Edition and Translation*, 2 vols. (Aldershot, 2009)

Keene, D. J., and V. Harding, ed., *Historical Gazetteer of London before the Great Fire: Cheapside; Parishes of All Hallows Honey Lane, St Martin Pomery, St Mary le Bow, St Mary Colechurch, and St Pancras Soper Lane* (London, 1987)

Kellaway, W., 'John Carpenter's *Liber Albus*', *Guildhall Studies in London History* 3:2 (1978), 67–84

Ker, N. R., '*Liber Custumarum* and Other Manuscripts Formerly at the Guildhall', *Guildhall Miscellany* 1:3 (1954), 37–45

―― *Medieval Libraries of Great Britain: A List of Surviving Books*, 2nd edn (London, 1964)

―― *Medieval Manuscripts in British Libraries*, 4 vols. (Oxford, 1969–92)

―― '*Liber Custumarum*, and Other Manuscripts Formerly at the Guildhall', in *Books, Collectors and Libraries: Studies in the Medieval Heritage*, ed. A. G. Watson (London, 1985), pp. 135–42

Kerby-Fulton, K., 'Professional Readers of Langland at Home and Abroad: New Directions in the Political and Bureaucratic Codicology of *Piers Plowman*', in *New Directions in Later Medieval Manuscript Studies: Essays from the 1998 Harvard Conference*, ed. D. Pearsall (York, 2000), pp. 103–29

―― 'Langland in his Working Clothes', in *Middle English Poetry: Texts and Traditions, Essays in Honour of Derek Pearsall*, ed. A. J. Minnis (York, 2001), pp. 139–61

Kerby-Fulton, K., and S. Justice, 'Langlandian Reading Circles and the Civil Service in London and Dublin, 1380–1427', *New Medieval Literatures* 1 (1997), 59–83

―― 'Scribe D and the Marketing of Ricardian Literature', in *The Medieval Professional Reader at Work: Evidence from Manuscripts of Chaucer, Langland, Kempe and Gower*, English Literary Studies 85 (Victoria BC, 2001), pp. 217–37

Kölbing, E., and M. Day, ed., *The Siege of Jerusalem*, EETS OS 188 (1932; repr. 2001)

Langland, W., *Piers Plowman: The B Version*, ed. G. Kane and E. Talbot Donaldson (London, 1975)

Le Goff, J., *Time, Work and Culture in the Middle Ages*, trans. A. Goldhammer (Chicago, 1980)

Leyerle, J., 'Thomas Usk', in *Dictionary of the Middle Ages*, ed. J. R. Strayer, vol. 12 (New York, 1989), pp. 333–5

Liber Albus: The White Book, trans. H. T. Riley (London, 1861)

Lindenbaum, S., 'London Texts and Literate Practice', in *The Cambridge History of Medieval English Literature*, ed. D. Wallace (Cambridge, 1999), pp. 284–309

London Assize of Nuisance, 1301–1431: A Calendar, ed. H. M. Chew and W. Kellaway, London Record Society 10 (London, 1973)

London Possessory Assizes: A Calendar, ed. H. M. Chew, London Record Society 1 (London, 1965)

Masters, B. R., 'The Town Clerk', *Guildhall Miscellany* 3 (1969–70), 55–74

―― *The Chamberlain of the City of London, 1273–1987* (London, 1988)

Matheson, L. M., *The Prose 'Brut': The Development of a Middle English Chronicle* (Tempe, 1998)

Matheson, L. M., and L. R. Mooney, 'The Beryn Scribe and his Texts: Evidence for Multiple-Copy Production of Manuscripts in Fifteenth-Century England', *The Library*, 7th series 4 (2003), 347–70

McIntosh, A., M. L. Samuels and M. Benskin, ed., *A Linguistic Atlas of Late Medieval English*, 4 vols (Aberdeen, 1986)

Mooney, L. R., 'Professional Scribes? Identifying English Scribes who had a Hand in More than One Manuscript', in *New Directions in Later Medieval Manuscript Studies*, ed. D. Pearsall (York, 2000), pp. 131–41

—— 'Chaucer's Scribe', *Speculum* 81 (2006), 97–138

—— 'Some New Light on Thomas Hoccleve', *Studies in the Age of Chaucer* 29 (2007), 293–40

—— 'Locating Scribal Activity in Late-Medieval London', in *Design and Distribution of Later Medieval Manuscripts in England*, ed. M. Connolly and L. R. Mooney (York, 2008), pp. 183–204

—— 'A Holograph of Hoccleve's *Regiment of Princes*', *Studies in the Age of Chaucer* 33 (2011), 263–96

—— 'Vernacular Literary Manuscripts and their Scribes', in *The Production of Books in England, 1350–1500*, ed. A. Gillespie and D. L. Wakelin (Cambridge, 2011), pp. 192–211

Mooney, L. R., and D. W. Mosser, 'Hooked-g Scribes and Takamiya Manuscripts', in *The Medieval Book and a Modern Collector: Essays in Honour of Toshiyuki Takamiya*, ed. T. Matsuda, R. A. Linenthal and J. Scahill (Cambridge, 2004), pp. 179–207

Mosser, D. W., '"Chaucer's Scribe", Adam and the Hengwrt Project', in *Design and Distribution of Late Medieval Manuscripts in England*, ed. M. Connolly and L. R. Mooney (York, 2008), pp. 11–40

Munimenta Gildhallae Londoniensis: Liber Albus, Liber Custumarum et Liber Horn, ed. H. T. Riley, 3 vols. in 4, Rolls Series 12 (London, 1859–60)

Nightingale, P., 'Capitalists, Crafts and Constitutional Change in Late Fourteenth-Century London', *Past and Present* 124 (1989), 3–35

—— *A Medieval Mercantile Community: The Grocers' Company and the Politics and Trade of London, 1000–1485* (New Haven CT, 1995)

Owen, C. A., *The Manuscripts of 'The Canterbury Tales'* (Cambridge, 1991)

Parkes, M. B., *Scribes, Scripts and Readers: Studies in the Communication, Presentation and Dissemination of Medieval Texts* (London, 1991)

—— 'Archaizing Hands in English Manuscripts', in *Books and Collectors, 1200–1700: Essays Presented to Andrew Watson*, ed. J. P. Carley and C. G. C. Tite (London, 1997), pp. 101–41

—— 'Richard Frampton: A Commercial Scribe, *c.* 1390–*c.* 1420', in *The Medieval Book and a Modern Collector: Essays in Honour of Toshiyuki Takamiya*, ed. T. Matsuda, R. A. Linenthal and J. Scahill (Cambridge, 2004), pp. 113–24

Pearsall, D., 'The "Ilchester" Manuscript of *Piers Plowman*', *Neuphilologische Mitteilungen* 82 (1981), 181–93

—— *The Canterbury Tales* (London, 1985)

—— *The Life of Geoffrey Chaucer: A Critical Biography* (Oxford, 1992)

—— 'The Manuscripts and Illustrations of Gower's Works', in *A Companion to Gower*, ed. S. Echard (Cambridge, 2004), pp. 73–97

—— 'The *Canterbury Tales* and London Club Culture', in *Chaucer and the City*, ed. A. Butterfield (Cambridge, 2006), pp. 95–108

Pedes Finium, or Fines Relating to the County of Surrey, ed. F. B. Lewis, Surrey Archaeological Society extra vol. 1 (Guildford, 1894)

Prescott, A., 'Administrative Records and the Scribal Achievement of Medieval England', *English Manuscripts before 1400*, ed. A. S. G. Edwards and Orietta da Rold, English Manuscript Studies 17 (London, 2012), pp. 173–99

Ramsey, N., and J. M. W. Willoughby, ed., *Corpus of British Medieval Library Catalogues*, vol. 14: *Hospitals, Towns, and the Professions* (London, 2009)

Rand Schmidt, K. A., *The Authorship of 'The Equatorie of the Planetis'* (Cambridge, 1993)

Reddaway, T. F., *The Early History of The Goldsmiths' Company, 1327–1509,* bound with *The Book of Ordinances, 1478–83,* ed. L. E. M. Walker (London, 1975)

The Register of Henry Chichele Archbishop of Canterbury, 1414–1443, vol. 2: *Wills Proved before the Archbishop or his Commisaries*, ed. E. F. Jacob and H. C. Johnson, Canterbury and York Society 42 (Oxford, 1937)

Richmond, C., 'Religion and the Fifteenth-Century English Gentleman', in *The Church, Politics and Patronage in the Fifteenth Century*, ed. R. B. Dobson (Gloucester, 1984), pp. 193–208

Riley, H. T., ed. and trans., *Memorials of London and London Life in the Thirteenth, Fourteenth and Fifteenth Centuries* (London, 1868)

Roberts, J., 'On Giving Scribe B a Name and a Clutch of London Manuscripts from c. 1400', *Medium Aevum* 80:2 (2011), 247–70

Robinson, P. R., *Catalogue of Dated and Datable Manuscripts, c. 888–1600, in London Libraries*, 2 vols. (London, 2003)

Root, R. K., *The Manuscripts of Chaucer's 'Troilus'*, Chaucer Society 1st series 98 (London, 1914 for 1911)

—— *The Textual Tradition of Chaucer's 'Troilus'*, Chaucer Society 1st series 99 (1916)

Samuels, M. L., 'The Scribe of the Hengwrt and Ellesmere Manuscripts of the *Canterbury Tales*', *Studies in the Age of Chaucer* 5 (1983), 49–65; repr. in *The English of Chaucer and his Contemporaries*, ed. J. J. Smith (Aberdeen, 1988), pp. 38–50

Sánchez-Martí, J., 'Adam Pynkhurst's "Necglygence and Rape" Reconsidered', *English Studies* 92:4 (2011), 360–74

Scase, W., 'Reginald Pecock, John Carpenter and John Colop's "Common-Profit" Books: Aspects of Book Ownership and Circulation in Fifteenth-Century London', *Medium Aevum* 61 (1992), 261–74

Scott, K. L., *Survey of Manuscripts Illuminated in the British Isles*, vol. 6: *Later Gothic Manuscripts, 1390–1490*, 2 vols. (London, 1996)

—— 'An Hours and Psalter by Two Ellesmere Illuminators', in *The Ellesmere Chaucer: Essays in Interpretation*, ed. M. Stevens and D. Woodward (San Marino CA, 1995; repr. 1997), pp. 87–119

—— *Dated and Datable English Manuscript Borders, c. 1395–1499* (London, 2002)

Seymour, M. C., *Selections from Hoccleve* (Oxford, 1981)

—— *A Catalogue of Chaucer Manuscripts*, vol. 1: *Works before 'The Canterbury Tales'* (Aldershot, 1995)

Skeat, W. W., ed., *The Vision of William Concerning Piers the Plowman in Three Parallel Texts, Together with Richard the Redeless*, 2 vols. (Oxford, 1886)

Smith, J., 'Studies in the Language of Some Manuscripts of Gower's *Confessio Amantis*' (unpublished PhD dissertation, University of Glasgow, 1985)

Somerville, R., 'The Cowcher Books of the Duchy of Lancaster', *English Historical Review* 51 (1936), 598–615

—— *History of the Duchy of Lancaster*, vol. 1 (London, 1953)

Spurgeon, C. F. E., *Five Hundred Years of Chaucer Criticism and Allusion, 1357–1900*, 8 vols., Chaucer Society 2nd series 48–50 and 52–6 (Cambridge, 1908–17)

Staley, L., 'Gower, Richard II, Henry of Derby, and the Business of Making Culture', *Speculum* 75 (2000), 68–96

Steer, F. W., ed., *Scriveners' Company Common Paper, 1357–1678, with a Continuation to 1678*, London Record Society Publications 4 (London, 1968)

Steiner, E., *Documentary Culture and the Making of Medieval English Literature* (Cambridge, 2003)

Stow, J., *A Survey of London*, STC 23341 (London, 1598)

—— *A Survey of London*, STC 23343 (London, 1603)

—— *A Survey of London* [1603 edition], ed. W. J. Thoms (London, 1876)

Strohm, P., *Social Chaucer* (Cambridge MA, 1989)

—— 'Politics and Poetics: Usk and Chaucer in the 1380s', in *Literary Practice and Social Change in Britain, 1380–1530*, ed. Lee Patterson (Berkeley CA, 1990), pp. 83–112

Stubbs, E., ed., *The Hengwrt Chaucer Digital Facsimile*, Scholarly Digital Editions (Leicester, 2000)

—— 'A New Manuscript by the Hengwrt/Ellesmere Scribe? Aberystwyth, National Library of Wales, MS Peniarth 393D', *Journal of the Early Book Society* 5 (2002), 161–8

—— *A Study of the Codicology of Four Early Manuscripts of the Canterbury Tales; Aberystwyth, National Library of Wales MS. Peniarth 392D (Hengwrt), Oxford, Corpus Christi College, MS. 198 (Corpus), London, British Library MS. Harley 7334 (Harley 4), and California, San Marino, Huntington Library MS. El. 26 C 9 (Ellesmere)*, The Norman Blake Editions of *The Canterbury Tales*, HRI Online, University of Sheffield (forthcoming)

—— '"Here's One I Prepared Earlier": The Work of Scribe D on Oxford, Corpus Christi College MS 198', *Review of English Studies* NS 58 (2007), 133–53

Stubbs, E., and L. Mooney, 'A Record Identifying Thomas Hoccleve's Father', *Journal of the Early Book Society* 14 (2011), 233–7

Sutton, A. F., 'The Mercery Trade and the Mercers' Company of London from the 1130s to 1348' (unpublished PhD dissertation, University of London, 1995)

—— 'Merchants, Music and Social Harmony: The London Puy and its French and London Contexts, *circa* 1300', *The London Journal* 17 (1992), 1–17

—— *The Mercery of London: Trade, Goods and People, 1130–1578* (Aldershot, 2005)

Tatlock, J. S. P., *The Harleian Manuscript 7334 and Revision of the 'Canterbury Tales'*, Chaucer Society 2nd series 41 (London, 1909)

—— 'The *Canterbury Tales* in 1400', *PMLA* 50 (1935), 100–39

Taylor, J., *English Historical Literature in the Fourteenth Century* (Oxford, 1987)

—— 'Favent, Thomas', in *Oxford Dictionary of National Biography* (Oxford, 2004)

—— 'Whittington, Richard', in *Oxford Dictionary of National Biography* (Oxford, 2004)

Tucker, P., *Law Courts and Lawyers in the City of London, 1330–1550* (Cambridge, 2007)

Turner, M., *Chaucerian Conflict: Languages of Antagonism in Late Fourteenth-Century London* (Oxford, 2006)

—— 'Conflict', in *Middle English*, ed. P. Strohm, Oxford Twenty-First Century Approaches to Literature (Oxford, 2007), pp. 258–73

—— 'Usk and the Goldsmiths', *New Medieval Literatures* 9 (2007), 139–77

Usk, T., *The Testament of Love*, ed. R. A. Shoaf, TEAMS Middle English Texts series (Kalamazoo MI, 1998)

The Victoria History of the County of Surrey, vol. 3, ed. H. E. Malden (London, 1911)

Wakelin, D. L., 'Writing the Words', in *The Production of Books in England, 1350–1500*, ed. A. Gillespie and D. L. Wakelin (Cambridge, 2011), pp. 34–58

Warren, F., and B. White, ed., *The Dance of Death*, EETS OS 181 (1931)

Windeatt, B., 'The Text of the *Troilus*', in *Essays on 'Troilus and Criseyde'*, ed. M. Salu (Cambridge, 1979), pp. 1–22

—— 'The Text of the "Troilus"', in G. Chaucer, *Troilus and Criseyde: A New Edition of 'The Book of Troilus'*, ed. B. A. Windeatt (London, 1984), pp. 36–54

—— *Oxford Guides to Chaucer: 'Troilus and Criseyde'* (Oxford, 1992)

Index of Manuscripts Cited

Pages that include illustrations of the manuscript listed are shown in boldface.

Aberdeen, University Library, MS 21 60 (n. 53)

Aberystwyth, National Library of Wales
Peniarth 392D ('Hengwrt manuscript') 3, 59 (n. 47), 63, 67–8, 72–5, **125**, 126
Peniarth 393D 68

Cambridge, Pembroke College, MS 307 61, 120, 136

Cambridge, Trinity College Library
B.15.17 68
R.3.2 3, 5, 38, 43, 69, **75**, 82, 84, 122–7, 130, 132–3, 136, 141
R.3.20 69 (n. 15), **70**

Cambridge, University Library
Dd.4.24 74 (n. 37)
Dd.8.19 86, 93, 96, **97**, 100, 136
Kk.1.3, Part XX 69, 71, 79, **80**
Mm.5.14 108, 116

Durham, University Library, MS Cosin V.iii.9 131

Edinburgh, National Library of Scotland, Advocates 18.1.7, 120

Exeter, Devon Record Office, MS 2507 116

Glasgow, University Library
Hunterian S.1.7 (7) 136
Hunterian T.4.1 (84) 107

Hatfield House, Herts., Cecil Papers, Box S/1 68, 79, 106

Kew, The National Archives
C 49/10/3 79 (n. 45)
C 81/1394/87 71 (n. 21), **72–3**
C 146/9532 102 (nn. 39, 41, 44)
DL 42/1–2 108, 111–12, **114**
DL 42/192–3 108, 111–12
E 40/1292 28 (n. 25)
E 40/2360 **53**
E 40/12349 29 (n. 28), 55 (n. 29), **87**, 131 (n. 90)
E 159/159 57 (n. 37)
E 356/14 57 (n. 37)
SC 8/20/997 79, 82, 118, 137–40
SC 8/20/998–1000 79 (n. 45), 118
SC 8/21/1001B **78**, 79, 82, 118, 140
SC 8/21/1001–6 79 (n. 45), 118
SC 8/94/4664 79 (n. 45)

Lichfield, Lichfield Cathedral Library, MS 29 120

London, British Library
Additional Charter 40542 **81**
Additional MS 27944 38–9, **40**, 42, 44–6, 48, 59, 133 (n. 5), 141
Additional MS 35157 3 (n. 11)
Additional MS 35287 68
Arundel 119 120
Cotton Caligula A.ii 116
Cotton Claudius D.ii 107, 139 (n. 45)
Egerton 1991 38, 45, 62, 133 (n. 5), 136
Harley 3943 4, 18, 21, **22**, 31–3, 35–7, 134, 141
Harley 7334 38, 55, **56**, 59, 63–5, 133 (n. 5), 134
Lansdowne 851 63 (n. 77)
Royal 18 C.xxii 136
Royal 18 D.vi 32 (n. 40)
Sloane 1686 63 (n. 77)
Sloane 3501 120

London, Goldsmiths' Company Archives, MS 1642 (Register of Deeds) 9, 24, **25**, 27, 34–5, 80

London, Guildhall Library
MS 5370 (Scriveners' Company Common Paper 3, **66**, 67, 75–6, 82
MS 31692 (Register of the Worshipful Company of Skinners, Book of the Fraternity of the Assumption of Our Lady) 120

London, Lambeth Palace Library, MS 491 4, 17–18, **22**, 31–4, 60, 116

London, Mercers' Company Archives, Account Book of 1347, 1391–1464 67, 80, 82, 83 (n. 51), 98

Index of Manuscripts Cited

London, Metropolitan Archives
    Charter 50   **109**, 111–12, 115, 139
    CLA 023/DW/01/113 (Husting Rolls of Deeds and Wills, items 97, 98)   67 (n. 3)
    CLA 023/DW/01/117 (Husting Rolls of Deeds and Wills, mem. 10v, item 96)   54, **55**
    CLA 023/DW/01/126 (Husting Rolls of Deeds and Wills, mem. 26–28 [item 117])   81 (n. 48)
    CLRO, COL/AD/01/007 (Letter Book G)   16, 50, 53, **54**, 56
    CLRO, COL/AD/01/008 (Letter Book H)   4, 9, 16, 25, **26**, 27–8, **50–1, 52**, 122 (n. 50)
    CLRO, COL/AD/01/009 (Letter Book I)   5, 16, 18–19, **22**, 23, 29 (n. 30), 48, **49**, 50, 75, **76**, 77, 82–4, 87, **88**, 89, **90**, **91**, 93, 96, 98
    CLRO, COL/AD/01/010 (Letter Book K)   50, 87
    CLRO, COL/CS/01/006 (*olim* Cust. 6; *Liber Custumarum*)   129 (n. 75)
    CLRO, COL/CS/01/008 (*olim* Cust. 8; *Statutes*)   107, 112, 139 (n. 45)
    CLRO, COL/CS/01/012 (*olim* Cust. 12; *Liber Albus*)   4, 5, 7, 9–16, 18–19, 23, **24**, 27, **47**, **48**, **49**, **92**, 93, **95**, 99–100, 109, **110**, 111–12, 115–16, 136, 139

London, University College, MS Frag. Angl. 1   136, 141

London, University Library, MS SL V.88 ('Ilchester' manuscript)   38–9, **40**, 44, 54, 58, 121, 133 (n. 5), 134

Manchester, University of Manchester, John Rylands Library, MS Eng. 103   38–9, **41**, 44, 60, 133 (n. 5), 134

New York, Columbia University Library, MS Plimpton 265   38, 133 (n. 5), 136

New York, Pierpont Morgan Library & Museum
    M.125   136
    M.817 ('Campsall' manuscript)   5, 86, 93, **94**, 100–1, 133

Oslo and London, Schøyen Collection, MS 615   120

Oxford, Bodleian Library
    Ashmole 59   83
    Bodley 294   38, 42, 133 (nn. 4–5), 136
    Bodley 693   136, 141
    Bodley 902   38, 61–2, 133 (nn. 4–5), 136, 141
    Bodley misc. 2963 (Rolls 9)   **117**, 118, 140
    Digby 102   121
    Laud misc. 609   136, 141
    Rawlinson C.86   31 (n. 36)

Oxford, Christ Church, MS 148   38, 133 (nn. 4–5), 136

Oxford, Corpus Christi College
    MS 67   38, 133 (nn. 4–5), 136
    MS 198   38–9, 42, **47**, 48, 54, 59, 63–5, 73, 133 (n. 5), 134

Oxford, Exeter College, MS 129   32 (n. 40), 33

Paris, Bibliothèque nationale de France
    Lat. 919   91 (n. 8)
    Lat. 3603   107

Petworth House, Sussex (The National Trust), MS 7   120

Philadelphia, Rosenbach Museum and Library, MS 1083/29   62, 86, 93, **96**, 100, 136

Princeton, Princeton University Library, Department of Rare Books and Manuscripts, MS Taylor 5   38–9, **41**, 44–5, 60, 62, 133 (n. 5), 136

San Marino, CA, Henry E. Huntington Library
    EL 26 C.9 ('Ellesmere manuscript')   3, 59 (n. 47), 63, 67, 69, 72–3
    HM 111   127–30
    HM 114   4, 16, 17–19, **20**, 21, 30–7, 101 (n. 34), 116
    HM 143   121, 122 (n. 46)
    HM 19920   107, **113**, 115

Tokyo, Senshu University, MS 1   141

Tokyo, Takamiya Collection
    MS 45   120
    MS 54   120, 121

Tokyo, Waseda University, MS NE 3691   121

General Index

Alexander the Great: *Liber magni Alexandri*, 107, 108
Anne (Queen of England, wife of Richard II), 81
archaizing script, 115 (& n. 16), 147
Ashurst farm (Surrey), 85 (& n. 29)
Awnters of Arthur, 30

Bamme, Adam (Goldsmith and Mayor of London), 119
Barbers' Company of London, 121
Barnet, Richard (Common Clerk of the City of London), 99
Barron, Caroline, viii, 5 (n. 21), 7 (n. 2), 8 (& nn. 5-6, 9), 9 (& nn. 12, 14), 10 (& nn. 19-22), 12 (n. 27), 18 (n. 4), 23 (& n. 18), 27 (n. 22), 28 (nn. 24-6), 29 (& nn. 29-30), 30 (nn. 31-2), 38 (n. 2), 51 (& n. 22), 65 (n. 88), 74 (& nn. 33-4), 77 (& nn. 40-2), 79, 81 (n. 48), 86 (n. 2), 87 (n. 3), 93 (& n. 11), 98 (& nn. 15-19, 21), 118 (& n. 25), 122 (n. 30), 136 (& n. 24), 137 (n. 25), 142
Beaufort, Henry, 137
Berkeley, Thomas (knight), 59 (& n. 52), 60 (n. 53), 116 (n. 19), 132 (n. 1), 137 (& n. 29), 145
Betchworth (Surrey), 83
Blake, Norman, 59 (n. 47), 63 (& n. 78), 126 (n. 61), 142
Blount, Robert (clerk), 101 (n. 37), 104, 106
Boccaccio, Giovanni: *Il Filostrato*, 36
Boethius: *De consolatione philosophiae*, 119, 120
Bolton Abbey (Yorkshire), 116
Bonjohn, William (citizen of London), 52, 53
Book of Hunting, 17, 18, 30, 33, 34
Bowers, John, 2 (n. 4), 39 (& n. 8), 58, 59 (n. 46), 73 (n. 31), 74 (& n. 33), 116 (n. 17), 132 (n. 1), 142
Bowyers' Company of London, 121
Brembre, Nicholas (Mayor of London, 1383-4, 1384-5), 67, 78-80, 82, 118, 137-8, 140
Brewer, Thomas, 87 (& n. 5), 89 (n. 7), 93 (n. 9), 96 (& n. 12), 97 (n. 14), 99 (n. 24), 100 (n. 30), 101 (n. 35), 102 (& nn. 38, 40, 42, 44), 103 (nn. 45-6, 48), 104 (nn. 52, 54, 57-8), 105 (nn. 61, 64, 66)
Brewers' Company of London, 5, 98, 121, 150
Brewers' Hall, ix, 121
Bromleigh (Surrey), 84
Brusendorff, Aage, 2 (& n. 6), 142
Brut chronicle (prose), 4, 7 (n. 1), 17-18, 21, 30, 33-4, 37-9, 41, 58 (n. 38), 60 (& n. 54), 133 (n. 5), 134, 146

Brynchley, John (clerk of the Tailors' Company), 119
Burrow, John, 19 (n. 15), 98 (n. 16), 128 (nn. 68-9), 130 (& nn. 82, 86), 131 (& n. 91), 134 (n. 7), 142, 145
Bury, William of, 103

cadels (strapwork), 89-91, 93, 96
Carpenter, John (Common Clerk of the City of London, 1417-38), 4, 5 (& n. 19), 6, 8-11 (& n. 26), 12 (nn. 27-8, 30), 13 (& nn. 33, 37), 14 (& n. 38), 15-16 (& n. 42), 18, 23-4, 27-8 (& n. 25), 29, 38, 47 (n. 17), 48, 50, 61-2, 65, 79, 84 (n. 54), 86-7 (& nn. 3-5), 88-9 (& n. 7), 90-3 (& nn. 9, 11), 94-6 (& n. 12), 97 (& nn. 13-14), 98 (& nn. 17, 19), 99 (& nn. 22-8), 100 (& n. 30), 101 (& nn. 34-6), 102 (& nn. 38-44), 103 (& nn. 45-50), 104 (& nn. 51-8), 105 (& nn. 59-64, 66), 106, 109 (n. 8), 111 (& nn. 9, 12), 129-31 (& n. 90), 133-4, 136, 138, 140, 142-3, 145-6, 148
  books bequeathed by, 86, 99, 101 (& n. 37), 102-3 (& n. 46), 104-6
  will of, 99, 101-2 (& n. 38), 104-6
Carpenter, John (elder brother of John Carpenter, Common Clerk), 102 (& n. 39)
Carpenter, John (warden of the hospital of St Anthony in Threadneedle Street, then Bishop of Worcester), 102 (& nn. 41, 43-4)
Carpenter, Katherine, 96 (n. 12), 99 (& n. 25), 101-2 (& n. 38), 104
Carpenter, Richard, 96 (n. 12), 97, 102
Carpenter, Robert, 102
Castre, John (Ironmonger of London), 53
Cecil, William (secretary to Lord Protector Somerset), 68, 79 (n. 46), 106 (& n. 69), 150
Chamberlain of London, 4, 8 (& n. 5), 9-10, 14, 16, 23, 25, 27 (& n. 22), 28 (& n. 25), 51 (& n. 21), 54, 61, 74, 77 (& n. 42), 93 (n. 11), 135-6, 146
Charles d'Orléans, 107
Chaucer, Geoffrey, 1 (& n. 1), 2 (& nn. 4-6, 8), 3 (& nn. 14-16), 4 (& n. 18), 5 (& n. 21), 7, 9-10 (n. 16), 16 (& n. 43), 17 (n. 2), 18 (& nn. 12-13), 30, 33, 35 (& n. 48), 36 (& nn. 49-50), 37-8 (& n. 4), 39 (n. 8), 47, 55 (& n. 29), 56 (& n. 32), 57 (n. 37), 59 (nn. 46-7), 60, 63-4 (& nn. 80-1, 83), 65, 67 (nn. 1-4), 68 (nn. 5, 9-10), 69 (nn. 11, 13-15), 70 (& nn. 16, 18), 71 (nn. 19-22), 72 (& nn. 23-6), 73 (& nn. 27, 29, 31), 74 (& nn. 32-3, 36-7), 75-6 (n. 39), 79 (& nn. 44-6), 80-1 (n. 47), 82 (nn. 49-50), 83 (nn. 51-2), 84 (& n. 57), 85 (& n. 59), 86, 93-4, 106, 119 (& nn. 29, 32-3), 120, 122, 126, 127 (& n. 65), 129 (& nn. 74-5, 77, 79), 132 (& n. 1), 133 (& nn. 5-6), 134 (& nn. 10-11), 135, 136, 137 (nn. 25, 29), 138-9 (& nn. 39-41), 140-9
  dwelling over Aldgate, ix, 9, 134, 135
  dwelling in Westminster Cathedral close, 73 (& n. 31), 126
  Boece (trans. of Boethius, *De consolatione philosophiae*), 68, 70-2, 84, 119
  Canterbury Tales, 1, 2 (nn. 6, 9), 3 (& n. 13), 4-5, 16, 19 (n. 12), 38 (& n. 4), 39, 47, 54-5 (& n. 30), 56, 59 (nn. 46-7), 60, 62-3 (& nn. 77-8), 64 (nn. 80, 82, 85), 67 (n. 2), 68 (& n. 3), 69 (& n. 13), 71-2 (& n. 26), 73-4 (& nn. 32, 37), 79-80, 85, 119 (& nn. 33-4), 120, 122 (& nn. 47, 50), 125-6 (n. 61), 129 (nn. 74-5, 77), 132 (n. 1), 133 (n. 5), 134, 138, 142-5, 147-9
  'Chaucer's Wordes unto Adam His Owne Scriveyn', 69-70
  Troilus and Criseyde, 4-5, 9, 10 (n. 16), 17 (& n. 2), 18-19 (n. 12), 30-5 (& n. 48), 36 (& nn. 49-51), 37, 68, 70-2 (& n. 23), 74 (& nn. 36-7), 79, 84, 86, 93, 94, 100-1 (n. 34), 106, 119, 133-5, 145, 148-9
Chaucer, Phillipa (wife of Geoffrey Chaucer), 137
Chaucer, Thomas, 74, 129 (n. 79)
Cheffon, Peter: *Epistola Luciferi ad Cleros*, 18, 30
Cleve, William, 103
Clifford, Thomas (earl of Skipton), 116
Colop, John, 5 (n. 19), 103 (n. 50), 104 (& n. 53), 105 (nn. 60-2), 148
Comberton, Robert, 81
common profit books, 5 (n. 19), 103 (n. 50), 104 (& nn. 53, 55), 105 (& nn. 60-2), 148
Cooper, Helen, 129 (& nn. 74-6), 143
Court de Bone Conpaignie, 128-30 (n. 81), 131
Cresswyck, William, 81 (& n. 48)
Curriers' Company of London, 121

Davies, Matthew, viii, 5 (n. 19), 103 (nn. 47-9), 119-20 (n. 35), 143
Debate between the Body and the Soul, 121 (& n. 40)
'Delta' (scribe), 5, 43 (n. 13), 45 (& n. 15), 60 (& n. 53), 136, 141
Dempster, Germaine, 2 (& n. 6), 143
Dodd, Gwilym, 118 (& nn. 21-2), 143, 152
Dorking (Surrey), 83

General Index

Doyle, A. I., viii, 2 (& n. 9), 3 (& n. 13), 4 (& n. 17), 5 (& nn. 20, 22), 13 (& n. 36), 16–17 (n. 1), 18 (n. 3), 19 (& n. 15), 23, 38 (& n. 1), 39 (& nn. 6, 9), 43 (& n. 13), 44 (& n. 14), 45, 53 (& n. 30), 58 (& nn. 38–9), 60 (n. 53), 64 (& nn. 82–3), 67 (n. 2), 68 (nn. 9–10), 69 (nn. 11–13), 73, 83 (n. 53), 87 (n. 3), 93 (& n. 10), 100 (& n. 31), 106 (n. 68), 107 (n. 1), 108 (& n. 7), 112 (n. 14), 120 (n. 37), 122 (& nn. 48–9), 123 (& n. 51), 124–6 (n. 60), 127 (nn. 65–6), 131, 134 (n. 7), 136, 141, 143–5, 153

Dunstone, or Dustone, John (Chamber Clerk of London, 1382), 51–2

Dutschke, Consuelo, 18 (& n. 9), 32 (n. 41), 33 (n. 43), 34, 108 (n. 4), 144

Dymok, Roger, 195
   Contra duodecim errores et hereses Lollardorum, 105 (n. 66)

Edmonton (Middlesex), 81
Edward III (King of England), 17, 50, 84 (& n. 55), 85, 93 (n. 10), 143, 152
Edward of Norwich (Duke of York): *Master of Game*, 120
Essex, William (Draper of London), 57, 119
Exton, Nicholas (Mayor of London), 137

Favent, Thomas: *Historia sive narracio de modo et forma mirabilis parliamenti apud Westmonasterium*, 117 (& n. 21), 118 (& nn. 21–2, 24), 140, 143–4, 149
Fisher, John, 2 (& n. 8), 3 (n. 11), 10 (n. 17), 39, 129 (n. 73), 132 (n. 1), 135 (& nn. 12–19), 136 (& nn. 20, 22), 137 (& nn. 28–9), 138 (& n. 30), 139 (& nn. 42–4), 144
Fishmongers' Company of London, ix, 8
Flamel, Jean (scribe), 91
Forde, Thomas, of Canterbury, 87, 89
Forster (Forester), Richard, attorney, 134, 136
Frampton, Richard, 5, 12, 30–1, 35 (& n. 47), 42 (& n. 10), 107 (& nn. 1, 3), 108 (& nn. 3, 5), 109 (& n. 8), 110–12 (& nn. 14–15), 113–18 (& n. 21), 134, 139 (& n. 45), 140, 147
Fredell, Joel, viii, 62 (& nn. 73, 75), 144
Furnivall, Frederick J., 63, 119 (n. 33), 127 (n. 66), 128 (n. 69), 130, 144

Gamalin, John, 104
Gaunt, John of (Duke of Lancaster), 56 (& n. 32), 81, 137–9, 140
Geffray, Adam, de Horsham, 83
Gesta Romanorum, 131
Gillespie, Alexandra, 1 (n. 2), 69 (n. 15), 70–1 (n. 19), 132 (n. 3), 144, 147, 149
Gilte Legende, 120
Girdlers' Company of London, 52–3, 121
Goldsmiths' Company of London, ix, 5, 8–9, 24 (& n. 19), 25 (& n. 21), 27, 34–5, 65 (n. 88), 80, 118 (n. 25), 119 (n. 28), 134, 139, 140 (n. 47), 142, 145, 147, 149–50

Gower, John, 1–2 (& nn. 7–8), 4 (& n. 18), 5, 7, 9–10 (& n. 17), 16, 38 (& n. 3), 39, 41, 58 (n. 45), 59 (n. 47), 60 (nn. 53, 59), 61 (& nn. 63–6, 68–9), 62 (& nn. 70, 73–5), 65, 69, 75, 79, 82 (& n. 49), 85–6, 93, 96–7, 100 (& n. 31), 119–20, 122–5, 127 (& n. 65), 129 (n. 75), 132 (n. 1), 134–5 (& nn. 12, 14–18), 136 (& nn. 20, 22), 137 (& n. 29), 138–9 (nn. 40, 42–4), 140–1, 144, 146–8
   Confessio Amantis, 2 (& n. 9), 4–5, 10, 38 (& n. 3), 39, 41, 43 (n. 12), 58 (n. 45), 59 (n. 47), 60–1 (& n. 69), 62–3, 69, 75, 82 (n. 49), 85–6, 93, 96–7, 100–1 (n. 34), 120, 122–3, 125–7, 132–3 (& nn. 4–5), 136–7, 139, 141, 144, 148
   Mirrour de l'omme, 7 (n. 1), 120 (& n. 37), 121, 143
Grandes Heures de Jean, Duc de Berry, 91
Griffiths, Jeremy, 32 (n. 40), 38 (n. 3), 62 (n. 72), 120 (& n. 36), 121, 144
Grocers' Company of London, ix, 8, 80 (n. 47), 104, 147
Guido della Colonna: *Historia destructionis Troiae*, 107–8
Guildford (Surrey), 84 (& n. 57)
Guildhall of London, ix, 1–5, 7 (& n. 8), 9, 10 (& n. 23), 11, 12 (n. 29), 15–18 (& n. 6), 19, 23–5, 27–9 (& n. 30), 30 (& nn. 31–2), 31–2 (n. 40), 34–5 (& n. 45), 37–8, 43, 48–51 (& n. 21), 52 (& n. 25), 56–60 (& n. 56), 61 (& n. 60), 62–9, 73–5, 77, 79–80, 82–4, 86, 93, 95–7 (n. 13), 98 (n. 15), 99 (& n. 28), 101 (& n. 37), 103 (& nn. 47, 49), 104–6 (& nn. 67, 69), 107, 109, 111–12, 115, 117–19, 121 (& n. 42), 122–3, 127–8 (& n. 73), 129, 131–3 (& n. 4), 134–42, 146, 150
   chapel, 29–30, 106 (& n. 69), 128 (& n. 73)
   library, 10, 30, 35, 66, 86, 103 (& n. 49), 104–6 (& nn. 67, 69)
   reconstruction (1411), 29–30, 102–3
Guy de Rouclif (Clerk of the Office of the Privy Seal), 127

Hanna, Ralph, viii, 3 (n. 12), 8 (n. 8), 12 (n. 29), 16 (n. 45), 17 (n. 2), 18 (& nn. 3, 5, 7), 19 (& nn. 10–12, 14), 23 (& n. 17), 27, 30 (n. 34), 31 (& nn. 36–8), 32 (& n. 39), 33 (& nn. 42–3), 34 (& n. 44), 35 (& nn. 46–8), 36 (& n. 50), 59 (& n. 52), 60 (& nn. 53, 55–6), 61 (& nn. 60–2), 74 (& nn. 36–7), 79, 108 (n. 3), 116 (& nn. 17, 19–20), 132 (n. 1), 137 (n. 29), 145, 154
Henry IV (King of England), 5, 12, 14–15, 23, 48–9, 74–5 (& n. 38), 108 (& nn. 5, 7), 109–1 (& n. 11), 112, 115–16, 127, 129, 131, 137–9 (& n. 40), 140, 142, 148, 152
   Inspeximus of charters to the City of London, 12, 14–15, 108–11 (& n. 11), 112, 115–16, 139–40

Henry V (King of England), 12, 14–15, 23, 55 (n. 29), 74, 87 (& n. 3), 100–1, 108 (& n. 7), 111, 131 (& n. 90), 133, 137–8
   Inspeximus of charters to the City of London, 12, 14
Hoccleve, Thomas, 2 (& n. 3), 5, 7 (n. 1), 19 (& n. 15), 21 (& n. 15), 45 (n. 16), 98 (n. 16), 122–5 (& n. 59), 126–7 (& nn. 62–3, 65–7), 128 (& nn. 68–72), 129–30 (& nn. 81–6), 131 (& nn. 88, 91), 132–4 (& n. 7), 136–7, 140–2, 144–5, 147–9
   'Balade to Master John Carpenter', 129–30 (& n. 83), 131
   'Balades to Sir Henry Somer', 128 (& n. 72), 130 (n. 81)
   Dialogue with a Friend, 131 (& n. 91), 145
   Regiment of Princes, 21 (n. 15), 133–4 (n. 7), 147
   Tale of Jereslaus' Wife, 131
Hoccleve, William (Draper of London), 127
Holgrave, William (tailor), 119
Horn, Andrew (Chamberlain of London, 1320–8), 8, 10, 12 (& n. 29), 14, 23, 61, 111, 128 (n. 72), 129, 143, 147, 150
   Liber Custumarum, 8 (& n. 8), 12 (& n. 29), 14, 111, 128 (n. 72), 129 (& n. 75), 146–7, 150
   Liber Legum, 8
Horobin, Simon, viii, 5, 21 (n. 16), 38 (n. 4), 41, 58 (n. 38), 59 (n. 47), 65 (n. 86), 68 (nn. 5, 7–8), 69 (n. 13), 71 (& n. 21), 72 (& nn. 23, 26), 73 (& n. 27), 74 (& nn. 32, 37), 79, 121 (& nn. 39, 41–5), 141, 145
Hospital of St Thomas of Acon, Cheapside, 67
Husting, Court of, 7, 8, 16 (n. 42), 18, 28 (& n. 25), 52 (n. 25), 53–5 (& n. 29), 67, 81 (n. 48), 87 (& n. 3), 98, 131 (n. 90), 132, 142, 150

John, Lewis (Vintner of London), 129 (& n. 79)
John of Lancaster (Duke of Bedford), 131
Jubilee Book, 14, 137 (& n. 25)
Justice, Steven, 4 (& n. 18), 39 (& n. 7), 59 (& n. 51), 60 (& nn. 57–8), 62 (& nn. 70, 72), 122 (n. 49), 132 (n. 1), 140 (& n. 47), 146

Kellaway, William, 10 (& n. 23), 11 (& n. 26), 12 (& nn. 28–30), 13 (& nn. 33–5, 37), 14 (& nn. 38–9), 47 (& n. 17), 86 (n. 2), 87 (& n. 4), 93 (& nn. 9, 11), 97 (nn. 13–14), 98 (n. 19), 99 (& nn. 23–8), 100 (n. 30), 109 (& n. 8), 111 (& nn. 9, 11–12), 142, 145, 146
Ker, Neil R., viii, 2 (& n. 9), 8 (n. 8), 12 (n. 29), 106 (n. 69), 144, 146

153

Kerby-Fulton, Kathryn, 3 (n. 11), 4 (& n. 18), 39 (& n. 7), 58 (& n. 44), 59 (& nn. 48, 51), 60 (& nn. 57–8), 62 (& nn. 70, 72), 122 (n. 49), 132 (n. 1), 140 (& n. 47), 146

Kelom, Martin (Mercers' scribe), 83 (n. 51)

Killum, John (Grocer of London), 104

Lancaster, Duchy of, 5, 108 (& nn. 5–6), 111–12 (& n. 14), 114, 116–17, 122 (n. 49), 139 (n. 42), 148

Langland, William, 1, 3 (n. 3), 4 (& n. 18), 7, 16–17, 30, 38, 39 (n. 8), 40, 58 (& n. 44), 59 (& nn. 46, 48), 60, 68 (& n. 8), 69, 121 (& nn. 39–40), 122 (n. 49), 132–3, 138, 140 (& n. 47), 141, 142, 145, 146

Piers Plowman, 1, 3 (& n. 11), 17, 21 (n. 16), 30, 33, 35 (& n. 46), 38–40, 44, 48, 54, 58 (& nn. 39–40), 68 (& nn. 7–8), 69 (n. 13), 121 (& nn. 39–40), 122, 133 (& n. 5), 134, 140, 143–8

Lawton, David, 16 (n. 45), 17 (n. 1), 18 (n. 3), 19 (n. 14), 23 (n. 17), 31 (& nn. 36–7), 35 (n. 47), 108 (n. 3), 116 (& nn. 18, 20), 143, 145

le Botoner family, 55 (& n. 29)

Leathersellers' Company of London, 78–9, 82, 84, 118, 138, 140

Leventhorp, John (Receiver General of the Duchy of Lancaster), 112

Liber Albus, 4–5, 8 (& n. 8), 9 (& n. 11), 10 (& n. 23), 11 (& nn. 25–6), 12 (& nn. 27–31), 13 (& nn. 33, 37), 14–16 (& n. 44), 18 (n. 3), 19, 23 (& n. 17), 24, 27, 30, 34, 47 (& n. 17), 48–9, 61, 77 (& n. 41), 86 (& n. 4), 92–3 (& nn. 9, 11), 95–7 (nn. 13–14), 98 (nn. 17–19), 99 (& nn. 23–9), 100 (& n. 30), 108–9 (& n. 8), 110–11 (& nn. 9, 12), 112, 115–16, 128–9, 136 (& n. 21), 137 (& n. 25), 146–7

Lichfield, William (rector of All Hallow's Church, London), 103–6

Lindenbaum, Sheila, 65 (& n. 88), 137 (n. 25), 138 (& n. 35), 139 (n. 36), 146

livery of city of London officials, 8, 77, 99, 101, 136, 139

Lollards / Lollardy, 58 (& n. 45), 59 (& n. 46), 105

Love, Nicholas, 7, 120 (& n. 37), 121, 143

Mirror of the Blessed Life of Jesus Christ, 7, 120 (& n. 37), 121, 143

Lydgate, John, 7 (n. 1), 32 (n. 40), 86 (& n. 1), 102, 120, 137, 141

'Danse of the Macabre', 86 (& n. 1), 102

Siege of Thebes, 120

Lynford, Robert (clerk of the Brewers' Company), 121

Macaulay, G. C., 2 (& n. 7), 39, 62, 132 (n. 1), 135 (& n. 14), 144

Maidstone, Richard, 121 (& n. 40)

Seven Penitential Psalms, 121 (& n. 40)

Mandeville, John: *Travels*, 17, 30–1, 33, 107

Manly, John, 2 (n. 6), 3 (n. 13), 55 (n. 30), 63 (n. 77), 67 (n. 2), 68 (n. 9), 69 (n. 11), 72 (n. 26), 74 (n. 32), 119 (nn. 33–4), 122 (& n. 47), 143

Marchaunt, John (Common Clerk of the City of London, 1399–1417), 4–6, 8, 10, 13–14, 16 (& n. 42), 28 (& nn. 24–5), 29–30, 38–43 (& n. 12), 44–50 (& n. 20), 51–2 (& n. 25), 53–4 (& n. 28), 55 (& nn. 29–30), 56–7 (& nn. 33, 37), 58 (& nn. 38, 45), 59–60 (& n. 53), 61–2 (& n. 72), 63 (n. 77), 64–5, 73–4, 79, 83, 85–7, 89, 96–7 (& n. 14), 98–9 (& n. 22), 100–1, 103, 117, 119 (n. 29), 121–3, 130–1 (& n. 90), 133 (n. 4), 134 (& n. 8), 135–41

dwelling within Guildhall Close, 10, 98 (& n. 15)

will of, 16, 29 (n. 28), 55 (& n. 29), 86–7 (& n. 3)

Marcus Paulus: *De Oriente*, 107

Mercers' Company of London, ix, 3, 5, 8, 31 (n. 36), 52 (n. 25), 55 (n. 29), 67 (& n. 4), 68, 79, 80–1 (& n. 47), 82, 83 (n. 51), 84, 98 (& n. 20), 99 (& n. 24), 101 (& n. 35), 118, 119, 137–40, 143, 145, 149–50

Merciless Parliament (1388), 117 (& n. 21), 118, 137, 140

More, John (Mercer of London), 57, 119

Mooney, Linne, 1 (& nn. 1–2), 2 (& nn. 4–5), 3 (& nn. 10, 16), 4, 7 (n. 1), 16 (& n. 43), 19 (n. 15), 21 (n. 16), 32 (n. 40), 45 (n. 16), 67 (& nn. 1–4), 68 (nn. 5, 7, 9–10), 69 (& nn. 11, 13–14), 70 (nn. 16, 19), 71 (& n. 22), 72 (& nn. 24–5), 76 (n. 39), 79 (& nn. 44–6), 80, 81 (n. 47), 82 (& nn. 49–50), 83 (& nn. 51–2), 84 (& n. 57), 85 (n. 59), 86, 116 (n. 17), 127 (& nn. 62–3), 128 (& n. 68), 134 (nn. 7, 10), 137 (n. 25), 138–9 (n. 39), 141, 143, 145–7, 149, 154

Morden, Richard, 104

Mosser, Daniel, viii, 32 (n. 40), 59 (n. 47), 65 (n. 86), 72 (& n. 25), 73, 126 (n. 61), 145, 147

Newgate (city of London gate and prison), ix, 102

Norbury, Richard (Mercer of London), 57, 119

Northampton, John of (Draper and Mayor of London, 1381–2, 1382–3), 51, 57, 80–1 (& n. 48), 82, 117–19, 134, 137–40

Norwich, 101

Odericus: *Itinerarium*, 107

Odiham, Richard (Chamberlain of London, 1383), 51, 54

Organ, John (Mercer of London), 67 (n. 4), 82

Osbarn, Richard (Chamber Clerk of the City of London, 1400–37), 4–6, 8–10, 12 (& n. 32), 13 (& nn. 33, 37), 14–18 (& n. 4), 19–20, 22–4 (& n. 20), 25–8 (& nn. 24–5), 29–31 (& n. 36), 32 (& n. 40), 33 (& n. 43), 34 (& n. 44), 35–7, 39, 49–50, 53–4, 56, 58, 60–1, 63, 65, 75, 77, 79–80, 83, 96, 98 (& n. 16), 101 (& n. 34), 116 (& n. 17), 117, 122, 134–5, 138, 140–1

house within Guildhall Close, 29–30, 49

Parkes, Malcolm B., 2 (& n. 9), 3 (& n. 13), 4 (& n. 17), 5 (& n. 22), 13 (& n. 26), 38 (& n. 1), 39 (& nn. 6, 9), 42 (& n. 10), 43 (& n. 13), 44 (& n. 14), 45, 48 (& n. 18), 53, 58 (& n. 38), 60 (n. 53), 64 (& nn. 82–3), 67 (n. 2), 68 (nn. 9–10), 73, 106 (n. 68), 107 (& nn. 1, 3), 108–9 (& n. 8), 111–12 (& nn. 14–15), 115 (& n. 16), 122 (& nn. 48–9), 123 (& n. 51), 124–6 (& n. 60), 127 (n. 65), 136, 139 (n. 45), 141, 144, 147

Patsall, John and Thomas (of Barking), 31 (n. 36)

Pearsall, Derek, viii, 1 (n. 1), 2 (n. 3), 3 (n. 11), 32 (n. 40), 58 (& nn. 40–1, 43, 45), 59 (n. 48), 60 (n. 59), 61 (& nn. 63–6, 68–9), 62 (& nn. 70, 74), 64 (n. 80), 71–2 (n. 23), 119 (n. 32), 129 (& nn. 77–80), 144, 146–7, 152–3

Pecock, Reginald (rector of St Michael Paternoster, Warden of Whittington's Hospital), 103–6

Perot, Henry (Common Clerk of the City of London, 1375–94), 14, 28 (& n. 24), 134 (& n. 8)

Pinkhurst (Pynkhurst), Adam (clerk of the Guildhall), 3, 6–7, 16, 21 (& n. 16), 38 (n. 4), 39, 60 (n. 53), 63 (& n. 79), 64, 66–7 (& nn. 3–4), 68 (& nn. 5–10), 69 (& nn. 11, 13–15), 70 (& n. 17), 71 (& nn. 21–2), 72 (& nn. 23–5), 73–4 (& nn. 32, 37), 75–81 (& nn. 47–8), 82 (nn. 49–50), 83 (& nn. 51–2), 84–5 (& n. 59), 106, 117, 119, 122–3 (& n. 55), 125 (n. 59), 126–7, 133–4, 136–41, 145

Pinkhurst (Penkhurst), Adam (King's Archer), 82–4 (& nn. 54, 56)

Pinkhurst (Pynkhurst), Joanna, 82–3

Pinkhurst, John, 84 (n. 56), 85

Pinners' Company of London, 79 (n. 45), 121

Pontefract (Yorkshire), 116

Porland, William (clerk of the Brewers' Company), 121

Pui (or *Puy*) of London, 65 (n. 87), 128 (& nn. 72–3), 129 (& nn. 74–5), 142, 149

Pykworth, Thomas (knight), 103

General Index

Recorder of London, 4, 7–8, 77 (& nn. 40, 42), 80, 82, 122 (& nn. 49–50), 134–6
Reynold, John, 102 (& n. 38)
Richard II (King of England), 9, 28 (n. 25), 50 (n. 20), 51–2, 57 (n. 37), 67 (n. 3), 71, 79–80 (n. 47), 81, 85 (& n. 59), 96 (n. 12), 99 (n. 24), 101 (n. 35), 107–8, 116, 118, 120, 137, 139 (& n. 40), 140, 142, 148
Rickert, Edith, 3 (n. 13), 55 (& n. 30), 63 (& n. 77), 67 (n. 2), 68 (n. 9), 72 (n. 26), 74 (n. 32), 119 (& nn. 33–4), 122 (& nn. 47, 50), 143
Riley, H. T., 12 (n. 29), 15 (n. 40), 16, 23 (n. 17), 112 (n. 13), 146–8
Roberts, Jane, 68 (n. 4), 82 (n. 49), 83 (n. 51), 148
Root, R. K., 19 (& n. 12), 33, 35 (& n. 48), 36, 148

St Bartholomew's Hospital, Smithfield, ix, 102
St Martin's Church, Outwich, 96 (n. 12), 105
St Michael Paternoster, Riola, ix, 103–4
St Mary Overie, Southwark, ix, 2, 135
St Paul's Cathedral, London, ix, 86, 102
St Thomas of Acon's Hospital, Cheapside, 67
Saunders, Ann, 119–20 (& n. 35), 143
Scase, Wendy, 5 (n. 19), 103 (& n. 50), 104 (& nn. 53–6), 105 (& nn. 60–3), 106, 148
Scheerre, Herman, 61
Scogan, Henry, 129 (& n. 78)
  Moral Balade, 129 (& n. 78)
Scriveners' Company of London, 1, 3, 66, 67 (& n. 3), 71, 82, 148
  Common Paper of, 3, 66, 67 (& n. 3), 75, 76, 82, 148
Serjeant-at-Law of London (Common Serjeant), 9, 27 (& n. 22), 28, 48, 54, 77 (n. 42), 93 (n. 41), 122, 135–6
Seymour, John (citizen of London), 27
Seymour, Michael C., 19 (n. 12), 36 (n. 50), 127–8 (nn. 68–9, 71–2), 130 (& nn. 81, 85–6), 148
Shirley, John, 69 (& nn. 14–15), 70 (& n. 16), 71 (n. 18), 83 (& n. 53), 129, 143
Shoreditch (Middlesex), 81
Siege of Jerusalem, 4, 16 (n. 45), 17–18 (& n. 3), 19 (n. 14), 23 (n. 17), 30–1 (& nn. 36–7), 33 (& n. 42), 34–5 (& n. 47), 108 (& n. 5), 116 (& nn. 18, 20), 117, 132, 145–6
Sifrewas, John, 61
Skinners' Company of London, ix, 5, 120, 121 (& n. 38), 136, 139
  Guild Book of the Fraternity of Our Lady's Assumption, 120
Somer, Henry (Chancellor of the Exchequer, 1410–37), 127–8 (& nn. 69, 71), 130 (n. 81)
Somerville, Richard, 107 (n. 1), 108 (& nn. 5–6), 112 (n. 14), 148
Sotheworth, Matthew (Recorder of London, 1398–1404), 122 (& n. 50)

Sotheworth, Richard, 122
South English Legendary, 121
Spaldyng, John (citizen of London), 54
Staley, Lynn, 139 (& n. 40), 148
Statutes of England, 107, 108, 111–13, 115, 129, 139
Stopyndon, John, 122
strapwork, *see* cadels
Strode, Ralph, 9, 36, 48, 54, 65, 135
  dwelling over Aldersgate, ix, 9, 135
Stubbs, Estelle, 3 (n. 15), 4, 13, 16, 59, 62–3 (& nn. 76, 79), 64 (& nn. 81, 83), 68 (n. 6), 73 (n. 30), 81 (n. 48), 127 (n. 62), 128 (n. 68), 134 (& n. 9), 141, 149
Sudbury, John (Grocer of London), 103–4
Susanna, 17, 30, 33
Suso, Heinrich: *Horologium sapientiae divinae*, 107
Swynford, Katherine (later Duchess of Lancaster), 137

Taillour, William (knight), 104–5
Tailors' Company of London, 79, 119–20, 139
Tatlock, J. S. P., 3 (& n. 13), 59 (& n. 47), 64 (& n. 85), 67 (n. 2), 68 (n. 9), 69 (n. 11), 149
Three Kings of Cologne, 17–18, 30–1, 33, 34
Thursley (Surrey), 85 (& n. 59)
Tottenham (Middlesex), 81, 82 (& n. 48)
Trevisa, John, 7, 16, 38, 40, 54, 59, 61, 132, 137, 141
  De proprietatibus rerum (trans. of Bartholomeus Anglicus), 38, 40, 59, 137
  Polychronicon (trans. of Ranulph Higden), 137, 141
Tucker, Penny, 18 (nn. 4, 6), 28 (n. 23), 52 (& n. 26), 54 (n. 28), 56–7 (& n. 33), 97 (n. 13), 132 (& n. 2), 134 (nn. 8, 11), 149
Turner, Marion, 65 (n. 88), 119 (& n. 30–2), 137 (n. 25), 138 (& nn. 33, 35), 139 (& nn. 36–7), 149
Turpin (Archbishop of Reims): *Itinerarium*, 107

Ursewyke, Thomas (Recorder of London, then Chief Baron of the Exchequer), 122 (& n. 49)
Usk, Thomas, 5 (& n. 21), 6, 57, 65 (& n. 88), 118 (& nn. 26–7), 119 (& nn. 29–32), 134, 137–8, 140 (& n. 47), 142, 146, 148–9
  Testament of Love, 118, 119, 149

van Neweden, John (weaver), 98

Wade, Robert (scrivener of London), 71
Walton, John, 120
  trans. of Boethius, *De consolatione philosophiae*, 120
Walwayn, Philip, 85
watermarks, 18 (& n. 9), 19, 31–3 (& n. 42), 34 (& n. 44)

Whittington, Richard, 4, 9–11, 86 (& n. 2), 98 (n. 19), 99 (n. 24), 101 (& n. 35), 102–4, 142, 149
  will of, 4, 86, 99 (n. 24), 101 (& n. 35), 102–3
Whittington's Hospital, Riola, ix, 103–4
Windeatt, Barry, 35–6 (& nn. 49, 51–4), 37, 149

YORK MEDIEVAL PRESS PUBLICATIONS

God's Words, Women's Voices: The Discernment of Spirits in the Writing of Late-Medieval Women Visionaries, Rosalynn Voaden (1999)

Pilgrimage Explored, ed. J. Stopford (1999)

Piety, Fraternity and Power: Religious Gilds in Late Medieval Yorkshire, 1389–1547, David J. F. Crouch (2000)

Courts and Regions in Medieval Europe, ed. Sarah Rees Jones, Richard Marks and A. J. Minnis (2000)

Treasure in the Medieval West, ed. Elizabeth M. Tyler (2000)

Nunneries, Learning and Spirituality in Late Medieval English Society: The Dominican Priory of Dartford, Paul Lee (2000)

Prophecy and Public Affairs in Later Medieval England, Lesley A. Coote (2000)

The Problem of Labour in Fourteenth-Century England, ed. James Bothwell, P. J. P. Goldberg and W. M. Ormrod (2000)

New Directions in Later Medieval Manuscript Studies: Essays from the 1998 Harvard Conference, ed. Derek Pearsall (2000)

Cistercians, Heresy and Crusade in Occitania, 1145–1229: Preaching in the Lord's Vineyard, Beverly Mayne Kienzle (2001)

Guilds and the Parish Community in Late Medieval East Anglia, c. 1470–1550, Ken Farnhill (2001)

The Age of Edward III, ed. J. S. Bothwell (2001)

Time in the Medieval World, ed. Chris Humphrey and W. M. Ormrod (2001)

The Cross Goes North: Processes of Conversion in Northern Europe, AD 300–1300, ed. Martin Carver (2002)

Henry IV: The Establishment of the Regime, 1399–1406, ed. Gwilym Dodd and Douglas Biggs (2003)

Youth in the Middle Ages, ed. P. J. P Goldberg and Felicity Riddy (2004)

The Idea of the Castle in Medieval England, Abigail Wheatley (2004)

Rites of Passage: Cultures of Transition in the Fourteenth Century, ed. Nicola F. McDonald and W. M. Ormrod (2004)

Creating the Monastic Past in Medieval Flanders, Karine Ugé (2005)

St William of York, Christopher Norton (2006)

Medieval Obscenities, ed. Nicola F. McDonald (2006)

The Reign of Edward II: New Perspectives, ed. Gwilym Dodd and Anthony Musson (2006)

Old English Poetics: The Aesthetics of the Familiar in Anglo-Saxon England, Elizabeth M. Tyler (2006)

The Late Medieval Interlude: The Drama of Youth and Aristocratic Masculinity, Fiona S. Dunlop (2007)

The Late Medieval English College and its Context, ed. Clive Burgess and Martin Heale (2008)

The Reign of Henry IV: Rebellion and Survival, 1403–1413, ed. Gwilym Dodd and Douglas Biggs (2008)

Medieval Petitions: Grace and Grievance, ed. W. Mark Ormrod, Gwilym Dodd and Anthony Musson (2009)

St Edmund, King and Martyr: Changing Images of a Medieval Saint, ed. Anthony Bale (2009)

Language and Culture in Medieval Britain: The French of England, c. 1100–c. 1500, ed. Jocelyn Wogan-Browne et al. (2009)

The Royal Pardon: Access to Mercy in Fourteenth-Century England, Helen Lacey (2009)

Texts and Traditions of Medieval Pastoral Care: Essays in Honour of Bella Millett, ed. Cate Gunn and Catherine Innes-Parker (2009)

The Anglo-Norman Language and its Contexts, ed. Richard Ingham (2010)

Parliament and Political Pamphleteering in Fourteenth-Century England, Clementine Oliver (2010)

The Saints' Lives of Jocelin of Furness: Hagiography, Patronage and Ecclesiastical Politics, Helen Birkett (2010)

The York Mystery Plays: Performance in the City, ed. Margaret Rogerson (2011)

Wills and Will-Making in Anglo-Saxon England, Linda Tollerton (2011)

The Songs and Travels of a Tudor Minstrel: Richard Sheale of Tamworth, Andrew Taylor (2012)

Sin in Medieval and Early Modern Culture: The Tradition of the Seven Deadly Sins, ed. Richard G. Newhauser and Susan J. Ridyard (2012)

Socialising the Child in Late Medieval England, c. 1400–1600, Merridee L. Bailey (2012)

Barking Abbey and Medieval Literary Culture: Authorship and Authority in a Female Community, ed. Jennifer N. Brown and Donna Alfano Bussell (2012)

YORK STUDIES IN MEDIEVAL THEOLOGY

I *Medieval Theology and the Natural Body*, ed. Peter Biller and A. J. Minnis (1997)

II *Handling Sin: Confession in the Middle Ages*, ed. Peter Biller and A. J. Minnis (1998)

III *Religion and Medicine in the Middle Ages*, ed. Peter Biller and Joseph Ziegler (2001)

IV *Texts and the Repression of Medieval Heresy*, ed. Caterina Bruschi and Peter Biller (2002)

YORK MANUSCRIPTS CONFERENCE

Manuscripts and Readers in Fifteenth-Century England: The Literary Implications of Manuscript Study, ed. Derek Pearsall (1983) [Proceedings of the 1981 York Manuscripts Conference]

Manuscripts and Texts: Editorial Problems in Later Middle English Literature, ed. Derek Pearsall (1987) [Proceedings of the 1985 York Manuscripts Conference]

Latin and Vernacular: Studies in Late-Medieval Texts and Manuscripts, ed. A. J. Minnis (1989) [Proceedings of the 1987 York Manuscripts Conference]

Regionalism in Late-Medieval Manuscripts and Texts: Essays celebrating the publication of 'A Linguistic Atlas of Late Mediaeval English', ed. Felicity Riddy (1991) [Proceedings of the 1989 York Manuscripts Conference]

Late-Medieval Religious Texts and their Transmission: Essays in Honour of A. I. Doyle, ed. A. J. Minnis (1994) [Proceedings of the 1991 York Manuscripts Conference]

Prestige, Authority and Power in Late Medieval Manuscripts and Texts, ed. Felicity Riddy (2000) [Proceedings of the 1994 York Manuscripts Conference]

Middle English Poetry: Texts and Traditions. Essays in Honour of Derek Pearsall, ed. A. J. Minnis (2001) [Proceedings of the 1996 York Manuscripts Conference]

MANUSCRIPT CULTURE IN THE BRITISH ISLES

I *Design and Distribution of Late Medieval Manuscripts in England*, ed. Margaret Connolly and Linne R. Mooney (2008)

II *Women and Writing, c. 1340–c. 1650: The Domestication of Print Culture*, ed. Anne Lawrence-Mathers and Phillipa Hardman (2010)

III *The Wollaton Medieval Manuscripts: Texts, Owners and Readers*, ed. Ralph Hanna and Thorlac Turville-Petre (2010)

HERESY AND INQUISITION IN THE MIDDLE AGES

Heresy and Heretics in the Thirteenth Century: The Textual Representations, L. J. Sackville (2011)

Heresy, Crusade and Inquisition in Medieval Quercy, Claire Taylor (2011)